THE GOLDEN
HOME AND

THE GOLDEN HOME AND HIGH SCHOOL ENCYCLOPEDIA, while sufficiently comprehensive and detailed for family use, has been created principally for students at the high school level.

The aim of this reference work is twofold: first, to serve the student's immediate need for authoritative information on a wide range of subjects, and, second, to set forth and explain the many areas of knowledge, so that a student may explore them and thus more competently plan his educational future.

Arranged alphabetically in twenty volumes, here are thousands of full, accurate entries, written and reviewed by experts. The text is abundantly illustrated with full-color photographs and paintings.

Designed to complement the high school curriculum, this encyclopedia offers help with assignments and valuable guidance in the use of other reference tools —dictionaries, atlases, and various library materials. Extensive cross-references and a complete index direct the reader quickly to the information he seeks. A special feature of this work is the sound career information it offers in scores of job and professional fields.

Among the many subjects encompassed in these volumes are the newest developments in science, from microbiology to radioastronomy; fine arts and literature; history and government; religion and philosophy; the physical world, its plants and animals; the social sciences; invention and industry. Four-color maps and latest census figures contribute to an up-to-date view of the world, its continents, nations, and peoples.

Every care has been taken to make *The Golden Home and High School Encyclopedia* lively and stimulating, without sacrifice of accuracy. It is the hope of the editors that these volumes will be used with both advantage and pleasure.

Volume X

HIGH SCHOOL ENCYCLOPEDIA

in 20 Volumes

Jaundice · Logrolling

GOLDEN PRESS · NEW YORK

FIRST PRINTING, 1961
Library of Congress Catalog Card Number: 61-13292
© Copyright 1961 by Golden Press, Inc. Designed and produced by Artists and Writers Press, Inc. Printed in the U.S.A. by Western Printing and Lithographing Company. Published by Golden Press, Inc., New York.

Illustrations from GOLDEN BOOKS, © 1947, 1954, 1955, 1956, 1957, 1958, 1959, 1960, 1961 by Golden Press, Inc.; and from the Basic Science Education Series (Unitext), published by Row, Peterson and Company, Evanston, Illinois, © 1944 by Row, Peterson and Company.

JAUNDICE is a disease condition marked by the presence of bile pigment in the skin and mucous membranes, giving a yellow appearance, especially to the whites of the eyes. Jaundice is of several types—obstructive, hemolytic, and hepatic being examples.

Obstruction of the normal bile flow from the gallbladder into the intestines is one common cause of jaundice. The obstruction may result from gallstones, inflammation of the lining of the bile duct, pressure on the duct from some outside source (such as a tumor), or another cause. When the particular cause of the obstruction has been found, and if the condition does not improve, surgery is often necessary. In some cases the gallbladder has to be removed.

Some poisons act on the liver to prevent passage of the bile pigments, which then accumulate in the blood. In some cases excessive amounts of bile pigment are produced by increased destruction of red blood cells; if the pigments are not eliminated fast enough, jaundice results.

In newborn infants jaundice occurs from excessive destruction of red blood cells, which may be a result of incompatibility between the blood of the infant and that of the mother or which may be of functional origin.

JAY, JOHN (1745-1829), American statesman and diplomat, was born into a wealthy and prominent New York family. He was privately educated, was graduated from King's College (now Columbia University), and became a lawyer.

Jay first entered public affairs in 1773, when he was made a member of a commission that determined the New York-New Jersey boundary. He then became a member of the New York Committee of Correspondence and of the First and the Second Continental Congress. (See COMMITTEE OF CORRESPONDENCE; CONTINENTAL CONGRESS.) In 1776 he played an important part in writing the New York constitution, and from 1776 to 1779 he served as chief justice of the state of New York. Late in 1778 he returned to the Continental Congress and served several months as its president.

In 1779 Jay was appointed ambassador to Spain, where he arrived early the following year. His mission was to secure recognition of American independence and to obtain loans from the Spanish government. The Spanish government, unfortunately, was not interested; Jay's mission was from the start hopeless. In 1782 he was summoned to Paris, where he, Benjamin Franklin, and John Adams negotiated the Treaty of Paris (1783), which ended the Revolutionary War and guaranteed American independence.

Library of Congress

Chief Justice John Jay's influence on the Supreme Court was distinctly conservative.

Upon his return to America in 1784 Jay became secretary of foreign affairs for the Continental Congress, an office he held until the Constitution went into effect. In this office he was made acutely aware of the faults of the Articles of Confederation and consequently urged adoption of the Constitution, in support of which he wrote five of the papers of *The Federalist*. (See ARTICLES OF CONFEDERATION; CONSTITUTION OF THE UNITED STATES; FEDERALIST, THE.) When the Constitution took effect, President Washington appointed Jay the first chief justice of the Supreme Court.

In 1794 Jay again traveled abroad on a diplomatic mission, this time to England, where he negotiated a treaty with the British government. The treaty was very unpopular, but it helped maintain peace and stability when both were very important to the new country. Upon his return from England Jay found he had been elected governor of New York, an office he held six years. In 1800 he was again offered the position of chief justice, but he declined the honor and retired to his farm in Westchester Co., New York, where he died at the age of 83.

JAYS, MAGPIES, CROWS, RAVENS, members of a bird family of exactly 100 species, many from other lands being known by such names as rooks, jackdaws, choughs, and nutcrackers. Birds of this family are medium to large in size, active and noisy, and usually omnivorous, feeding on carrion, seeds, fruits, insects, eggs of reptiles and birds, and even small reptiles. Generally they build substantial, well-lined nests, often in treetops.

The jays of North America are usually beautiful birds. The blue jay, for instance, is a handsome, crested bird, bright blue on the back and whitish gray below. Its repertoire of calls is large, and it even imitates well the call of the red-shouldered hawk. The gray (or Canada) jay, also called whiskyjack, is a bird of the northern spruce forests. Another of its names is camp robber, for it takes bait from traps and anything shiny or edible from camps and homes. Other jays are the piñon jay of the western and southwestern United States; the scrub jay, a crestless bird inhabiting the dense brush or scrub of the western United States and central Florida; the green jay of thickets and undergrowth from Texas to South America; the Steller's jay, a bird of the pine forests of the west; and the Mexican jay of the southwestern United States and Mexico.

Magpies are long-tailed birds, widely distributed in the Northern Hemisphere. The yellow-billed magpie is found only in a small area in California. The range of the black-billed magpie, however, extends from Alaska and Canada into the western United States. This 20-inch bird is black and white, with a greenish-black, wedge-shaped tail. It is a noisy bird with harsh notes, and a flock keeps up a constant chatter. Its domed nest of sticks, mud, hair, and feathers has two side openings, probably designed to accommodate the magpie's very long tail.

Crows are large, ebony-black birds with a deep, steady wingbeat and a raucous "caw," probably one of the best known bird calls. Crows habitually gather odd bits for their nests. At night they return to communal roosts from distances up to 50 miles. North American species include the common crow of the United States and Canada; the northwestern crow, which ranges from southern Alaska to Oregon; and the fish crow of the Atlantic and Gulf coasts.

Ravens look so much like crows that they are often wrongly identified by many who are familiar with them in legend and poetry. Formerly the raven was considered a bird of ill omen, a bringer of bad luck and death. Like crows they are black. However, they have a rough, shaggy throat; they are larger than crows; and they alternate flapping with sailing. The common raven is found from subarctic Alaska and northern Canada to the western United States. Besides being a scavenger it feeds on berries, insects, and small mammals. The white-necked raven of the southwestern United States is black except when the wind ruffles the neck feathers and shows their white bases.

Clark's nutcracker is another North American bird in this family. A gray bird with white face and black-and-white wings, it feeds on nuts, seeds, berries, and insects. It is noisy and inquisitive about camps and becomes very tame in some of the national parks.

These representatives of an interesting bird family include some species found in North America—black-billed magpie, Clark's nutcracker, blue jay, common raven, and common crow. The others are from other parts of the world. Many of the birds of this family are noted for their so-called intelligence. Crows, for instance, learn to solve puzzles and to repeat words and phrases.

JAY'S TREATY, a treaty that was signed Nov. 19, 1794, between Great Britain and the United States and that settled several disputes between the two nations arising out of the Treaty of Paris (1783) and the later issue of neutral rights on the high seas. The chief issues were Great Britain's refusal to evacuate the frontier posts in the Great Lakes region, difficulties in collecting prewar debts owed to British creditors, and a dispute over the boundary in the north. Relations between the two countries reached a crisis in 1794, when Britain, at war with France, began seizing U.S. vessels suspected of trading with the enemy.

U.S. Chief Justice John Jay was sent to London on a special peace mission. In negotiations with William Grenville, the secretary for foreign affairs, he succeeded in reaching agreement on most of the major problems. Britain agreed to give up the frontier posts by June 1, 1796; the United States guaranteed payment of the debts; and two boundary commissions were set up to establish the correct boundary in the northwest and in the northeast. The first commission never met, but the other one agreed on the frontier between Maine and Canada. In the matter of the naval seizures Jay gave in to the British and agreed to accept their policy for the duration of the Anglo-French war.

When presented to the Senate, the treaty met strong opposition on the grounds that Jay had not been firm enough with the British government and had compromised U.S. rights. It was finally approved after strong pressure from President George Washington.

JAZZ, a type of music, of predominantly American Negro origin, that has become popular not only in the United States but throughout the world.

Perhaps the most definite characteristic of jazz is its pulsating rhythm. Jazz is also marked by the employment of improvisation on an established melodic line and the use of various harmonic alterations. The jazz performance involves a freedom of melodic intonation, a complexity of syncopation, and a vocal quality that defy notation by conventional means.

Jazz evolved from the body of music that was popular in the South after the Civil War. The early jazz musician drew most heavily upon the music of the ragtime piano player, the wandering blues singer, and the Negro brass band. Although the origin and early evolution of jazz are generally associated with New Orleans, there is reason to believe that music of a similar nature was being evolved simultaneously in other areas where similar social and cultural conditions existed. The earliest New Orleans jazz bands, direct descendants of the popular marching bands of the late 19th century, generally consisted of a trumpet or cornet, trombone, clarinet, banjo or guitar, piano, and string bass or tuba. A band of this instrumentation is still called a Dixieland band. Among the musicians associated with the early days of jazz in New Orleans were Bunk Johnson, Buddy Bolden, Sidney Bechet, King Oliver, Jelly Roll Morton, and Louis Armstrong.

Jazz music had a very limited audience, even in the South, until

JAZZ

Benny Goodman, clarinetist and band leader

Shown here is the jazz combo.

almost the third decade of the 20th century. Three events, all of which occurred in 1917, marked the beginning of the public's awareness of the new music. In that year the first phonograph records of jazz music were made; the Original Dixieland Jazz Band performed at Reisenweber's Cafe in New York; and the notorious Storyville district of New Orleans was shut down. This last event resulted in an exodus of jazz musicians from New Orleans. By the end of World War I jazz had become popular in several cities of Europe, including Paris and London. In addition to the Original Dixieland Jass Band, the bands of the period included King Oliver's Creole Jazz Band and the New Orleans Rhythm Kings. Few members of the earliest jazz bands were musically literate. By the 1920's the proportion of jazzmen who could read music had increased. However, since improvisation on familiar melodies was the basis of the jazz performance, written arrangements were rarely used.

During the 1920's the so-called Chicago style of jazz arose. The saxophone was added to what had already become the traditional instrumentation. Solo rather than ensemble improvisation was stressed. Among the exponents of the Chicago style were Gene Krupa, Bud Freeman, Joe Sullivan, and Eddie Condon. Meanwhile, such personalities as Louis Armstrong, Fats Waller, Duke Ellington, Fletcher Henderson, and Earl Hines were acquiring a popular following. Bands of the period included the Hot Seven and the Hot Five, both featuring Armstrong; the Wolverines, with Bix Beiderbecke; and, in the later 1920's and early 1930's, the Paul Whiteman Band.

In 1924 Paul Whiteman introduced George Gershwin's *Rhapsody in Blue*, perhaps the best known attempt at incorporating elements of the jazz idiom into a symphonic framework. Symphonic jazz, as it was called, became particularly popular among European composers, but it was never considered a part of the mainstream of American jazz.

The next decade, especially the second half of it, is remembered as the era of swing, a type of music that was, in reality, a fusion of jazz of the New Orleans tradition with commercially popular dance music. From the standpoint of instrumentation the 13-piece to 15-piece swing band of the late 1930's was basically an expansion of the jazz band of the 1920's. However, unlike the latter, the swing bands played from written arrangements. Swing music was characterized by dazzling solo passages, elaborate ensemble work, and, most important, a steady four-four beat. Among the most successful band leaders of the swing era were Benny Goodman, Glenn Miller, Artie Shaw, Tommy Dorsey, and Woody Herman. Boogie-woogie, a type of piano music combining a repeated "eight-to-the-bar" rhythmical bass figure and a contrasting melody line, became popular during the last years of the decade.

By the early 1940's it was apparent that the swing era was over. With the notable exceptions of the Count Basie and the Duke Ellington bands, big bands were relying more and more on commercial dance music at the expense of the vital jazz spirit. Attention turned to the small-band field. New York's small nightclubs, which during the 1930's had featured such swing musicians as Teddy Wilson, Art Tatum, Lionel Hampton, and Coleman Hawkins, now became the center of a new jazz cult. Building upon the musical concepts of such innovators as Lester Young, Jimmy Blanton, Charlie Christian, and Roy Eldridge, a small circle of musicians that included Charlie Parker, Dizzy Gillespie, Thelonious Monk, Kenny Clarke, Bud Powell, and Oscar Pettiford developed the jazz style that came to be called bop. Bop was essentially a reaction against swing music. The steady, unvaried four-four beat of swing gave way to more subtle rhythmical patterns in which the beat was often merely implied. Horizontal rather than vertical structure was stressed, and traditional concepts of harmonic structures and progressions were greatly extended.

The years that followed were marked by further definition and development of the bop idiom. In the big-band field it was reflected in the music of the bands of Stan Kenton and Woody Herman. During the late 1940's bop became somewhat refined and restrained in the so-called cool style of Miles Davis, Stan Getz, Shelly Manne, Lennie Tristano, Lee Konitz, and others. The work of such small groups as the Gerry Mulligan Quartet, the Modern Jazz Quartet, and the Chico Hamilton Quintet, as well as that of such individuals as Shorty Rogers, Johnny Mandel, and others of the West Coast group, is representative of more progressive trends in jazz following the mid-1950's.

Louis "Satchmo" Armstrong, trumpeter, singer, band leader, one of the great jazz musicians
Columbia Records

JEEP, a U.S. military vehicle that was used by all Allied armies during World War II. The jeep was employed for reconnaissance, the mounting of machine guns and antitank guns, the carrying of wounded from the areas of battle, and scores of other tasks.

Officially designated as a quarter-ton 4-by-4 truck, the jeep was intended to replace motorcycle-side-car pieces and to enable military strategists to bridge the gap between heavy, advance units and infantry. The jeep was originally called the peep. Another vehicle, the command car, was called the jeep. The newer quarter-ton 4-by-4 trucks, because of their versatility, replaced the command car but adopted the name jeep.

Built from a design by Willys-Overland Motors, Inc., the jeep has basically the Willys commercial-car powerplant with special carburetor and manifold, developing 61 horsepower at 3,800 revolutions per minute. The engine's cooling capacity has been highly developed. The radiator is protected by a special heavy grill, and the engine is protected from mud and dust by a special heavy-duty oil-bath cleaner. Application of the engine's power through a four-wheel-drive mechanism gives the car unusual pulling ability on slippery roads and in deep mud, snow, or sand. Regular transmission gears, three forward and one in reverse, are operated by a gearshift lever on the floorboards beside the driver's seat. A special gearbox, giving an additional 2-to-1 reduction, is brought into operation when a special transmission lever, also on the floor of the jeep, is thrown forward; it is thus possible to obtain a total of six forward speeds and two reverse speeds. Another lever on the transfer case permits selection of either four-wheel drive or rear-wheel drive only. Designed to use either low-grade or high-grade gasoline, the car's 12-gallon fuel tank under the rear seat provides a high-speed cruising radius of 175 miles or better. Employing a wheel base of only 80 inches, the jeep has exceptional road clearance and at the same time an exceptionally low center of gravity.

In a postwar modification the jeep has been adapted to many industrial and farm uses. Because of its exceptional pulling power and its ability to move over rough ground, it has been employed as a farm tractor, pulling such equipment as plows, harrows, and various harvesting machines.

JEFFERSON, THOMAS (1743–1826), third president of the United States, was one of the outstanding figures of his time. He was a scientist, philosopher, author, architect, and inventor as well as a diplomat and a statesman.

Jefferson was born in what is now Albemarle Co., Virginia, on Apr. 13, 1743. A graduate of the College of William and Mary in

Thomas Jefferson

1762, he studied law and was admitted to the bar in 1767. After 1769 he sat in the Virginia House of Burgesses, where he actively opposed English policy toward the colonies, was responsible for the establishment by law of religious freedom and the separation of church and state, and helped revise inheritance law and criminal law. He was a member of the Continental Congress in 1775 and 1776, and while serving there he drafted the Declaration of Independence. He later helped draw up the Virginia constitution, and in 1779 he became governor of that state.

In 1783 Jefferson returned to the Continental Congress and was important in drafting the land ordinance in 1784 that became the basis of the Ordinance of 1787. He also secured the installation of the decimal system of coinage. His draft peace treaty served as a basis for negotiating the Treaty of Paris (1783), which ended the American Revolutionary War. He served as minister to France from 1785 to 1789, when he returned to the United States. Shortly afterward, President George Washington appointed him the first secretary of state under the Constitution. Jefferson soon found himself at odds with Alexander Hamilton, who was pro-British and who sought to undermine Jefferson's office. Jefferson became the leader of the Republican faction in opposition to Hamilton, who, as leader of the Federalists, favored a strong federal government. (See DEMOCRATIC-REPUBLICAN PARTY.) In 1794 Jefferson retired to Monticello, his home near Charlottesville, Va.

In 1796 Jefferson was elected vice president of the United States in which position he continued to build his party. He was elected president by the House of Representatives in 1800 as a result of a tie in the electoral vote between him and Aaron Burr. Jefferson's cabinet was harmonious, and his financial policies aimed at economy. He was reelected in 1804. He maintained peace for the United States during his terms in office by pursuing a policy of neutrality in the wars between the France of Napoleon I and other nations. The Embargo Act countered British and French pressures on U.S. neutral commerce. Jefferson's administration negotiated the purchase of the Louisiana territory in 1803, which doubled the size of the United States.

Jefferson retired in 1809 and devoted himself to scientific and literary pursuits and to other matters that pressed for his attention. Throughout his life his interest in science had led him to studies in botany, geography, and paleontology. He was skilled in both ancient and modern languages; as a patron of the arts he amassed one of the finest private collections of paintings and statuary in the country. Monticello, the University of Virginia, and a good many Virginia houses testify to Jefferson's love of architecture, particularly of classical design. It is no exaggeration to say that he was the father of American architecture.

Jefferson's interest in education, an interest that began while he was governor of Virginia, bore fruit after he retired from the presidency. His proposals for elementary education as well as for university education were adopted by the state of Virginia. He lived to see his plans for the University of Virginia realized, though its student body was somewhat more aristocratic than he would have wished it to have been. Jefferson died on the 50th anniversary of the Declaration of Independence, at Monticello.

JEFFERSON CITY, capital of the state of Missouri, on the Missouri River, 120 miles west of St. Louis. It is a farming, manufacturing, retail trading, and governmental center. Manufactures include shoes, bricks, clothing, and products made from grain and wood. Lead, zinc, and clay are found in the vicinity. The city has railroad shops and some river traffic. It is the seat of Lincoln University, founded for Negroes in 1866. The state penitentiary and a boys reformatory are located here. The site of the city was chosen for the capital in 1821. The population in 1960 was 28,228.

JELLYFISH, a translucent, umbrella-shaped marine invertebrate that is not a fish at all. Much lower than fish on the evolutionary scale, jellyfish are related to corals and sea anemones. They often float or propel themselves in great numbers along the surface of the sea. They vary in diameter from less than 1 inch to several feet. In color they vary from white through rainbow hues to deep red or bright blue. They are frequently phosphorescent; when irritated, they emit a bright light that is visible at night. This is best seen where the sea is stirred by a passing vessel. Then the light given off by jellyfish shines like globes of fire, sparkles like stars, or spreads into a pale glow that marks the vessel's course.

The body of the jellyfish is watery and jelly-like and is held together by a simple framework of cells. The mouth, located on the underside of the body, opens into a cavity, within which food is digested. Digested food is then carried by radiating canals to all parts of the body. Surrounding the mouth of some jellyfish are four long, dangling feelers, or oral arms, which seize little sea animals for food. Often the edge of the body is fringed with other feelers that bear tiny stingers. These stingers sweep through the water and pierce and paralyze little sea animals, which are then eaten.

JENKINS' EAR, WAR OF, a war between England and Spain from 1739 to 1742, received its name from a brutal Spanish act. The Spanish, on catching an English trading ship in the Caribbean, cut off the ear of the master of the ship, Robert Jenkins. The Spanish did this and similar acts because England had violated an agreement to send only one trading ship a year to the Spanish colonies. The fighting took place in the Spanish colonies in the New World. Many English colonists participated, including George Washington's older brother. Settlers from Georgia, who had won the friendship of the Indians of Florida, were especially successful in their attacks on that Spanish colony. Their success, under their leader James Edward Oglethorpe, greatly strengthened the British against the French and Spanish in America. The War of Jenkins' Ear merged into King George's War. See KING GEORGE'S WAR.

Fisher Sci. Co.

Edward Jenner

JENNER, EDWARD (1749-1823), an English physician who discovered vaccination. He was a pupil of the famous John Hunter. Jenner lived almost all his life at Berkeley, in Gloucestershire, caring for sick country people.

The great devastating disease of the 17th and 18th centuries was smallpox. Those who lived after they contracted the disease had pitted and scarred skins. In Jenner's time nobody knew of the existence of microbes or how they are propagated. It was noticed, however, that milkmaids who contracted cowpox while milking did not catch smallpox. After 20 years of patient observation, Jenner was able to supply the true explanation, namely that cowpox and smallpox are closely related diseases. On May 14, 1796, Jenner performed the first vaccination by inoculating cowpox into an eight-year-old boy. Later, the same boy was vaccinated with smallpox, but the disease did not develop. Jenner's method of vaccine inoculation was rapidly adopted by other doctors. He was offered many honors and much money, but he continued to prefer to live the life of the simple country doctor.

The translucent, milky-blue, moon jellyfish (directly below) is often washed by the surf onto the beaches between Maine and Florida. The pink jellyfish (lower right) has many long, stringy, trailing tentacles.

Jordan Tourist Dept.
The Garden of Gethsemane, the site of Christ's betrayal by Judas, is located in Jerusalem.

JERUSALEM, an ancient city of Palestine, is now divided between Israel and Jordan. It stands on a rocky ridge about 2,500 feet above sea level. Held in turn by Jews, Christians, and Moslems, it is a sacred city to all. Eastern Jerusalem, held by Jordan, contains the Old City, which is surrounded by a 16th-century wall with eight gates. Within the walls are most of the holy places of the three faiths. The Old City is divided into four sections: Christian, Moslem, Armenian, and Jewish. The Israeli part of the city lies in the west. In 1950 Israel declared Jerusalem as its capital.

Jerusalem is a very old city. About 1000 B.C. David captured it and made it the capital of his kingdom. It had a glorious era under Solomon, who built the great Temple. In 586 B.C. the Babylonians captured the city, destroyed the Temple, and took the Jews into captivity. When the Jews were allowed to return, they rebuilt the Temple.

In 333 B.C. Jerusalem submitted to Alexander the Great. Three centuries later it came under Roman domination. Events of Christ's life during the Roman period made Jerusalem the holy city of the Christian world. The Romans destroyed Jerusalem A.D. 70 and rebuilt it as a Roman city. Under the rule of Emperor Constantine it became a Christian shrine. Constantine's mother had churches built on sacred sites, including the Church of the Holy Sepulcher.

The Arabs took Jerusalem in 637. With great slaughter the Crusaders conquered the city in 1099 and set up the Latin Kingdom of Jerusalem. Moslems regained Jerusalem in 1187. It remained in Moslem hands until the British captured it from the Turks in 1917. When the British withdrew in 1948, the Jews and the Arabs fought for control. An armistice, arranged by the United Nations, left the city divided into Jewish and Arab sections. Population of the Israeli sector is about 155,000; that of the Jordanian sector is probably about 50,000.

JESTER, a buffoon installed at a king's palace or in a nobleman's household to amuse the master and divert his attention from heavy cares. Jesters were colorfully and fantastically dressed, usually in the official colors and designs of the royal or noble family. They made use of their folly in different ways. Some exaggerated a natural deformity or simple-mindedness to arouse laughter. Others held the attention of court society with their quick-witted comments and observations, for they were allowed complete freedom of expression. The Aztec emperor Montezuma is reputed to have said of jesters that "more instruction was to be gathered from them than from wiser men, for they dared to tell the truth."

These fools, as they were often called, had been known in all parts of the world from early times. However, they were firmly established and most influential in Europe just after the Crusades. The suppression of fools at court was started in France about the 16th century, when France took an independent stand against Italy in several matters of taste and etiquette. Jesters gradually disappeared in the rest of Europe afterward, since more and more of the European nobility began to look to France for social and cultural examples.

JESUIT, a member of the Society of Jesus, a religious order founded in 1540 by the Spaniard St. Ignatius of Loyola. The aim of the society was twofold: to support the papacy and the Roman Catholic Church against the Protestants and to do missionary work among pagans. The rules of the society emphasized self-discipline: Every Jesuit was to be a soldier of Christ, loyal, if necessary, even unto death. The society was headed by a superior general who had great authority and was directly accountable to the pope.

The Jesuits appeared in Europe when many people exchanged the Roman Catholic religion for Protestantism. The Jesuits sought to reconvert these people to Roman Catholicism, even sacrificing their lives to this end. When Roman Catholic religious practices were outlawed in England, Jesuit priests trained on the Continent were sent to minister to English Catholics. Because they worked secretly in the realm, Jesuits were hunted men and were sometimes accused of plotting against the government. In other parts of Europe Jesuits became advisers to kings. Their power and their aggressive methods earned them many enemies, and their loyalty to papal supremacy brought them into conflict with the forces of nationalism. During the late 18th century they were expelled from France, Spain, Portugal, and Italy. To avoid discord Rome officially suppressed them in 1773. However, they were restored in 1814.

The Jesuits emphasize achievement in two fields: education and foreign missions. One of the first Jesuits, St. Francis Xavier, gained many converts in India and Japan as early as 1550. The Jesuits also introduced a system of education based upon the study of Greek and Roman classical writers. At present the Jesuits are to be found in most countries of the world.

JESUS (5 B.C.?—A.D. 30?). Christian religions consider that this Jew of simple origin was the Son of God and that he appeared on earth as a human being and suffered and died for the salvation of mankind. *Christ* is the Greek word for "Messiah," or the great king whom the Jews expected to come and lead them in establishing a universal kingdom. But from the beginning Jesus stated clearly that he did not wish to become a Jewish national hero; his kingdom was to be spiritual, not political, and would include not only the Jews but also people of all nations who believed in his teachings. He usually called himself the Son of Man or the Son of the Father, rather than the Messiah, in order to avoid this misunderstanding about his person and mission. Non-Christians do not deny the historical existence of Jesus, but they do deny his and his followers' claim to his divinity.

Jesus was born in Bethlehem, a small town in Judea, which became a Roman province after the death of King Herod the Great in 4 B.C. According to the Four Gospels, which contain the story of Jesus' life, Joseph, a carpenter, was merely Jesus' foster father. Jesus was born to Mary, Joseph's wife, by divine intervention. The Four Gospels say little about Jesus' childhood. Like all Jewish boys he was presented in the Temple at Jerusalem and was blessed by the priest soon after his birth. Joseph was warned in a dream that King Herod wanted to take the child's life. The family fled to Egypt and remained there until after the death of Herod. Then Jesus was brought back from Egypt, and the family settled in the village of Nazareth in the province of Galilee. There Jesus spent most of his life, probably helping his father. He is said to have developed in wisdom and to have been an obedient son. Some Christians believe that he was an only child, while others think that he had brothers and sisters. When Jesus was 12 years old, he went with his parents on a pilgrimage to Jerusalem and, after the departure of his parents, stayed in the Temple to discuss religion with the learned priests. Some stories from Jesus' childhood are contained in the Apocrypha.

The first three Gospels—Matthew, Mark, and Luke—were written for the Jews, the Romans, and the Greeks respectively. The Fourth Gospel, John, presents a more spiritual than factual picture of Jesus' personality and teaching. All of the Four Gospels were written after Jesus' death and before the end of the 1st century. Some of the letters of the missionary Paul date from before the earliest of the Gospels (Mark or Matthew), which was composed around A.D. 65. When taken together, the Gospels supplement each other and record the important facts about Jesus with simplicity, directness, and surprisingly little disagreement. About A.D. 27 or 28 a Jewish prophet named John the Baptist preached repentance and baptized people in Judaea. He baptized Jesus in the Jordan River. On this occasion it is said that God's voice was heard proclaiming Jesus to be his beloved son. After his baptism by John, Jesus spent 40 days in solitude in the desert south of Jerusalem, preparing himself and doing penance. Tempted by Satan, Jesus refused to be turned aside and instead started on his mission.

In a little less than two and a half years Jesus covered on foot

"The Risen Christ," a statue by Michelangelo

most of the provinces of Galilee, Samaria, and the region around Jerusalem. He preached that the kingdom of God had arrived with his own coming. He healed the sick, expelled evil spirits, and revived the dead. Through these miracles he wanted all to see the power of God manifested in his actions. He often talked of God as a loving father and taught his hearers how to pray to God. In the story of the prodigal son he described the limitless goodness of God, who will forgive the sins of a repenting sinner. The God Jesus talked about was quite different from the just but severe Yahweh of the Old Testament. God invited everybody to the marriage feast—one of the many stories Jesus told to illustrate his teaching—and only those who disregarded the invitation and rejected his appeal would be condemned. The wealthy would have a difficult time entering the kingdom of God. But this would be easy for those who were pure in heart and who loved God above all else and their fellow men as themselves. Jesus criticized the Pharisees and the Sadducees for devoting their time to the observance of external ceremonies and enforcing the letter of the law. Instead, Jesus emphasized the virtues of charity, humility, and sincerity. He claimed to have come not to reject but to fulfill the law given by God in the Old Testament, to transform the letter of the old law by a new spirit. He chose his disciples from among the simple and even the sinful and sent them out to teach the commandments of God in the new spirit. Soon he gained many followers. His success made the Jewish religious leaders jealous and apprehensive, for Jesus flouted many of the Jewish traditional religious customs. He denied the importance of the Sabbath and forgave sins, which the Jews said God alone had the power to do. Finally, the Jewish leaders captured Jesus, using the treachery of Judas Iscariot, one of his disciples. Jesus was accused of having called himself the Son of God, a charge that he did not deny. The Jewish high priests delivered him to the Roman procurator, who alone had the power to condemn him to death. Pilate reluctantly gave orders for Jesus to be crucified, a method of punishment reserved for criminals.

Jesus is said to have predicted his own death to his disciples. He emphasized that the shedding of his blood would result in a new relationship between men and God; that everyone who believed in him could again become the child of God. Since the Jews rejected his message, Jesus ordered his disciples to go forth and preach his teachings to all people. Although the disciples at first did not seem to have understood Jesus' self-sacrifice, their faith in the Master was reestablished when he rose from the dead three days after his execution. Jesus is said to have spent 40 days among his disciples after the Resurrection. After that time he is said to have returned to heaven and, in the words of the Apostles' Creed, sits at the right hand of God the Father.

JET AIRCRAFT

JET AIRCRAFT, the first type of aircraft to use a propulsion force other than the propeller, or airscrew, driven by a reciprocating engine, which all other powered aircraft, including lighter-than-air aircraft, use. The propeller-driven airplane is incapable of speeds much over 400 miles per hour. During World War II the need for faster warplanes forced the rapid development of jet aircraft.

The first successful jet-propelled aircraft was flown in Germany in 1939. It was developed by Heinkel and Von Ohain. The first British jet flew in 1941, using an engine designed by Frank Whittle. In 1942 the United States flew its first jet, which was developed from the British models. By the end of World War II Germany, Great Britain, and the United States were producing jet fighter planes.

Courtesy of American Airlines, Inc.

Several types of jet propulsion have been and are being used. Airplanes are powered by turbojet engines. Some guided missiles are powered by ramjet engines. The V-1, a World War II German guided missile, used a pulsejet engine. Rockets are propelled by a jet reaction, but they are usually not thought of as jet aircraft. Jet aircraft need air to function; rockets do not need air. See JET PROPULSION; ROCKET.

Formerly, the jet-propulsion engine, because of its high fuel consumption and short range, was confined to high-speed fighter planes. The jet-propulsion engine is now also used in long-range bombers and in transports.

The Boeing 707 is the first U.S. commercial jetliner to go into operation.

Convair's B-58 supersonic Hustler carries armament in a pod, which may be dropped to increase the plane's performance.

General Dynamics

JET AIRCRAFT

The first jet aircraft were for military uses. Commercial airlines are now using more and more jet aircraft for long-distance flights. The first commercial jet service was established in 1952 between London and Rome. The first transatlantic jet passenger service started in 1958. Jet aircraft also carry freight.

Besides turbojets, airlines use turboprop aircraft—aircraft that have jet engines in which the turbine shaft is connected to turn a propeller as well as to turn an air compressor.

Jet aircraft have achieved great speeds. In December, 1959, Major Joseph Rogers of the U.S. Air Force made a speed record of 1,520.9 miles per hour in a Convair F-106.

The small X-15 rocket plane is launched from a B-52 jet bomber. The X-15 is an experimental airplane and is launched in the air to save fuel for flight and testing.

North American Aviation, Inc.

The Lockheed T-33 jet trainer was developed from an older jet fighter, the F-80 Shooting Star, America's first operational jet aircraft. This design was in continuous production for 15 years. The T-33 can be equipped with cameras for aerial reconnaissance.

Lockheed Aircraft Corp.

JET AIRCRAFT ASSEMBLY

1. PLASTIC NOSE
2. RADAR ANTENNA
3. RADAR MODULATOR
4. OXYGEN BOTTLE
5. RADAR RANGE SERVO GEAR BOX
6. AMMUNITION BOXES (4)
7. C-1 POSITION LIGHT FLASHER
8. AN/ARC-3 AND AN/ARN-6 RADIO RECEIVERS
9. GUN-SIGHT
10. PILOT'S RADAR INDICATOR
11. INSTRUMENT PANEL
12. PILOT'S SEAT
13. AN/ARN-6 RADIO COMPASS LOOP ANTENNA
14. RADAR INDICATOR POWER SUPPLY
15. RADAR MANUAL CONTROL
16. OPERATOR'S RADAR INDICATOR
17. RADAR OPERATOR'S SEAT
18. FUSELAGE FUEL TANK
19. ELEVATOR CONTROL ROD
20. J33-A-33 ENGINE
21. FUSELAGE AFT-SECTION ATTACHING POINT
22. AFTERBURNER
23. AN/ARC-3 RADIO ANTENNA
24. AFTERBURNER TRACK
25. AFTERBURNER EYELID ACTUATOR
26. ELEVATOR TAB MOTOR
27. GYROSYN COMPASS FLUX VALVE
28. AILERON BOOSTER UNIT
29. WING BEAMS
30. DIVE FLAPS
31. TURBINE AND COOLER UNIT
32. AILERON TORQUE TUBE
33. CABIN AIR MIXING VALVE
34. INTERPHONE AMPLIFIER
35. D-2 INVERTER
36. RADAR INVERTER
37. RADAR VERTICAL GYRO
38. RADAR
39. BATTERIES
40. AILERON-ELEVATOR CONTROL ASSEMBLY
41. RUDDER PEDALS
42. NOSE ALIGHTING GEAR
43. FUSELAGE NOSE-SECTION ATTACHING POINT
44. CASE EJECTION DOOR
45. MACHINE GUNS (4)
46. AIR-SPEED PITOT
47. GUN-SIGHT COMPUTER
48. GUN-SIGHT AMPLIFIER SERVO

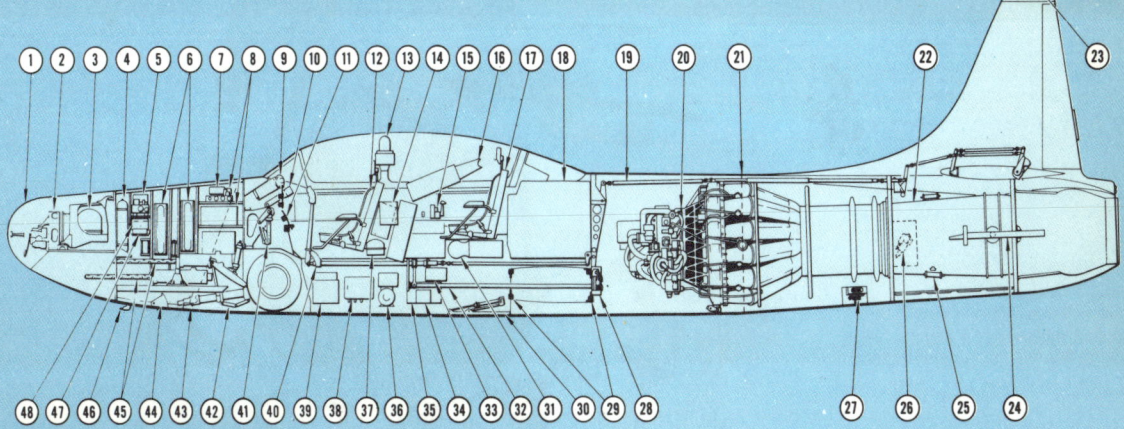

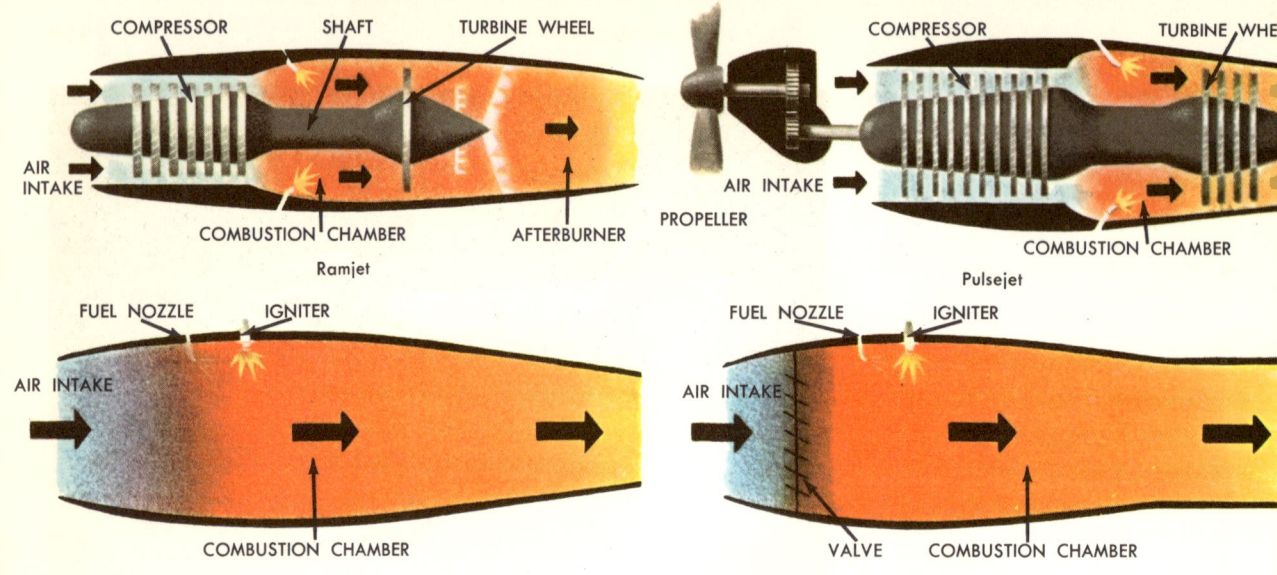

Above are four types of jet engine. All jet engines require air to operate, unlike the rocket engine, which will operate in a vacuum.

Four F-100 Super Sabres fly in tight formation. The F-100 was the first operational supersonic airplane in the United States Air Force.
U.S.A.F.

Jet propulsion involves the principle that every action has an equal and opposite reaction. This principle was clearly stated by Newton in the 17th century; however, the Greek mathematician Hero of Alexandria devised this machine in the 1st century. Water was boiled in the cauldron. Steam entered the globe through the supporting pipes and escaped through bent nozzles. The force of the escaping steam caused the globe to rotate.

JET PROPULSION 1357

Courtesy of North American Aviation, Inc.

The ZEL zero-length launcher hurls an F-100 Super Sabre into the air. The rocket motor fastened to the underside of the airplane falls off when the plane is safely airborne.

JET PROPULSION involves the high-speed ejection of a fluid from an engine through a nozzle. The force required to eject the fluid has a reaction that is the thrust that propels a jet airplane, missile, or spaceship. The idea of such propulsion is based on Isaac Newton's third law of motion: To every action there is an equal and opposite reaction.

If a balloon is filled with air and then closed at the stem, the air inside the balloon is under pressure and tries to expand in every direction. Much force is exerted by the air, but since this pressure is equal in every direction, the balloon does not move. If the stem is opened, air rushes out of the balloon in one direction, and the balloon is propelled in the opposite direction by the reaction to the rushing air.

The first practical application of jet propulsion was made by the ancient Chinese, who employed the exhaust gases of burning powder as a means of propelling rockets in warfare. In Europe during the late Middle Ages such rockets were used but were discarded when the more efficient and accurate rifled artillery piece was introduced. In the War of 1812, however, British use of the rocket successfully routed U.S. forces defending Washington, D.C., and resulted in the capture and burning of the city. During World War II jet-propulsion engines for missiles and aircraft were developed. Jet-propulsion devices are divided into two basic classes—the air-breathing jets that get oxygen from the atmosphere for burning fuel and rockets that carry oxidizers as well as fuel. In the mechanical jet, which is rarely used, air is pumped in from the atmosphere, compressed, and ejected with an increase in velocity. In the thermal jet the air is compressed and heated by fuel combustion. Modern jet engines are usually thermal-jet units and contain three main features—an air compressor, a combustion chamber for heating the air, and a discharge nozzle for the escape of expanding exhaust gases. See ROCKET.

Two types of jet engines that do not require mechanical compressors but obtain compression by special design of the air-intake section are the ramjet engine and the pulsejet engine. In the pulsejet the air-and-fuel mixture flows in cycles; in the ramjet this flow is continuous.

The most commonly used jet engine is the turbojet, which contains a turbine through which the exhaust gases pass. Air is taken in at the front of the engine, compressed, and forced into the combustion chamber by the compressor. It is mixed with fuel and ignited. The gases that form expand rapidly under pressure and rush out the rear of the engine, providing the thrust that pushes the airplane forward. As the gases escape, they pass through and turn a turbine connected to the compressor. The turbine's rotation provides power to rotate the compressor once the engine is started.

Turbojets used in fast military aircraft are often equipped with afterburners, or reheaters. In the afterburner additional fuel is injected between the turbine and exhaust nozzle. Greater temperature, pressure, and thrust are produced. The bypass-turbojet, or turbofan, used in heavy transport planes, is designed to pass part of the compressed air around the combustion chamber and turbine. This air is mixed with the exhaust gases before ejection. The exhaust jet thus has greater mass and slower speed. These conditions produce better fuel economy in slower flying jet aircraft.

The turboprop engine combines jet propulsion and propeller action. In this jet engine the turbine is attached by a shaft to a propeller; thus it rotates both a compressor and a propeller. The turboprop produces more power than a piston engine of the same weight.

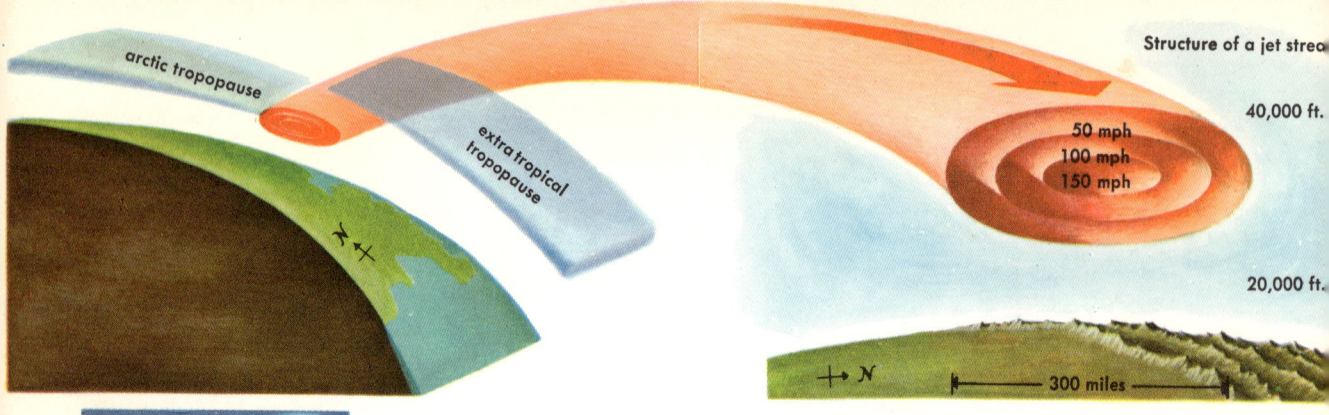

Structure of a jet stream

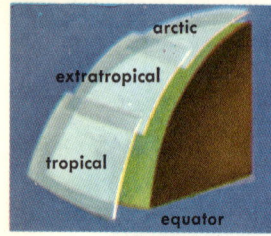

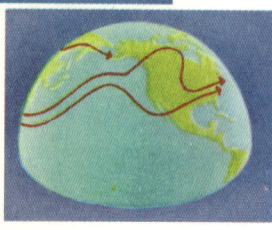

The jetstream is a wide, shallow ribbon of wind that flows in a meandering path around the earth in the tropopause, the region of the earth's atmosphere between the troposphere and the stratosphere. The jetstream was discovered in World War II by high-flying bombers. Modern long-range jetliners sometimes fly in the jetstream to add its speed to theirs and shorten flying time.

JETSTREAM. When B-29 pilots began to fly over the western Pacific during World War II, they encountered winds so strong that they could not reach their target areas. At first, people were skeptical about these wind speeds, which were reported to be up to 200 miles per hour. Meteorologists, or weather experts, began to learn more about these winds with the aid of new weather instruments. They called these winds the jetstream.

The jetstream is a narrow, ribbonlike current, some 300 miles wide and about 4 miles high, that moves around the earth in wavelike patterns. Sometimes it encircles the globe, but more often it is broken into several segments. The wind speeds within the jetstream vary from about 50 to 250 miles per hour. In fact, polar jetstreams have been measured at 350 miles per hour. The jetstream generally appears at an altitude of about 20,000 to 40,000 feet, or, in other words, in the turbulent tropopause.

The location and speed of the jetstream and its northward and southward shifts are important to the weatherman, who can use this knowledge to predict whether certain storm systems will become stronger. The aviator can also use the jetstream to give him a boost on long, high-altitude flights.

JEWELRY, a collective name for some articles intended for personal adornment. They are made of precious metals and may be enriched with stones or enamels. Objects not intended for personal use, such as caskets, when decorated with precious stones are said to be jeweled. Popularly, there is much confusion of the terms *gem* and *jewel*. The former belongs specifically to cut and polished stones. The latter is a stone or other substance, cut, polished or otherwise prepared for use or beauty.

Before the use of metals was known, jewelry, if it can be so termed, consisted of carved beads and fragments of such bright substances as were at the command of early man. Gold is the first metal mentioned in literature, and there is no doubt that, being usually found in a native state, it was the first to be used by mankind.

The art of making jewelry attained a high state of development in the countries of the Orient, probably because of the abundance of precious stones and pearls. The Egyptians were notable jewelry craftsmen, as shown by the excellent examples found in tombs that date from 3000 B.C. The scarab, or sacred beetle, and the lotus are the principal motifs found in this type of jewelry. The ancient Greeks were skilled in the art of jewelry making, especially in the use of gold and the engraving of precious stones to form intaglio rings. The Romans originated the cameo type of jewelry. The Byzantine jewelers also were noted for their craftsmanship. During the Renaissance jewelry was brought to a high degree of artistry by European jewelers, the most noteworthy of whom was Benvenuto Cellini. At that time great emphasis was placed on the design of jewelry. Greek and Roman styles of jewelry were revived in the 18th century, and the wearing of expensive jewels by the wealthy classes was extensive throughout Europe. With the advent of the 20th century new interest was brought to bear upon gold and silver work, and the pearl has become one of the most prominent jewels, second only to the diamond. In addition, a great deal of so-called costume jewelry, utilizing semiprecious stones and imitation, synthetic, and cultured gems, has been produced.

The distinction between jewelry of the present day and that of earlier times is found in the fundamental

This Mexican jeweler works with the aid of a blowtorch, one of the many tools used by the modern jeweler in his ancient craft.
David Forbert—Shostal

fact that the old work is the creation of the craftsman, while the modern jewel is the product of a manufacturer who adopts many laborsaving machines and appliances for the economical finishing of his wares.

JEWS. See HEBREWS.

JIG, a spirited, fast-stepping dance, popular throughout the British Isles before Shakespeare's time but now almost exclusively Irish. The Irish jig is performed by one or more dancers and is characterized by jumping, hopping, tapping and shuffling motions to music of triple rhythms. The solo jig is difficult, with great emphasis on rapid and intricate footwork.

JOAN OF ARC, SAINT (about 1412-1431), the national heroine of France, often called the Maid of Orléans, largely responsible for the liberation of France in the 15th century from English occupation and domination, born in the village of Domrémy-la-Pucelle. The illiterate daughter of very pious peasant parents, Joan was also very devout. She spent much of her time in prayer and meditation. She was considered a very gentle, kind, and good person by the people of her village. She is supposed to have begun hearing celestial voices and seeing visions in 1425, at the age of 13. Joan claimed the voices belonged to the archangel Michael and to St. Catherine and St. Marguerite.

At first the voices simply urged her to be good and pious and to trust in God; later, they told her she would lead the French forces against the English and would have the dauphin consecrated at Rheims. After a period of doubt and hesitation Joan accepted her heavenly command, and in 1428 she sought the aid of Robert de Baudricourt, the royal captain at Vaucouleurs.

With some difficulty Joan finally persuaded him to give her a letter of introduction to the dauphin, at Chinon. She arrived there Mar. 6, 1429, and her claim of having been sent by God was again received with skepticism. At her first meeting with the dauphin, Joan successfully passed a test devised for her: The dauphin tried to hide among a group of lords, but she recognized him immediately, even though she had never seen him before. Joan also passed an examination of her religious faith by several theologians.

Joan's confident personality and her insistence that he was the rightful heir to the throne of France buoyed up the spirits of the lethargic and faint-hearted dauphin and flattered his vanity. The prophecy that France would be delivered from her enemies by a maid also helped him decide to accept Joan's help.

Joan was given armor, a horse, and a small army. Carrying her famous white banner—with its pictures of angels, its fleur-de-lis, and the phrase Jesus Maria,—Joan of Arc led her forces into Orléans on April 29; by May 8 the siege was broken and the English were driven off. This victory was extremely important psychologically because it gave the French generals, soldiers, and people new confidence. Other victories followed.

On July 17, 1429, the dauphin was crowned Charles VII at Rheims, and he thus became the legitimate ruler of France. Joan continued fighting the English until she was captured at Compiègne on May 24, 1430. The Count of Luxembourg sold her to the English on November 21, and she was taken to Rouen. She was put on trial before an ecclesiastical court, judged a heretic and witch, and burned at the stake on May 30, 1431.

In order to clear his royal title Charles VII, who had made no attempt to save Joan, used his influence to have a retrial held in 1455; the pope reversed the verdict, and Joan was rehabilitated. On May 16, 1920, Joan of Arc was canonized. Since 1919 the first Sunday following May 8 has been a French national holiday in her memory.

JOB, a biblical character and the hero of one of the great dramatic poems in world literature, the Book of Job. Ancient Jewish tradition ascribed the book to Moses, but modern scholars believe it was written between the 6th and 4th centuries B.C. by an unknown author (or authors). Its theme is found in Egyptian and Babylonian literature, but the biblical version may be independent.

The Book of Job has 42 chapters, of which the first two and part of the last are in prose; the rest is poetry. The first two chapters (the prologue) present Job as a wealthy man, a prince, who lives in the land of Uz—probably near the territory of Edom, southeast of Palestine, near the Dead Sea. He is a pious and God-fearing man—wise, honest, and charitable—one who takes good care of his family and helps the needy. Even God praises Job's many virtues, but Satan challenges God's judgment by saying that Job is loyal to God only because he is happy, respected, and prosperous. God disagrees and gives permission to Satan to try Job. Four disasters strike Job in quick succession. His servants, oxen, and asses are carried away by raiding Sabeans, his sheep are lost in a desert storm, his camels are stolen, and his sons and daughters perish in a hurricane. Job himself is stricken with a kind of leprosy. But in spite of all this, Job does not lose his faith in God and resigns himself to his fate. Then three of Job's intimate friends, Eliphaz, Bildad, and Zophar, visit him. For seven days and seven nights the friends mourn silently with the grief-stricken and despairing Job.

The poetic part begins with Job's cursing the day he was born and expressing his desire to die rather than to lead a life of misery and suffering. His friends try to console him but slowly turn against him, charging his fate to his sins. Job, on the other hand, maintains his innocence and even goes so far as to lay all blame on God. Later, however, Job realizes that God is just, even though Job cannot see the reason for his misfortune. After Job's repentance God appears in thunder and storm, vindicates Job's innocence, restores his wealth, and condemns his friends, who had presumed to judge Job for his sins, which God alone could know.

JOHN XXIII (1881-   ), bishop of Rome and pope of the Roman Catholic Church. He was born Angelo Giuseppe Roncalli in Sotto il Monte, a small village in the province of Bergamo, Italy. He was the oldest son of a farmer. In 1892 he entered the seminary in Bergamo to study for the priesthood and was ordained in Rome in 1904. For ten years he was secretary to the bishop of Bergamo. During World War I Roncalli served first with the medical corps and then as a chaplain in the Italian army. After the war Roncalli was called to the Vatican and reorganized the Roman Catholic society for international charitable work. In 1925 he was made a bishop and was appointed the papal diplomatic representative in Bulgaria, Greece, and Turkey. In 1944 Roncalli was made Vatican ambassador to France, where he distinguished himself as a diplomat. He became a cardinal and the patriarch of Venice in January, 1953. Cardinal Roncalli was elected pope by 49 of his fellow cardinals on Oct. 28, 1958, following the death of Pope Pius XII. He assumed the name of John XXIII.

JOHN (1167-1216), king of England and youngest son of Henry II, was born at Oxford. When a boy he was nicknamed "Lackland" from his lack of Continental possessions. As his father's favorite son he was later given huge territories in both France and England. He waged war (1184) against Richard, his brother, in an attempt to take from him the duchy of Aquitaine. Having been declared king of Ireland in 1177, John was sent to that country in 1185 but soon returned to England in disgrace, having antagonized the people by his insolence. In 1189 he joined Richard and Philip II of France in war against Henry II, and this treachery was the final blow that killed the old king. During Richard's absence on the third Crusade John tried to supplant him on the throne by claiming that Richard had died. Richard forgave this treacherous act after their mother intervened in John's behalf (1194) and named John his successor, passing over Arthur, the young son of an older brother.

John's reign (1199-1216) was a complete failure. He was suspected, with good cause, of murdering his nephew Arthur in 1203. In the next year he became involved in a disastrous war with France in which England lost all of Normandy and most of Poitou. By 1206 he was forced to give up all the English possessions in France north of the Loire River. In a dispute with Rome over an appointment to the archbishopric of Canterbury, John seized the properties of the English bishops and was excommunicated by Pope Innocent III in 1212. A year later John gave in and promised to pay an annual tribute to the Holy See and receive back the exiled bishops. In 1215 the English barons saw their opportunity to deal with John and forced him to sign the Magna Charta, or Great Charter. (See MAGNA CHARTA.) The king soon repudiated the charter, raised an army, and attacked the barons. In the midst of the ensuing civil war John died at Newark, possibly of poison, and was succeeded by Henry III, his son by his second queen, Isabella of Angoulême.

JOHN HENRY, a Negro folk hero of 19th-century United States, as well as the title of a folksong about him. John Henry was a workman who helped build the Big Bend Tunnel of the Chesapeake and Ohio Railroad. According to the folksong he died while working "with his hammer in his hand," although the real John Henry supposedly died in a cave-in. The legend of this strong man traveled from West Virginia to many places in the southern United States.

The tune of the song is probably derived from a Scottish tune and is often sung to the accompaniment of a banjo or a guitar.

JOHNNY APPLESEED. See APPLESEED, JOHNNY.

Andrew Johnson

JOHNSON, ANDREW (1808-1875), American statesman and 17th president of the United States, was born Dec. 29, 1808, in Raleigh, N.C. Johnson had to go to work while very young and could not go to school. He educated himself with the help of his wife. He married her in 1827, shortly after he settled in Greeneville, Tenn. First alderman, then mayor of Greeneville, Johnson became known beyond his town. He was elected successively to the state legislature, to the U.S. House of Representatives (where he served from 1843 to 1853), to the governorship of Tennessee, and to the U.S. Senate. He worked for economy in government, for popular election of federal senators and judges, for the abolition of the electoral college, and for laws favoring the working people and frontiersmen. While a U.S. senator, he ardently advocated the Union cause. In 1864 he was elected vice president, under Lincoln; on the assassination of Lincoln in April, 1865, he became president by succession. Both houses were demanding harsh measures against the Southern states, but Johnson adopted the merciful policy of Lincoln. Before Congress met, the seceding states had reorganized their governments in accordance with the Lincoln-Johnson program, but Congress delayed the recognition of congressmen elected under the new state governments and passed severe measures for the treatment of the South. In the struggle that followed, Congress continued to pass bills over the President's veto. The House of Representatives finally impeached Johnson. But since the Senate in trying him could muster only 35 of the 36 votes necessary to convict him and remove him from office, Johnson served the rest of his term. When his term expired, he retired to Tennessee. In 1875 he was again elected to the U.S. Senate.

JOHNSON, LYNDON BAINES (1908-   ), vice president of the United States, was born near Stonewall, Tex., the son of a pioneer Texas family. He attended public schools in Blanco Co., Texas, and was graduated from Southwest Texas State Teachers College and the law school of Georgetown University in Washington, D.C. After a brief period of schoolteaching he was secretary to U.S. Representative Richard M. Kleberg from 1932 to 1935 and Texas state director of the National Youth Administration from 1935 to 1937. In 1937 he was elected to the U.S. House of Representatives and served six terms. Three days after the outbreak of war with Japan in 1941 Johnson enlisted in the Navy and was commissioned a lieutenant commander. He served as an observer on bomber missions in the South Pacific until 1942, when a presidential order banned congressmen from duty with the armed forces.

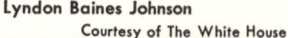

Lyndon Baines Johnson
Courtesy of The White House

He was elected to the U.S. Senate in 1948 and was reelected in 1954. From 1953 to 1955 he served as minority leader in the Senate and from 1955 as majority leader. As Democratic leader of the Senate he showed great ability in carrying through such legislation as the compromise filibuster rule of 1959 and the Civil Rights Act of 1960.

Johnson sought the Democratic presidential nomination for the first time in 1956 but ran third in the balloting. He was defeated for the nomination in 1960 by Senator John F. Kennedy and then accepted the vice presidential nomination. In the election of Nov. 8, 1960, he was elected vice president and also was reelected senator from Texas, a position from which he resigned. He married Claudia Alta Taylor, a wealthy Texas landowner, in 1934.

JOHNSON, SAMUEL (1709-1784), the dominant figure in English literary life in the middle years of the century, was born at Lichfield, where his father ran a bookstore. As a child he was large and awkward, traits that steadily increased as he grew older, and early in his life he contracted a disease that left him permanently scarred. However, as a child he demonstrated his remarkable mind. He read voluminously and by sheer force of his learning and personality made numerous friends. He distinguished himself in grammar school and at Oxford, which he was forced by poverty to leave without taking a degree. At 26 he married a widow 20 years older than himself and shortly thereafter moved to London, where he spent most of the rest of his life.

For several years Johnson supported himself by doing literary hack work. He also published poems, a play, and numerous essays but did not achieve real fame until his *Dictionary of the English Language* was published in 1755. This remarkable work, on which he and a few assistants had worked for nine years, was not only the first great English dictionary but was also a literary masterpiece. The success of the dictionary prompted the government to grant Johnson a pension. Freed from the need to write for a living, Johnson produced comparatively little during his last 25 years. The only important works were the parable *Rasselas, Prince of Abissinia*, an edition of Shakespeare, and the *Lives of the Poets*.

Johnson loved conversation. After the death of his wife in 1752 he found no greater pleasure than sitting in a tavern with a group of intelligent and literate friends with whom he could talk for hours on end. Although neither his manner nor his appearance was particularly appealing, he attracted a wide circle of followers who were fascinated by his brilliant wit and stimulating ideas. In 1764 an informal organization called simply The Club was founded. Its members included Oliver Goldsmith, Joshua Reynolds, and several other leading literary and artistic figures of the time. Johnson's influence upon these and others was so great that his era has since become known as the Age of Johnson. Fortunately, many of his great conversations, which in the final analysis are more important than any of his writings, were recorded by Johnson's faithful disciple James Boswell, who incorporated them into his *Life of Johnson*. This work, among the greatest of all biographies, presents Johnson's brilliant personality far more thoroughly than do any of his own works. See BOSWELL, JAMES; ENGLISH LITERATURE.

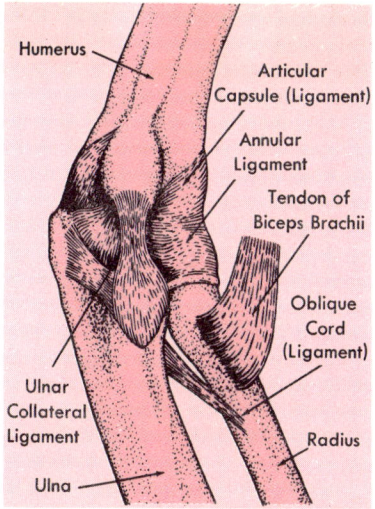

The elbow joint is a good example of a hinge joint. The articular capsule and ligaments associated with it connect the ends of the three long bones of the arm.

JOINT, or articulation, the place of union between two or more bones, usually admitting motion in some of the parts. Joints are classified as immovable joints, slightly movable joints, and freely movable joints. The most familiar examples of immovable joints are the sutures found in the skull. Here union between the various bones forms jagged lines of contact. The slightly movable joints are formed when adjoining bony surfaces are connected by pads of fibrocartilage. The third main class of joints, the freely movable joints, makes up the largest number of joints found in the body. These joints connect adjoining bony surfaces by ligaments. The opposing surfaces are usually covered with articular cartilage, which in turn is connected with a membrane that secretes a lubricating fluid. The types of joints included in the freely movable classification are named by the kind of motion they permit. Those permitting only gliding motion are called gliding joints. Hinge joints have the motion of a door on hinges. Condyloid and saddle joints permit movement in two directions. Pivot joints have a ringlike structure rotating around a pivot. Ball-and-socket joints have a pivot movement as well as an angular motion in all directions.

JOLLIET, LOUIS (1645-1700), Canadian explorer, was born either in Quebec or near Beaupré in New France (now the province of Quebec). He was educated by the Jesuits in Quebec and spent a year studying scientific subjects in Europe. On his first trip to the Great Lakes region in 1669 he met Father Jacques Marquette at Sault Sainte Marie. Guided by an Iroquois Indian, his party returned to Quebec by way of Lake Huron, Lake St. Clair, and the Detroit River, thereby establishing a new all-water route to the West.

Jolliet made other voyages to the western country, and by 1672 he was more familiar with the area than any other Canadian. That year he was selected to lead an expedition in search of the great river that many Indians talked of. Father Marquette was named chaplain of the expedition. See MARQUETTE, JACQUES.

Upon returning from the Mississippi expedition Jolliet left for Quebec to report his discoveries. His canoe overturned in the Lachine Rapids above Montreal, and consequently all his maps, journals, and souvenirs were lost. He was able to draw several maps from memory, but the principal record of the voyage is Marquette's journal.

Jolliet married in 1675 and established his home on Anticosti Island in the Gulf of St. Lawrence. His later explorations included trips around the Gulf of St. Lawrence, along the Labrador coast, and into Hudson Bay. At the time of his death Jolliet held the position of royal mapmaker at Quebec.

JONES, JOHN PAUL (1747-1792), American naval officer, was born in Scotland. His name was originally John Paul. He first went to sea when 12 years old, and by the age of 19 he was third mate on a slave ship. He first commanded merchant ships from 1769 to 1770, when he made two voyages to the West Indies. In 1773, on another voyage to the West Indies, his crew mutinied at the island of Tobago, and while attempting to suppress the mutiny, Jones killed its ringleader. Since the crew remained unfriendly and his life was in danger, he fled to America where, presumably to escape detection, he added Jones to his name.

Jones was unemployed at the beginning of the American Revolution. He went to Philadelphia and on Dec. 7, 1775, secured a commission as lieutenant in the navy. He made his first voyages under the American flag early in 1776. Later that year he received his first command of a ship and was promoted to captain. In 1777 he was sent on a mission to France, and in 1778 he conducted a highly successful raiding expedition along the west coast of England and Scotland. In 1779 he took command of an old French ship, the *Duras*, which he rechristened *Bonhomme Richard* in honor of Benjamin Franklin. On his first voyage with the *Bonhomme Richard* his fleet encountered a British fleet in the North Sea. It was in this battle that Jones, before capturing the British flagship *Serapis*, declared "I have not yet begun to fight."

Jones saw little action during the rest of the war. In 1783 the navy was disbanded, and the following year Jones was sent on a diplomatic mission to Paris, where he remained several years. In 1787 he went to Denmark and from there to Russia, where in 1788 he was commissioned rear admiral in the Russian navy. After a few engagements with the Turks in the Black Sea, Jones was relieved of his duties because of a dispute with his superior officer. In 1790 he returned to Paris, where he died two years later. In 1905 his body was returned to the United States and was later buried at the U.S. Naval Academy situated at Annapolis, Md.

John Paul Jones
C. W. Peale—Independence National Historical Park

© National Portrait Gallery, London
Ben Jonson

JONSON, BEN (1572-1637), Elizabethan dramatist, was born probably in Westminster. He was educated there and later saw military service in Flanders. In 1597 he began working as an actor with Philip Henslowe's company. Jonson began developing his comedy of humors with his first play, *Every Man in His Humor*, which was performed in 1598 with Shakespeare in the cast. *Every Man Out of His Humor* appeared the following year, and in 1600, *Cynthia's Revels*. *The Poetaster* appeared in 1601, and his first extant tragedy, *Sejanus*, was done by Shakespeare's company in 1603. For his part in writing the play *Eastward Ho* Jonson was imprisoned but was released through the intercession of friends.

Between 1606 and 1616 appeared five of Jonson's great plays: *Volpone*, *Epicoene*, *The Alchemist*, *Bartholomew Fair*, and *The Devil Is an Ass*. James I awarded Jonson a pension in 1616. *The Staple of News* appeared in 1625. Other works of Jonson's include his tragedy *Catiline* and his prose work *Timber; or Discoveries Made upon Men and Matter*.

JORDAN is a constitutional monarchy in southwestern Asia. The greater portion of it consists of former Trans-Jordan, east of the Jordan River. It includes also the central portion of Arab Palestine, west of the Jordan River. Jordan's border with Israel is not recognized by any of the Arab states, and it remains sealed to practically all traffic. The Jordanian region was the home of the Old Testament prophets and the scene of Christ's birth and death. It served as a springboard for the widespread conquests of Islam. Places of religious and historic importance in Jordan include Jerusalem (divided with Israel), Bethlehem, Jericho, Hebron, Petra, and Amman. Amman is Jordan's capital. The only port is Aqaba, on the country's short coastline on the Gulf of Aqaba of the Red Sea. Jordan covers about 37,500 square miles. Its population is about 1,700,000.

Most of the population lives in or near the Jordan Valley. A section of the Jordan River flows southward from the Sea of Galilee to the Dead Sea, whose shores are the lowest place on the earth's surface.

Above are the flag, adopted after World War I, and the coat of arms of Jordan.

The Jordan River forms part of the boundary with Israel; Israel also includes part of the Dead Sea. Steep cliffs rise on both sides of the Jordan Valley. To the west lies a region of rounded hills and wide valleys; to the east, a rolling plateau falling to a wide desert plain that accounts for most of the country.

The climate of western Jordan is influenced by the Mediterranean. Summers are hot and dry; winters, mild with occasional heavy showers. Snow sometimes falls at the higher elevations. Eastern Jordan has a desert climate, with places where no rain falls at all in some years.

Although Jordan is mostly desert, farming is the chief occupation, often carried on by primitive methods. The main crops are wheat, olives, barley, vegetables, and fruits, including bananas, oranges, figs, and pomegranates. Tobacco is the industrial crop of significance. Livestock raising, especially of goats and sheep, is very important. Much livestock is raised by desert tribes. Camels are essential in the desert, being used for work, transportation, and food.

The principal exports are fresh fruits, vegetables, and raw wool shipped to neighboring states. Tourism is an important source of income, but Jordan's economy is not self-supporting and requires foreign assistance.

The people of western Jordan are Palestinians, persons of mixed origin whose ancestors settled there countless generations ago. Several hundred thousand Palestinian Arab refugees, who lost their homes in Israel as a result of the conflict in Palestine, live in camps in western Jordan. They live mainly on subsistence rations provided by the

The shepherd drives his flock of goats over the dry and barren land of Jordan.
Roubat, Réalites—Photo Researchers

Inge Morath, Magnum Photos, Inc.
These hills along the Jordan River valley figured prominently in biblical history.

United Nations. The people of eastern Jordan are descendants of Arabian Bedouin tribes. Many are still desert nomads. The country's population is overwhelmingly Moslem, but there are other religions. Arabic is the national language.

Before coming under British control in World War I, the area now comprising Jordan had been under Turkish rule for 400 years. After the war it became part of the British mandate of Palestine. In 1923 Trans-Jordan (the land east of the Jordan River) was set up as a semi-independent nation under British protection. It became an independent kingdom in 1946. When the Palestine mandate ended in 1948, Jordan's army invaded the newly proclaimed state of Israel and occupied the central region of Palestine. See PALESTINE.

The 1949 truce permitted Jordan to retain the area, which was then formally annexed. The country became known as the Hashemite Kingdom of the Jordan. In 1958 it joined a short-lived federation with Iraq to counteract the anti-Western activities of the United Arab Republic, but the federation dissolved with the Iraqi revolution. To prevent overthrow of Jordan's government, British troops were brought to the country for several months. For detailed map, see ISRAEL.

JORDAN

Area: 37,500 sq. mi.
Population: 1,700,000
Capital: Amman
Largest cities: Jerusalem, Amman
Chief rivers: Jordan, Yarmuk
Chief lake: Dead Sea
Climate: Hot, dry summers and mild winters—winter rainfall in northwest—little rain in east and south
National flag: Three horizontal stripes of black, white, green—red triangle containing white star on pole side
Form of government: Constitutional monarchy
Unit of currency: Jordan dinar
Language: Arabic
Chief religion: Moslem
Chief economic activity: Agriculture, including livestock raising
Chief crops: Wheat, barley, vegetables, fruits, olives
Chief minerals: Potash (from the Dead Sea), phosphates
Chief exports: Fresh fruits, vegetables, wool
Chief imports: Foodstuffs, petroleum products, automobiles, iron and steel manufactures

JOULE, JAMES (1818-1889), an English physicist, was born in Lancashire. He studied under the chemist John Dalton. Joule's father, who was a well-to-do brewer in Manchester, was so pleased with his son's progress that he fitted out a laboratory for him. Joule worked in his private laboratory all his life and never accepted a teaching or other academic position.

Joule's researches provided the basis for the modern science of thermodynamics. He proved that heat is energy, that work can produce heat, and that heat can do work. This identity of heat and work established by Joule is the basis of the theory of the conservation of energy. Joule's experiments strengthened the idea that energy can be transformed but cannot be created or destroyed.

The joule, the unit of work equivalent to 10,000,000 ergs, is named for Joule.

The presidential White House press secretary holds press conferences with news reporters in order to make official announcements of the U.S. government's policies on all important domestic and international matters.

UPI

JOURNALISM is the collection and dissemination of information, especially of news, to a mass audience. The major journalistic media are the newspaper, the magazine, the radio, television, and the motion picture. All individuals engaged in gathering, writing, and editing news for these media are called journalists. They may be editors, reporters, rewrite men, columnists, photographers, radio and TV commentators, foreign correspondents, critics or reviewers of drama, music, and art, free-lance writers, or political cartoonists.

News is defined as anything timely that is of interest and importance to the greatest number of people. A good journalist is one who has a nose for news. He is able to select from a mass of events those that will interest his audience, his treatment often creating such interest.

No journalistic publication is more varied in its contents than is a daily newspaper. But its primary function has been and still is the reporting of news. It is for most people their main source of such information. See NEWSPAPER.

The news reporter is the eyes and ears of the newspaper as well as of the radio and television broadcaster.

OCCUPATION: Journalist
NATURE OF WORK: Gathering and writing of subject matter for publication
PERSONAL FACTORS—ABILITIES, SKILLS, APTITUDES: An interest in people and events is essential. The ability to use words properly and a good knowledge of rhetoric are very important. Journalists must have open minds, integrity, a sense of humor, perseverance, and the ability to get along well with people.
EDUCATION AND SPECIAL TRAINING: A bachelor's degree from a school of journalism is necessary. Additional training in radio and television is helpful for specialization. On-the-job education is the best training.
WORKING CONDITIONS:
1. **INCOME:**
    COMPARED WITH OTHER CAREERS WITH EQUAL TRAINING: Average to high
    COMPARED WITH MOST OTHER CAREERS: Average to high
2. **ENVIRONMENT:** Varying from noisy newspaper office and news scenes to quiet editorial office or broadcasting studio
3. **OTHERS:** Irregular hours; possible travel; opportunities for excitement, considerable prestige, and recognition
RELATED CAREERS: Reporter, editor, copyreader, rewrite man, columnist, news analyst
WHERE TO FIND MORE INFORMATION: American Newspaper Publishers Association, 750 Third Avenue, New York 17, N.Y.; American Council on Education for Journalism, 119 Gregory Hall, University of Illinois, Urbana, Ill.; leading universities having schools of journalism.

Up-to-the-minute news reports of election returns are broadcast on radio and TV.
NBC Television

It is his job to go out and get the news, either by personal observation of the events or by interviewing eyewitnesses. Reporters also work for large news agencies (United Press International, Reuters, Tass) that collect and make available to the various news media a steady supply of news. See NEWS AGENCY.

Most of the news gathered by reporters and agencies is transmitted to the newspaper office by telephone, telegraph, cable, or wireless. It is then rewritten and edited to meet space requirements and edition deadlines, given headlines, set in type, made into pages, printed, and finally distributed to the public.

The use of photographs is important in news reporting, especially in such printed media of mass communication as newspapers and news magazines. A press photographer often works with the reporter. Journalistically, photographs can be used in several ways. They may be subordinate to, and serve as illustrations for, stories; they may appear alone with only short explanatory texts; or they may be equal in news importance to the accompanying stories.

The invention in the 20th century of radio and television and their development as effective journalistic media caused a revolution in news reporting. Radio added a new element, sound, to reporting. It enabled a reporter to carry a microphone to the scene of a news event and to broadcast accounts over the air direct to the public. On-the-scene coverage of sports contests, political debates and conventions, and disasters—such as fires and floods—became very common. Recording devices, which came into use during the mid-1940's, enabled newscasters to play back reports of all kinds at times most convenient for listeners. With the advent of television, audiences could actually see the news taking place.

But broadcasting direct from the scene is only one of numerous ways in which radio and television present news. Others include the reading of summaries of the latest news by commentators, roundtable discussions of important news features by specialists, the presentation of long special-events programs on domestic and foreign news, dramatizations, and interviews with important citizens in such fields as politics, athletics, entertainment, science, medicine, education, and religion. Newsreels and documentary films, which were originally shown only in motion picture theaters, are also used on TV.

JOYCE, JAMES (1882-1941), Irish novelist, was born in a suburb of Dublin. He was educated at Jesuit schools and a Jesuit college, where he distinguished himself as a writer and as a scholar, particularly in Latin and several modern languages. For a time he considered becoming a priest, but by 1902 he had lost faith not only in his church but also in his family and his country, and, determined to become a writer, he left Ireland for Paris. He returned to Ireland in 1903 but left again in 1904 and spent the rest of his life in Trieste, Zurich, and Paris.

Joyce's writings were so advanced that he had great difficulty getting them published, and after publication they were usually misunderstood and therefore sold very poorly. Consequently, his life was in part a struggle with poverty. His masterpiece, *Ulysses*, was published in France in 1922 but was banned in all English-speaking countries for over ten years. Finally it was admitted to the United States in 1933 after a famous court decision overruled the earlier charges of obscenity. *Ulysses* was subsequently published in Great Britain, but it is still banned in Ireland. The royalties obtained from the American publication of *Ulysses* enabled Joyce to spend a few of his later years in comparative comfort.

Ulysses is one of the most complex novels ever written. It describes in very great detail the principal events of a single day in the lives of three Dubliners. Every character and event parallels in some way a character or event in Homer's *Odyssey;* thus Leopold Bloom, the middle-aged advertising-salesman hero, parallels Odysseus; his wife Molly, Penelope; and Stephen Daedalus (a young man patterned to a large extent on Joyce himself), Telemachus. The novel is divided into 18 episodes, each written in a style peculiarly appropriate to its content. Several employ the stream-of-consciousness, or internal monologue, a technique perfected by Joyce, in which not only a character's speech but also his stray thoughts and impressions are recorded in full detail.

Joyce's other major works are *Dubliners*, a volume of short stories; *A Portrait of the Artist as a Young Man*, a short autobiographical novel; and *Finnegans Wake*, a novel even more complex than *Ulysses*, in which Joyce attempted with astonishing success to set down on paper the dream world of the unconscious. He also published three small volumes of poetry and one play.

JUÁREZ, BENITO PABLO (1806-1872), a Mexican revolutionary leader, born near the city of Oaxaca, in Mexico. His parents were full-blooded Indians. Both parents died when he was but three years old, and he was brought up tending his uncle's sheep. When some of these sheep were stolen, he escaped from his uncle's anger into the city of Oaxaca, where a Franciscan brother gave him work and aroused his interest in studying. By the time he was 25, Juárez had taught himself enough law to enter a law office as clerk. For the next several years he gave legal advice to Indian farmers who were too poor and illiterate to compete with the big landowners.

As governor of his native state of Oaxaca from 1847 until 1852, Juárez established an honest and efficient administration. After the return of the dictator Santa Anna in 1853, Juárez was arrested, jailed, and banished. He went to New Orleans and helped plot Santa Anna's overthrow.

In January, 1858, Juárez was one of the presidents of Mexico, and the following May he established his capital in the liberal stronghold of Veracruz. The conservative forces and their president, Félix Zuloaga, ruled in Mexico City. In 1859 Juárez decreed a land reform, depriving the church of its lands and assigning them to the poor. With the majority of the people behind him, he and his troops occupied Mexico City. But when Juárez refused to pay the country's debts, England and France invaded Mexico; and in 1864 Napoleon III, the French emperor, sent Archduke Maximilian of Austria to be emperor of Mexico. Juárez escaped to the border; three years later he was back in Mexico City as president, and Maximilian was executed. By this time Juárez was a sick old man. One of the generals, Porfirio Díaz, led a revolution against the government. However, Juárez was reelected to the presidency. He died a few months after his third term began.

Benito Pablo Juárez, revolutionary

Paul's Photos

JUDAISM, the religion of the Jewish people. The heart of Judaism is belief in one God, who is both beyond the universe and within it. Man, although he is bound within the chain of natural causation, is regarded in Judaism as an active agent in the establishment of God's kingdom of peace and justice for all mankind. Judaism is a dynamic religion that regards God's revelation as expressed continuously through the prophets, sages, poets, mystics, priests, and scholars of the Jewish community.

Judaism had its early roots in rich Semitic religious traditions, which included taboos, a belief in spirits and demons, animism, and ritual connected with ancestor worship. Monotheism may be traced from the time of Abraham, but it was during the life of Moses that Judaism became definitely monotheistic and developed a body of rites and laws connected with the belief in one God. (See ABRAHAM; MOSES). In Canaan Judaism developed a priesthood, sacrificial rituals, and festivals. Prophets arose who maintained the pure concept of monotheism and stressed the moral quality of righteousness. The dispersal of the Jews began after the Babylonian captivity. The destruction of the second Temple by the Romans (A.D. 70) left the Jews without a political homeland. The Torah (the first five books of the Bible) became the spiritual homeland of each Jew, and his community life centered on the synagogue. Rabbis replaced priests. After the rise of Islam in the 7th century the Talmud gradually became a common possession of all Jews, although the Karaites opposed it and stressed a return to the Torah. The period highlighted by the work of Maimonides was one of codification and organization on the one hand and of the mystical influence of the cabala on the other hand. (See MAIMONIDES). In the 18th century Moses Mendelssohn initiated the modern liberalization of Judaism that led to Reform Judaism. Orthodox Judaism held to a stricter form of the religion, while conservative Judaism adopted a middle ground.

Judaism is made up of four major elements—the community, the Torah, a morality, and a creed. The community, which is Israel in a spiritual sense, is the whole Jewish people, bound together by ties of history and kinship. The community welcomes converts who join of their own free will, and in free nations it identifies with the culture of its neighbors. The synagogue is the organized core of the community. (See SYNAGOGUE.) The festivals (such as Passover), solemn days (Rosh Hashana and Yom Kippur), days of sorrow, and joyous holidays (Hanukkah) commemorate historical events and provide each Jew with the living presence of his faith and his community.

The Torah—for Jews, the revealed will of God—contains the past religious experience of Judaism and provides a moral law for the present and future. The Mishnah is a detailed interpretation of the Torah. The Talmud, which contains scholarship and discussion pertaining to the Mishnah, is a record of Halakah, or legal debate; and Haggada, or folklore, legends, ethical and theological discussions, parables, prayers, and aphorisms.

The morality of Judaism is based on the ethical monotheism stated in the Torah. Judaism affirms the goodness of human life and holds that mankind is perfectible and that moral striving is best expressed through the family, the Jewish community, and society at large.

The creed of Judaism consists in a reliance upon God, or faith, tempered by reason. The fundamental prayer of Judaism is taken from the Torah: "Hear, O Israel: The Lord our God is one Lord: And thou shalt love the Lord thy God with all thine heart, and with all thy soul, and with all thy might." Man's soul is regarded as indestructible and thus lives beyond the grave.

JUDGE is the official who presides over the trial of a lawsuit. Judges may preside alone; with a jury; or in reviewing courts, such as the U.S. Supreme Court, and in multijudge trial courts. The judge sees that the trial or suit is conducted according to the proper rules. He controls what may be accepted as evidence. He decides any questions regarding the law that may come up during the case. The judge advises the jury, before it retires to find the verdict, about matters of law bearing on its decision. When there is no jury, he gives the decision himself or with other judges.

In the United States there are two types of judges: federal judges and state judges. Federal judges are appointed by the president and remain in office so long as their behavior is good. They may voluntarily retire with full pay after the age of 70 if they have been in office ten years. Most state judges are elected for a specific term.

JUDICIAL REVIEW, the power of the court system of a nation to decide whether legislative acts accord with its constitution. The most notable exercise of this power is that by the U.S. Supreme Court. The Federal Constitutional Court of West Germany also has this power. The Supreme Court of Canada and of many other nations may advise on questions of constitutionality but do not exercise judicial review.

There are three types of judicial review in the United States. The first of these is the power of the courts to decide the constitutionality of congressional legislation. The second is the duty of the courts to uphold the Constitution in cases of conflict with state laws and state constitutional provisions. The third is the power of state courts to rule on the conformance of state laws with state constitutions.

The power of judicial review, which is not specifically granted by the Constitution, became constitutional law as a result of the decision handed down in 1803 by Chief Justice John Marshall in the case of *Marbury* vs. *Madison*. Marbury, a judge appointed by President John Adams, was denied his position by the newly elected president, Jefferson. Marbury sued for a writ that would compel James Madison, Jefferson's secretary of state, to carry out the appointment. A section of the Judiciary Act of 1789 empowered the court to issue such a writ. Marshall declared this section unconstitutional and therefore void.

The Basic Law of the Federal Republic of Germany empowers the Federal Constitutional Court to decide on the interpretation of the constitution in case of disputes concerning the extent of the rights and duties of the highest federal organ, in cases of differences of opinion on the compatibility of federal law or *Land* law with the constitution, and in cases of differences of opinion on the rights and duties of the Federation and the *Laender*. The Federal Constitutional Court is therefore the guardian of the constitution. French tradition has held that the legislature is supreme. The Constitutional Committee of the Fourth Republic was rarely used and was not completely independent of Parliament. The constitution of the Fifth Republic, however, created a Constitutional Council composed of former presidents of the republic and nine additional members. The Council has full power to rule on the constitutionality of organic laws and parliamentary regulations.

JUJITSU is a form of wrestling, first practiced in Japan. Another common name for the sport is judo.

Jujitsu is based on the idea of using the strength of one's opponent to overcome him. The jujitsu expert must learn certain grips, blows, and motions that will allow him to take advantage of his opponent most effectively. Three basic methods are often used to win a jujitsu contest. The first method requires the wrestler to grasp his opponent and hurl him to the ground. This result is often achieved by using the opponent's own forward motion in such a way that he sends himself flying to the ground. The second basic method requires the wrestler to gain a grip on his opponent so that the latter cannot move. Victory is achieved in the third method by striking or kicking one's opponent in a vital and sensitive part of his body.

Jujitsu became widely known in the United States when it was taught to the troops during World War II for purposes of self-defense. It remained popular in the United States as a useful form of self-defense rather than as a competitive sport. In Japan, however, competitive exhibitions are held frequently and attract large audiences. A jujitsu match ends when one opponent gives up for fear of serious injury. Jujitsu is thought to have originated in Japan during the 1600's.

Jujitsu is both a sport and a form of self-defense. It should be practiced under an expert, such as this YMCA instructor.
Photo, Jerry Cooke, YMCA

JULIUS CAESAR (100?-44 B.C.), Roman statesman and general. Caesar was one of the great military leaders of history. He made Gaul a Roman province and prepared the way for the establishment of the Roman Empire. Caesar was a man of vision and versatility. Shakespeare pictured Caesar at his worst, after power had corrupted him.

Sources for the life of Caesar include biographies by Suetonius and Plutarch (Shakespeare's source). Caesar himself wrote *Commentaries* on the Gallic and civil wars. These works, written in a clear and incisive style, created a new literary genre. As an orator he was excelled only by Cicero.

Caesar was born into a patrician family. In 84 he married Cornelia, daughter of an enemy of the dictator Sulla. Deprived of property and rank for refusing to divorce his wife, Caesar fled Rome. He served in military campaigns in Asia and returned to Rome in 78 following Sulla's death. In Rome he plunged into politics and won favor with the populace, who elected him pontifex maximus in 63.

Following a period of valuable military experience as propraetor in Spain, he returned to Rome in 60. The Senate, influenced by Cato the Younger, refused Caesar's request to stand for the consulate, whereupon Caesar refused the triumph granted to victorious generals and joined with the great general Pompey and the wealthy Crassus in the First Triumvirate. Caesar secured the consulate in 59. He was granted the governorship of Cisalpine Gaul (northern Italy), Illyricum, and Transalpine Gaul (the huge territory bounded by the Mediterranean, the Pyrenees, the ocean, the Rhine River, and the Alps). The German tribes in Transalpine Gaul were on the verge of seeking mastery of the territory, and for nine years Caesar was occupied with subduing them. He also conducted inconclusive campaigns in Britain in 55 and 54. His defeat of Vercingetorix settled the fate of Gaul, which became an orderly province by 51.

In 54, however, Julia, daughter of Caesar and wife of Pompey, died. Crassus was killed in 53. In league with the Senate, Pompey worked to undermine Caesar's power. In 49 Caesar, with one legion, crossed the Rubicon, a river on the northern boundary of Italy proper. Pompey fled to the East, where he was renowned, and Caesar overran all of Italy. After subduing Pompey's lieutenants in Spain, Caesar sailed to meet Pompey. On the plain of Thessaly his hardened veterans defeated decisively Pompey's larger army. Pompey fled to Egypt, where he was murdered. In Egypt Caesar became involved in the Alexandrine War, which he successfully resolved in favor of Cleopatra. In 47 Caesar defeated Pharnaces II at Zela (now Zile) in Asia Minor and sent to Rome his succinct report, "*Veni, vidi, vici*" (I came, I saw, I conquered). In 46 Caesar crushed the Pompeian forces that had united under Scipio in Africa. In Rome in 46 Caesar celebrated his great triumphs and won the people with festivals, gifts, and games. In the same year he fought Pompey's sons, whom he defeated in Spain in one of his most difficult battles.

Against all Roman tradition Caesar was made dictator for life in 44. His head appeared on Roman coins of 45 and 44, and he aspired to a monarchy. Because of public disapproval Caesar reluctantly refused the crown placed on his head by Mark Antony in February, 44. On Mar. 15, 44, Caesar fell beneath the knives of conspirators led by Marcus Brutus and Gaius Cassius. Caesar's new government had seemed to portend a world empire in which the old republican institutions would have no place. For this reason Julius Caesar was assassinated by the senatorial aristocracy. See BRUTUS, MARCUS JUNIUS; CICERO, MARCUS TULLIUS; CLEOPATRA; MARK ANTONY; POMPEY THE GREAT.

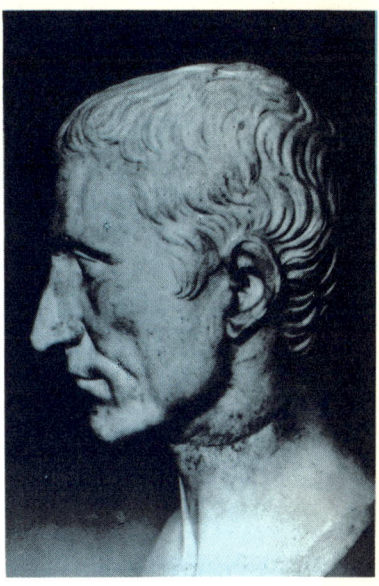

The versatile and cultured Julius Caesar was a general, statesman, writer, and orator.

Steve McCutcheon

Juneau, Alaska's capital, is a sea and fishing port, ice free the year round.

JUNEAU, the capital of Alaska, in the southeastern part of the state, on the Gastineau Channel, near the border of the Yukon Territory of Canada. The city is beautifully situated in a region of bays, islands, and snowcapped mountains. It is a seaport and fishing center and has a large trade in gold and furs from the surrounding area. Other important industries are salmon canning and lumber milling. Average temperatures at Juneau range from 21° F. in January to 63° F. in July. The harbor remains open all year. Within easy reach of Juneau by boat, car, or plane are some of the state's finest fishing and hunting areas. The Alaska Historical Library and Museum in Juneau has an extensive Eskimo collection.

Founded in 1880 following the discovery of gold nearby, the city became the capital of the Alaska Territory in 1900. The population (1960) is 6,797.

JUNGLE, a thick growth of trees and underbrush found in many tropical regions. Often the growth is so dense that men must cut it down in order to pass through. Tall grasses, ferns, and woody vines called lianas abound. Heavy rainfall, high temperatures, and sunlight penetrating to the ground are necessary to make the vegetation grow with such luxuriance. Much of the tropical rain forest does not have the dense undergrowth of the jungle because the thick overhead foliage of the trees prevents sunlight from reaching the forest floor. But jungles occur, for example, along the large streams. Jungles are found in parts of South America, Central America, Africa, and Asia and in some islands of the South Pacific. See TROPICAL RAIN FOREST.

JUNIOR ACHIEVEMENT, in the United States and Canada, a nonprofit program designed to instruct young persons in practical business operation. The participants, boys and girls from 15 to 21 years of age, set up miniature corporations, which they run in accordance with the principles of senior corporations. These companies provide services or products for sale, and the members learn to keep business and production records, organize advertising and publicity campaigns, and prepare financial statements. The motto of Junior Achievement is "Learn by doing."

The Junior Achievement program was founded in 1919 by Horace A. Moses, president of a paper company. Moses had been active in the 4-H Club program and conceived the Junior Achievement program as a means of doing for city young people what the 4-H program was doing for rural youths. The national program was launched in 1941, but its real expansion began in 1946. Well over half the states in the United States have a Junior Achievement program as do two provinces of Canada.

At the local level the program is developed by labor, business, civic, and educational leaders. These people comprise a local Junior Achievement Committee, which guides and directs the finances of the program. The direct management of a company is guided by a local, trained director, who is paid by the local committee. The actual operation of the company, however, is in the hands of the young people. They decide on the service or product they want to sell and on the name of the company. Capital is obtained by selling stock at 50 cents a share. Once a week the company meets for two hours at a regular meeting place in order to conduct business operations. Each member is a stockholder, manager, and wage earner. Members are advised in business procedure by adult advisers who are expert in the fields of management and accounting, production, and sales. Once a year the company holds a stockholders meeting at which it decides on the dividends to stockholders and bonuses to employees. Each company competes for national awards in various

This Junior Achievement company assembly line is producing coasters and snack trays.
Junior Achievement of Southeastern Wisconsin, Inc.

business fields. The members compete for scholarship awards. The companies are in business from October to May each year.

The local operations are autonomous, but they are aided by the national organization, Junior Achievement, Inc. The national board of directors provides information and assistance to local groups. A national advisory council, composed of outstanding representatives from many fields of endeavor, offers advice on policies and awards.

JUNO was the queen of the gods in Roman mythology. She was the wife of Jupiter, the king of the gods and lord of the heavens. Her name in Greek mythology was Hera.

The Romans and Greeks believed that she was the most queenly of the goddesses, and they described her as sitting on a golden throne and

Sculptured head of the goddess Juno

driving a golden-wheeled chariot. Roman women held a special celebration in her honor every year on March 1.

Juno was a jealous goddess. She tried to kill Hercules, the son of Jupiter and Alcmene. When she failed, she caused Hercules to perform the difficult twelve labors. (See HERCULES.) At another time Juno became jealous when Jupiter paid attention to the maiden Callisto. She changed Callisto into a bear.

Jupiter, a sculptured head from Pompeii

JUPITER was the king of the gods and lord of the heavens in Roman mythology. His name in Greek mythology was Zeus. Both the Romans and the Greeks considered him the wisest and most glorious of the gods. They believed that he controlled the winds, rains, clouds, and seasons. Lightning and thunder were thought to be caused by Jupiter hurling his thunderbolts across the sky.

Jupiter was the son of the Titan, Saturn (or Cronus) and Rhea. Saturn was the lord of all the heavens and of earth. But a prophecy told him that one of his children would overthrow him. He tried to prevent this by swallowing each child as it was born. Rhea, however, tricked her husband by substituting a rock wrapped in baby clothes for him to swallow in place of Jupiter. After Jupiter had become a man, he attacked Saturn and defeated him. He freed his brothers and sisters and became king of the gods. One of his sisters, Juno, became his wife.

The children of Jupiter and Juno were the gods Mars and Vulcan and the goddess Hebe. His other children included the goddess Minerva, who sprang full-grown from his brain, the gods Apollo and Mercury, and the goddesses Diana and Venus. Jupiter was also the father of Hercules whose mother was Alcmene.

JUPITER is the largest planet of our solar system. All the other eight planets put together would fill a space only about two-thirds the size of Jupiter. Over 1,300 earths would be needed to equal Jupiter's size. Its diameter at the equator is 88,700 miles—over ten times the earth's diameter and actually one-tenth the diameter of the sun itself.

In spite of such huge size Jupiter turns completely on its axis in less than ten hours, which makes its day shorter than any other planet's. Its rapid rotation has caused enough bulging of the equatorial region to make the diameter there 7,000 miles greater than the diameter through the flattened poles.

Jupiter's mass, a measure of its amount of material, is over 2½ times larger than the combined mass of the other planets. A man weighing 200 pounds on earth would weigh over 500 pounds on Jupiter because of the greater gravitational pull of its mass. To escape this pull a spaceship would need the extremely high velocity of 133,000 miles per hour (37 miles per second), compared with 25,000 miles per hour (7 miles per second) on earth.

In spite of its great mass Jupiter's huge size means that it is only one-third more dense than water. Its atmosphere is known to contain some methane and ammonia, and the temperature above the clouds has been measured as about −130° C. Astronomers presently believe that the planet may be composed mainly of hydrogen under tremendous pressure, plus some helium. The great mass of the planet is

One of Jupiter's 12 satellites is shown (bottom left) crossing the planet's disk. In the first two phases, the satellite (white object) may be seen as well as its shadow. Jupiter's volume is greater than that of all the other planets combined (below).

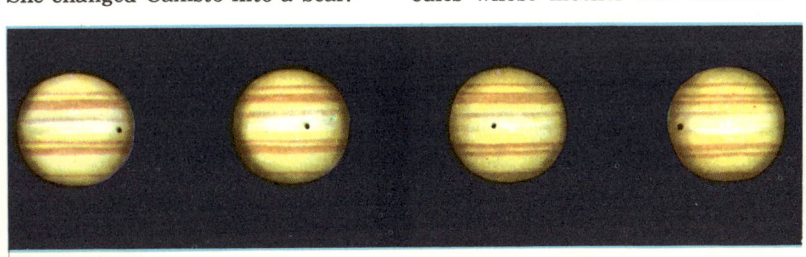

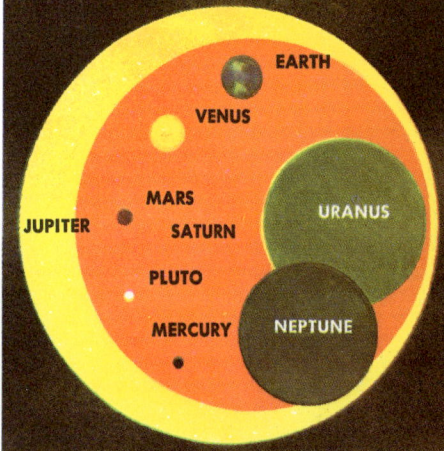

thought to lie near its center, for otherwise the high rotation speed would cause an even larger equatorial bulge. Strong radiowave emissions have been detected from Jupiter, but their cause is not yet known.

Jupiter is the fifth major planet in order of distance from the sun. It lies beyond Mars and the asteroid belt and closer than Saturn; its average distance from the sun is 483,000,000 miles, which is five times farther from the sun than we are on earth. Even when Jupiter is closest to us, it is about ten times farther away than the planet Mars at its closest approach.

Being farther from the sun than the earth Jupiter travels more slowly in its orbit—about 8 miles per second compared with the earth's 19 miles per second—and takes 12 years to make a complete trip around the sun.

Normally Jupiter appears as the second brightest object in the sky, excluding the sun and moon. Venus is always brighter. Occasionally Mars outshines Jupiter's brightest phase, and when Jupiter is dimmest, the bright star Sirius or occasionally the planet Mercury may outshine it.

Jupiter has 12 satellites—the largest number for any planet of our solar system. One of these, Ganymede, is the largest satellite in the solar system and, with a diameter of 3,100 miles, is actually larger than the planet Mercury (diameter 2,900 miles). Another of Jupiter's satellites, Callisto (diameter 2,800 miles), is almost the size of Mercury; two others, Io and Europa (diameters 2,000 and 1,800 miles), are nearly the size of our moon (diameter 2,160 miles). These four satellites are brightly visible in a small telescope and could even be seen by the eye alone except for Jupiter's glare.

These four of Jupiter's satellites are the only ones given official names. They are also numbered in order of their distance from Jupiter. Io is first, Europa second, Ganymede third, and Callisto fourth. Their orbits are located from 260,000 to 1,170,000 miles from Jupiter.

The rest of the satellites are numbered in order of their discovery. The fifth, sometimes called Amalthaea, is a tiny moonlet about 150 miles in diameter and is the only satellite actually closer to Jupiter than the four already discussed. It is but 113,000 miles from Jupiter. The swiftest satellite of the solar system, it moves some 60,000 miles miles per hour.

Millions of miles more distant from Jupiter than these five inner satellites are three more—the sixth, seventh, and tenth. They circle Jupiter at a distance of about 7,000,000 miles. In all the solar system only one other satellite (belonging to Saturn) revolves at such a distance from its planet. Yet Jupiter has four more satellites revolving at double this distance—about 14,000,000 miles. These outermost satellites—the eighth, ninth, eleventh, and twelfth—all have retrograde motion, that is, they revolve from east to west instead of from west to east. For this reason astronomers think they may be captured asteroids or perhaps satellites that at one time escaped and were later recaptured. All the outer seven satellites are small—100 miles or less in diameter.

JURY is a group of persons sworn to determine the facts on the basis of evidence given in a legal hearing or trial. The jury, of which there are three main types—the coroner's jury, the grand jury, and the petit, or trial, jury—originated in France in the 9th century but developed in England and spread to the various English colonies. Many European countries adopted the trial jury in the 19th century.

The coroner's jury examines evidence to determine whether a death was unnatural and if so how it was caused. In the United States the jury numbers from 12 to 23 and usually consists of people from the neighborhood where the death occurred. At least 12 members must agree on the verdict.

The purpose of the grand jury is to investigate crime and to indict suspects, when evidence points to them, so that they can be tried. Indictment in Canada and the United States is by majority vote. The number of jurors in the United States is determined by the individual state and ranges between 6 and 23. The grand jury was abolished in England in 1933.

The trial, or petit, jury—so called because it is usually smaller than the grand jury—is the most important part of the jury system. Trial by jury is guaranteed by the U.S. Constitution in all suits at common law, one type of noncriminal law, in which claims exceed $20.00 and in all criminal cases. However, one may decline jury trial in certain cases, and in other cases it has to be specially requested. In England the jury is used in many criminal cases but rarely in civil cases, though sometimes the parties can request a jury trial. In Canada jury trial is mandatory for certain high crimes; minor crimes are usually tried without jury; and in most of the criminal cases that come between, the defendant can choose the manner of trial. The various provinces determine the types of civil cases that must be tried by jury, but the parties can also request jury trial in other cases.

Though the jury trial in England and the United States springs from one tradition, there is a significant difference between trials in the two countries. In England the judge's instructions to the jury before it goes out to determine the verdict include a summary of the evidence, a statement of its relevance to the questions to be decided, and an evaluation of it, as well as an explanation of various points of law. In most of the states of the United States, on the other hand, the judge is forbidden to comment on the evidence and in many of them he is not allowed to summarize it.

In all criminal cases in England and Canada and in most of the states of the United States, the jury's verdict must be unanimous. In civil cases tried by jury in Canada and in certain states of the United States unanimity is not required.

The trial jury usually consists of 12 persons, though in some cases the number may be smaller. The jury is chosen from a list, made up by special officials, of those eligible for jury service. The lawyers on each side have the right to object to, or challenge, prospective jurors for various reasons and sometimes without giving a reason.

Those eligible for jury service in the United States are usually all literate citizens between 21 and 70 who have not been convicted of a major crime. Each state determines eligibility and the causes for excuse and exemption from jury service. In England jurors must be persons between 21 and 60 years old, must be citizens or persons who have lived in England for 10 years and must own some property. In the United States and Canada the juror usually is paid for his service and for traveling expenses.

Trial by jury exists in Belgium, Greece, Norway, Sweden, France, and Italy and throughout Latin America. In most of these countries it is used only in criminal cases, though in Sweden only press offenses are tried before juries. In France the system provides that only major crimes are tried before juries.

L. B. Prince

This building in Washington, D.C., houses the United States Department of Justice.

JUSTICE, UNITED STATES DEPARTMENT OF, one of the departments of the federal government, headed by the attorney general, who is a member of the president's cabinet. The office of attorney general was created in 1789 with cabinet rank, but the Department of Justice was not established until 1870. The chief purposes of the department are to provide means for the enforcement of federal laws, to furnish legal counsel in federal cases, and to interpret the laws under which other departments act. The department represents the government in legal matters generally and gives legal advice and opinions, upon request, to the president and to the heads of other executive departments. The Department of Justice conducts all suits in the Supreme Court in which the United States is concerned, supervises the federal penal institutions, and investigates and detects violations of federal laws. The attorney general supervises and directs the activities of the U.S. district attorneys and marshals in the various judicial districts throughout the country. The principal components of the department are the following: offices of the attorney general, deputy attorney general, solicitor general, legal counsel, pardon attorney, and office of alien property; antitrust, civil rights, civil, criminal, internal security, lands, tax, and administrative divisions; Federal Bureau of Investigation; Bureau of Prisons; boards of immigration appeals and of parole; and the Immigration and Naturalization Service.

JUSTINIAN I (A.D. 483–565), called the Great, who became Byzantine emperor in 527. His reign witnessed the last but temporary reunion of the western with the eastern part of the old Roman Empire. Justinian's chief claims to fame rest on his work as legislator, builder, and patron of the arts.

Justinian was born in a village in Macedonia, of Illyrian or Albanian origin. After 518 he was adviser to his uncle, Emperor Justin the Elder. Justinian married a former actress, the beautiful, witty, and intelligent Theodora, who until her death in 548 took an active part in the government. She and the brilliant general Belisarius saved Justinian's throne during the Nika Insurrection of 532, when the rebels destroyed a large part of the capital, Constantinople (now Istanbul).

Justinian considered himself the rightful heir of the Roman Caesars and aimed at the restoration of the Christian Roman Empire. In three long wars his armies and navies conquered North Africa from the Vandals (533–543), Italy from the Ostrogoths (535–554), and a part of Spain from the Visigoths (554). However, these conquests were short lived and exhausted the economic and financial resources of the Byzantine Empire. Justinian neglected the eastern half of the empire, whose prosperity was more vital for the empire. He bought a humiliating treaty from the powerful Persian emperor by paying him large sums of money. While his armies were fighting in the west, Justinian could not prevent the ravages of Slavic and Hunnian tribes in the Balkan Peninsula.

Justinian was an able theologian, but he wavered between Roman and Monophysitic Christianity, dominant in the eastern provinces, and could not achieve religious unity in the empire. But with the policy of caesaropapism, in which all the temporal and spiritual power of the Byzantine Empire was combined in the emperor, he subjected the church to serve the needs of the state.

Justinian's greatest achievement was the collection and revision of the existing codes of Roman law, including the imperial constitutions and the works of all the classical jurists. The new code, called the Digest, or Pandects, was published in 533. This became known during the Middle Ages as the corpus of civil law and is a basis for the laws regulating modern societies.

Justinian's costly building programs culminated in the construction of the great church of St. Sophia in Constantinople.

JUTE, a fibrous plant grown in Pakistan and India on rich, damp soil. When jute prices are low or food prices are high, rice production tends to replace that of jute.

Jute fibers are long and silky, but, unlike flax fibers from which linen is made, they are weak. Compared to cotton and wool, jute is of minor commercial importance. However, jute is used for many products in which fibrous strength is not important.

In India and Pakistan the cheapest clothes are made of jute. In Scotland, Belgium, and the United States burlap bags and light twine take a large portion of the jute crop each year. When it is soaked with tar, jute is called oakum and is used in calking ships. Thousands of miles of tar-soaked jute insulate and cushion the copper wires of submarine cables. Linoleum and other floor coverings are frequently built up from a jute base, which need not be strong but must provide a resilient cushion. Since the rise of molded plastics, jute has found a new market as a bulk filler.

Jute fibers are being washed in Pakistan. The fibers are obtained from the tall, slender stalk of the jute plant. After being cut, the stalks must be soaked for many days before the fibers can be extracted. They are often extracted manually.

Embassy of Pakistan

JUVENILE DELINQUENCY, in a legal sense, the commission by young persons of antisocial acts as defined by law. In most states juvenile delinquents are regarded as those offenders between the ages of 6 and 18. Under the legal definition juvenile delinquency might include habitual truancy, conduct endangering the person or morals of others, infraction of governmental laws and regulations, and uncontrollable disobedience. The delinquent typically displays disrespect for socially accepted values concerning property and the person. Although a delinquent may engage in vandalism and violence, he frequently desires and envies both material wealth and social position.

The ultimate cause of juvenile delinquency is unknown Some possible explanations for delinquency include rebellion against authority, group friction that affects newcomers to city life, the impersonality of modern industrial cities, maladjusted parents, poverty, inadequate living quarters, lack of recreation facilities, and improper values and goals. It would be tempting to stress just one factor as the major cause of juvenile delinquency, but most criminologists and sociologists are wary of accepting any single explanation. Some sociologists have suggested that juvenile delinquency is not necessarily a deviation from social standards but is rather a reflection of problems that beset society as a whole. For example, the urge to be accepted by one's peers at any price may reflect an overall social stress on status or security. The concept of a delinquent subculture—a group within a larger society that has its own modes of dress and speech, commands loyalty from its members, and has its own norms and values that may be opposed to the norms of the larger society—has been the most fruitful basis to date for an explanation of juvenile delinquency.

Juvenile delinquency is not confined to any one nation, but there is a tendency toward greater frequency in city environments. Sweden, where poverty has been well-nigh abolished, has a delinquency problem with which it has tried to cope by sending children to comfortable re-education centers or by sending some to work with the lumbermen in the forests. Argentina, Brazil, Chile, Mexico, and Uruguay have developed good institutional systems. France, which was once relatively free of a major delinquency problem, experienced an outbreak of juvenile gang violence in 1959. London has its "teddy boys," the Soviet Union its "hooligans," Germany its "halfsalted ones," and Japan its "sun tribes" or "moonlight tribes."

The treatment of juvenile offenders includes foster-home placement, casework studies, probation, supervised recreation, disciplinary measures, and child-guidance clinics. In no nation are these adequate to cope with the problem. However, the treatment of juvenile delinquents, while important, does not appreciably affect the rate of delinquency. Preventive measures are necessary. The indirect approach—slum clearance, attempts to eliminate social frictions, and general health and welfare plans—is much needed, but it will not prevent delinquency, as the case of Sweden indicates. The direct method of trying to reach predelinquents in order to orient them toward a meaningful life may be the best preventive measure. This demands comprehensive community and federal programs, but above all it demands an interest in the delinquent as an individual and an examination of the goals of society.

New York City Youth Board

The U.S. Children's Bureau and the nonprofit Community Research Associates have conducted studies about the cause of juvenile delinquency. Above is a meeting of a New York City Youth Board street club. The Youth Board provides skilled social workers to establish contact with teenage gangs and to turn their energies into constructive channels.

These young people are probably not juvenile delinquents. Yet, roughly 2.3 percent of young people from ages 10 to 17 appear in court each year in the United States. The typical delinquent comes from a home broken by divorce, death, or desertion.

Rus Arnold

K is the 11th letter of the English alphabet. In chemistry K is the symbol for the element potassium; the symbol derives from the Latin name of potassium, *kalium*. In physics K indicates temperature (°K) on the Kelvin scale, a scale of absolute temperatures. Lowercase italic K (*k*) often denotes a constant in mathematics.

KABUKI THEATER, Japan's most popular theater and its classic art form, was a blending of song, dance, and drama. It originated 350 years ago when a female dancer, O-Kuni, performed erotic dances on the stage. The government, in a strait-laced mood, banned all women from the stage, and feminine roles have since been played by men, even though the ban was lifted at the close of the 19th century.

This is the late Kichiemon Nakamura, appearing as the hero in a kabuki play.

Japan Tourist Assoc.

In the 19th century kabuki borrowed from the ancient no plays, to which were added dance interludes and lively music. It adopted from the puppet theater a narrator and his musical accompanist, who sat in full view of the audience; and from the Western theater, elements of realism.

The three kinds of plays performed were historical tragedies; dance-dramas; and love stories in which ordinary people were caught in a conflict between their desires and the demands of society.

The kabuki theater was rectangular, wide, and shallow. On its left ran a *hana-michi* (platform), which connected the stage with the auditorium. This ramp was used for major entrances and exits. The Kabuki-Za in Tokyo featured a stage 91 feet wide and a proscenium arch only 21 feet high. A Westerner might also have been surprised to see the curtain pulled aside rather than raised.

The costumes and scenery were lavish and extravagant. The actors wore beautiful wigs, masks, and conventionalized makeup. The kabuki theater represented the nostalgia of the Japanese people for their past, for their traditions, and for their indestructible sense of beauty.

KAFKA, FRANZ (1883-1924), a 20th-century novelist born in Prague, Bohemia (now in Czechoslovakia). In 1906 he took a law degree at the University of Prague and later worked for the government of Austria-Hungary. Kafka suffered severely from tuberculosis and spent several years in sanitariums. During his lifetime Kafka published only a few short stories, but these reveal his brilliant sense of the unreality of existence, conveyed in a subtle and precise German prose. Kafka is so much a writer who uses symbols and whose work is so laden with implications that numerous interpretations of his writings, ranging from the psychoanalytical to the religious, have been offered. Usually forgotten, however, is his humor. Kafka's three novels, all incomplete, are *The Trial, The Castle,* and *America.* Among his many notable stories are "In the Penal Colony," "Metamorphosis," and "The Hunter Gracchus." His diaries have also been published.

KALB, JOHANN (1721-1780), known as Baron de Kalb, was a German-born French officer who became a major general in the American Continental army and lost his life in the Revolutionary War. De Kalb was born into a peasant family in Hüttendorf, in Germany. During his early years he was educated at Kriegenbronn. He worked as a waiter while still a boy and left home at the age of 16. In his early 20's he served as a lieutenant in the French infantry under the name of Jean de Kalb. Despite his lack of formal education De Kalb undertook the study of modern languages, mathematics, and military strategy.

Baron de Kalb was one of the most famous of the foreign soldiers who volunteered to fight for the independence of the American colonies. He was sent by the French government on a secret mission to America in 1768; he returned again on July 27, 1777, with Lafayette. He was commissioned a major general on September 15 of the same year. De Kalb fought at Valley Forge, and in 1780 he was sent to relieve Charleston, S.C. He was in the southern army, which was defeated in the Battle of Camden on August 16, 1780. Three days later, near that city De Kalb gave his life for the American cause.

Franz Kafka, a great modern novelist

KANGAROO, a marsupial mammal of Australia that carries its newborn young in an abdominal pouch. Newborn kangaroos are extremely immature. They are blind, hairless, and about 1 inch long. Their legs are flipper-like, with little indication of toes. Immediately after birth they crawl into a large pouch located on the underside of the female's abdomen. There they grow and suckle milk from the female's teats, which are in the pouch. When about four months old they first venture from the pouch and play on the ground near their mother. At the least sign of danger, however, they immediately scamper back to the safety of the pouch. A kangaroo is sometimes seen peeping from its mother's pouch as she leaps along. When pursued, the mother will throw her young from her pouch in order to save both its life and her own.

KANSAS

Leaping is the kangaroo's method of locomotion. Sitting erect on its hindlegs and tail, it springs forward by means of the powerful muscles of its large hindlegs. When it goes at normal speed, the leaps of a large species are about 5 feet long. When it flees rapidly from a pursuer, the leaps of the same large species may be as long as 25 feet. A large species can jump over a 5-foot-high fence. After each leap it alights erect on its hindlegs and then bounds forward again. Its front legs, which are much smaller and weaker, are not used for leaping. They support the forepart of the body while the animal is

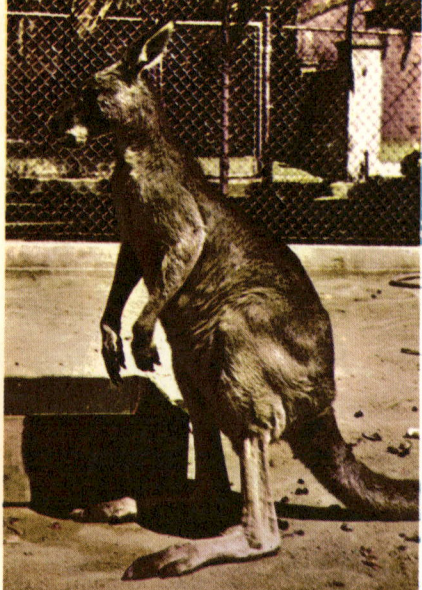
Bucky Reeves
Kangaroos leap by means of their hind legs.

browsing grass and sometimes are used as hands to move small objects. The forepart of the kangaroo's body is no larger than that of a big dog, while the hindpart is much larger. The kangaroo has a long, thick tail, which helps it balance while leaping.

Kangaroos are native only to Australia and New Zealand. The great gray kangaroo may attain a height of 5 feet and a weight of 200 pounds. Certain smaller breeds of kangaroo are called wallabies. Most kangaroos are as timid as deer and flee fearfully when man approaches. In Australia hunting kangaroos with greyhounds is a favorite sport. Kangaroo flesh is relished by Australian aborigines and is also eaten by white men. If chased and cornered, a kangaroo will turn and desperately fight both hounds and hunters before being captured or killed.

Chamber of Com., Topeka, Kan.
Topeka, an important trade center, was founded in 1854 on the Oregon Trail.

KANSAS, the Sunflower State, is a leading wheat-producing region. It lies in the vast Great Plains region in the central United States. Topeka, the capital, and Kansas City and Wichita are its chief cities.

Kansas, with an area of approximately 82,000 square miles, ranks 14th in size among the states. It measures about 200 miles from north to south and about 400 miles from east to west. In 1960 it had a population of 2,178,611.

The state is topographically divided into three different regions. In the west are high, treeless plains. The land becomes low plains with erosional forms, as buttes and cliffs, in the central area. In the east the land is rich, forested or in grassland, and marked by broad, shallow valleys and low hills. The principal rivers in Kansas are the Kansas, Missouri, and Arkansas.

Kansas' continental-type climate varies in different sections of the state. There are often extremes in summer and winter temperatures. Annual rainfall averages about 15 inches in the extreme west, while about 40 inches is normal in the southeast. Wichita has an average temperature of 32° F. in January and 81° F. in July. Duststorms and tornadoes occur on the open plains.

Because of the varying land surface and climate, certain areas are devoted to one crop. The great wheatfields cover the western plains. Grazing land and farmland, with much corn, are found in the east.

The history of Kansas began 79 years before the Pilgrims landed on Plymouth Rock. Coronado rode from Mexico to central Kansas in 1541. Three centuries later the great trade route of the Santa Fe Trail stretched across 500 miles of Kansas.

Construction on the state Capitol of Kansas, in Topeka, was started in 1866.
Kansas Industrial Development Commission

KANSAS

In 1854 Kansas was organized as a territory. Whether Kansas would enter the Union as a slave state now became a point of much controversy, which within two years turned Kansas into a battleground between proslavery and antislavery forces.

The state was admitted to the Union in 1861. The nation expanded westward, and many persons settled in Kansas. Agricultural, industrial, and mineral production hastened the building of modern Kansas. Soldiers were trained at Fort Leavenworth and Fort Riley during World War II.

KANSAS

Nickname: Sunflower State
Seal: Farmer and cabin to represent agriculture—river and steamboat in background to stand for commerce—wagon train and herd of buffalo with Indians in pursuit shown in center—34 stars at top representing number of states when Kansas entered Union
Flag: State seal on blue field with sunflower above
Motto: *Ad Astra per Aspera* (To the Stars Through Difficulties)
Flower: Native sunflower
Bird: Western meadowlark
Capital: Topeka
Largest cities: Wichita, Kansas City
Area: 82,276 sq. mi. (including 168 sq. mi. inland waters)
Rank in area: 14th
Population: 2,178,611
Chief universities: University of Kansas, Kansas State University of Agriculture and Applied Science
Chief rivers: Arkansas, Kansas, Missouri
Average temperature: Wichita, 32° F. (Jan.), 81° F. (July)
Average annual rainfall: 40 inches in southeast, 10 to 20 inches in extreme west
Chief economic activities: Agriculture (including livestock raising), manufacturing
Chief crops: Wheat, corn, grain sorghums
Chief minerals: Oil, natural gas
Chief manufactures: Airplanes, food products, chemicals
Notable attraction: Eisenhower Museum at Abilene
Important historical dates:
- 1541 Kansas explored by Coronado
- 1827 Fort Leavenworth established
- 1854 Kansas organized as territory
- 1861 Kansas admitted to Union as 34th state
- 1867 Chisholm Trail opened

Kansas Industrial Development Commission

Kansas Industrial Development Commission

Irrigation is important for the farmlands in the dry areas of Kansas (above). The state is primarily agricultural, with over 90 percent of the total area in farms and rangeland. Kansas is the largest producer of winter wheat in the country. Because of its great stretches of level ground in the central and western parts, almost all of the wheat is mechanically harvested (right). Kansas is a leader in flour milling and grain storage. Grain elevators (below) dot the landscape. In addition to wheat, the state's leading crops include corn, grain sorghums, and oats. A major portion of the farm income is derived from livestock and poultry raising. Huge stockyards are at Kansas City and Wichita.

Kansas Industrial Development Commission

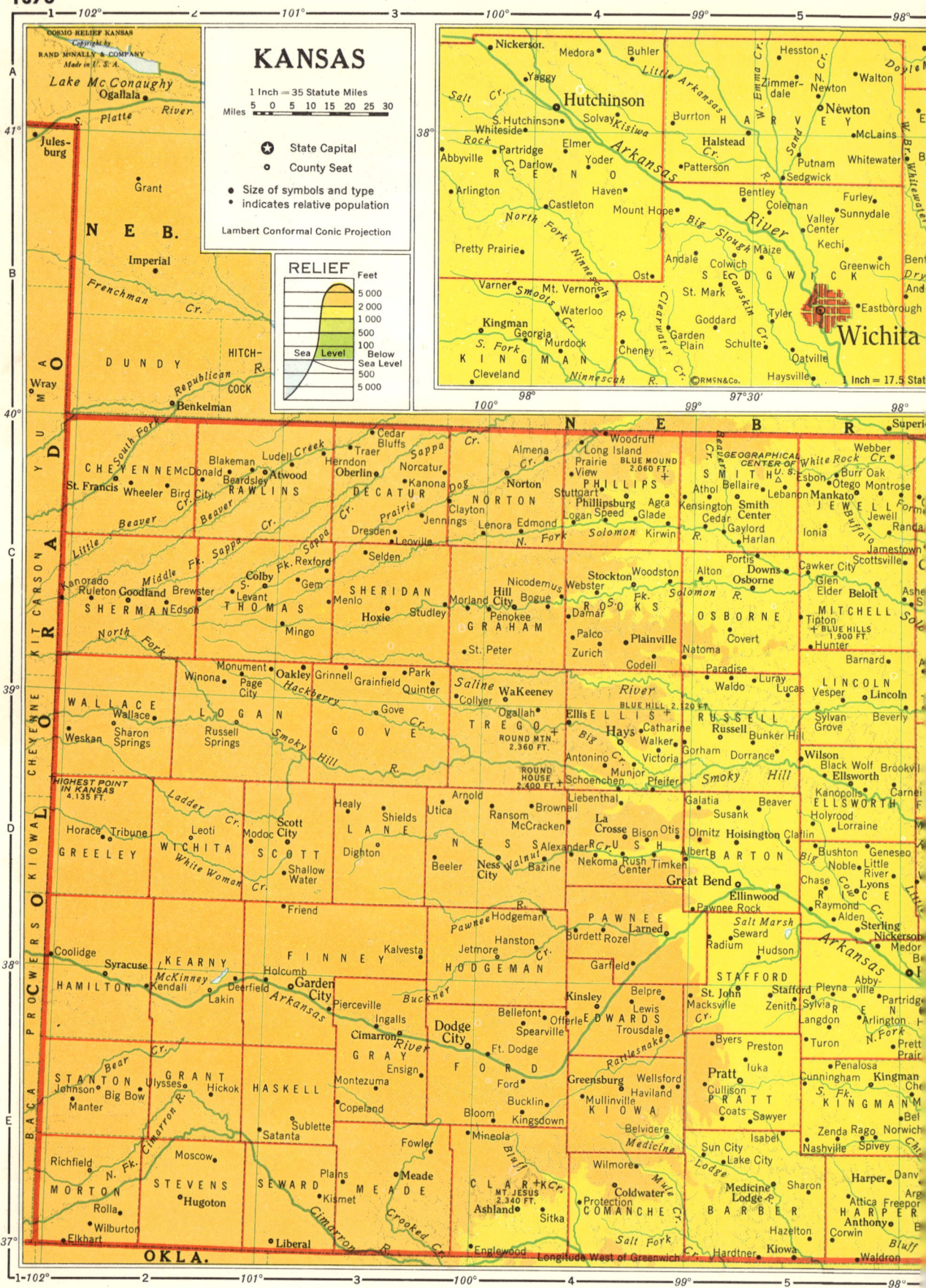

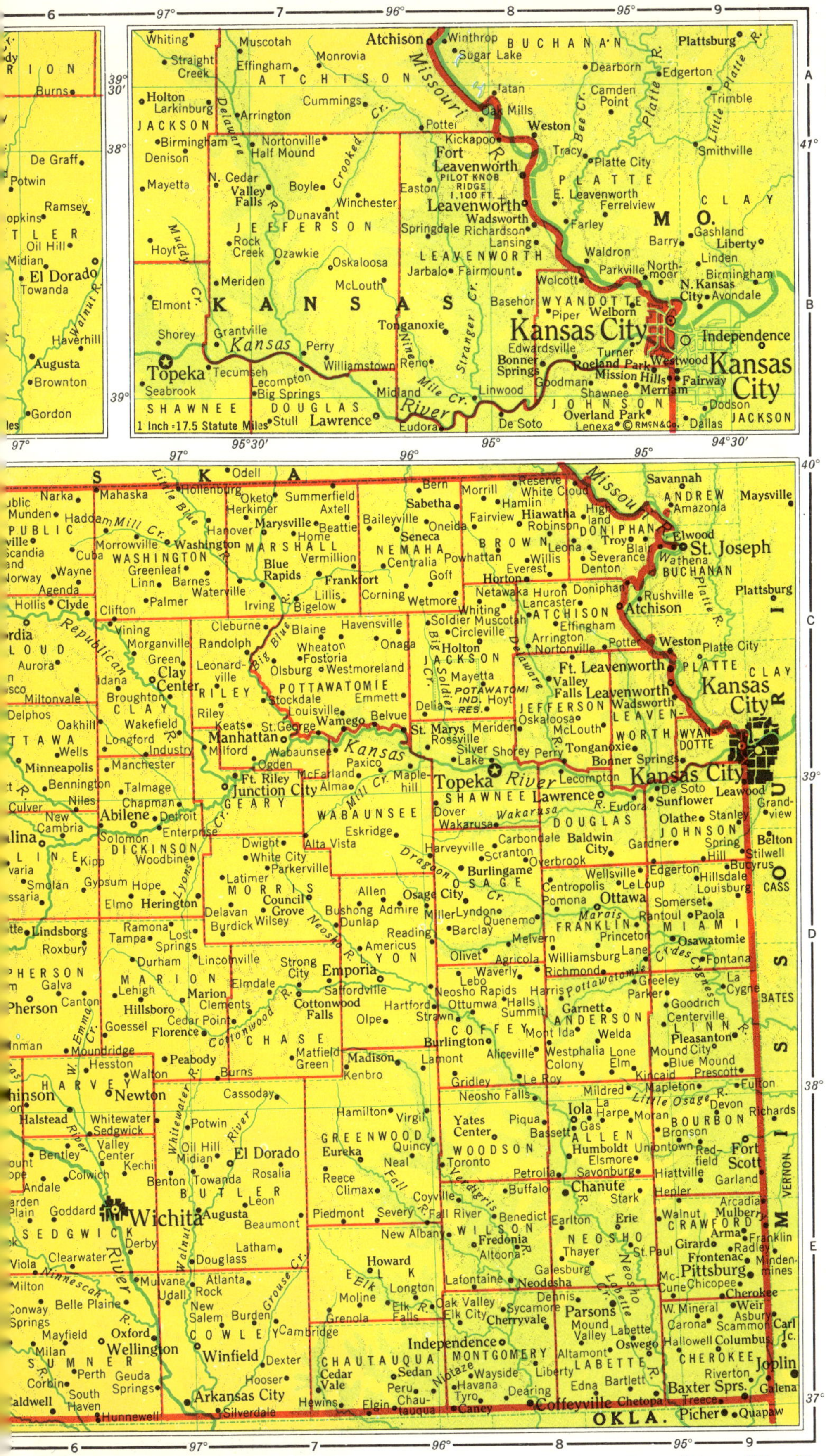

1377

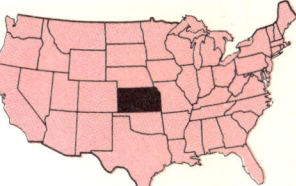

Location map

The western meadowlark, a native of the prairie states, is the state bird of Kansas.

The official state seal was adopted in 1861 by an act of the Kansas legislature.

The native sunflower is the flower of the Sunflower State.

The official seal and flower of Kansas are on the state flag.

For map index, see Volume 20.

KANSAS CITY, the name of two cities that form a single, extensive industrial, trade, and transportation center serving a vast plains area. Kansas City, Kan., is one of the largest livestock markets in the United States. It has stockyards and meatpacking plants and is an important grain-storage area and flour-milling center. Adjacent Kansas City, Mo., has the offices of this major livestock industry. The University of Kansas City is here. In 1960 Kansas City, Kan., the largest city in the state, had a population of 121,901 while Kansas City, Mo., had a population of 475,539.

KANSAS-NEBRASKA ACT, a bill passed by Congress in 1854, during the administration of President Franklin Pierce, for the purpose of organizing the territories of Kansas and Nebraska. It provided, among other things, that the question of slavery should be left to the people of the territories. Further, so far as this region was concerned, the Missouri Compromise of 1820, which excluded slavery from the Louisiana territory north of 36°30′ N latitude except for the state of Missouri, was declared repealed.

With the decision for or against slavery left to the people of the territories the scene was set for the troubles that were to be called the "Kansas question." Antislavery settlers rushed into Kansas from the northern and eastern states and proslavery men came in from Missouri and other Southern states. The Northern people were armed with "Beecher's Bibles" (improved rifles nicknamed after the abolitionist preacher Henry Ward Beecher), and the Southerners were supported by raiding armed bands from neighboring Missouri. Each group elected its own government. In 1856 the situation exploded into armed conflict. Delegates elected by the proslavery people met in the fall of 1857 and wrote the Lecompton Constitution, which would have permitted slavery in the new state. (See LECOMPTON CONSTITUTION.) It was during the bitter struggle for "Bleeding Kansas" that John Brown first gained fame by the massacre of five unarmed settlers on Pottawatomi Creek, in Kansas. In Congress the Kansas question erupted in emotion-charged speeches and physical violence. Kansas was eventually admitted as a free state in 1861. The Kansas-Nebraska Act and the resulting struggle inflamed both the North and the South and foreshadowed the Civil War.

KANT, IMMANUEL (1724-1804), probably the greatest and most influential of German philosophers, was born in Königsberg, Prussia (now Kaliningrad, U.S.S.R.). After studying mathematics, philosophy, physics, and theology at the University of Königsberg, he spent nine years as a private tutor. Kant then returned to Königsberg, where he received his degree in 1755. Following graduation he devoted his time to lecturing on logic, physics, metaphysics, mathematics, and politics; eventually he expanded his scope of subjects to include anthropology, physical geography, pedagogy, and natural theology. A bachelor, Kant lived a prosaic private life, spending practically all his time in Königsberg. He displayed profound thought, wit, and humor in his lectures and was noted for his veracity and honor, austere principles of morality, and fearless support of political liberty. He had great faith in human progress.

The purpose of his philosophy was to reconcile the claims of science with faith in God, immortality, and freedom. He attempted to show how all sensations are organized into objects of perception and how these perceptions are related through the synthesis of imagination and under the organization of intellect. His conclusion was that dialectical procedure is a discipline of reason, rather than a means of perceiving reality, and that objects of perception exist only in relation to the mind. Kant regarded morality as the supreme cause and obedience to the moral law as binding on every rational will. His philosophy is presented in his *Critique of Pure Reason*, *Critique of Practical Reason*, and *Critique of Judgment*.

KAPOK is a downy material obtained from the inside of the seed pods of the silk-cotton tree. It is used to stuff cushions and, being impervious to water, is used in lifesaving apparatus. Kapok oil is pressed from the seeds as an edible oil. Kapok was first introduced into Europe in 1851. It is mostly obtained from tropical Africa, the East Indies, and the Philippine Islands. A related Central American tree is also a source of kapok.

KARAT, a measurement to indicate the purity of gold. A karat is $\frac{1}{24}$ part. Pure gold is said to be 24 karat. Most things made of gold have another metal, called a base metal, mixed with the gold. Thus, a bracelet of 18-karat gold is 18 parts gold and 6 parts base metal. It is usually stamped 18K. Something made of half gold is 12 karat.

When the word is spelled *carat*, it is a unit for measuring the weight of gems. The international standard carat is 0.2 of 1 gram. The greater number of carats a gem weighs, the more valuable it is. The carat is used for indicating the weight of the diamond, ruby, sapphire, emerald, opal, topaz, and garnet. Other gems, such as the moonstone, amethyst, lapis lazuli, and high-grade malachite, are sold by the gram. Pearls are usually sold by the grain ($\frac{1}{20}$ of 1 gram, or $\frac{1}{4}$ of a carat).

KÁRMÁN, THEODOR VON (1881-   ), aerodynamicist and physicist who has greatly influenced the development of high-speed and supersonic aircraft in the United States.

Von Kármán was born in Budapest. He studied at the University of Budapest and at the University of Göttingen, in Germany. From 1912 to 1930 he was director of the Aeronautics Institute at the University of Aachen, in Germany. From 1930 to 1949 Von Kármán was head of the Guggenheim Aeronautics Laboratory at the California Institute of Technology. He became a United States citizen in 1936. Since 1951 Von Kármán has been chairman of NATO's advisory group on aeronautics.

Von Kármán has written many books and papers on aerodynamics and has originated theories about the behavior of air when high-speed objects move through it. His best known theory is the Kármán vortex trail theory, which states that within a certain range of velocities through air a bluff object will leave a certain pattern of air disturbance be-

hind it. During World War II and afterward Von Kármán worked with the U.S. Army and Air Force in programs of research and development concerning jet propulsion and rocket motors. In the early 1940's Von Kármán and four associates founded a company to manufacture parts and motors for rockets and guided missiles.

KARTING. See AUTOMOBILE RACING.

KAYAK. See CANOE.

A portrait of John Keats by William Hilton
©National Portrait Gallery, London

KEATS, JOHN (1795-1821), an English poet, was born in London. He was the son of a stablekeeper, and at an early age he was left an orphan. He was apprenticed to a surgeon, studied medicine, and began practice in a London hospital in 1816. However, Keats soon left the medical profession for poetry. In 1816 he contributed his first poems to Leigh Hunt's *Examiner*, and the next year he published his first volume of *Poems*. He followed with his poetic romance *Endymion* (1818). Many of his greatest poems were published in *Lamia, Isabella, The Eve of St. Agnes, and Other Poems* (1820). This volume contained the poems "Hyperion," "Fancy," "Ode to Psyche," "Ode on a Grecian Urn," "Ode on Melancholy," "Ode to a Nightingale," and "To Autumn." Among Keats's many sonnets were "On the Sea," "When I Have Fears That I May Cease to Be," and "On First Looking into Chapman's Homer." The latter is considered one of the finest sonnets in the English language. His odes are also among the best written by any Englishman. While on a tour in the English Lake District he contracted a cold that developed into tuberculosis in 1820. He was nursed by his fiancée, Fanny Brawne, but his condition grew worse, and he went to the milder climate of Italy. He died at the age of 25 and was buried in the Protestant Cemetery in Rome. He was mourned by his friends the Hunts and by Percy Bysshe Shelley, who addressed his beautiful elegy *Adonais* (1821) to Keats.

KEELBOAT. See FLATBOAT AND KEELBOAT.

KEKULE, FRIEDRICH (1829-1896), German chemist, whose work in theoretical organic chemistry provided the foundation of modern aromatic chemistry, the chemistry of carbon-ring compounds related to benzene.

He was born in Darmstadt, in Germany. At the University of Giessen, Kekule studied architecture; he later turned to the study of chemistry under Dumas. He was later professor of chemistry at the universities of Ghent, Belgium, and Bonn, Germany.

Kekule found that carbon atoms can be tetravalent and that they can link with other carbon atoms in molecules. He proposed that the structure of benzene was a closed chain, in which the carbon atoms were grouped in a ringlike pattern. This theory led to new methods of chemical synthesis and provided an insight into the composition and decomposition of numberless organic compounds. Kekule is also credited with the synthesis of acetylene.

KELLER, HELEN (1880-   ), famous American writer, lecturer, and humanitarian, was born in Tuscumbia, Ala.; she was stricken deaf and blind in her second year. In 1886 she became the pupil of 20-year-old Anne Sullivan. Miss Sullivan, a teacher from Boston's Perkins Institute for the Blind, taught Helen Keller to "see" with her fingertips, to "hear" with her feet and hands, and to communicate with other people.

It is difficult to imagine the patience and determination that must have been displayed both by the child and by her devoted teacher. By spelling the names of objects into Helen's hand, Anne Sullivan succeeded in arousing her interest and curiosity. One day, while a stream of water flowed over one hand, the teacher spelled *w a t e r*

Amer. Foundation for the Blind, Inc.
Helen Keller

into the other hand. This was Helen's first step toward understanding speech and the world around her.

Helen Keller was an eager and intelligent child. She learned quickly. In only three years she had mastered both the manual and the braille alphabet and could read and write. She heard rumors that other deaf and dumb people had learned to speak, and in 1890 she herself began speech lessons with Sarah Fuller. By 1894 Helen had made such rapid progress that she was able to enter the Wright-Humason School for the Deaf in New York. There she studied vocal culture, lip training, arithmetic, physical geography, French, and German. In 1896 she attended the Cambridge School for Young Ladies, and in 1900 she entered Radcliffe College.

Helen was a friendly girl and was elected vice-president of her freshman class. She completed her studies and was graduated with honors in 1904. Throughout these school years Anne Sullivan was at Helen's side. The faithful teacher used the manual alphabet to interpret classes, lectures, books, and references for her pupil.

After she was graduated, Helen Keller began to study the problems of the blind. During her long and active career she gave many public lectures and toured the United States, Europe, and Asia, speaking on behalf of the handicapped. She worked with the American Foundation for the Blind and began the Helen Keller Endowment Fund for that organization. Helen Keller also wrote many books and magazine articles. Among them, in addition to an autobiography of her early years, were *Midstream: My Later Life* and *Let Us Have Faith*.

KELLOGG-BRIAND PACT, a multilateral treaty for renunciation of war, known also as the Pact of Paris and the Pact of Peace. It was named for its sponsors, Frank Billings Kellogg, U.S. secretary of state, and Aristide Briand, French minister for foreign affairs. The countries signing the pact in Paris on Aug. 27, 1928, were Australia, Belgium, Canada, Czechoslovakia, France, Germany, Great Britain, India, the Irish Free State, Italy, Japan, New Zealand, Poland, South Africa, and the United States. The 15 signatories declared that they "condemn recourse to war for the solution of international controversies and renounce it as an instrument of national policy in their relations with one another."

KELLY, EMMETT (1898-   ), became one of the most famous circus clowns in the United States. He specialized in playing the role of "Weary Willie," a ragged little tramp who wandered sadly around the circus arena.

Kelly was born in Sedan, Kan. He grew up on a farm in Missouri and in 1917 went to Kansas City to try to become a newspaper cartoonist. He failed to get a newspaper job and worked as a sign painter and as manager of a sideshow in a carnival. He began his career as an entertainer by giving a cartoon talk in whiteface clown makeup for the Frisco Exposition Shows in Kansas City.

Emmett Kelly as "Weary Willie"
Wisconsin State Historical Society

Kelly joined Howe's Great London Circus in 1923 as a clown and a trapeze performer. He gave up his trapeze act in 1931 and concentrated on becoming a leading clown. In 1933 he created his famous sad tramp, "Weary Willie." Kelly first performed in England in 1937 and returned in 1938 and 1939. He played in a musical comedy, *Keep Off the Grass*, in 1940.

Kelly joined the Ringling Brothers, Barnum and Bailey Circus in 1942 and became one of the outstanding attractions. In 1952 he appeared in the motion picture *The Greatest Show on Earth*. He wrote *Clown*, his autobiography.

KELVIN, WILLIAM THOMSON, 1st Baron (1824-1907), an English mathematician, physicist, and engineer, who was responsible for the successful laying of telegraph cable across the Atlantic Ocean. He was born at Belfast, Northern Ireland, and was educated at the universities of Glasgow, in Scotland, and Cambridge, in England. By the age of 22 he had published several scientific papers. At the same time, in 1846, he became a professor at the University of Glasgow and remained at that institution until his retirement.

His interests at first were directed toward the problems of electricity and magnetism. He invented the mirror galvanometer, which was later used in the reception of cable messages, and the Kelvin standard balance, a dynamometer by which mechanical moments are balanced by electrical moments. Kelvin's experiments in turning heat into work resulted in the formulation of the second law of thermodynamics. Lord Kelvin also made major contributions to the study of heat engines.

Kelvin was a genius in his ability to turn scientific theories into practical inventions. He improved the mariner's compass, which made navigation safer, and he devised sounding instruments by which the ocean floor could be found and mapped. He defined the absolute scale of temperature, named for him.

KEMAL ATATÜRK (1881-1938), the Turkish military leader and statesman who founded modern Turkey. His vigorous reforms of Turkish economic and social life changed Turkey from a backward country into a modern industrialized one.

Mustafa Kemal (he took the title "Atatürk," or "chief Turk," in 1934) was born in Salonika, Greece, where his father was a customs

© National Portrait Gallery, London

William Thomson Kelvin

official for the Ottoman Empire. While in his early teens he enrolled in a military college in Salonika. He left the senior military school at Monastir (now Bitolj, Yugoslavia), where he excelled in mathematics, to attend the War College at Constantinople, the training center for officers destined for the Turkish general staff. On being graduated he was exiled to Damascus because of his revolutionary activity at the college, but his revolutionary activities did not cease. He served in the Tripolitan War in 1911, winning the rank of major for his service as a guerrilla chief at Tripoli. During World War I, while Turkey was allied with the Central Powers, Kemal earned the title of "pasha" for his leadership on the Russian front and at the Dardanelles. At the end of the war, when Turkish power seemed in complete collapse, a Greek landing at Smyrna began the campaign of the Allies to divide Asia Minor into protectorates. Kemal, who had formed a national assembly at Angora (now Ankara) in defiance of the sultan, forced the Greeks to retreat. In the patriotic fervor that swept Turkey he was able to depose the sultan and to become president in 1923 of the new Turkish Republic.

Kemal Atatürk's reforms, often ruthlessly carried out, included the adoption of the Swiss legal code to replace Moslem law, the adoption of Western dress, the abolition of polygamy, and the introduction of Latin written characters. An educational program was inaugurated, and women were emancipated. Kemal remained president until the time of his death in 1938.

KENNEDY, JOHN FITZGERALD (1917-   ), 35th president of the United States, born in Brookline, Mass., May 29, 1917, the son of Joseph Patrick and Rose Fitzgerald Kennedy. His father was a banker, real estate owner, and ambassador to Great Britain. Kennedy was educated in Boston private schools and at Harvard University. On a leave of absence from Harvard he worked for his father in the U.S. Embassy in London. His senior-honors thesis was a description and explanation of England's lack of preparedness for war. This was later published in book form under the title *Why England Slept* (1941). He donated most of the profits from the book to help rebuild the bombed city of Plymouth, England.

Kennedy was rejected for army enlistment at the outbreak of World War II because of a back injury, but later (1941) he received a commission as lieutenant junior grade in the Navy. In the Solomon Islands campaign of 1943 he was decorated for heroism after rescuing a crewman when his PT boat was sunk by a Japanese destroyer. He was discharged from the Navy in 1945 after spending several months in a hospital with a recurrence of the back injury.

He was first elected to public office in 1946, when he won a seat in the U.S. House of Representatives. After serving three terms he was elected to the Senate in 1952, defeating Henry Cabot Lodge, Jr. He underwent two spinal operations in 1954-1955, and during his long convalescence wrote a book, *Profiles in Courage*, which won the Pulitzer prize in 1957. In 1958 he was re-elected to the Senate with the largest majority ever won in Massachusetts. After a vigorous campaign for delegates he was nominated for president by the Democratic National Convention of 1960. Kennedy won a close election against Vice President Richard M. Nixon, the Republican nominee, and became the youngest man ever to be elected president of the United States and the first president of the Roman Catholic faith. In 1953 Kennedy married Jacqueline Lee Bouvier, daughter of a New York financier.

KENSINGTON STONE, a stone with runic inscriptions found near Kensington, Minn., in 1898. The stone is now in Alexandria, Minn. At one time it was believed to be a record of the visits of 30 Norsemen to Minnesota in 1362.

A Swedish farmer was said to have found the stone. It was under the roots of a poplar tree on his farm. Nobody was able to read it. Years later the inscription was translated, and the stone was sent to scholars in Europe. Many archaeologists believed that the writing was not authentic.

Here is the translation of the inscriptions on the stone:

> Eight Goths and 22 Norwegians upon a journey of discovery from Vinland westward. We had a camp by two skerries (islands) one day's journey north of this stone. We were out fishing one day. When we returned home we found ten men red with blood and dead. AVM (Ave Virgo Maria) save us from evil. [We] have ten men by the sea to look after our vessel fourteen days' journey from this island. Year, 1362.

In 1907 Hjalmar R. Holand, a Norwegian-American, acquired the stone and wrote a series of publications in an attempt to prove its authenticity. There followed a controversy that lasted 50 years. Recent study indicates that the inscriptions on the stone were not sufficiently weathered to have been carved in the 14th century. The conclusions were that the Kensington inscription was planned as a deliberate hoax.

KENT, ROCKWELL (1882-   ), an American artist and author, was born at Tarrytown Heights, N.Y. After several years of study at the Columbia University school of architecture he turned to painting. His travels to such parts of the world as Alaska, Newfoundland, Tierra del Fuego, Ireland, and Greenland provided the scenes for many of his paintings. He wrote and illustrated several books about his tours. Kent also became noted for his magazine illustrations, lithographs, and wood engravings. His works may be found in many museums, including the Metropolitan Museum of Art in New York and the Art Institute of Chicago. Kent's books include *Voyaging*, *N by E*, *Salamina*, *This Is My Own*, and *It's Me O Lord*.

John Fitzgerald Kennedy

The Kensington Stone is now regarded by scholars as a deliberate hoax.
Minnesota Historical Society

Rockwell Kent, with one of his paintings
Wide World Photo

Location map

The great seal of Kentucky was adopted in April, 1893.

The cardinal, or redbird, was adopted as the state bird of Kentucky in 1926.

The goldenrod became the official state flower of Kentucky in March, 1926.

The state flag, adopted in March, 1918.

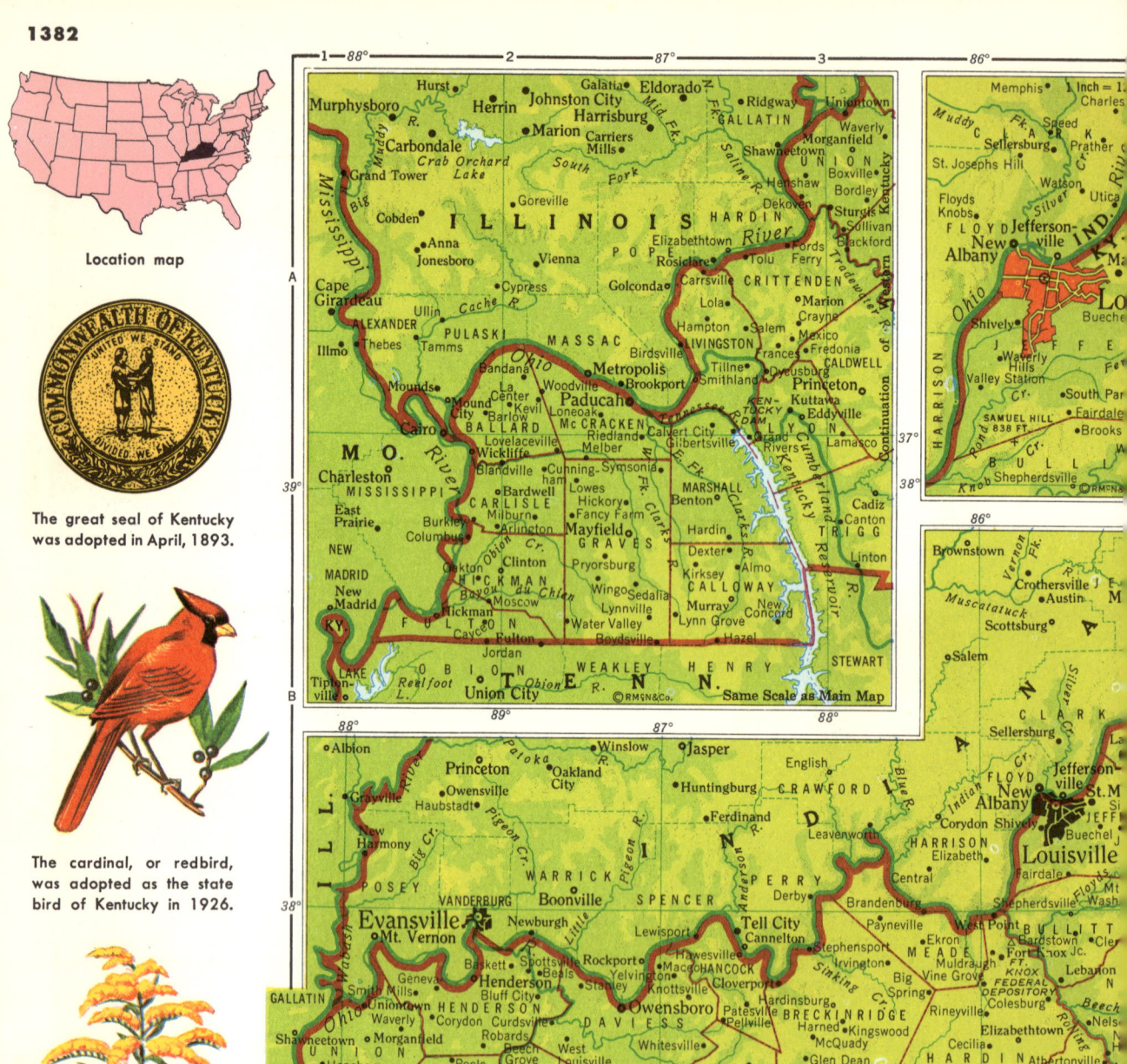

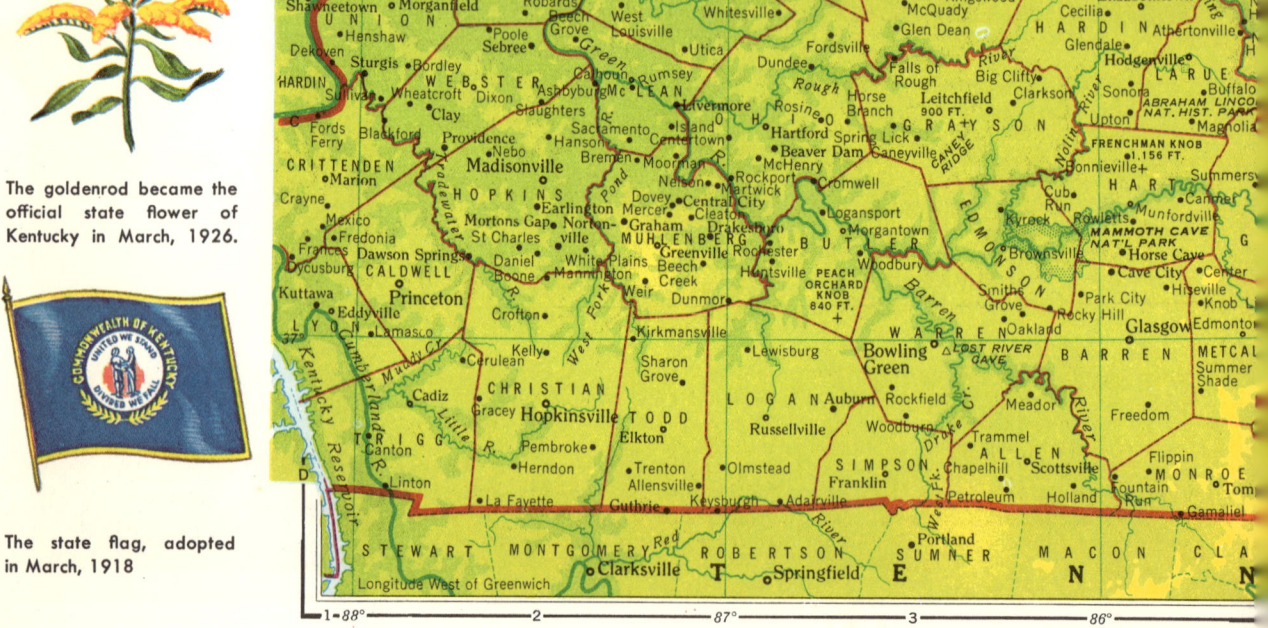

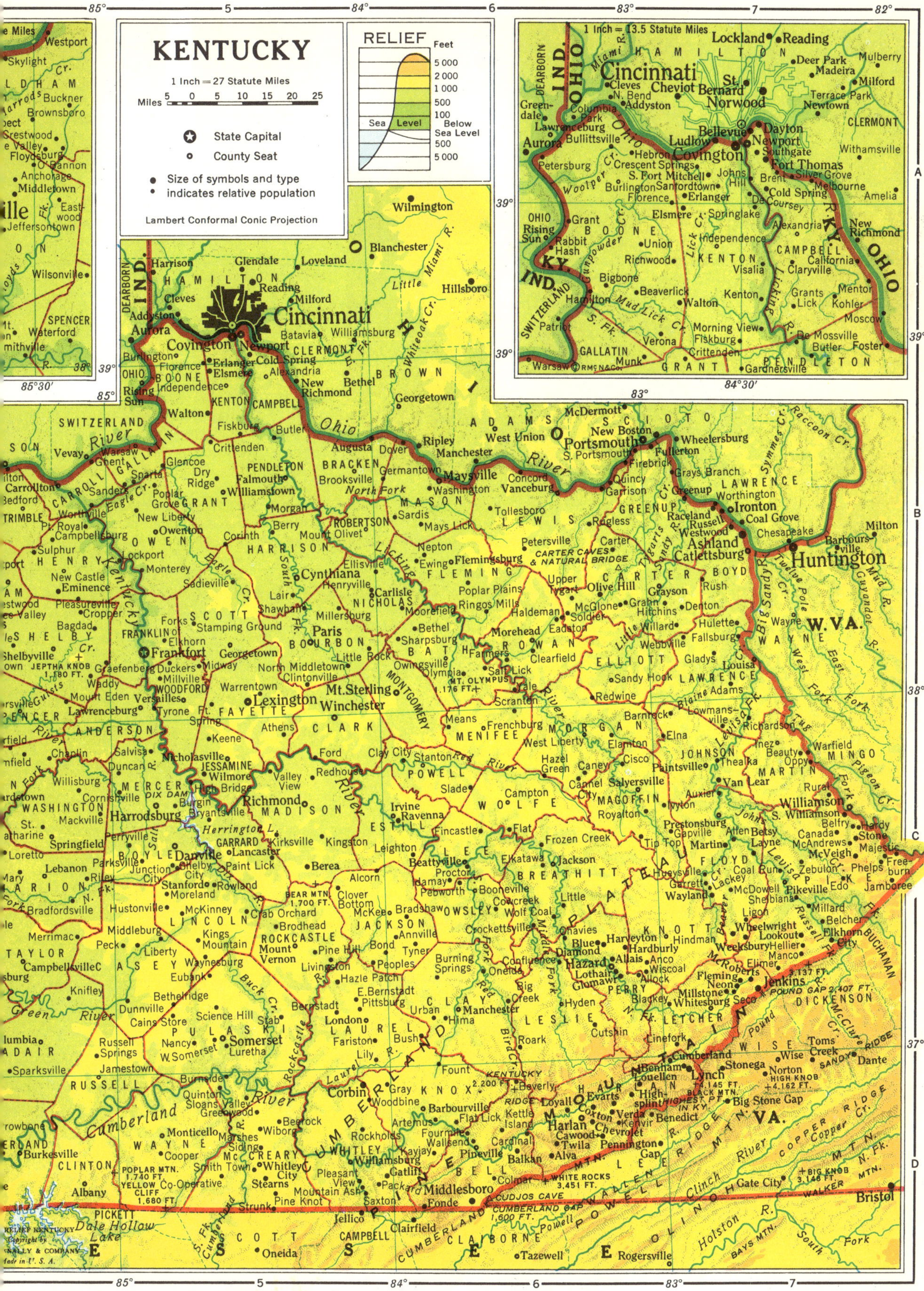

For map index, see Volume 20.

This horse-breeding farm is near Lexington, Ky., in the center of the famous Bluegrass region. (Courtesy of the State of Kentucky)

KENTUCKY is called the Bluegrass State after its famous farming, grazing, and distilling region. Situated in the north-central part of the state, this area contains Frankfort, the capital, and the three largest cities—Louisville, Lexington, and Covington.

Located in the south-central United States, Kentucky ranks 37th in size among the states. It has an area of about 40,400 square miles. In 1960 Kentucky had a population of 3,038,156. The state has a continental type of climate, with extremes in temperature and precipitation. The summers are hot, and the winters are cold and short.

Kentucky has several different economic regions. Its mineral production is of national importance. Coal, its chief mineral, is mined in the east and in the west. The eastern coalfield, especially in Harlan County, is more productive. Kentucky is the third largest coal producer in the United States. Other state minerals include fluorspar, rock asphalt, limestone, clay, petroleum, and natural gas. Forests cover the east.

In central Kentucky distilling and food processing are major industries. The state heads the nation in the production of rye and bourbon whiskies and is a leader in tobacco products. Other state industries include metal goods, textiles, chemicals, and furniture. Many of the manufacturing centers are located on the Ohio River.

Many scenic and historic places of interest are found in Kentucky. Mammoth Cave National Park has subsurface streams, sinks, and caves, which have been carved out of limestone. Abraham Lincoln National Historical Park preserves Lincoln's birthplace.

The first explorers came to Kentucky in the middle of the 18th century. Daniel Boone crossed the state in 1767 and led the way for the coming settlers in 1775. Boonesboro was established the same year. When the Civil War began, popular sentiment was divided between the Confederacy and the Union, which managed to keep the strong pro-slavery forces from seceding and joining the Southern States. Important battles were fought at Mill Springs and Perryville.

The depression of 1929-1933 brought severe suffering and wage curtailment to the miners in Harlan County. Both miners and operators resorted to the use of guns during the strike that began in 1931. A great part of the federal government's gold reserve is kept at Fort Knox, near Louisville.

KENTUCKY

Nickname: Bluegrass State
Seal: Two men exchanging greetings—"United We Stand," above them; "Divided We Fall," below them
Flag: State seal on blue field
Motto: United We Stand, Divided We Fall
Flower: Goldenrod
Bird: Cardinal
Capital: Frankfort
Largest city: Louisville
Area: 40,395 sq. mi. (including 531 sq. mi. inland waters)
Population: 3,038,156
Chief universities: University of Kentucky; University of Louisville
Chief rivers: Ohio, Kentucky, Green
Chief lake: Kentucky
Average temperature: Louisville—36° F. (Jan.), 79° F. (July)
Average annual rainfall: 45 inches
Chief economic activities: Agriculture (including livestock raising), mining
Chief crops: Tobacco, corn, hay
Chief minerals: Coal, fluorspar, rock asphalt, petroleum, natural gas
Chief manufactures: Food, wood, tobacco, metal products, textiles
Notable attractions: Mammoth Cave National Park, Abraham Lincoln National Historical Park, Fort Knox, Kentucky Lake
Important historical dates:
1750 First major exploration of region by English
1764 Daniel Boone's first visit to Kentucky
1774 First permanent settlement at Harrodsburg
1792 Kentucky admitted to Union as 15th state

Kentucky Dam, on the Tennessee River near Paducah, provides for flood control and navigation. The dam forms Kentucky Lake, which is some 184 miles long. (TVA)

KENTUCKY AND VIRGINIA RESOLUTIONS, passed by the legislatures of Virginia on Dec. 24, 1798, and of Kentucky Nov. 16, 1798, and Nov. 22, 1799. The Kentucky Resolutions were written by Thomas Jefferson and the Virginia one by James Madison. They were issued to protest against the Alien and Sedition Acts passed by the Adams administration. See ALIEN AND SEDITION ACTS.

The resolutions stated that only the states had the power to decide whether a federal law or an action of the federal government was in violation of the Constitution. This opinion was later used by John C. Calhoun to support his doctrines of state sovereignty and nullification. At the time that the resolutions were passed by the two legislatures they were sent for comment to the legislatures of the other states. These took a different position, some states replying that the power to judge the constitutionality of federal laws belonged to the federal courts. This is where that power came to be placed.

KENTUCKY DERBY is one of the most famous horseraces in the United States. It is held each year in early May at Churchill Downs Racetrack in Louisville, Ky. Only three-year-old horses are eligible to compete. The race is 1¼ miles in length and is run over a flat dirt track. The Kentucky Derby was first run in 1875. Among the famous horses that have won the race are Gallant Fox (1930), War Admiral (1937), Whirlaway (1941), Assault (1946), and Citation (1948). About 100,000 spectators attend the Derby, and the owner of the winning horse generally receives a prize of about $75,000.

KENYA is a British colony and protectorate in eastern Africa. The protectorate consists of a 10-mile-wide strip along much of the coast; it is leased from the sultan of Zanzibar. The rest of Kenya constitutes the colony. During the 1950's Kenya was terrorized by the Mau Mau—a secret, native organization dedicated to driving the white settlers out of the country. Nairobi, a center for big-game hunters from all over the world, is Kenya's capital and chief city. Mombasa is the principal seaport. Kenya has an area of 225,000 square miles and a population of about 6,500,000.

The surface gradually slopes up from a hot, marshy coastal plain to the temperate highlands of the interior. The interior plateau is between 3,000 and 10,000 feet high. In central Kenya Mt. Kenya rises to 17,000 feet. Mt. Elgon on the western border reaches 14,000 feet. Forests are found in the higher elevations. There are large stretches of grassland with scattered trees. They abound in big game. The Great Rift Valley cuts southwestern through Kenya and holds Lake Rudolf. Lake Victoria lies on the western border. The chief rivers, including the Tana, flow into the Indian Ocean.

The climate varies according to the altitude and ranges from hot in the lowlands to cool in the highlands. Rainfall is seasonal. It is light in the north but increases southward. The northern half of the country is arid and unproductive. As a result, economic activity and population are concentrated in the south.

Agriculture is the main occupation and provides the principal exports: coffee, sisal, and tea. Pyrethrum (for insecticides), corn, cotton, and other crops are also grown for export. Because of the different climatic conditions at different altitudes, a wide variety of crops can be grown. Livestock provide butter, bacon, and ham as well as hides and skins for export. Kenya's principal mineral export is soda ash, obtained from Lake Magadi. Trade is largely with the United Kingdom.

The people in the coastal section are mainly Arabs and Swahili. The African tribes of the interior are both Bantu and non-Bantu. There are many tribal languages, but Swahili is widely understood. In the coastal area Islam is the chief religion; the interior tribes are mostly pagan. Christianity is spreading. Besides the Arabs living on the coast, Indians, who are Hindus and Moslems, and Europeans are among the important minority groups in Kenya.

Arabs had occupied the east African coast for several centuries before the Portuguese established trading posts there in the 1500's. After bitter fighting most of the coastal area came under the rule of the sultan of Zanzibar. The British and the Germans became active in eastern Africa in the late 1800's. They obtained concessions from the native chiefs and made boundary agreements. The British formed the British East Africa Company, which leased the Kenya coastal strip from the sultan of Zanzibar.

In 1895 the British government took over administration of the company's territory and called it the East African Protectorate. This territory, except for the leased coastal area, became Kenya Colony in 1920; the coastal section became Kenya Protectorate. From 1952 to 1956 violence raged in Kenya as a result of the activities of the Mau Mau. This was an organization of Kikuyu tribesmen who wanted to expel the European settlers. The government repressed the movement. Eventual self-government is the goal for Kenya. For detailed map, see UNITED ARAB REPUBLIC.

Nairobi, capital of Kenya, has wide avenues and modern office buildings. It grew up from a railhead camp and stores depot that developed when a railroad was constructed from Mombasa to Uganda in 1899.

Safari Productions—Photo Researchers

KEPLER

Johannes Kepler

The Bettmann Archive

KEPLER, JOHANNES (1571-1630), a German astronomer and mathematician, influenced by Copernican principles. He discovered three important rules about planetary motion.

Johannes Kepler was born at Weil, Württemberg. He was educated at the Protestant seminary at Tübingen, Württemberg. From 1594 to 1600 he taught at the seminary at Graz, Austria. In 1600 all Protestants were banished from Graz. Kepler went to Prague, where he was the assistant of Tycho Brahe, a famous Danish astronomer. After Brahe's death in 1601 Kepler became imperial mathematician and court astronomer to the Holy Roman emperor Rudolf II. In 1612 Rudolf was forced to abdicate. Kepler fled to the Austrian town of Linz, where he worked for many years as a schoolteacher and district mathematician. Because of the wars and unrest of the Counter Reformation Kepler was forced to leave Linz in 1626. He lived in Ulm until 1628, when he moved to Sagan, in Silesia.

Kepler attempted to give reasons for the number of planets, the size of planet orbits, and the motions of the planets. When Tycho Brahe died, he left his papers and observations to Kepler. Kepler used many of Brahe's observations in his *Astronomia Nova . . . de motibus stellae Martis*, published in 1609. This work contained the first two of Kepler's laws. The first law is that each planet moves around the sun in an ellipse. The sun is at one of the foci of the ellipse. The second law states that a planet does not move with uniform velocity but in such a way that a line drawn from it to the sun sweeps out equal areas in equal times. In other words, when a planet is closer to the sun, it has a greater velocity than when it is farther away. In 1619 Kepler published *De harmonice mundi*, which contained his third law. The third law states that the squares of the periods of revolution of any two planets are in the same proportion as the cubes of their mean distances from the sun. In 1627 Kepler published the *Rudolphine Tables*, lists of stars and planets and their positions. Much of the information in the tables was inherited from Tycho Brahe.

Kepler's three laws, together with Newton's law of universal gravitation, form the basis of modern celestial mechanics. Celestial mechanics is a branch of astronomy that studies the motions of bodies in space under influence of gravitational attraction.

KEROSENE is a product of petroleum distillation. Once a principal derivative and much used for illumination, kerosene now represents only about 6 percent of the total petroleum production. Kerosene is used as fuel for jet aircraft. It may be distilled from any crude mineral oil that will boil between 175° F. and 325° F. Its flash point is 150° F., making it safe for domestic use. The occasional mistaking of gasoline for kerosene, however, when quick fires are needed, has resulted in many explosions. In a lamp kerosene burns with a steady, luminous flame, but when it is deprived of air or lacks a chimney, combustion is incomplete, and the unburned carbon forms an oily soot.

When kerosene is distilled, it is subjected to chemical treatment to remove sulfur compounds with their unpleasant odor and to remove color. This is done by using a strong sulfuric acid to dissolve out the sulfur derivatives and impurities.

Refilling the kerosene lamps was at one time a routine chore in many households.
Standard Oil Co. (N.J.)

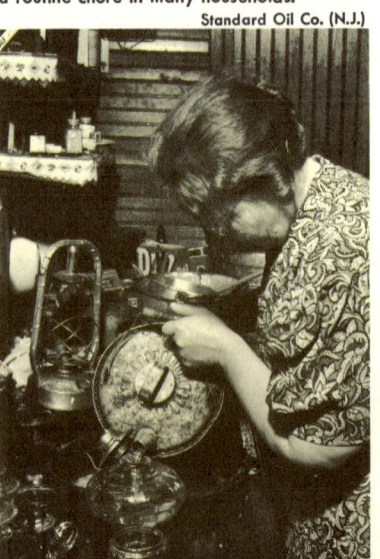

KETTLEDRUM, a percussion musical instrument, so named from its resemblance to a hemispherical kettle. It is also known as the tympano (plural, *tympani*). Formed of thin copper, it has a head of parchment, or vellum, or plastic. Kettledrums were at one time used in pairs, slung on each side of the withers of a cavalry horse. One drum was tuned to the keynote, and the other to the fifth of the key in which the piece that was to be played was written. Tuning was once done by means of a hoop and screws that tightened or loosened the head. Kettledrums are now tuned by pedals. Kettledrums have been used in symphony orchestras since about the 17th century. In the modern orchestra as many as five or more such drums may be employed.

Two of the four kettledrums in this set have pedal mechanisms for quick tuning.
Ludwig Drum Co.

KEY, FRANCIS SCOTT (1779-1843), American lawyer and author of "The Star Spangled Banner," was born in Carroll Co., Maryland. He was graduated from St. John's College in Annapolis, Md., studied law, and opened a law practice in Frederick, Md., in 1801. The following year he married and moved to Georgetown (now part of Washington, D.C.), where he lived the rest of his life.

In 1814 the British occupied Washington. (See WAR OF 1812.) During their retreat from the city they seized a prominent physician, Dr. William Beanes. Key and an army colonel, J. S. Skinner, were sent to negotiate his release. They accomplished their mission but were detained in Chesapeake Bay by the British, who were planning an attack on Baltimore. Consequently, Key and his companions spent the night of Sept. 13-14, 1814, on a British ship, from which they observed the bombardment of Baltimore. At dawn Key was overjoyed to see the American flag still flying over Fort McHenry, and he com-

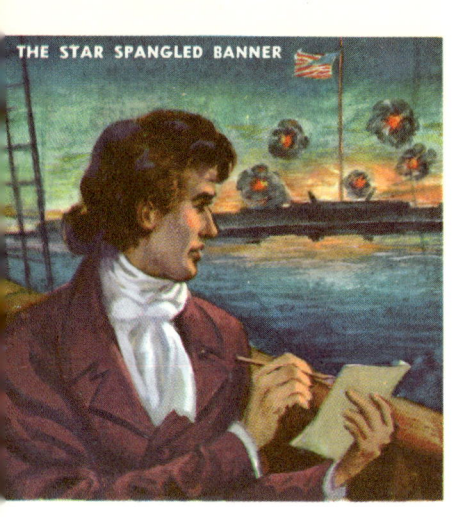

Francis Key, aboard a British ship off Fort McHenry, writes "The Star Spangled Banner."

posed his poem while still highly excited. He wrote the words to be sung to the tune of "To Anacreon in Heaven," an English drinking song whose melody had been used during the Revolutionary War for a song called "Adams and Liberty."

Key wrote a few other poems later in his life, but none of them is of the high quality of "The Star Spangled Banner." He was a devout and enthusiastically active member of the Episcopal Church, which he served in several capacities. From 1833 until 1841 he was United States attorney for the District of Columbia. In 1833 President Jackson sent him to Alabama to negotiate a treaty with the Creek Indians, a mission that he accomplished. He died of pleurisy at the age of 63. See FORT MCHENRY; STAR SPANGLED BANNER.

KEY, in geography, a small, low coral island like those off the southern coast of Florida. The ones in the West Indies are called cays or *cayos,* the Spanish form of the word, meaning "islet."

The Florida keys stretch south and west in a 200-mile arc from Miami to the Dry Tortugas. They are connected by U.S. Highway 1.

Florida State News Bureau

KEYNES, JOHN MAYNARD (1883-1946), an English economist. Keynes has been called by some people the most stimulating and gifted of 20th-century economists. His theories were influential in the United States. Keynes's method of preventing an outbreak of inflation after World War II, the deferred-saving plan, was the basis of Great Britain's defense-economy policy in 1941. Politically, Keynes was associated with the British Liberal party.

John Maynard Keynes was born at Cambridge. He attended Eton College and went on to graduate with highest honors from Cambridge University in 1905. He returned to Cambridge to teach economics. He was on the staff of the British Treasury during World War I and was appointed a Treasury representative at the Versailles Conference after the war. He withdrew from the conference in 1919 when he became convinced that the financial measures adopted by the Allies could not lead to peace. His study *The Economic Consequences of the Peace* created heated controversies among economists. His *Treatise on Money* analyzed the causes of depressions. Keynes believed that savings invested to expand factories resulted in increased consumer purchases, and increased need for new investments, and general economic prosperity. When pessimism caused people to hoard savings, however, banks gathered idle reserves, investment ceased, and national income declined. This state of affairs contributed to depressions. Thus, Keynes emphasized the need in a healthy economy for individual and corporate investment opportunities. During the depression of 1929-1933 Keynes advised the promotion of government spending in order to build up mass purchasing power. Government spending in Keynes's view would initiate private investment, which would increase in rate toward a healthy economy. These views were later presented by Keynes in *The General Theory of Employment, Interest, and Money.* Some of Keynes's suggestions were adopted by the New Deal. However, Keynes did not advocate government spending for its own sake. During World War II he advised against government spending for the purpose of stimulating business, for conditions had changed.

UPI

Khrushchev headed the Soviet Union's delegation to the 15th UN General Assembly in New York. Beating the desk with his fist or his shoe was his way of expressing disapproval.

KHRUSHCHEV, NIKITA (1894-   ), leader of the Soviet Union. Khrushchev, the son of a coal miner, was born in the town of Kalinovka (now in Russian S.F.S.R.), near Kursk. As a boy Khrushchev worked as a shepherd, and later he became a locksmith. He joined the Communist party in 1918 and fought in the Russian Revolution. Following the revolution, Khrushchev attended a high school established by the party and directed the work of the party at Stalino and then at Kiev, the capital of the Ukraine. In 1929 Khrushchev was called to Moscow to study at the Industrial Academy. By 1934 he had become the first secretary of the party's committee at Moscow and had been elected to the central committee of the Communist party of the Soviet Union. He was the successor of Lazar Kaganovich as head of the Moscow Communist party in 1935. In 1938 Khrushchev became a candidate member of the Politburo and went to the Ukraine as secretary of the party there. During World War II he organized guerrilla warfare in the Ukraine and later administered the Red Army's political section during the defense of Stalingrad.

After the war Khrushchev returned to the Ukraine, but in 1949 he was transferred to Moscow as first secretary of the party committee there. He also became a secretary of the All-Union party's central committee. His chief task was to reorganize agriculture, but his plan of "farm cities" was not successful. On Stalin's death in 1953 Khrushchev devoted his time to the central committee's affairs. In the same year he became the first secretary of the central committee of the Soviet Communist party. Thus, he held the post from which Stalin had wielded his power.

In 1955 Georgi Malenkov was replaced as premier by Nikolai Bulganin. In 1956 Khrushchev delivered to the 20th party congress his famous speech on the cult of personality, denouncing certain aspects of Stalin's rule. In 1958 Khrushchev succeeded Bulganin as premier and became the most powerful leader in the U.S.S.R. after the death of Stalin.

KIDD, CAPTAIN. See PIRACY.

KIDNAPING, a felony that includes seizing, confining, or carrying off persons without the authority of law. Kidnaping appears in a number of special forms besides the holding of a person for ransom. At one time kidnaping was used to complete the crews of ships. This practice was called shanghaiing. The slave trade, which still exists in Saudi Arabia, is often supplied by kidnaping persons. Kidnaping also includes illegal arrests.

In the early 1930's in the United States, kidnaping was engaged in by underworld criminals, who would seize underworld leaders or wealthy persons and hold them for ransom. However, after the child of Charles A. Lindbergh was kidnaped and slain in 1932, a law was passed by which kidnaping was made a federal offense. The Federal Bureau of Investigation (FBI) is now authorized to enter a case after 24 hours. The Lindbergh Act, as it is called, also made kidnaping punishable by death, on the recommendation of a jury, if the victim is not returned unharmed. The result was that professional kidnaping almost ceased. Nevertheless, there have been some 600 cases of kidnaping in the United States since the Lindbergh Act went into effect.

Kidnaping is an ancient offense. It was covered by Hammurabi's code of laws, which dates from almost 2000 B.C. In Great Britain kidnaping is most generally considered the detaining or luring away of a minor from the person having legal charge of the child. This offense is considered a felony punishable by a prison sentence. In the German Federal Republic the kidnaping of a child (*Kinderraub*) is punishable by a prison sentence ranging up to ten years. The holding of a minor for ransom is punishable by a sentence of not less than three years. The kidnaping of an adult (*Menschenraub*), which includes forcing a person illegally into military service, is punishable by a prison term up to 15 years. Austrian law punishes kidnaping with terms up to 20 years. The Swiss have laws protecting people from the illegal deprivation of their freedom, but they recognize no special category of kidnaping. Since the partition of Germany following World War II the German Federal Republic has also regarded as kidnaping the luring or the carrying by force of a person across the country's border for purposes of political persecution.

The kidneys remove waste products, particularly urea, in their important role of regulating the composition of the blood. Large volumes of fluid are filtered out in the outer part of the kidney, but only about 1/70 of this becomes urine. The remainder of the fluid is reabsorbed into the blood.

KIDNEY, either of two bean-shaped organs located one on each side of the spine beneath the lowermost ribs. The kidneys are situated outside the peritoneal cavity. They are the principal organs of the urinary system and remove water and waste products from the blood to form urine. They also play a part in controlling the composition and acid-base equilibrium of the blood. Paired kidneys of various forms are characteristic of all vertebrates.

The kidneys are known to be associated with certain types of high blood pressure, or hypertension. However, the way in which the blood pressure becomes elevated is not entirely understood. A decrease in the blood supply to the kidneys appears to be a causative factor. The blood pressure also tends to become elevated when large amounts of kidney tissue are destroyed by disease.

Because the kidneys have the capacity to perform their functions far in excess of the normal requirements, the removal of one diseased kidney does not endanger life, provided the remaining kidney is unimpaired. Kidney infection is determined clinically by the qualitative and quantitative composition of the urine and by the subject's ability to excrete certain dyes injected into the bloodstream.

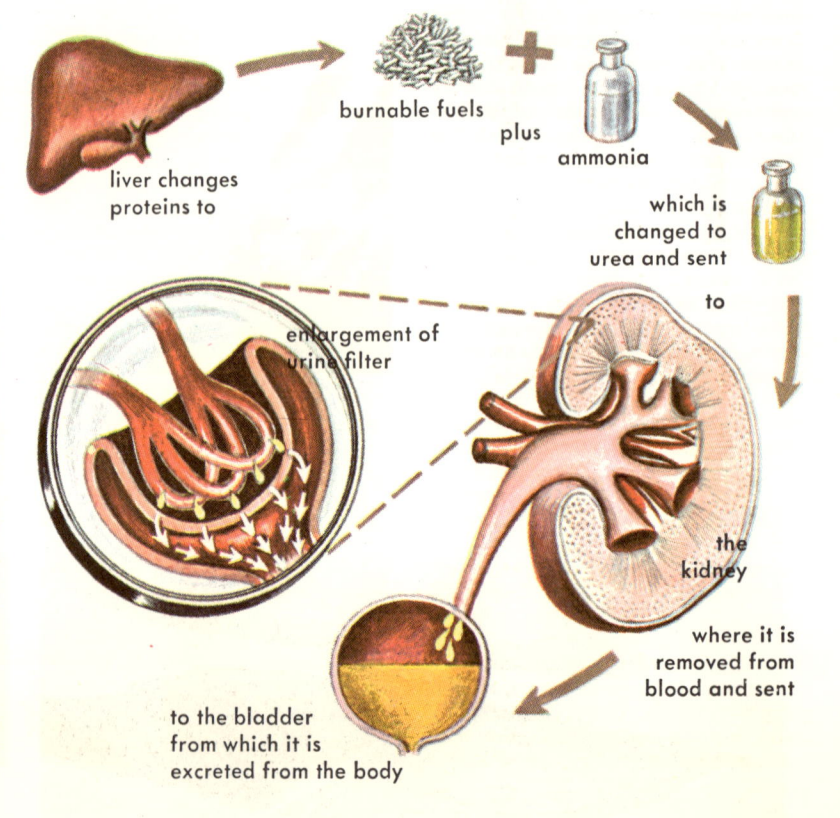

liver changes proteins to burnable fuels plus ammonia which is changed to urea and sent to the kidney where it is removed from blood and sent to the bladder from which it is excreted from the body

enlargement of urine filter

KINETIC THEORY

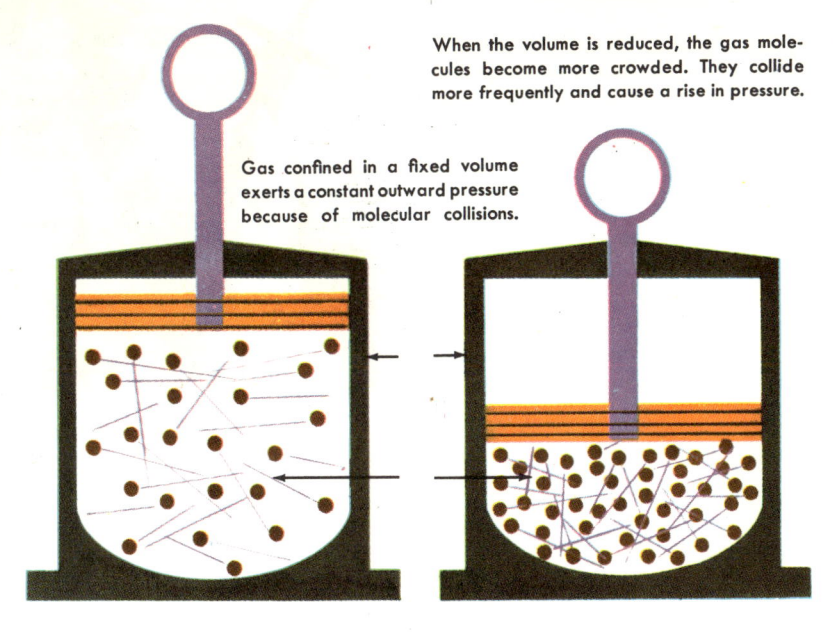

Gas confined in a fixed volume exerts a constant outward pressure because of molecular collisions.

When the volume is reduced, the gas molecules become more crowded. They collide more frequently and cause a rise in pressure.

Gas molecules move about randomly, colliding with each other and with the container walls.

KILIMANJARO is the highest mountain in Africa. It lies in northeastern Tanganyika near the border with Kenya. An enormous extinct volcano, it has two principal summits, Kibo and Mawenzi. Kibo, the higher, rises to about 19,500 feet. At about 15,000 feet it is connected by a broad saddle to Mawenzi, which reaches approximately 17,000 feet. The southern slopes of Kilimanjaro are densely settled. Coffee, corn, and bananas are grown. Between 6,000 and 10,000 feet, forests are found. Grasses grow above the forest zone to about the 12,000-foot level. On the heights are glaciers and snow. Although Kilimanjaro was first seen by Europeans in 1848, it was not climbed until Kibo was scaled by Hans Meyer and Ludwig Purtscheller in 1889.

KINETIC ENERGY is the energy of a moving body due to its weight and motion. There are two kinds of mechanical energy: kinetic and potential. Potential energy is energy at rest—a tank of compressed air, a stretched spring, or a heavy block of wood resting on a table, which will fall with great force if pushed over the edge. Whenever potential energy is released, it is changed into kinetic energy. A ball has kinetic energy when it has been thrown into the air. At its highest level, however, it has only potential energy. When it falls toward the earth again, its potential energy is changed into kinetic energy. When the ball lands, the kinetic energy becomes some other form of energy. See ENERGY.

KINETIC THEORY. According to the kinetic theory, each body consists of a large number of extremely small particles (atoms or molecules) moving at high speed and separated from each other by empty space. The molecules of a gas move through space with random motion and very frequently collide with each other.

The particles of a liquid behave in the same fashion, but the particles do not move as fast or as far as gas molecules. Particles of a solid have random motion about a fixed point. Because the atoms and molecules are moving, they possess kinetic energy. The amount of kinetic energy any one particle possesses depends on its mass and velocity. The average kinetic energy of the atoms or molecules in a body is related to the temperature of the body. An increase in temperature causes an increase in the average velocity of particles in a body. The molecules in warm water move with greater velocity, and therefore have a higher average kinetic energy, than the molecules in cold water.

The simplest and most direct evidence for the kinetic theory is shown in Brownian movement, first observed by a Scottish botanist named Brown. He saw, through a microscope, the rapid, random movement of very fine particles suspended in water. The only possible explanation for such random motions was that the fine particles were being bombarded by the surrounding water molecules. The smaller the particles were, the more freely they moved. Since that time Brownian movement has been observed in many types of suspensions.

Kilimanjaro can be climbed from either Moshi or Marangu in from three to six days. The ascent of Kibo is much easier than the ascent of Mawenzi. Although the lower of the two summits, Mawenzi requires definite climbing experience and the use of a rope.

Felix Julen—Monkmeyer

KING, WILLIAM LYON MACKENZIE (1874-1950), Canadian statesman, born in Berlin (now Kitchener), Ontario, and educated at the University of Toronto, Harvard University, and the University of Chicago. While studying in Chicago, he did social work under Jane Addams at Hull House. From 1900 to 1908 he was deputy minister of labor and editor of the *Labour Gazette*. From 1908 to 1911 and from 1919 to 1949 he was active in Canadian political affairs as a member of Parliament and as minister of labor. From 1914 to 1917 he was an investigator of industrial relations under the auspices of the Rockefeller Foundation. In 1919 he succeeded Wilfred Laurier as leader of the Liberal party. In 1921 King became prime minister, president of the Privy Council, and secretary of state for external affairs. He remained in these offices until 1930, except for a few months. He was a member of the Council Assembly and vice-president of the League of Nations in Geneva in 1928 and 1936. His party was defeated in the general elections of 1930, and King again became leader of the Liberal opposition in Parliament. In 1935 his party returned to power, with King as prime minister for the third time. His government was reelected in 1940 and in 1945. A joint defense board with the United States was formed in 1940. King headed the Canadian delegation to the United Nations Conference at San Francisco. With British Prime Minister Clement Attlee and President Harry S. Truman he signed the Atomic Energy Declaration. In 1948 he resigned as prime minister after a longer period in office than any other Canadian.

KING, THE (constellation). See CEPHEUS.

KING ARTHUR AND HIS KNIGHTS OF THE ROUND TABLE are the legendary figures in a group of adventure stories first written in English during the Middle Ages. The deeds of King Arthur were related in French romances as well as in English tales; in both languages the stories were cast into the popular form of the romance in verse. Notable French authors of the Arthurian legends were Chrétien de Troyes, Wace of Jersey, Marie de France, and Robert de Boron. The Welsh historian Nennius, in his *Historia Britonum*, refers to Arthur by name as a 6th-century chieftain, so that there is some basis for believing that King Arthur was an actual person.

Sir Thomas Malory's popular *Morte d'Arthur* (1470) was based on French sources, but an earlier English author who wrote a romance about King Arthur was Geoffrey of Monmouth. By the time that his *Historia regum Britanniae* was written (1139) Arthur had become the focus of a body of popular stories, in which he appeared as a mythical ruler and a chivalrous knight, whose origin and death were shrouded in mystery.

According to the tales, his parents were Uther Pendragon and Igraine of Cornwall; his teacher was the magician Merlin. The elves granted him long life, wealth, and virtues. Heroic deeds fill the pages of Arthurian legends. He leads his knights in battle; they engage in tournaments and set out upon arduous errands; and they become involved in magical predictions. When the knights reached the age of 21 they went through a ceremony and pledged themselves to valor, courtesy, and loyalty. They promised to be foes of evil and friends of the weak; to be brave, honorable, loyal, and merciful, and never to fight in a bad cause. Gawain, Launcelot, and Tristram were among King Arthur's bravest and most chivalrous knights.

Included in the legends of Sir Thomas Malory's *Morte d'Arthur* are the stories of the Holy Grail and the loves of Launcelot and Guinevere and of Tristram and Iseult. Malory's work provided inspiration for many later English poets. William Morris and E. A. Robinson wrote fine poems dealing with Arthurian figures, but Tennyson's *Idylls of the King* is the most familiar version.

King Arthur receives the sword Excalibur.

This is a 14th-century miniaturist's conception of King Arthur's Round Table at Camelot.
La Croix

- Gray-Headed Kingfisher
- Kookaburra
- Belted Kingfisher
- Ceylon White-Breasted Kingfisher
- Common Kingfisher
- Amazon Kingfisher

Kingfishers are of two kinds: true kingfishers and wood kingfishers. True kingfishers have sharp, pointed bills; they usually feed by diving for fish. Wood kingfishers, such as the kookaburra above, have large, flat bills; they generally feed on small land animals.

KINGFISHER. An unusual North American bird is the belted kingfisher, so named because of the belts, or bands, of color across its light breast. Its head has a big, shaggy crest; its bill is large; and its call is a hoarse rattle. It is blue gray in general color and about a foot long. This is one of the few species in which the female wears brighter color than the male. A chestnut band across her breast and down the flanks is in addition to the blue-gray breastband worn also by the male. These kingfishers range from Alaska and Labrador to the Gulf coast. They always live near water—a brook, pond, or larger body—and sometimes defend as much as a mile of feeding territory. They dive headlong for fish; the prey is carried to a perch where it is twisted or tossed so it can be swallowed headfirst. Five to eight white eggs are laid in a chamber at the end of a long passageway dug horizontally in a steep bank. The young birds are fed on fish or tadpoles.

About 80 other species of kingfishers, sparrow-sized to crow-sized and often very beautiful, are found around the world, mostly in tropical regions. A famous one is the Australian kookaburra, or laughing jackass. This bird is startling with its raucous screams and chuckles.

The European kingfisher is a symbol of calm seas and still air. This symbolism comes from the Greek myth of Halcyone, who grieved piteously for her drowned husband; in compassion the gods changed her and her husband into kingfishers. The legend says that while their nest was floating on the water, the seas were quiet. The word *halcyon* comes from the Greek *halkyon*, meaning "kingfisher"; and halcyon days, which in the myth were the calm days when the kingfishers' nest rested on the water, are now days of peace and calm.

KING GEORGE'S WAR, a war fought by Great Britain and its American colonies against France and its Indian allies during the reign of King George II. The war, which began in 1743 and lasted until 1748, was an extension to America of the War of the Austrian Succession. The fighting was confined to the Nova Scotia–New England frontier. Its principal event was the capture of Louisburg, on Cape Breton Island, the strongest and most important French fortress in America except Quebec. By the Treaty of Aix-la-Chapelle Louisburg was returned to France for Madres in India. This was one of a series of colonial wars between France and England for control of North America.

New England forces, below, land on Cape Breton Island to capture the French fortress of Louisburg, during King George's War.
Pub. Archives of Can.

KINGLETS AND GNATCATCHERS

male, yellow in the female. In the ruby-crowned, however, only the male has the bright-ruby crown, and it is often concealed. This species is best identified by the white eye ring, which gives the eye a prominent, staring look. The ruby-crowned has an extraordinary volume of song for such a small bird, and it sings even on migration. The golden-crowned sings only on the breeding ground.

Gnatcatchers have a long tail, often cocked upward like a wren's. The blue-gray gnatcatcher, which resembles a tiny mockingbird, is grayish above and light below, with a long black-and-white tail and a white eye ring. Tops of high forest trees are preferred by this active, insectivorous bird. It breeds throughout the warmer part of the United States. The black-tailed gnatcatcher, similar except for its darker tail, occurs only in the southwestern United States and northern Mexico.

KING PHILIP'S WAR, a conflict between the New England colonists and the confederated Indian tribes—the Narragansets, the Wampanoags, and the Nipmucs—carried on in 1675 and 1676. The war was primarily caused by the expansion of the colonists into the western New England Indian lands and to the attempts of the colonists to disarm and civilize the tribes. Philip was the Christian name given to Metacomet, the chief of the Wampanoags, whose young warriors began the raiding parties along the frontier. After the war the Indians ceased to be a serious problem in southern New England.

Kings Canyon National Park in California is a mountain wilderness dominated by the summit peaks of the Sierra Nevada and by two canyons of the Kings River. Glacial lakes and flowering alpine meadows dot the park.

KINGS CANYON NATIONAL PARK is an area of impressive canyons, massive peaks, and giant trees. It is situated in east-central California and adjoins Sequoia National Park, which lies to the south. Kings Canyon National Park covers approximately 700 square miles. Kings River Canyon, along the South Fork of Kings River, is over 3,000 feet deep. This gorge is overlooked by Sentinel Dome (9,127 feet) from the south. General Grant National Park, established in 1890 to protect magnificent groves of giant sequoias, was absorbed in Kings Canyon National Park when it was established in 1940.

KING WILLIAM'S WAR, name for the American part of the War of the League of Augsburg (1689-1697). It was the first of the series of colonial struggles between England and France for control of North America. In America the war was fought in the western area between the French and the Iroquois Indians, who were allied with the English, from the Mohawk River to the St. Lawrence River and as far north as Hudson Bay. The English colonists, under Sir William Phips and his Massachusetts troops, managed to gain, and later to lose, Port Royal. A general seesaw battle was fought all along the lines until the Treaty of Ryswick in 1697 restored the status quo. The struggle resumed with the outbreak of Queen Anne's War in 1702.

KINSHIP is a relationship between two or more persons recognized on the basis of heredity, marriage, or adoption. Ties of kinship provide certain social and economic benefits for members of a kinship group. Systems defining kinship vary considerably from society to society.

National Park Service Photo

The blue-gray gnatcatcher (top), the Formosan kinglet (center), and the ruby-crowned kinglet are active little birds about 4 or 5 inches long. Ruby-crowned kinglets often travel in bands with other kinglets or with such small birds as warblers and creepers.

KINGLETS AND GNATCATCHERS are tiny birds, smaller than warblers but somewhat resembling them in their busy feeding activity among the tree branches. They belong to the family of Old World warblers. In the New World there are only two species of kinglets and two species of gnatcatchers.

Both kinglets—the golden-crowned and the ruby-crowned—are sprightly mites with short tails, short bills, and olive-gray plumage. The nest, a pendant ball with top opening, contains from five to ten creamy eggs. Nest and eggs of the two species are similar, but the birds are easily distinguishable. In the golden-crowned the crown patch is always obvious; it is orange in the

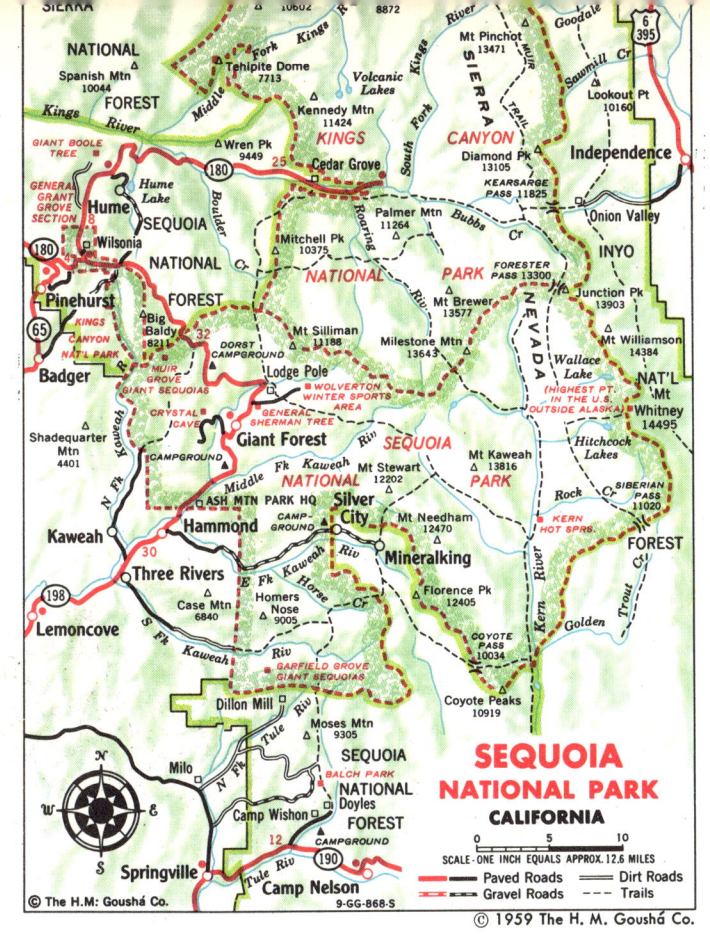

Kings Canyon National Park lies to the north of Sequoia National Park.

Through kinship a person may, from birth, expect certain benefits from relatives that he may not expect from nonrelatives. Socially, a person may expect special considerations from his kin; for example, he may expect hospitality from persons he has never met if they are his kin. Financially, a person may expect his kin to help him out of extreme difficulties, help him to get a job, and so forth. Strong kinship ties necessarily impose obligations as well as offer benefits. Especially in modern urban societies, many people come to feel that the obligations outweigh the benefits and so tend to loosen kinship ties.

To see what a kinship system is like in Western society, let us trace the kin of a hypothetical man, Mr. Martin. At the center of Martin's kinship group is his immediate family. He will probably belong to two such families during his lifetime—the family into which he is born and the family he creates by marriage. The first of these includes Martin, his father, mother, brothers, and sisters; the second includes Martin, his wife, sons, and daughters.

Martin's parents' parents are his grandparents; his grandparents' parents are his great-grandparents. For each generation we go back, another *great* is added. The system works similarly for Martin's direct descendants. His children's children are his grandchildren, his grandchildren's children are his great-grandchildren, and so forth.

Brothers of Martin's parents are his uncles; sisters of his parents are his aunts. Brothers and sisters of his grandparents are his great-uncles and great-aunts. Martin is a first cousin to all grandchildren of his grandparents, a second cousin of all great-grandchildren of his great-grandparents, and so forth. Children of his first cousins are Martin's first cousins once removed. Sons of Martin's brothers and sisters are his nephews; daughters of his brothers and sisters are his nieces.

Martin is related to his in-laws through marriage. His wife's father is his father-in-law; her brother is Martin's brother-in-law. (The suffix *-in-law* originally referred to the canon law that prohibits marriage to close relatives. Thus a mother-in-law is a person who, in canon law, is as unmarriageable for one as one's mother. This original significance can be seen in Dickens' writings, where *mother-in-law* may refer to a stepmother.)

This kinship system, like most in Western societies, tends to distinguish fairly sharply the immediate family from more distant kin. In many other societies kinship is figured differently. The paternal and maternal relatives are distinguished in some societies, such as that of the Eskimo. Among some peoples, such as the Iroquois, children of paternal uncles and maternal aunts are treated as brothers and sisters, while children of other uncles and aunts are treated as cousins. Polynesians and some other peoples group the members of one generation, so that no distinction is made between brothers or sisters and cousins.

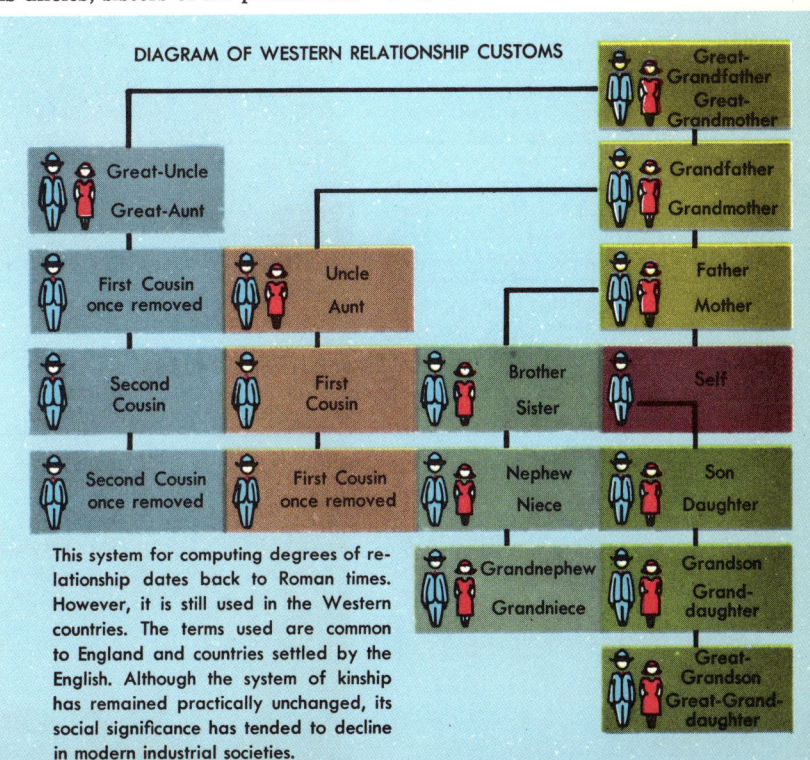

DIAGRAM OF WESTERN RELATIONSHIP CUSTOMS

This system for computing degrees of relationship dates back to Roman times. However, it is still used in the Western countries. The terms used are common to England and countries settled by the English. Although the system of kinship has remained practically unchanged, its social significance has tended to decline in modern industrial societies.

1393

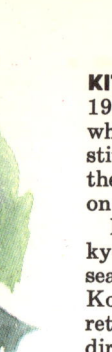

KIPLING, RUDYARD (1865-1936), was an English author and poet. He became famous for his short stories, poems, and novels, dealing with such subjects as India, the jungle, army life, and the sea. He received the Nobel prize for literature in 1907.

Kipling was born in Bombay, the son of an official in the British government. He was sent to England as a child and was educated at the United Services College in Devonshire. He later wrote about his childhood and school experiences in *Stalky & Co.*

Kipling returned to India in 1883 and became a reporter and editor for a newspaper in Lahore. His first book, a collection of poems called *Departmental Ditties*, was published in 1886. From 1887 to 1889 he worked on a newspaper in Allahabad. He wrote several books of short stories during this time, including *Plain Tales from the Hills* and *Soldiers Three*. He returned to England in 1889 and wrote the novel *The Light That Failed* and *Barrack-Room Ballads*, which includes the famous poem "Gunga Din."

Kipling married an American woman in 1892 and moved to Brattleboro, Vt., where he lived until 1897. During this period he wrote two famous books of short stories, *The Jungle Book* and *The Second Jungle Book*, and the novel *Captains Courageous*. He returned to England in 1897 and lived there for most of the remainder of his life. He had gained much fame by this time and was able to support himself by his writings.

Kipling's later books include *Kim* (considered by many to be his finest novel), *Just So Stories*, and *Songs of the Sea*. He actively supported the British cause in World War I and wrote several military books, including *The New Army in Training* and *France at War*. Among his best known single poems are "If," "Danny Deever," and "Recessional."

KITAZATO, SHIBASABURO (1852-1931), a Japanese bacteriologist who, as director of the Research Institute of Contagious Diseases, laid the foundation for Japanese research on epidemics and bacteriology.

Kitazato was graduated from Tokyo University in 1883. He did research in Germany under Robert Koch from 1885 to 1891. When he returned to Japan, he was appointed director of the Research Institute of Contagious Diseases, a government laboratory. In 1914 he founded his own research institute, named Kitazato Laboratory. Later he was dean of the medical faculty of Keio University in Tokyo, a member of the Imperial Academy, president of the Japan Medical Association, and a member of the House of Peers. He was created a baron in 1924.

Kitazato isolated the tetanus bacillus and the bacillus of symptomatic anthrax in 1889. In 1894 he discovered the bacillus responsible for bubonic plague. In 1898 he isolated the dysentery bacillus. He prepared a diphtheria antitoxin in 1890. He also did research on the tubercle bacillus, which is the cause of tuberculosis.

Shibasaburo Kitazato

KITE (bird). See HAWKS, KITES, EAGLES.

KIWI, a most unbirdlike bird, about 2 feet long, related to the extinct moas. Having no noticeable wings, it cannot fly; but it runs faster than a man. It has no tail, and its feathers are hairlike. It has poor daytime vision but a good sense of smell, its nostrils being at the tip of the long, slender bill. It feeds only at night, digging up insect larvae, worms, and snails, which it detects in the earth by smelling. A burrow is its daytime hiding place. Kiwis waddle when they walk; they travel in pairs and seem to mate for life. To defend themselves they kick forward and use their sharp claws. The nest, hidden in a hole at the base of a tree, normally contains only one egg—but it is the largest known egg in relation to the size of the bird, being one-fourth the weight of the female. Its incubation (by the male only) is

The kiwi's wings are too small for flight.

one of the longest known—about 80 days. Sometimes, as soon as one egg has hatched, the female lays another; the male must then start incubating again. The male also does the nest building, after some help from the female in digging the hole.

This oddity, found only in New Zealand, was named by the Maoris from its peculiar cry. Once almost extinct, it now flourishes under government protection. It is the national emblem; its name is given to New Zealand soldiers and airmen; its picture adorns the coins, stamps, and paper money of the country; and the government forbids its further export.

KLEE, PAUL (1879-1940), was a Swiss painter noted for painting fanciful and dreamlike scenes and objects. Born near Bern, Switzerland, he took violin lessons as a boy but went to Munich, Germany, at the age of 19 to study painting. His first works were painted in a realistic style, but he gradually became more fanciful and abstract. Klee often tried to paint objects as he thought children or mentally disturbed people would imagine them. Many of his later paintings reveal a world of strange, fantastic, brightly colored creatures and objects.

KLONDIKE GOLD RUSH. During the years 1897-1899 about 100,000 people dropped their work and left their homes for the Yukon area of the Canadian Northwest Territories. Gold had been discovered there on Bonanza Creek of the Klondike River in 1896. The newspapers gave the gold strike much publicity, and transportation companies, seeing profit to be gained, conducted a great campaign advertising the gold finds. The publicity was largely responsible for the size of the rush. After the surface gold had been mined, most of the miners sold their claims to large companies and moved into Alaska to search for more gold or to settle down. The Klondike gold rush, therefore, had an important effect on the growth and development of Alaska.

KNEELER, THE (constellation). See HERCULES.

KNIGHTHOOD AND CHIVALRY, terms referring to a system of manners or social arrangement in medieval Europe. Chivalry was the code of conduct to which the knights subscribed. Knights were pledged to protect the weak and the oppressed and to serve their feudal lord, the church, and their sovereign. The ideals of chivalry were never fully heeded, but they worked as a civilizing influence. The golden age of knighthood and chivalry was in France during the 13th century.

Chivalry was characteristically European. The Arabs, however, had a similar way of life that was never a social institution, as it was in Europe. Saladin, the heroic foe of the Crusaders, was the great representative of Arabic chivalry. In Japan the samurai, with their knightly code of Bushido, somewhat resembled the knights of Europe.

The origin of knighthood is obscure. The military base of chivalry arose in Christendom after the death of Charlemagne in 814. Europe, which had already fought to stave off the Moors, had to battle the vikings, the Magyars, and the Slavs. The only military forces capable of coping with the invasions were cavalry units formed by freemen, who in return for protection had pledged themselves to serve local lords. A military chivalric code developed, based on courage, prowess, loyalty, and generosity. However, these early knights displayed the most terrible cruelty to all who were not included in the code of chivalric obligation. By about 1000 the invaders of Europe had been driven off, and knighthood and chivalry ceased to be militarily useful. Instead, groups of knights entrenched themselves in castles and carried on local wars.

Tournaments were the recreation of knights.

The second element of chivalry was rooted in Christian virtues, which the church attempted to instill in these crude warriors. It was the church's motive to try to make the knights an instrument for carrying out the will of God on earth. As a result of the Crusades the church was partially successful in imbuing chivalry with the virtues of defending the poor, the widow, and the orphan. The quasi-religious nature of knighthood was symbolized in the lengthy ceremony involved in becoming a knight. The prospective knight symbolized his purification from sin by bathing. He donned garments of white, red, and black to signify purity, sacrifice, and death. Following an all-night vigil in church, the knight attended a confession, Mass, and sermon. His sword was consecrated to the service of the church, which he swore to obey. Only then was the knight given over to the feudal lord, from whom he received the accolade. The great religious orders of knighthood approached most closely the church's ideal. These were the Knights Templars, the Hospitalers, and the Teutonic Knights. As a rule, most prospective knights did not undergo the entire religious-secular ceremony. In England the accolade was almost always the entire ceremony of dubbing a knight, except in those cases in which knights were dubbed during state occasions. In England knights who underwent the full ceremony, which included the bath, came to be called Knights of the Bath.

The last addition to the chivalric code was gallantry, by which a knight became a courtier. The troubadours of Provence, in the south of France, were the first to add poetic embellishments to gallantry. Each knight was supposed to have his secret lady love, for whom he performed feats of valor.

By the 14th century chivalry had developed a regular educational system. Knighthood was not hereditary: It was a reward for valor or for proper training. However, the

These two European knights in full armor, including helmet, have met in single combat.

When knights were not engaged in real combat, they organized jousting tournaments. Such simulated battles were sometimes dangerous.

knights did come to be an almost closed class of nobility. Because of the custom of primogeniture the younger sons of the nobility had only two callings open to them: soldiering and the priesthood. Those who longed for adventure chose military service. The schools for knighthood were the feudal courts and castles. At about the age of seven a boy began his education as a page, who was a constant personal servant of his master and mistress, from whom he learned elements of religion and comportment. The master and his squires taught the page to throw a spear, to manage a shield, and to march. He also learned hunting and falconry, estate management, a little law, and—since he was expected to entertain—singing, dancing, and poetry. The page became a squire when he was 16 years old. Although he continued to attend his master, much of his day was spent in developing military skills. He tilted at the quintain, practiced with the battleax and sword, swam, climbed, learned to wear armor, and became accustomed to hardships. He also chose a lady love. After enough training the squire could have his sword blessed by a priest, after which he became a squire of the body, either for his old master or for one of his own choosing. The squire of the body accompanied his leader into battle and assisted him in many ways. Following six or seven years of service as a squire, a man might become a knight. Some, however, preferred to remain squires for the rest of their lives.

The decline of chivalry occurred during the 14th and 15th centuries. Economic considerations eroded chivalric customs—children of five years of age were knighted to protect their estates, for example. Chivalry had never provided an effective military system, and the use of infantry (with crossbows) and artillery rendered the heavily armored knights obsolete. Even the Hundred Years' War was fought largely by national armies. The terrible Thirty Years' War and the Wars of the Roses in England saw little chivalric practice. The chivalric orders became mere decorations, which, like the English Order of the Garter, were used by sovereigns to honor outstanding services by subjects. When Cervantes wrote *Don Quixote*, poking fun at chivalry, the chivalric system was already a thing of the past.

The major legends of chivalry include the Arthurian legends and the *Song of Roland*. The best overall picture of chivalry in the 14th century can be found in Jean Froissart's chronicles. See COAT OF ARMS; CRUSADES, THE; FEUDALISM; KING ARTHUR AND HIS KNIGHTS OF THE ROUND TABLE; TOURNAMENT.

KNIGHTS OF LABOR, a labor organization in the United States and Canada, founded as a secret society in Philadelphia in 1869. It was organized on a national basis in 1878. Its outstanding leader was Terence Vincent Powderly. It was an industrial union, as opposed to a craft union, and included all kinds of labor, skilled and unskilled. Its membership reached a peak of over 700,000 in 1886. After that time a rapid decline occurred as a result of unsuccessful strikes, internal friction, and depletion of union finances. In the meantime the American Federation of Labor had been organized and was competing successfully for trade-union members. The Knights of Labor became involved in reform movements not related to trade unions, and by 1900 the organization had virtually ceased to exist.

KNIT GOODS, fabrics made on machines that intertwine threads by looping rather than by weaving or by heat and pressure. In trade, the term "knit goods" generally refers to stockings, underwear, sweaters, and knit gloves, all of which stretch to fit the contours of the body.

The ceremony of knighting a squire was often richly symbolical. The white linen tunic, for example, represented purity.

The knit-goods industry, as distinct from weaving and felting, is remarkably modern. It seems to have been existing in England during the reign of Henry VII. A parliamentary act of that time referred to knitted woolen caps. Other vague references occur during the following 100 years, but it was not until 1598 that the first real knitting machine, the stocking frame, was built by an English parson, William Lee, of Cambridge. On his machine he made a pair of silk stockings for the queen. His invention consisted of knitting needles set in a machine in such a way that a series of continuous loops could be intertwined to make a fabric. All knitting machines since have been merely additions to and modifications of his basic invention. Lee died in poverty and was buried in an unknown grave in Paris.

During the 19th century seamless circular knitting machines were perfected, so that now any textile article can be reproduced on the knitting, or loop-structure, principle. About one-fifth of American textiles are produced in knitting mills.

The technique of casting on is shown in 1 through 4; that of knitting, in 5 through 8.

KNITTING, the use of needles and a thread to form fabric by interlocking a single thread in a series of joined loops. Knitting thread may be woolen yarn or rayon, cotton, linen, or any synthetic-fiber thread of various twists, sizes, and textures. These threads come in all colors and shades. At one time the needles, which are eyeless, were carved out of wood, bone, or ivory, but now they are usually made of steel, aluminum, or plastic. Heavy needles should be used for thick yarn and smaller ones for thinner yarn. Consult the directions given in your knitting pattern for the choice of needles and yarn; directions must be followed exactly if the finished product is to be satisfactory. Circular needles may be used to make skirts or to avoid seams in other garments. Stockings, mittens, and hats are usually made on two, three, or four double-pointed needles.

Knitting has been known in parts of the Middle East from the time of Christ. From there it spread to Europe by way of the Mediterranean ports. Centuries later, knitting guilds were organized throughout Europe. Apprentices, after six years of instruction, were required to produce several elaborate and colorful articles before their work was approved by the guildmaster. One such article was a woolen carpet in a floral design, with birds and animals—all knit in their natural colors.

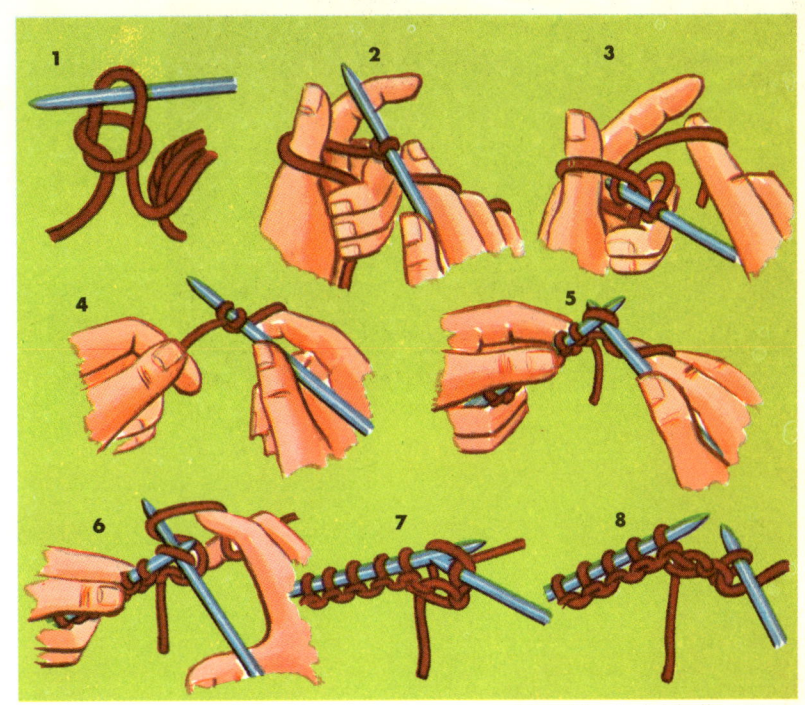

The basic knitting stitches are the knit, or garter, stitch and the purl stitch. The purl stitch is made in the same manner as the knit stitch except that the needle is inserted from back to front of the stitch on the left-hand needle instead of from front to back as in the plain stitch. The thread is kept in front of the work as long as purling is being done. These two stitches may be used in alternating rows to give a ribbed surface to a garment. The stockinette stitch is the simplest combination of knit and purl, although it may also be done on a circular needle or by going around and around on three double-pointed needles instead of back and forth on two single-pointed needles. In this case purling is omitted except where it is called for in the directions for making the piece. The moss and cable stitches are among other combinations of knit and purl. The cable stitch produces a spiral ribbing on the surface of the work and is especially attractive on sweaters.

Increasing and decreasing stitches and casting on or off make possible the pleasant variety and elaborate designs in knitting. The number of stitches may be increased when called for in the instructions by knitting a second stitch in the loop on the left-hand needle before the loop is slipped off. A decrease is accomplished by simply knitting two stitches off the left-hand needle as a single stitch instead of knitting one at a time.

When the work is finished, the stitches in the final row are cast off to make a finished edge that is comparable to the beginning, or cast-on, edge. When casting off stitches the thread should be held very loosely; otherwise, the finished edge will be too tightly drawn. Expert knitters sometimes use a larger size needle to cast off in order to avoid tightness. When the last row of work has been finished, turn the work as if to begin a new row. Knit two very loose stitches onto the right-hand needle; pass the first over the second after both are on the right-hand needle; knit another stitch onto the right-hand needle and pass the one already there over it. Continue in this manner until only one stitch remains. Break the thread, leaving an end about 6 inches long. Make a loop knot through the remaining stitch and pull taut, thus finishing the piece. This method is also used when only part of a row is to be cast off, as when making armholes and necklines or shaping body pieces. However, the thread is not broken, as the remainder of the row will be knit in the usual manner.

Stitches dropped accidentally are easily recovered by using a crochet hook and working on the plain surface of the knitting.

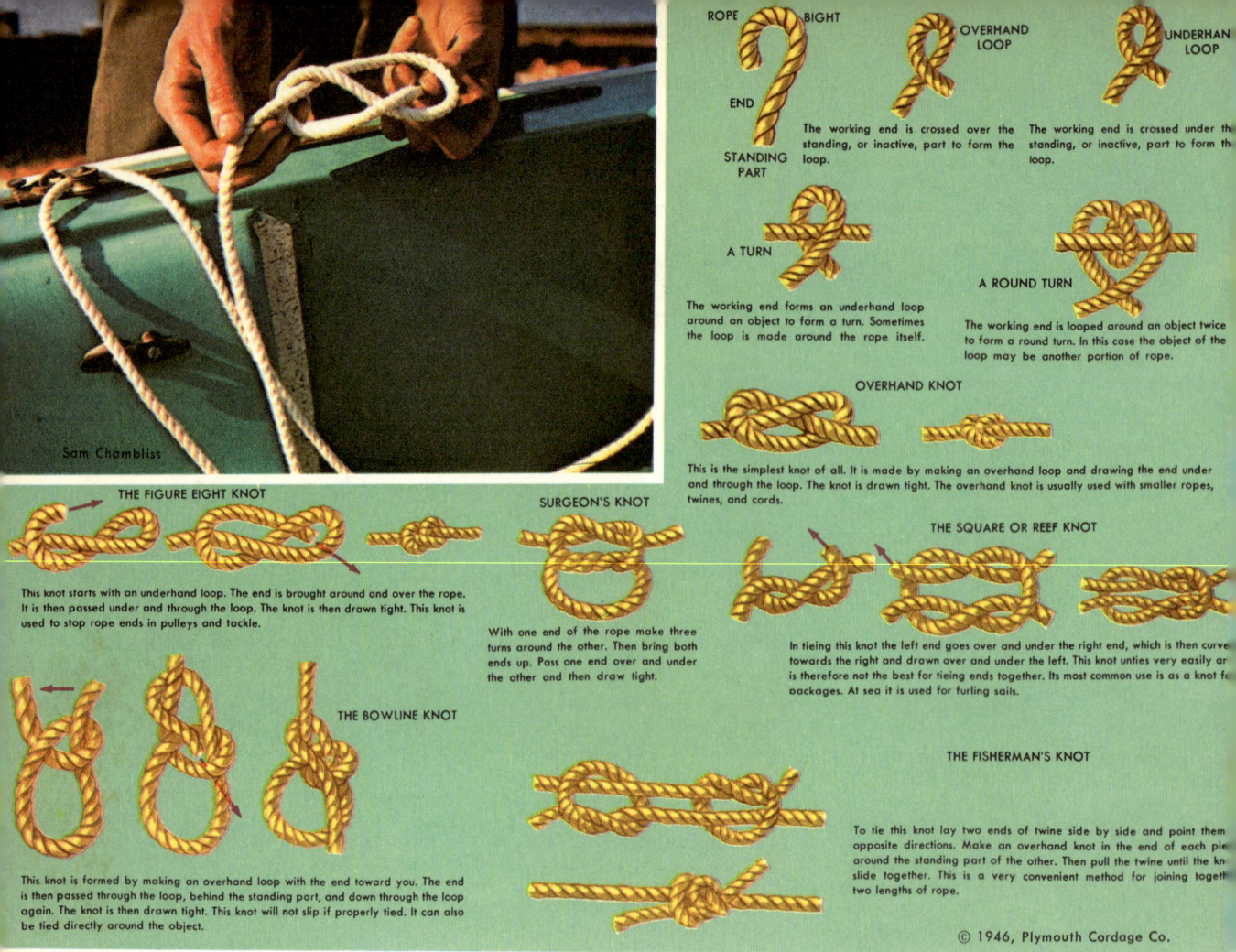

Several knots are illustrated above. The sailor (inset) has tied a figure-eight knot.

KNOTTING, the bending, looping, intertwining, and tightening of string, twine, and rope for many purposes, such as decorating, connecting lengths of rope, fastening rope to an object, and binding or lashing two or more things together. Lacemakers, clerks, campers, farmers, construction workers, longshoremen, and sailors use scores of kinds of knots, slings, splices, and hitches for their specific needs.

Knotting is more than a pleasant development of personal competence. Upon the correct knot may depend the safety of a towed ship, the speed in getting in a crop of hay, or the life of a man on a mountainside. In stump pulling, the wrong knot can break the rope, stop the day's work, or even kill a bystander.

To learn how to tie and to use the common knots, such as the overhand, the square, the slip, the halter, the bowline, the half hitch, and the clove hitch, take two lengths of rope about 7 feet long and, referring to a rope manual, practice each type of knot until it becomes thoroughly familiar. Tying knots is the only way to learn knotting. Ninety percent of temporary tying needs can be met by the square knot, the half hitch, the clove hitch, and the bowline knot.

Knots and splices weaken the original strength of the rope. An eye splice over an eye iron has only 90 percent of the rope's original strength; a bowline knot, only 40 percent; a square knot, less than half of the rope's breaking strength. See ROPE AND TWINE.

KNOW-NOTHING PARTY, or American party, an American political party originally known as the secret Order of the Star Spangled Banner. It was founded in New York in 1849 by native Protestants. When questioned by outsiders, its members, who were subject to an elaborate ritual and to rigid discipline, answered, "I know nothing." The rise of the party was occasioned by the disruption of older party lines over the Kansas-Nebraska Act, by a growing fear of Catholicism (a fear considerably augmented by the visit of a tactless papal nuncio), and by the preaching of the doctrines of Comte de Saint-Simon by German radicals. Out of its fears of foreign subversion of the republic, the party espoused a program that pledged its members to vote only for natives, to agitate for a 21-year probationary period preceding naturalization, and to combat the menace of the papacy. During the early 1850's the party grew so strong that in the election of 1854 it almost captured New York and did win Massachusetts, where it elected a legislature that spent most of its time investigating Catholic schools and nunneries. The same legislature passed a literacy test qualification for voting. At its national convention in 1855, the party, which by then had taken the name of the American party, passed under the control of the South and proceeded to pass proslavery resolutions. This turn of events so weakened the party that in the presidential election of 1856 its candidate, Millard Fillmore, carried only the state of Maryland. Thereafter the party came rapidly to an end.

KOCH, ROBERT (1843-1910), a Nobel prize–winning German bacteriologist. He was an outstanding figure in the history of modern medicine, especially in microbiology, and his studies in the problems of surgical infection were fundamental. He studied medicine at Göttingen and later became professor at the University of Berlin and director of the Institute for Infectious Diseases. In 1882 Koch described to the Berlin Physiological Society his discovery of the tubercle bacillus. He was later thought to have found a sure cure for tuberculosis in tuberculin, but this drug proved to be only of diagnostic value. Koch made extensive researches into the causes and treatment of tropical diseases. After spending some time in Egypt, he discovered the comma bacillus of cholera and also investigated the causes of malaria and other diseases prevalent in Africa.

Robert Koch, the great bacteriologist, studied sleeping sickness in East Africa. — Brown Brothers

KOLKHOZ, in the Soviet Union, a collective farm. The kolkhozy (plural of *kolkhoz*) grew out of the Soviets' scheme to nationalize all means of economic production and their belief that large, scientifically cultivated farms would outproduce many small peasant holdings. Since 1929, despite bitter peasant opposition, all but a small percentage of the cultivated land in the U.S.S.R. has been absorbed by the kolkhozy.

Although the land is owned by the state, it is given to the kolkhozy for permanent use. The collective farms also own the buildings, livestock, seed, and fodder. Originally they owned only smaller items of equipment. Other organizations, the machine-tractor stations, supplied the larger machinery and performed the heavier operations. Since 1958, however, the collective farms have been permitted to buy heavy equipment, and the machine-tractor stations are being abolished. Member families of the kolkhozy are permitted to own their homes, small garden plots, and some livestock.

Ostensibly, the highest authority on the kolkhoz is the general assembly of members. It elects the president of the kolkhoz, as well as lesser officials, and it approves the plans and budgets of the administrators. Actually, these decisions are always strongly influenced by the Communist Party and the government of the Soviet Union.

The kolkhoz draws up its annual plan on the basis of the government's overall agricultural plan. The members are divided into brigades and assigned specific tasks. Of the annual crop the kolkhoz is required to sell a designated quantity to the state at a fixed price. The remainder is divided among the members on the basis of the quality and quantity of their work. They may either consume it or resell it. This choice also applies to the yield from their private garden plots.

Another type of Soviet farm is the sovkhoz, or state farm. The sovkhoz engages in highly specialized agriculture and is worked by hired labor under state-appointed management. In 1954 many of these sovkhozy were established in Kazakhstan and western Siberia to bring the so-called Virgin Lands under cultivation.

KORAN, the sacred book of Islam, believed by Moslems to be the direct word of God. It is probably one of the most widely read books in the world. Moslems believe that the original text of the Koran is kept in heaven and that Mohammed received it, piece by piece, from the dictation of the angel Gabriel.

The Koran has been regarded for centuries as a perfect example of written Arabic. Parts of it are vigorous and poetic. Even the passages on civil law and inheritance are rendered in a poetic style, which was probably well adapted to Mohammed's audience. The rhythm of the Koran is more or less spontaneous when it occurs, but the rhyme is always maintained. The great beauty of the book is revealed if it is read aloud, and professional Moslem reciters give artistic readings of the Koran.

The Koran describes the glory of Allah and shows his workings in nature. The pleasures of heaven and the torments of hell are vividly depicted. The law is laid down for the followers of Mohammed, and answers are given to questions that were asked of Mohammed during his lifetime. There are also stories of former prophets and saints, which are used to illustrate Mohammed's teachings. Many biblical characters can be found in the Koran—Adam, Noah, Abraham, Ishmael, Moses, David, Solomon, Job, John the Baptist, and Jesus.

The Koran was probably written in part immediately after Mohammed's revelations. However, when Mohammed died A.D. 632, the Koran existed only in scattered written portions and memories. Islam had to have these separate sections brought together in one book. This was even more urgent because many who had known the Koran by heart had fallen in battle in 633. The duty of compiling the Koran was given by the caliph, Othman, to Zaid ibn Thabit, who had served as Mohammed's secretary. From narratives written on leather, flat stones, and the ribs of palm leaves and from men's memories, Zaid collected the Koran. Controversies arose as to which of the many versions of the sections was the correct one. About 651 Zaid was instructed to prepare a single authoritative text. All other texts were destroyed, and it is Zaid's compilation that has come down to the present. See ISLAM; MOHAMMED.

This Arab sheik is reading the Koran. — Religious News Service

KOREA

KOREA, a peninsular country in the heart of the Far East. It is mainly agricultural, although its being mountainous makes farming somewhat difficult. Korea is bounded on the east by the Sea of Japan, and Japan itself is only about 120 miles southeast. About 120 miles west across the Yellow Sea lies China. Manchuria, a territory of China, lies to the north beyond the Yalu River, and the Soviet Union touches Korea in the northeast along the Tumen River. Thus, Korea lies among all the great far-eastern powers. It has historically been a bridge between Asia's mainland and the Pacific. For these reasons Korea's history has been both interesting and tragic. Since Japan's defeat in World War II Korea has been divided into North Korea and South Korea. The capital of North Korea is Pyongyang. Seoul is South Korea's capital. The other major cities, all in South Korea, are Pusan, a port in the southeast; Taegu, in the southeast; and Inchon, the port city on the Yellow Sea for Seoul. Cheju Island, off the southern coast, also belongs to Korea. The peninsula of Korea is about 480 miles from north to south and some 200 miles wide. Korea has an area of 85,000 square miles. Its total population is about 30,000,000; but about two-thirds of the people live in South Korea, which is slightly smaller in area than North Korea.

United States jeeps, seen on the streets of Seoul, the capital of South Korea, contrast with the traditional tile-roofed houses.

Ewing Krainin—Photo Researchers

The emblem in the center of the South Korean flag is the yang and yin sing, symbolizing the two opposing principles of existence.

North Korea's flag carries a red star, the typical emblem of Communist countries.

Korea is closed in on the northern and eastern sides by rugged mountains and cliffs, which extend the length of the peninsula. The mountainous area extends throughout the central area and gradually tapers off into rolling hills and scattered plains in the southwestern portion of the peninsula. The western and southern coasts have many good harbors, although jutting reefs present many hazards and navigational problems. The rapid currents among the islands along the western coast make piloting hazardous. The rivers are shallow but swift, with many sandbanks and rapids. Korea has four distinct seasons. Spring and

Rice is Korea's chief crop. Although farmland is limited, there are numerous small rice paddies, many located on terraced mountain slopes.

autumn are ideal, but the winters of northern Korea are severe. Seoul in central Korea has an average temperature of about 75° F. in August, its hottest month. Its average January temperature is about 22° F., although the thermometer occasionally falls below zero. Korea's rainy season occurs regularly during the months of July and August.

This old man is wearing the white clothing and black horsehair hat typical of Korea.

Timber is important to Korea. It furnishes material for building and fuel for homes and industries. Most of the present forests are artificially planted and include fir, pine, alder, spruce, oak, birch, maple, larch, cypress, and bamboo. About 70 percent of the forest is in North Korea.

Three-fourths of the people are engaged in agriculture. Because of its mountains, Korea has limited area for farming, and a family of five may eke out a living from $2\frac{1}{2}$ acres. Farming methods are primitive yet remarkably efficient. One-third of Korea's agricultural lands are rice paddies, terraced into mountainsides or forming great steppes among fertile valleys. Grains, such as millet and barley, and fruit are also grown. Livestock is relatively unimportant. South Korea has the most fertile farmlands. Since Korea is surrounded by water, it also reaps a valuable harvest of fish.

Making use of its swift rivers for hydroelectric power, Korea has developed chemical industries, steel mills, textile mills, and food-processing plants. Most of these industries are in the north, because that is where the rivers are located. Seoul and Pusan are the industrial centers for South Korea. Koreans also make lacquer ware, pottery, paper, and metalwork in small shops.

The Koreans are racially related to the Chinese and Japanese. Ruddy, yellow-brown complexions, dark-brown hair, and hazel eyes are common features. The people are friendly. They usually maintain a sober countenance like other Orientals, but they are also given to mirth and joviality. The Korean language is unique, although there have been many borrowings from Chinese and Japanese. The alphabet is simple and phonetic. It was invented 500 years ago by King Sei-Chong, who wanted to make writing easier for his people. The clothes of the people are usually white. The men wear wide trousers and short, loose jackets. The women's dress is like the men's, and women also wear pleated skirts. The children's clothing is more highly colored, and the sleeves of children's jackets may look like rainbows.

The principal religions of Korea are Confucianism, Buddhism, and Christianity. Shamanism is also common. Korean life revolves around the village, and the family is the basic social unit. The man is the head of the family, but grandmother exerts a strong influence from behind the scenes. Sports are popular and include baseball, soccer, wrestling, judo, boxing, ice skating, and top spinning.

Korean civilization developed some 24 centuries before the birth of Christ. The nation was founded, according to legend, by Tangoon. Koreans drew heavily on Chinese culture, but they were also the first to make use of gunpowder and movable type. They also published an

Disturbances such as this occurred in South Korean cities as people demonstrated in 1960 against election fraud. Syngman Rhee's government toppled, and he fled to Hawaii.

encyclopedia long before any appeared in Europe. Korea experienced a cultural revival in the 15th century, during the Yi Dynasty. A short time later Korea was transformed into a vassal state by Japanese and Chinese invasions. The nation completely shut itself off from the rest of the world and became known as the Hermit Kingdom. The United States finally negotiated a trade treaty with Korea in the 19th century. Korea again found itself dominated by the Japanese in 1904. The Japanese developed roads, railroads, and industries but allowed the Koreans no freedom. After World War II Korea was divided temporarily at the 38th parallel by arrangements among China, the United States, the U.S.S.R., and Great Britain. North Korea, under U.S.S.R. auspices, developed a communist government; South Korea, under Syngman Rhee, became a democratic republic. The United States signed a mutual-defense pact with Korea after the Korean War. Rhee was overthrown in 1960, and in 1961 the regime of Premier John M. Chang was deposed. For detailed map, see CHINA.

KOREA

Area: South Korea, 38,452 sq. mi.—North Korea, 46,814 sq. mi.
Population: South Korea, 23,000,000—North Korea, 10,000,000
Capital: Seoul (South Korea)—Pyongyang (North Korea)
Largest cities: Seoul, Pusan, Taegu, Inchon, Pyongyang
Highest mountain peak: Kwanmo (8,337 feet)
Chief rivers: Han, Naktong, Yalu
Climate: Hot summers, cold winters—adequate rainfall
National flag: White, with four black trigrams in corners—red and blue circle in center (South Korea)—red, with blue stripes (white-edged on inner sides) on upper and lower edges—white circle containing red star (North Korea)
Form of government: Republic (South Korea)
Communist people's republic (North Korea)
Unit of currency: Hwan
Language: Korean
Chief religions: Animist, Buddhist, Confucian
Chief economic activities: Agriculture, mining, fishing
Chief crops: Rice, barley, wheat, beans, tobacco, cotton
Chief minerals: Tungsten, graphite, coal
Chief manufactures: Textiles

KOREAN WAR. On June 25, 1950, North Korean troops crossed the 38th parallel to invade South Korea. The United States immediately called for a cessation of hostilities. This request was supported in the UN Security Council by all its members except Yugoslavia, which abstained, and the U.S.S.R., which had boycotted the council. On June 27 President Harry S. Truman of the United States ordered sea-and-air support for the South Koreans. The 24th Division was alerted and sent to Korea from Japan. Major General William F. Dean became the commander of U.S. forces in Korea, and General Douglas MacArthur was named commander in chief of the UN forces, which eventually included troops of South Korea, Australia, Belgium, Great Britain, Canada, Luxembourg, The Netherlands, New Zealand, Republic of the Philippines, Colombia, Ethiopia, France, Greece, the Union of South Africa, Thailand, and Turkey. The delaying action of the 24th Division allowed time for reinforcements to land at Pusan. General Dean, who had been captured, was replaced by Lieutenant General Walton H. Walker as commander of the UN ground forces.

The North Koreans were stopped at the Pusan beachhead, and while the Eighth Army pressed forward there, General MacArthur organized an amphibious landing on September 15 at Inchon, which cut off the North Koreans from their supplies. One month later the Eighth Army captured Pyongyang, the North Korean capital. On October 26 South Koreans met Chinese forces at the Yalu River, and the UN forces were attacked by the Chinese from Manchuria. The Eighth Army withdrew to Pyong-

U. S. soldiers guard the Naktong River, where North Koreans mass for an attack.

yang. Other troops fought through to Hungnam. From there they were evacuated by sea. General Matthew B. Ridgway replaced General Walker, who had died in a highway accident.

The new Chinese offensive pushed the Eighth Army across the 38th parallel. Seoul and Inchon fell, but they were recaptured. On April 11 General MacArthur was replaced by General Ridgway. General James Van Fleet was given command of the Eighth Army.

The failure of the Chinese spring offensive was followed by truce talks, which began at Communist-held Kaesong on July 8, 1951. Some of the bloodiest battles of the war were fought after this time. The talks, moved to Panmunjom, stalled on the prisoner-exchange issue, but an armistice ending hostilities was finally signed at Panmunjom on July 27, 1953.

The terms of the armistice were supervised by Sweden, Switzerland, Poland, and Czechoslovakia. The Chinese and North Koreans had had about 2,000,000 casualties. South Korea suffered about 2,000,000 killed or wounded. The UN forces had over 300,000 casualties; some 27,000 Americans were among the 74,000 dead. North and South Korea began to rebuild their devastated towns and cities. In Seoul alone there were over 4,000 orphans. North and South Korea were divided almost as they had been before 1950. However, the UN intervention may have prevented a series of conquests such as led up to World War II. See KOREA.

Collection of Mrs. John Nicholas Brown
Thaddeus Kosciusko was a leader in the revolutionists' cause in America and Poland.

KOSCIUSKO, THADDEUS (1746-1817), a Polish soldier and statesman, won distinction as a hero fighting for liberty on the battlefields of Poland and of the United States. Kosciusko was born in Lithuania. Educated at the expense of the Polish state in the best military schools of Europe, he became a captain of artillery in the Polish army in 1774. Two years later he volunteered to help the American Revolutionary army and distinguished himself as a colonel of engineers in Washington's army and as Washington's adjutant. In 1783 Congress offered Kosciusko U.S. citizenship and an annual pension, and he was raised to the rank of brigadier general. But Kosciusko could not sit idle while his native Poland was in danger of being divided among Russia, Prussia, and Austria.

He returned to Poland and fought the Russian armies in 1791-1792. Then he fled to Leipzig, in Germany, where he became the center of Polish emigration. He organized resistance against the Russians. When he returned to Poland in March, 1794, his army consisted of untrained squires and peasants. This army, equipped only with scythes and spikes, defeated a Russian army. But the Poles lacked money, artillery, and even food. Moreover, the Prussian king, who at first promised neutrality, treacherously joined the Russians. The Polish armies were defeated one by one. Warsaw was defended by Kosciusko, but his valiant resistance was of no avail against the superior forces of the enemy. Polish independence was lost, and the wounded Kosciusko was imprisoned in Russia. After his release in 1796 he visited the United States for the second time and lived in Philadelphia until 1798. Later he returned to Europe and died in Switzerland in 1817, a broken man whose hopes for the independence of Poland were shattered.

Lyon & Healy
Fritz Kreisler was perhaps the most famous violin virtuoso of his time. However, he was also known for his contributions to the literature of his instrument.

KREISLER, FRITZ (1875-   ), an Austrian violinist, was born in Vienna. He began to study at the Vienna Conservatory at the age of seven; when he was ten years old, he won a gold medal for playing the violin. He studied afterward in Paris and in 1888 began a successful concert tour in the United States. Kreisler resumed his studies on his return to Europe and made a second tour in 1899. He continued his concert tours until the outbreak of World War I in 1914. He served during the early part of the war in the Austrian army, but a wound

Soldiers of the Marine 1st Division stretch out to rest after a dangerous night patrol on the battlefront in South Korea. Patrols probed the enemy position each night.
UPI

L is the 12th letter of the English alphabet. As a Roman numeral L equals 50. In commerce L, written £, means *pound* or *pounds sterling;* the symbol derives from *libra,* the Latin word for "pound." In geometry and physics italic L (*L* or *l*) stands for length. In astronomy and geodesy L is used as a symbol for *longitude.*

LABOR, in economics, the human effort expended in the production of economic goods. Economic goods are commodities and services that may be sold to satisfy human wants. This labor may be physical or mental, highly skilled or unskilled, direct or indirect—it is productive labor so long as it produces want-satisfying goods. It must be noted that not all human effort results in productive labor. A swimmer expends much effort, but if he swims only for his own pleasure or necessity, he cannot be said to be laboring productively. A swimmer who exhibits his skill before a paying audience, however, is providing a service. In this case the swimmer's efforts are productive labor. The word *work* in common speech covers the idea of labor. Specifically, however, the word *work* should be reserved for the physical concept that work equals a force times the distance through which the force acts.

The dignity of labor is a concept that has changed many times in history. Judaism has always regarded labor as honorable. The dignity of labor was also upheld by the Christians, for Jesus himself had been a carpenter. This contrasts with the contempt for manual labor among the ancient Greeks. The guilds in the Middle Ages and the modern labor unions have also contributed to the idea of the dignity of labor.

Along with capital, land, and enterprise, labor is one of the factors of production. The physiocrats had thought that land was the most important of these, but Adam Smith in his great *Wealth of Nations* wrote that labor was the true source of a nation's wealth. Smith also stressed the importance of the division of labor, which was a new concept in his day. The division of labor, of assigning to each group of workers a specialized and limited task, has several economic advantages. It develops greater, albeit specialized, skill on the part of the worker; it saves time, for workers need not change from one task to another; it allows a more efficient adaptation of work to the worker; it allows a better use of capital goods; it stimulates automation; and it reduces the worker's learning time.

Smith suggested that the value of a commodity depended on the labor expended on it. However, he recognized the difficulty of measuring the effort that went into making articles and the part played by capital goods. David Ricardo also stressed labor as the major determinant of economic value, and Karl Marx developed this idea into the labor theory of value. In his opinion labor was not only the only measure of value, but value was simply embodied labor. The labor theory of value was made the crux of modern socialism. This theory was timely in pointing out that labor is produced by human beings, a fact that many early industrialists forgot. But as an exact measure of economic value the theory is not adequate. See LABOR MOVEMENT.

Charles Baptie

This building in Washington, D.C., houses the Department of Labor. It was designed by Arthur Brown and was completed in 1934.

LABOR, UNITED STATES DEPARTMENT OF, one of the executive departments of the federal government, headed by the secretary of labor, a member of the president's Cabinet. It was created in 1913. Its purpose as stated in the congressional act is to foster, promote, and develop the welfare of American workers. Principal fact-collecting agency is the Bureau of Labor Statistics. The placement of workers in jobs and the issuance of unemployment insurance benefits are the function of the Bureau of Employment Security in cooperation with state authorities. Special attention to employment opportunities for women and the standards governing their employment is given by the Women's Bureau. The Wage and Hour Division and the Public Contracts Division administer the minimum-wage law affecting interstate commerce and the establishment of prevailing rates on certain government contracts. The Bureau of Labor-Management Reports administers that part of the Landrum-Griffin Act dealing with the reporting of financial transactions between employers and labor unions. The promotion of improved labor standards in the states is the function of the Bureau of Labor Standards. The Bureau of Apprenticeship and Training promotes improved standards of industrial training. Special attention to veterans is given by the Bureau of Veterans' Reemployment Rights and the Veterans' Employment Service.

LABOR DAY is a national holiday in the United States. It is observed each year on the first Monday in September. Labor Day is celebrated by parades, speeches, and picnics, generally sponsored by labor organizations. The holiday has also become popular as a time for family parties and picnics.

The Knights of Labor originated Labor Day by holding a parade in New York on Sept. 5, 1882. Their purpose was to demonstrate the strength and enthusiasm of labor organizations. The idea quickly spread to other parts of the country. In 1887 the state legislature of Oregon voted to set aside the first Monday in September as a state holiday in honor of labor. Other states soon took the same action, and Labor Day is now observed as a legal holiday in all parts of the United States.

LABOR LAWS, UNITED STATES. The earliest labor laws were passed by the legislatures of the individual states in the 1830's and 1840's. Massachusetts led the way in 1836 by passing a law providing schooling for employed children. In 1842 the same state limited children under 12 years of age to a 10-hour working day. Massachusetts was also the first state to pass a 10-hour law for women (1874), the first to employ factory inspectors (1867), and the first to establish a state labor department (1869).

The other states lagged behind Massachusetts, and not until the 1880's did other industrial states generally follow its lead. By 1900 almost every state had laws regulating employment of children. Federal child-labor laws were passed in 1916 and in 1919, but both were declared unconstitutional by the Supreme Court.

Under the New Deal administration of President Franklin D. Roosevelt a large volume of legislation dealing with workers was passed. The National Labor Relations Act (Wagner-Connery Act) of July 5, 1935, declared it the national policy of the United States to encourage collective bargaining and to protect employees' freedom to organize and to negotiate with the employers through representatives of their own choosing. The act prohibited certain antiunion conduct of employers, stating that such constituted unfair labor practice. The law was administered by the National Labor Relations Board, which the act created. The New Deal labor laws were of major importance in the rapid growth of unions in the 1930's.

The next major piece of labor legislation passed by Congress was the Fair Labor Standards Act of 1938, which set a minimum wage of 25 cents an hour in business engaged in interstate commerce. This minimum was raised to 40 cents in 1945, to 75 cents in 1949, to $1 in 1955, and to $1.25 in 1961, effective in 1963.

The Labor-Management Relations Act of 1947 (Taft-Hartley Act) was passed by Congress, over President Truman's veto, after a bitter struggle during which it was called a slave-labor law by union leaders. It prohibited the use of union funds for political purposes, required a 60-day notice before a strike or lockout, outlawed the closed shop, and gave the government the power to serve injunctions against industry-wide strikes likely to imperil the nation's health or safety.

The Labor-Management Reporting and Disclosure Act of 1959 was passed following a long investigation of corrupt practices in some of the labor organizations. This act requires periodic reports by union officers regarding union finances and the officers' own financial interests in companies that have a bargaining relationship with their union. The act contains a bill of rights for union members and specifies procedures for democratic election of union officers. It also provides restrictions on certain picketing and boycotts.

Labor laws in the United States have developed in piecemeal fashion to control specific evils. The states, fearing the increase of federal power at their expense, have been reluctant to allow federal control over such matters. The labor laws of the individual states differ widely in their provisions, especially in regard to union organization, safety standards, public employment agencies, and social insurance.

LABOR MOVEMENT, an organized, conscious, and continuous effort of wage earners to improve their working conditions and their standard of living. The criterion for judging a genuine workers' organization within the labor movement is whether the workers recognize the organization as an expression of their own desires. Thus, the German Labor Front under the Nazis was not a manifestation of the labor movement because it did not represent the wishes of the workers. Although the aim of the labor movement is common to all national movements, in no two nations has the labor movement developed in the same way.

The modern labor movement arose in response to the Industrial Revolution. In the guilds of the Middle Ages the master was himself a worker, who employed several journeymen and apprentices. These employees, in accordance with the rules of the guilds, could look forward to becoming masters. (See GUILD.) The factory system of the Industrial Revolution created a permanent class of wage earners, who developed a consciousness of distinct group aims that separated them from their employers. In England, the first nation to experience the Industrial Revolution, the lot of former agricultural laborers and craftsmen who worked in the mines and factories was worsened. This was the situation described by Karl Marx in *Capital*. Conditions varied in different trades—the textile workers and miners experienced the worst conditions, while printers, tailors, and men in the building trades had relatively good conditions. The government, influenced by the dominant laissez-faire (hands off) philosophy of England's economists, refused to intervene on behalf of the wage earners and even prevented the organization of unions through its Combination Acts of 1799 and 1800, which prohibited union-employer agreements to increase wages or to shorten hours. It was natural, therefore, that a well-defined, permanent, and oppressed class of wage earners would begin to organize mutual-aid societies and unions when the Combination Acts were repealed in 1824 as a result of the efforts of the middle-class reformer Francis Place. Workers in nations such as Germany, France, Denmark, Sweden, and Norway did not suffer to the extent that the English workers of the early 19th century suffered. The tardiness of the Industrial Revolution in these countries afforded them the benefit of a more humanitarian viewpoint, which had developed as a result of England's prior experience. Moreover, the existence of credit facilities, the result of surpluses in nations that had industrialized earlier, meant that employers in the newly industrializing nations did not have to cut labor costs in order to obtain funds to put back into their industry. Nevertheless conditions in all industrializing nations were such that a defensive response developed on the part of workers.

Selig Perlman, in *A Theory of the Labor Movement*, suggested that a contributing cause of the labor movement was the wage earners' feeling of a scarcity of opportunity. The entrepreneur optimistically believes that society is filled with opportunity, but the wage earner, faced with the possibility of cyclical (depression) or technological unemployment, views the social order more pessimistically. He organizes in order to distribute the existing job opportunities evenly among workers in his trade. The individual is protected by such an organization, for which—in the interests of all—he sacrifices his freedom of unrestrained action.

The ultimate aim of the labor movement, betterment of workers' conditions, has been sought by radical and conservative means. Radical methods are often resorted to during periods of economic depressions or during periods of the suppression of the labor movement. The blind, loosely organized attacks against machines and factories of the English Luddite rioters during the early 19th century were one form of radical approach. Having accepted industrialization as inevitable, however, the radical element within the labor movement seeks to transform society for the benefit of the workers. The innumerable paths radicalism adopts in each nation arise from differences in the social origins of workers, from the form of the economic system that they face, and from the difference in viewpoint of the leaders of the movements. For example, Danish industrial workers were drawn from a preexisting farm-laborer group, already hardened to wage-labor conditions and tending toward a moderate form of socialism. Norwegian workers, however, had been mainly free farmers, and this origin inclined them to individualism and helps explain why they were drawn to the extreme radicalism of communism after World War I as well as why they soon severed their trade unions from international Communist affiliations. Faced with the aspect of small, independent producers and shopkeepers, the French labor movement was long influenced by the cooperative transformation of society advocated by the anarchist Pierre Proudhon. This belief in producers' cooperatives also was a major belief of the U.S. Knights of Labor. The Australian unionlabor movement, however, was faced almost from its inception with strong, large-scale industries, which encouraged the growth of large trade unions and a political inclination toward government nationalization.

In contrast to the radical outlook is the conservative viewpoint of "pure and simple" trade unionism, which seeks to improve the condition of the worker within the existing economic system. Exposed to the concrete situation of the daily shop routine, the worker and his trade-union leader tend to measure progress in immediate advantages: shorter hours, higher wages, and less pressure on the job. The conservative element in the labor movement tends to be skeptical of philosophies that regard the working class as an abstract force operating to bring society to a higher level. For this reason, the "pure and simple" unionist has often been at odds with branches of the labor movement that espouse Marxian socialism, syndicalism, or anarchism. The German trade unions, for example, led by Karl Legien, in 1906 severed their formal connections with the Social Democratic party, which was dominated by the Marxism of August Bebel and the influence of the state socialism of Ferdinand Lassalle. The "new model" unionism of England, which was dominant from 1850 to 1890, was a conservative reaction to the radical and unsuccessful revolution-oriented Chartist movement. Even the syndicalist General Confederation of Labor in France lost its faith in the efficacy of the general strike and following World War I adopted the conservative tactics of trade unionism. "Pure and simple" unionism in the United States and Canada was represented by the American Federation of Labor, founded in 1886 by Samuel Gompers. The unspectacular but steady success of the conservative labor movement together with the suppression of the independent labor movement in the Soviet Union (the example of Communist revolution) has caused many among the radical labor groups to regard "pure and simple" unionism with more respect. The vast importance of such conservative victories as the nationwide trade agreement between the German printers' union and the printing employers in 1896 came to be appreciated. Consequently, trade unionism had a mellowing effect on the Socialist parties in Scandinavia, Germany, and England.

The tactics of the labor movement in pursuance of its aims differ within each nation or section of the movement in accordance with the conservative or radical nature of the labor movement. Fundamental to the labor movement is organization itself, which molds individuals into concerted activity. The importance of wage-earner solidarity has caused the demand in many nations for the union shop or closed shop, in which all workers must belong to the representative union. The strike is used by unionists in order to increase wages, to lower working hours, to wrest control of shop and apprenticeship rules, or to force benefit concessions. The strikes of the conservative labor movement are a means of bringing about collective bargaining within the existing economic framework. Syndicalist groups, such as the French General Confederation of Labor before World War I and the Industrial Workers of the World in the United States, used strikes as training for the general strike, a strike of all the workers of a nation in order to bring about the transformation of society on syndicalist lines. The boycott has been employed to reduce the sales or access to raw materials of an employer deemed unfair to his workers. To enforce strikes or boycotts, picketing is sometimes utilized, a method usually not necessary in Scandinavia, where nearly all workers belong to unions. Anarchists in the labor movement sometimes used sabotage of machines. Revolution has been an instrument of some labor movements. The German revolution of 1918 was successful in elevating the Socialist Democratic party to power and obtaining a constitution and legislation favorable to the independent labor movement. The Russian revolutionary workers' and soldiers' councils, developed around originally weak union organizations, raised the Communists to power in Russia. The independent labor movement in the U.S.S.R., however, in spite of attempts by Mikhail Tomski to preserve it, was brought under the control of the state. In nations with universal suffrage, revolution tends to be replaced by the exercise of the vote. In New Zealand, Australia, Scandinavia, Germany, Switzerland, and Great Britain the vote is used to place Socialist parties in power. In the United States it is used by the labor movement to reward friends and punish enemies. The U.S. labor movement is also represented by a powerful lobby. The labor movement has also used propaganda effectively, and an active and intelligent labor press exists in the democratic nations. The propaganda efforts on behalf of labor of Christian organizations, Protestant and Roman Catholic; of the famous English Fabian Society; and of individual reformers like Robert Owen, Charles Kingsley, and Wendell Phillips did much to lend prestige to the cause of the labor movement. Finally, the French Bourse du Travail may be mentioned as a unique labor tactic. The bourses, numerous before 1914, were a type of workers' stock exchange, where information on labor supply and demand was collected and publicized. These bourses also founded libraries and workers' study groups.

The accomplishments of the labor movement are innumerable. Obviously, the increasing rate of productivity fostered by entrepreneurs, inventors, and scientists as well as by workers has also been crucial in improving working conditions. One of the labor movement's major accomplishments was winning the right of its organizations to exist. This occurred as early as 1824 for certain types of organizations in Great Britain, and in 1884 in France. In large part through the efforts of labor organizations, the average work week was reduced from 70 hours in England, 78 hours in France and the United States, and 83 hours in Germany, all in 1840, to about 40 to 48 hours. Higher real wages and paid vacations are in part a legacy of the labor movement. Conditions of health and safety in shops and mines were vastly improved. Child-labor laws exist in most nations, and women generally receive equal pay for equal work. The use of the vote has enabled the labor movement to influence a great body of social legislation, including that on public education, unemployment insurance, workmen's compensation, health insurance, social security, public housing, and minimum wages. Supplements to these benefits were also obtained from employers through collective-bargaining agreements. In nations such as Great Britain the labor movement has influenced the nationalization of certain industries. In the Scandinavian countries the labor movement has frequently pioneered new projects in order to foster economic prosperity. The labor movement has also been operative in raising the workers' cultural level, and following World War II Scandinavian unions considered this their next major endeavor in improving the workers' condition. See ARBITRATION; COLLECTIVE BARGAINING; COMMUNISM; COOPERATIVE; LABOR UNION; LABOUR PARTY, BRITISH; SOCIALISM; SOCIALIST PARTIES; STRIKE.

LABOR UNION, an organization of workers. The labor union is the product of the factory system that grew out of the Industrial Revolution. Prior to the development of the factory system the worker was a journeyman who labored side by side with the master craftsman. The status of journeyman was regarded as temporary, as a period of a few years of training, after which the journeyman himself became a master craftsman. Consequently, the journeyman had no distinct, or permanent, interest as an employee. Factory production with power machinery gave the worker permanent status as an employee and created a distinct worker interest. This widening gap between employee and employer led to the organization of labor unions, which could speak to the employer for the employee with a stronger voice than a single employee speaking for himself.

Although the primary function of labor unions is to bargain with employers for wages and working conditions, unions have at various times been established for a number of other reasons. For example, company unions—those formed and dominated by the employer—have been used to combat legitimate unions. In nations controlled by a single political party the unions exist to carry out the orders of implement the policies of the government. This is largely true in Fascist and Communist countries. In the early United States, unions supported social and political change. In 1828 unions in Philadelphia formed a Workingmen's Party, which supported such social reform legislation as restrictions on child labor and shortening of the workday. In several European countries unions have promoted more fundamental social change.

The basic aim of unions is to obtain higher wages, shorter hours, and better working conditions for workers. If the union and the employer cannot reach an agreement by bargaining, the union may call a strike. It is to the union's advantage to have all the workers who are employed by the same employer or who work in the same factory be members of the union. Therefore, unions generally favor a union shop in which all permanent employees must become union members.

Traditionally, there have been two kinds of union organization, the trade union and the industrial union. The trade union, or the craft union, organizes all the men of a particular trade. Thus, bricklayers would belong to one union, carpenters to another. It frequently happens, however, that many unskilled and semi-skilled workers are employed together with many skilled craftsmen in a single factory or industry. The industrial union brought these men together into a single organization. The industrial union would include in one union mineworkers, for example, no matter what their particular skill or job. The American Federation of Labor was predominantly an organization of craft unions. The Congress of Industrial Organizations was predominantly an organization of industrial unions. Great Britain has both trade unions, such as the Amalgamated Engineering Union, and industrial unions, such as the Miners' Federation, within its powerful Trade Union Congress. In the Federal Republic of Germany unions in the German Federation of Trade Unions are nearly all organized on industrial lines.

In some nations unions are closely connected to political parties. In France, for example, the General Federation of Labor tends to support Communist leaders, the Workers Force–General Federation of Labor inclines toward the Socialist left, and the French Federation of Christian Workers tends to be oriented toward the Popular Republican party (MRP). The German Federation of Trade Unions, while nonpartisan, tends to support the Social Democratic party. The American AFL-CIO is generally nonpartisan, basing its support on the individual candidates. There are, in addition, unions based on Christian principles but seeking traditional union ends. Switzerland, for example, has Catholic Christian-social unions and unions of Protestant workers and employees.

Unions offer more than collective bargaining to their members. They also offer publications, educational opportunities, life insurance, health benefits, pension benefits, recreation and social activities, cooperatives, credit unions, and housing projects. In the United States unions bargain with employers for life insurance, health benefits, and pensions which are paid for, in part or in whole, by the employer. The British Trades Union Congress, in fact, educates its workers in production and management subjects as well as in the practice of trade unionism. See AMERICAN FEDERATION OF LABOR AND CONGRESS OF INDUSTRIAL ORGANIZATIONS; INDUSTRIAL WORKERS OF THE WORLD; KNIGHTS OF LABOR; LABOR MOVEMENT.

Because of the labor movement, these workers are better off than those of the 19th century.
UPI

LABOUR PARTY, BRITISH, one of the major political parties of Great Britain, favors public ownership of industries and services. However, there has been disagreement within the party as to the degree of, and emphasis upon, nationalization. Chief party leader Hugh Gaitskell claimed in 1959 that nationalization was but one of many means to full employment, greater equality, and higher productivity. The party favors an increase in social services, particularly in the fields of retirement insurance, education, and housing. Until 1960 the party supported the development of nuclear weapons and British participation in NATO. In 1960 the Labour party conference voted to support British unilateral nuclear disarmament and the abolition of missile bases in Great Britain. The party also favored admission of Communist China to the United Nations.

In 1900 the Independent Labour party, other socialist groups, and the trade unions joined to form what in 1906 became known as the Labour party. The organization resulted from dissatisfaction with the previous political activity of trade unions in the Liberal party and from nearly 20 years of socialist propaganda by the Fabian Society and by James Keir Hardie of the Independent Labour party. The Fabian Society, formed in 1883, favored gradual, nonrevolutionary socialism and emphasized national economic planning and efficiency. It promoted its ideas through the writings of George Bernard Shaw, H. G. Wells, and Beatrice and Sidney Webb. The society, though small, was influential in converting the Labour party in 1918 to support of nationalization. Hardie—former miner, lay preacher, and temperance man—converted many union members through his emphasis on a socialism whose purpose was to create a moral society.

The Labour party's first two terms of office, 1924 and 1929-1931, were not notable. These governments, both headed by Ramsay MacDonald, did not produce a socialist economy. A financial crisis in 1931 caused the resignation of the Labour government. At the end of World War II the party again came into power. It nationalized the Bank of England and the gas, coal, iron, steel, and transportation industries; created the National Health Service to provide free medical care; and extended unemployment, sickness, and other types of social insurance. The Conservative party defeated the Labour party in 1951.

LACE AND LACEMAKING. Lace is an openwork tissue made with needle and fine linen, cotton, or silken threads. It results from the interlacing of threads. Lace made with a needle is called needlepoint or point lace. Examples are *point d' Alençon* and rose point lace. Lace made on a cushion with bobbins and pins is called bobbin or pillow lace. Bobbin laces include *point d'Angleterre*, Binche, Chantilly, Cluny, duchesse, torchon, and Valenciennes. In lacemaking by machine the threads may be arranged as in handmade lace or in another way to give a handmade impression.

A simple type of lacemaking was probably known to the ancient Egyptians. However, needlepoint lace did not really develop until the Venetians began to apply themselves to the craft. These lacemakers first sketched a pattern on parchment. Over this pattern a framework of threads was stitched and then worked over in buttonhole stitches to form ties or bars. To

This is an example of *point de gaze*, a type of lace made chiefly in Brussels, Belgium.

this background, or *réseau*, the solid parts of the pattern, or *toilé*, were joined. Then the finished piece—that is, the lace—was cut away from its parchment base. The Venetians used gold and colored silks until this luxurious practice was forbidden. Workers began to make lace exclusively with white threads. France and Flanders took the lead in needlepoint lacemaking during the 17th and 18th centuries.

Bobbin lacemaking also developed first in Italy—in Genoa and Milan rather than Venice—during the 17th century. In this manner of making lace, the *réseau* was made by twisting and braiding several threads with bobbins. The *toilé*, which consisted of crisscross threads, had a woven appearance. Flemish bobbin lace became prominent in the 17th century. English lacemaking derived from different European styles, owing to the skills of lacemaking refugees from Roman Catholic countries.

This woman is making lace by hand in Taormina, Sicily. Most lace is machine made.

Limerick lace is made by hand in homes in and near Limerick, Ireland.

Early in the 19th century, lacemaking began to be taken over by machines, and now it is rarely done any other way in most parts of the world.

This exquisitely delicate trimming, which at one time enriched the borders of garments and elegant household articles, is rarely seen today, even among those who can afford the price of handmade lace. But many can afford the price of machine-made lace trimmings on handkerchiefs, lingerie, blouses, and similar articles of apparel.

LACROSSE is a fast and exciting outdoor team sport. Invented by the Indians living in what is now Canada, it was adopted by the white settlers and later introduced into other parts of the British Commonwealth and the United States, where, with adaptations, it is still played.

Originally the game (called bagataway by the Indians) was played on the open prairie by as many as a thousand young men at one time. Games started at 9 A.M. (there was no break in the game, except for one minute after a goal had been scored) and terminated when one side had scored 100 goals or when the sun sank below the skyline—whichever happened sooner.

The National Lacrosse Association of Canada was formed in 1867. Lacrosse is considered to be Canada's national game. Lacrosse was introduced into the United States in 1880, Harvard and Princeton having teams in 1881 and 1882 respectively. The United States Intercollegiate Lacrosse Association was founded in 1882 and now has 50 member colleges.

In June, 1960, at the College of the Holy Cross in Worcester, Massachusetts, a team of young men representing 11 southern colleges defeated another team selected from 12 northern colleges by 13 goals to 12, giving the South a 10-to-8 lead in a series of annual all-star games dating from 1940.

The game is played on a field 110 yards long and between 60 and 70 yards wide. A center line parallel to the endlines divides the playing surface in half. A goal 6 feet wide and 6 feet high, having a net at the back, is placed 15 yards in from each end of the playing area. Ten players constitute a team; two teams contest a match. The game lasts for one hour and is divided into four quarters. It starts with a face-off, in which the opposing centers place the back of their sticks against the ball in the center circle. The referee then blows his whistle. The centers withdraw their sticks, and each tries to cradle the ball in his crosse and then pass it to his teammates, run with it, or kick it.

The stick, or crosse (so called because of its similarity in shape to a bishop's crosier), is substantially the same today as when used by its originators. Then, however, each player had two sticks, one in each hand; today players have but one stick. It consists of a hickory shaft with triangular head of meshwork. The mesh is made of rawhide and is shaped in the form of a hollow basket no wider than 12 inches at its widest part. Depending upon the position occupied by the player, the stick varies in length from 2 feet 6 inches to 6 feet. No metal is allowed on any part of the crosse; the rawhide is tied to the curved framework.

The aim of the game is to fling the ball from the crosse into the goal being attacked. Each goal scored equals a point, and the greater number of points at the end of the game determines the winning team. If a tie ensues, two overtime periods of five minutes each are played. Then, if the score is still tied, the game is declared a draw.

LADY IN THE CHAIR, THE (constellation). See CASSIOPEIA.

West Point cadets play the vigorous game of lacrosse, an invention of American Indians. Pub. Relations Off., W. Point, N.Y.

This painting by George Catlin shows lacrosse as it was played by the Choctaw Indians. Smithsonian Institution

LAENNEC, RENE (1781-1826), French physician, born in Quimper. After studying medicine at Nantes and Paris, Laennec became associated with Necker Hospital, Paris, in 1806. He devoted his life to the study of diseases of the lungs and heart. His major work, published in 1819, describes the stethoscope, which he had invented. It also describes mediate auscultation, the technique of detecting certain physical disorders or conditions by listening to the sounds within the body, particularly within the chest and abdomen, with the aid of the stethoscope. In 1822 Laennec was appointed professor of medicine at the College of France, in Paris.

Marquis de Lafayette

LAFAYETTE, MARQUIS DE (1757-1834), French statesman and soldier, was born in Auvergne into one of the oldest, noblest, and richest of French families. By the time he was 18 he had inherited the family fortune, married, and been commissioned in the French army.

When Lafayette first heard of the struggle of the American colonists against the British government, his enthusiasm was immediately aroused. He determined to help America fight for its liberty. In 1776 he resigned from the French army and, against the advice of his friends, began preparing to sail to America. The French king, prodded by the British ambassador, sent officers to prevent Lafayette's sailing, but Lafayette escaped and landed safely near Georgetown, S.C., on June 13, 1777. The Continental Congress welcomed him after he had offered to serve at his own expense, and he was commissioned a major general in the Continental army. He served with skill and courage at Valley Forge, at Brandywine, in the Virginia campaign that led to Cornwallis' surrender at Yorktown, and in several other campaigns, earning for himself the title "the soldier's friend" as well as great popularity in both America and France. After the entry of France into the war he was invaluable as the principal liaison officer between the forces of the two allies.

After the American Revolutionary War, Lafayette returned to France, where he worked tirelessly on behalf of the young United States. In 1789 the French Revolution began, and Lafayette immediately became one of its principal leaders. In 1790 he was undoubtedly the most popular man in France. Gradually, however, the French Revolution was taken over by radical elements, and in 1792 Lafayette was forced to flee France. In so doing he was captured by the Austrians, then at war with France, and was held prisoner by them until 1797, when his release was secured by Napoleon Bonaparte. Following his release, he stayed out of political affairs and was content to manage his estate at La Grange-Blénau. Late in his life he returned to French politics and was important in the July Revolution of 1830. He died in Paris and was buried there in a grave covered with earth from Bunker Hill.

LAFFITE, JEAN (1780?-1826?), French pirate and smuggler, believed to have been born in Bayonne. He first became known as the leader of a pirate band that had its headquarters on Barataria Bay, near New Orleans. An expedition sent out by the U.S. government in 1814 managed to destroy the pirate's stronghold and capture several of his vessels. However, Laffite and his companions escaped. In 1815 the British promised Laffite a reward if he would join their attack on New Orleans. Laffite not only refused but reported the British plans to the American authorities, to whom he then offered his services. Laffite and many members of his band fought on the American side in the ensuing Battle of New Orleans.

Following the War of 1812 Laffite resumed his illegal activities in the Gulf area. Little further is known of him except that, following another raid by U.S. authorities in retaliation for his attack on a merchant ship in 1820, Laffite moved the base of his illegal operations to the Spanish Main.

LA FONTAINE, JEAN DE (1621-1695), French poet and writer of fables, famed for his verse and for his delicate satire. He was born at Chateau-Thierry. He was educated for the church but did not enter this calling. For some time he resided alternately in Paris, where he found a patron in Nicolas Fouquet, and in his native village, where the duke and duchess of Bouillon held him in high esteem. The first book of his tales, published in 1664, found favor with Moliére, Racine, and Boileau, with whom he later formed a famous quartet of self-appointed dictators of literary taste. He increased his fame by the publication of his *Fables* and the final volumes of his tales. His *Fables* have been especially popular and have been translated into many languages. The American poet Marianne Moore made a complete translation of the *Fables* into English in 1954.

LAGERLÖF, SELMA (1858-1940), Swedish novelist, born in Värmland. She attended the Royal Women's Superior Training College and after completion of her studies taught for ten years in southern Sweden. Her first published work was *Gösta Berling's Saga*. It was followed by *Invisible Links*, *The Miracles of Anti-Christ*, *Jerusalem*, and other works. Especially well known is her trilogy, *The Ring of the Löwenskölds*. She was also the author of a popular book for children, *The Wonderful Adventures of Nils*. In 1909 she received the Nobel prize for literature. In her later years she devoted herself to writing of her childhood in *Memories of My Childhood* and *The Diary of Selma Lagerlöf*.

Laffite purchased booty from pirates and smuggled it to merchants in New Orleans. He was primarily a smuggler rather than a pirate.

In the atolls of the South Pacific, coral reefs enclose shallow lagoons, as shown above.

LAGOON, a shallow body of water that may be a pond, lake, or channel. It is usually near or communicating with the sea. In shallow coastal regions lagoons are formed gradually over a period of many years. This is done by the action of waves, which drag bottom material and pile it up offshore. At first small, narrow islands are formed. Then they are connected to form long bars. The bars are eroded by waves on the side along the sea and rebuild landward. The lagoon is the area between the bars and the shore. It fills up with material carried by rivers and gradually becomes shallower. Finally it becomes marshland and a part of a new beach. In tropical seas lagoons are formed by coral reefs that form off the shores of islands. See CORAL.

LAGRANGE, JOSEPH (1736-1813), an important French mathematician, who originated the calculus of variations. Born and educated in Turin, Lagrange became a professor of mathematics at the age of 19. While still a young man he solved the isoperimetric problem. An example of an isoperimetric problem is finding the geometric figure of maximum area for a perimeter of fixed length.

On the death of his patron, Frederick the Great, king of Prussia, in 1786, Lagrange was invited to France by the French king. While in Paris Lagrange worked to bring order to the confused French system of weights and measures.

Lagrange made important contributions to the theory of numbers and differential equations. He also did important work in the mathematics of sound. Lagrange's most famous book, *Mécanique Analytique*, was published in 1787. It dealt with the principles of virtual velocities and least action.

LAKE, a body of inland water. Most lakes contain fresh water, but some lakes in areas of arid climate contain salty water. Lakes form wherever water accumulates in a depression in the earth's surface. Most lakes are supplied with water from rainfall, rivers, and the ground. Some lakes are filled with water from melting glaciers.

Lake basins are formed in many ways. Some lakes accumulate in troughs formed by faulting. Lake Tanganyika and Lake Nyasa in Africa are examples of such lakes. Some lakes are formed when stream valleys are dammed up by lava flows or landslides. A large number of lakes in the middle and higher latitudes of the Northern Hemisphere occupy basins formed during the Pleistocene glaciation. The basins are shallow depressions in ground moraines, basins formed by moraines damming up valleys, basins scoured out of bedrock by moving glacier ice, valleys blocked by debris carried from glaciers by meltwater streams, and so on. Lakes also form in the craters of extinct volcanoes, in abandoned river channels, and in other places.

Salt-water lakes occupy basins of interior drainage in regions of arid climate. Streams flow into the lakes, but no streams flow out. Water evaporates rapidly in the hot, dry air, and the impurities of the original water are concentrated. Some salt-water lakes contain water only part of the year.

Above is a restored Neolithic lake dwelling.

LAKE DWELLING, a house constructed along the shore of a lake or raised on piles above its waters. The earliest known lake dwellings are from the Neolithic period in Switzerland, Germany, and other parts of Europe. Contemporary lake dwellings are found in South America and in New Guinea. The ancient

Below are eight types of lake basins. Some other types of basins are hollows in ground moraine, wind-eroded hollows, large hot-spring openings, and manmade depressions.

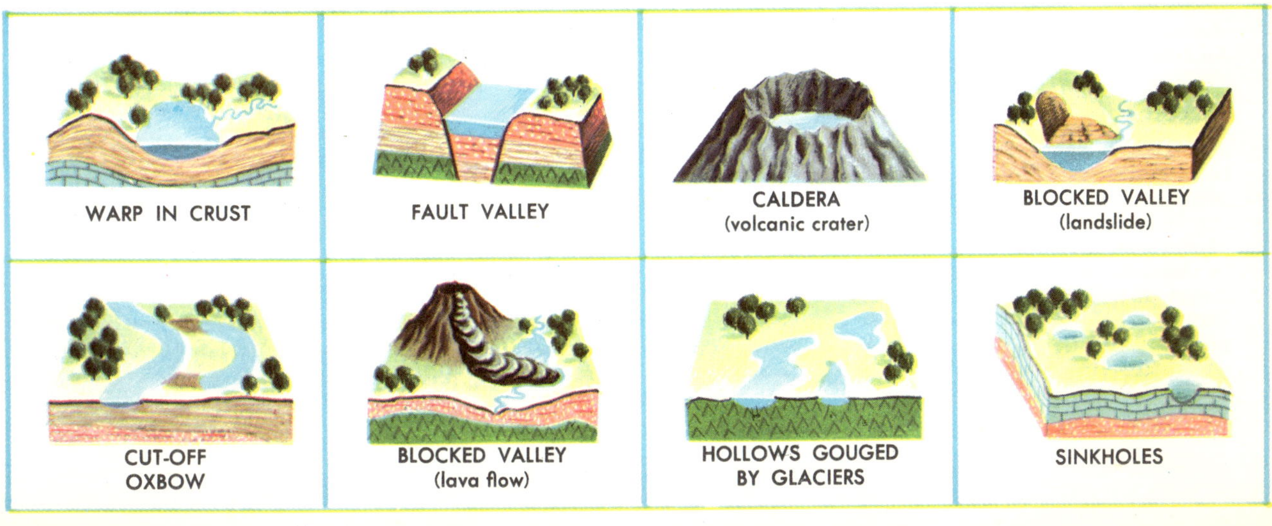

WARP IN CRUST | FAULT VALLEY | CALDERA (volcanic crater) | BLOCKED VALLEY (landslide)

CUT-OFF OXBOW | BLOCKED VALLEY (lava flow) | HOLLOWS GOUGED BY GLACIERS | SINKHOLES

Swiss lake dwellings, subsequent to 2500 B.C., were discovered in the winter of 1853-1854, when the level of certain lakes was low.

Once the remains of the houses were discovered, archaeologists found a wealth of informative material in the lakes, since the water preserved objects that are usually destroyed in the earth. Many articles of wood were found, including cups, bowls, combs, and clubs. Fragments of cloth, of netting, and of basketry indicated the way the people lived. On shore they grew wheat, barley, oats, and rye, as well as flax for linen. They raised cattle, pigs, sheep, and goats.

These dwellings were built until the end of the Bronze Age. In many ways they reflected a life similar to that of Swiss, German, or French peasants of the 19th century.

LAMA, DALAI, the Grand Lama who ruled Tibet from Lhasa from about 1641 to 1959. When Communist China crushed a rebellion of Lamaist monks in 1959, the Dalai Lama fled to India. The name lama refers to one of the clergy of Tibet and means "one who is superior."

When the Mongol Empire crumbled in China, the Tibetan monk Tsong-kha-pa seized the opportunity to reform Lamaism, the Buddhism of Tibet. He founded the Yellow Church and made himself its Grand Lama. The Grand Lama became the Dalai Lama in the 16th century. In that century So-nam Gya-tso traveled to Mongolia at the request of the Mongol chieftain Altan Khan and revived Buddhism in Mongolia. The chieftain rewarded the Grand Lama with the title "Dalai," which means "the sea." To the Mongol the Grand Lama was as profound and measureless as the sea. In 1640 the Mongol prince Gusri Khan conquered Tibet and presented it to the fifth Grand Lama, making him the temporal ruler of that country. This Grand Lama elevated in power the abbot of the large monastery of Shigatse, who, as Panchen Lama, came to hold the spiritual prestige in the Yellow Church.

Monks of the Yellow Church do not marry and may not have children. Therefore, when a Dalai Lama died, a successor had to be found. The monks believed that the soul of a Dalai Lama left his body and entered that of a child born at the moment the former Dalai Lama died. The search for the reincarnation of a Dalai Lama might continue for many years.

LAMARCK, CHEVALIER DE (1744-1829), a French naturalist, born Jean Baptiste de Monet in a village in Picardy. As a boy of 17 he proceeded to the front during the Seven Years' War with a letter of introduction to a colonel. The next day found him the head of some 14 survivors of a company that had not joined the general retreat of the French army. He was awarded a lieutenancy for his valor. Fortunately for science, a disease of the glands of the neck forced him to quit the military life. In 1778 he published the popular *French Flora,* which gained him admittance to the Academy of Sciences.

The naturalist Buffon succeeded in having Lamarck appointed botanist to the king. This position allowed Lamarck to travel throughout Europe to collect information for his *Dictionary of Botany.* In 1792 Lamarck was appointed to a chair of natural history at the Jardin des Plantes and turned his attention to the study of zoology. In spite of an impairment of his vision, which became blindness in the last 17 years of his life, Lamarck was able with his daughter's help to publish his greatest zoological achievement, the *History of the Invertebrate Animals.*

Lamarck's excellence as a zoologist rests on his abundance of ideas, his precise descriptions, and his clear style of writing. He claims a permanent place of fame in the field of zoology by his detailed work with fossil and living invertebrates. His speculations, unfortunately, outran the material he gleaned from his accurate observations. Consequently he is most famous for his theory of evolution. Lamarck's theory of organic evolution held that altered wants in animals led to altered habits and to the use or disuse of certain limbs and organs. The changes produced in the affected organs by use or disuse were inheritable, argued Lamarck. This theory was replaced by the body of evolutionary theory that began with Darwin. See DARWIN, CHARLES; EVOLUTION.

LAMB, CHARLES (1775-1834) and **MARY** (1764-1847), were English authors, brother and sister. Charles Lamb became especially noted for his series of essays, *Essays of Elia.*

Both of the Lambs were born and reared in London. In 1796 Mary Lamb suddenly became insane and killed her mother. From that time Charles Lamb devoted his life to caring for his sister. From 1792 until 1825 he worked in London as a clerk for the East India Company, a group of merchants who traded with India and eastern Asia.

Lamb began his career as an author in 1796 with the publication of four of his sonnets in a volume of poems by Samuel Taylor Coleridge. One of his best known poems, "The Old Familiar Faces," appeared two years later in *Blank Verse* by Charles Lloyd and Charles Lamb. He also wrote a well-known short story, "The Tale of Rosamund Gray and Old Blind Margaret," in 1798.

Lamb then turned to drama and wrote two plays, *John Woodvil* and *Mr. H.* He and Mary collected many of the plays by William Shakespeare and wrote interpretations of them for children in *Tales from Shakespeare* published in 1807. He then wrote *The Adventures of Ulysses,* a children's version of Homer's *Odyssey.* In 1809 he and his sister wrote *Mrs. Leicester's School,* a collection of ten short stories.

The essay "Recollections of the South Sea House" appeared in the *London Magazine* in 1820. This was the first of the essays written by Lamb that he signed "Elia." He continued writing these often witty and humorous essays until his death. Among the best known are "A Dissertation upon Roast Pig," "The Superannuated Man," and "Dream Children."

LAMP, a vessel used for the combustion of inflammable liquids to produce artificial light. Its invention is ascribed to the Egyptians. In early times shells were used to hold the liquid oils, but as late as the time of Homer torches and open fires were used for light. About the 5th century, in Greece, lamps for lower grades of olive oils were generally used. They were made of pottery, bronze, or some such material and had a dish for the oil and a spout for the wick. Vegetable and animal oils were used in this style of lamp until the 19th century and are still used where only poorer grades of oil may be had. Whale oil was popular before kerosene was introduced in the 19th century. Because there was too little combustion at the center of the flame, these lamps smoked greatly. The flat wick, which made less smoke, appeared near the end of the 18th century, but the light it produced was dim. About the same time the circular wick with an open center and the lamp chimney were introduced in France. The candle competed with the early lamps but not with kerosene lamps. Gas superseded kerosene, and in

mouth

DETAIL OF LAMPREY — gill slits, notochord, nerve cord

This man is inspecting a trap that prevents lampreys from leaving the Great Lakes and swimming up a river to spawn. — Mich. Dept. of Conservation

turn electricity generally superseded gas. The ancient lamp design has symbolized learning in literature and art, and honor to the divine in religious rituals.

LAMPREY, an eel-like fish that lives in fresh and salt waters. It has a long, slender body and smooth skin but no bony skeleton. The lamprey lacks the paired fins found in other fish. Instead of jaws it has a circular sucking mouth. The mouth is armed with horny, toothlike projections. By means of its peculiar mouth the lamprey attaches itself to other fishes, rasps away the flesh, and sucks the blood.

The sea lamprey, found in European waters and in the North Atlantic as far south as Virginia, is 3 feet long and dark brown, mottled with black flecks. In the spring it follows the shad up the rivers to lay its eggs in fresh water and seeks the sea again in the fall. Sea lampreys attach themselves also to salmon and sturgeon, and in Europe bathers have sometimes been attacked by them. In North America sea lampreys have become landlocked in the Great Lakes and in some of the Finger Lakes in New York. By the 1950's the lake-trout fishery of the Great Lakes, formerly important, had been almost ruined as a result of the parasitic activity of the landlocked sea lamprey.

Fresh-water lampreys, measuring 6 to 18 inches long, are found in streams in northern Europe, northern Asia, and also in the cooler parts of North America, Chile, and Australia.

LANCE, a weapon consisting of a long shaft with a sharp point. The lance was much used, chiefly by mounted fighters, during the Middle Ages. The typical cavalry lance had a shaft from 8 to 16 feet long with a steel point 8 or 10 inches long. Pennons, fastened at the point, were intended to frighten the enemy's horses.

A free lance was formerly a mercenary soldier—hence its meaning of a person who is free of allegiance and may assail any party or principle or work for any employer.

This map shows the extent to which each of the Great Lakes is infested with lampreys. The lampreys have killed millions of trout and other Great Lakes food fish.

Heavily infested
Moderately infested
Lightly infested

LAKE SUPERIOR — Soo Locks — LAKE MICHIGAN — LAKE HURON — LAKE ONTARIO — Welland Canal — Niagara Falls — LAKE ERIE

In carpentry the word *lance* means a pointed blade used to sever the grain on each side of the intended path of a chipping bit or router; in medicine the word means a surgical instrument.

LAND GRANTS. The U.S. government has given away parts of its land for many purposes. The most important purposes have been to promote public education, to help in the construction of railroads, and to aid settlers in obtaining land.

The Ordinance of 1785 provided the first land grants for educational purposes. This law governing the surveying and sale of lands north of the Ohio River gave 1 square mile out of every 36 square miles to the new states for use in supporting their school systems. After 1848 an increased amount of land was given. The government also gave land to the states for the creation of state universities, agricultural schools, normal schools, and many other types of schools.

Beginning with gifts to the Illinois Central Railroad in 1850, the U.S. government had by 1871 given 131 million acres to the railroads. Much of the land was given after the Civil War to the great transcontinental railroads. Some of these railroads made large profits from selling their land in the sparsely populated Great Plains to immigrants and other settlers. Because of the complaints of these settlers, the government stopped land grants to the railroads in 1871.

The Homestead Act of 1862 gave free public land to settlers, granting them 160 acres of free land if they would live on it and work it for five years. The sponsors of the act hoped to help workers from the East and farmers to acquire land. However, the workers had neither the experience nor the tools to start a homestead, and they could not afford the cost of transportation to the Great Plains, the area first affected by the Homestead Act. Even the farmers who went there were often disappointed in their hopes for free land. Much of the public land was snatched up at low prices by cattle ranchers and timber companies under laws enacted after the Homestead Act. Land speculators took advantage of loopholes in the Homestead Act and used other clever and often unfair tactics to buy up the best land cheaply and later to sell it at high prices to the homesteaders.

LANDRU, HENRI. See BLUEBEARD.

LANDS, UNITED STATES PUBLIC, or the public domain, lands owned by the federal government of the United States. The term should not be confused with the national domain—lands over which the federal government exercises political jurisdiction, but which it does not own. The states also own land.

When the 13 colonies declared their independence from Great Britain, several of them had land claims that extended all the way to the Mississippi River. Maryland refused to ratify the Articles of Confederation until these western lands were surrendered to the federal government, which they were on the stipulation that the lands be used to create new states equal to the old. These western lands were the original public domain. The Louisiana Purchase was the next addition to public lands, and it was followed by the acquisition of the Floridas, the Oregon Territory, the Mexican cession, and the Gadsden Purchase. The total cost of this more than 2,500,000 square miles of land was about 75 million dollars.

There were two views on the disposal of this land. Alexander Hamilton, always conscious of finances, wanted to sell the land to the highest bidders. Democratic-minded Thomas Jefferson, however, wanted to give the land to people who would use it. Hamilton's view carried the day until 1841, despite the pressure for free lands on the frontier. In 1841 the Preemption Act was passed. And in 1862 President Abraham Lincoln signed the Homestead Law, which gave free land to settlers in the West.

The public domain was also given to schools, colleges, and universities. Some of the land was given to builders of canals, roads, and other public improvements. A huge portion of the public domain was granted between 1850 and 1871 to the railroads. Unfortunately, the land grants were not well planned. Land that should never have been farmed or grazed was handed out to the taker, often to his own detriment. As one folksong has it, "I'm starvin' to death on my government claim." About 160 million acres of land remain in the public domain. Some of these lands are of great scenic beauty, but most of them are agriculturally useless. About 175 million acres of land are in national forests, which are used, where possible, as grazing lands. A large acreage has also come into the public domain through tax defaults. See LAND GRANTS.

LANDSCAPE, a type of drawing or painting that represents a section of the countryside as far as the eye can see or a certain extent of land with the objects and figures it contains. Just as a landscape gardener plots a garden on the grounds of a house, so a painter arranges the objects on his canvas as he chooses to see them. Such pictures, taken collectively, are often contrasted with seascapes, which are paintings that show various aspects of life or scenes on large bodies of water.

Early Chinese painters loved the landscape form for its own sake. Their paintings reflect both a deep love and a keen awareness of natural beauty; yet they were governed by strict conventions. For example, painters devised 16 different ways of drawing mountains. Each one varied according to the geological contours, the plant life, and the time of year.

For Italian painters of the Renaissance, landscapes in the background of a painting gave their subjects a definite position in space and could heighten dimension and volume as well. Their realistic approach to the structure of the human body, to the effects of light and shade on objects, and to perspective made demands on natural settings that medieval painters had ignored.

Not until the 17th century did landscape art come to be regarded as an independent art form. The Frenchmen Poussin and Claude Lorrain and the Dutchmen Van Ruisdael and Hobbema were the most prominent figures in that century. Both Lorrain and Poussin visited the countryside around Rome to capture the spirit of classical beauty. Their landscapes show idealized pastoral scenes. In the 19th century the English painters Constable and Turner devoted themselves to this form. Constable, like the Dutch, painted realistic scenes; his subjects were typical of the English countryside. Turner made more original studies and explored the dramatic, striking effects of light. The French impressionist Monet (and Cézanne somewhat later) and the Dutch painter Van Gogh are among the best known modern landscape painters, although their work includes a variety of other subjects. Landscape art has not been pursued with any particular fervor by contemporary painters. Rather, natural scenes are rendered, as are so many other subjects, in colored abstractions of objects and figures or in disordered shapes and strokes suggesting extremely personal emotion. See MODERN ART.

LANDSCAPE GARDENING. See GARDEN AND GARDENING.

Claude Monet's landscape "Basin at Argenteuil" was painted at a bathing and boating resort on the Seine near Paris. The use of small dotlike brush strokes and of the brilliant colors of the rainbow palette are characteristic of the impressionist technique.

Museum of Art, Rhode Island School of Design, Providence

A mass of rain-soaked volcanic dust slid down a valley in the San Juan Mountains, in Colorado, and dammed a river to form a lake. Soldiers, below, are trying to find two people trapped in the snow of an avalanche that occurred in Switzerland.

LANDSLIDE AND AVALANCHE, rapid movements of material downhill. During a landslide earth or fractured rock on a steep hill or mountain breaks away from its underlayers and slides rapidly downhill. An avalanche is a mass of material, usually snow or snow and included debris, rolling, sliding, or falling rapidly downhill.

Landslides ordinarily occur only on steep slopes, such as mountainsides or cliff faces. A landslide may be caused by the undercutting of a slope. After undercutting, some of the material on the slope is unsupported, except for its cohesion to other material, against the pull of gravity. If that cohesion is overcome, the unsupported material slides downhill. If material is water soaked, it becomes both heavier and slipperier. It may suddenly slip downhill on some water-lubricated surface. Earthquakes, which jar the earth, may break the cohesion of material on steep slopes and cause landslides. Most landslides are small.

Avalanches take place where snow lies on steep mountainsides. Vibration or jarring of the snow, added moisture, or undercutting of a snow slope may cause avalanches.

In 1903 Samuel Langley built a piloted, steampowered airplane for the U. S. War Department. The airplane was catapulted from a boat on the Potomac River. Two attempts at flight were made, but the plane crashed both times, and the government withdrew support.

All photos courtesy National Air Museum, Washington, D.C.

LANGLEY, SAMUEL PIERPONT (1834-1906), an American physicist and astronomer, born at Roxbury, Mass. He was graduated from Boston High School. For a time he was assistant professor of mathematics in the United States Naval Academy. Langley is best known for the numerous experiments he made to perfect an aerial machine that could support itself in midair and move freely without the aid of a balloon. One of the experiments that he performed by means of a crude steam-propelled machine was successful. Langley's machine was not manned. He became secretary of the Smithsonian Institute in 1887. His writings on flight included *Experiments in Aerodynamics* and *Internal Work of the Wind*.

LANGUAGE, broadly speaking, any conventional system, linguistic or otherwise, by which meaning is communicated. Signal flags, drums, gestures, codes, military bugle calls, traffic lights, and road signs are all nonlinguistic (not based on speech) means of communicating. In its more specialized use the word *language* is applied only to the numerous systems of meaningful human vocal sounds men use to communicate among themselves all feelings, thoughts, and experiences expressible in words. See CODE; SIGN LANGUAGE.

No one really knows how or when language, one of the great cohesive elements of human society, came into being. Speech varies from social group to social group, and although there are similarities among the many languages of the world, each is a unique system with a characteristic set of conventions that must be adhered to if one desires to communicate in it. There is no natural law that governs, or determines, the shape and character of languages. It is generally agreed that languages are human inventions and that the conventions of internal structure and vocabulary of these languages were arbitrarily established sometime in the past history of each. The one fixed law about living languages is that they are always changing, growing, and being modified. (See LANGUAGE FAMILY.) Language is learned and noninstinctive. There is no special "gift for languages" possessed by some and not by others. Every normal human being learns at least one language, and the particular language he learns depends on the culture or country in which he is reared and educated. The child begins by imitating the speech of his parents and other speakers about him; after years of trial and error, of experimentation and correction, he attains fluency. In most countries by the time a child is sent to school to learn to read and write he is able to speak quite well.

SPEECH

Speech historically preceded writing, as it does in fact with each individual child. Both are complex arts, employing symbols systematically to express all kinds of meanings: direct or remembered sense impressions; states of mind and feeling, remembered or observed actions of long or short duration, abstractions, relationships, and so forth. The relationship between a linguistic symbol and what it stands for is an arbitrary one. The meanings of words, parts of words, and groups of words are based on convention, on a kind of mutual understanding among the people who use them. Even onomatopoeic words, which are supposed to imitate natural sounds, show a considerable amount of variation from one language to another. See SEMANTICS.

The symbols of speech are sounds, and these sounds result from the action of organs whose primary functions are breathing and eating and only secondarily the production of speech. The organs of speech include the lungs, larynx, palate, nose, tongue, teeth, and lips. No one language utilizes all of the possible sounds the human vocal apparatus is capable of producing. Many of these sounds, such as coughs and

A student of ancient languages copies script from a reproduction of a tablet found at Pylos, Greece. The script, called Linear B, was deciphered only during the 1950's.

Mabel Lang

sneezes, are not used linguistically because they have no symbolic value. Each language represents a selection of only a few of the total number of available vocal sounds; a native speaker of one language often has difficulty pronouncing words in another language because his own language does not make use of a particular sound and he has never learned to produce it. See PRONUNCIATION.

Speech sounds can be classified in many different ways. One common distinction drawn is between vowels and consonants. As air passes from the lungs through the nose or mouth, the kind and quality of sound that is produced can be influenced by modifications in the shape of the oral chamber by movements of the tongue and lips. Vowels are sounds produced by tongue and lip modification of an unimpeded flow of breath. Consonants are sounds resulting from interference with the free flow of breath. This interference may take the form of complete momentary stoppage (for example, English *t, d, p,* called stops or explosives), of continuous obstruction resulting in friction (for example, English *s, z,* called fricatives or spirants), of partial stoppage (for example, English *l*), or of rapid alternating stoppages and releases (called rolled consonants or trills). See CONSONANT; VOWEL.

WRITING

The symbols of written language are graphic representations either of the sounds of speech or of thoughts, ideas, and objects directly. In the history of writing it is believed that nonphonetic pictorial symbols (pictographs and ideograms) preceded phonograms (characters representing single speech sounds, syllables, or words). See ALPHABET; CUNEIFORM; HIEROGLYPH; IDEOGRAM; PICTOGRAPH; SYLLABLE.

The earliest written records of a language are in Sumerian, a tongue spoken in Mesopotamia about 6,000 years ago. Speech antedates these records by many times that number of years. A written language differs in many ways from a spoken language, especially in vocabulary, sentence structure, and rhythm. Speech is normally characterized by the use of common words, colloquialisms, slang, and relatively short sentences; and when someone speaks in the manner of written works, he is said to sound "bookish." In writing there is time to express ideas with greater precision and to arrange them in more complex and subtle relation to one another. See COLLOQUIALISM; PARAGRAPH; SENTENCE; SLANG; VOCABULARY.

Individuals who are unable to read or write are generally not aware of the necessity of understanding the grammar of a language, because they use language for very simple, practical purposes. Fewer words and less complicated syntactical and grammatical structures are needed to express ideas in speech than is the case with written expression. The speaker can utilize supplementary aids to communication not available to the writer: facial expressions, gesticulation, and such elements of sound as pitch, accent, intonation, and dynamics. In addition, the speaker can make use of the physical environment in which he happens to be at the time he is talking; but a writer cannot pound a table or point for effectiveness. See GRAMMAR; SYNTAX.

It is commonly believed by people who know only one language that every other language parallels their own in structure and that languages differ only in their vocabularies. This, of course, is not correct. For information concerning the histories and characteristics of specific languages, see the separate entries in this encyclopedia on the various languages of the world. See UNIVERSAL LANGUAGE.

The importance of knowing how to read and write a language is recognized all over the world. The children below are attending a free primary school in South America.

Ernst Baumann—Birnback

LANGUAGE FAMILY

LANGUAGE FAMILY, a group of languages that have a common origin. Linguists establish kinships among languages by studying comparatively their sound systems, vocabulary, and grammar. Some important language families include the Malayo-Polynesian, Indo-European, Finno-Ugric, Sino-Tibetan (also called Indo-Chinese), and Semitic.

Various branches exist within language families. For example, in the Indo-European family Germanic and Italic are two of the subfamilies, and the Romance languages are a subgroup of the Italic. A conjectured language called proto-Germanic gave rise to certain tongues that in turn gave rise to Dutch, English, German, and the Scandinavian tongues. Another conjectured language called proto-Romance (closely related to Latin) gave rise to French, Italian, Spanish, Portuguese, and other tongues. French, Italian, and German are all Indo-European languages, but French and Italian are more closely related than French and German or Italian and German.

In tracing the development of the Romance languages linguists have had the help of written Latin texts. In studying other language groups linguistics is not always fortunate enough to possess written records.

One way in which linguists can trace the relationship of languages is by comparing words in one language with words having the same meaning in another language. For example, comparing words in English and German, we find *man* and *Mann*, *hand* and *Hand*, and *to drink* and *trinken*. In addition to similarities in sound, there exist similarities in grammatical construction: in English, "stand up"; in German, *stehe auf*.

Relationships of this kind are characteristic of languages that belong to the same language family; they do not exist across language-family lines. Thus it may be established that Greek, the Slavic languages (such as Russian), the Celtic languages (such as Irish), and some of the languages of India (such as Sanskrit) are members of the Indo-European family but that Finnish and Hungarian are not. Similarly, other groups of tongues, such as the languages of the American Indians, can be grouped into language families.

Dialects are branches of parent languages and when they become very different from those of the parent a new language results.

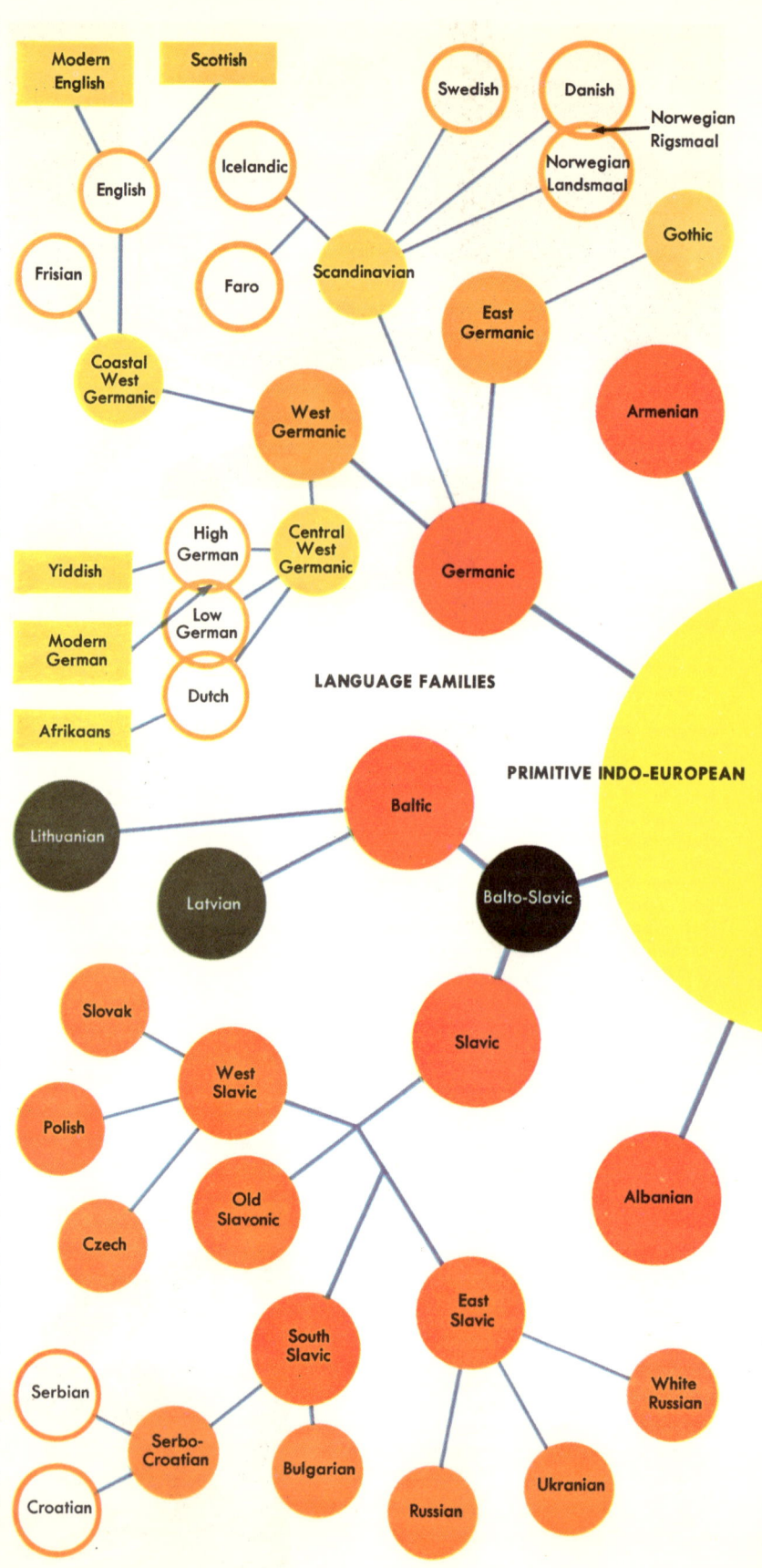

LANGUAGE FAMILIES

PRIMITIVE INDO-EUROPEAN

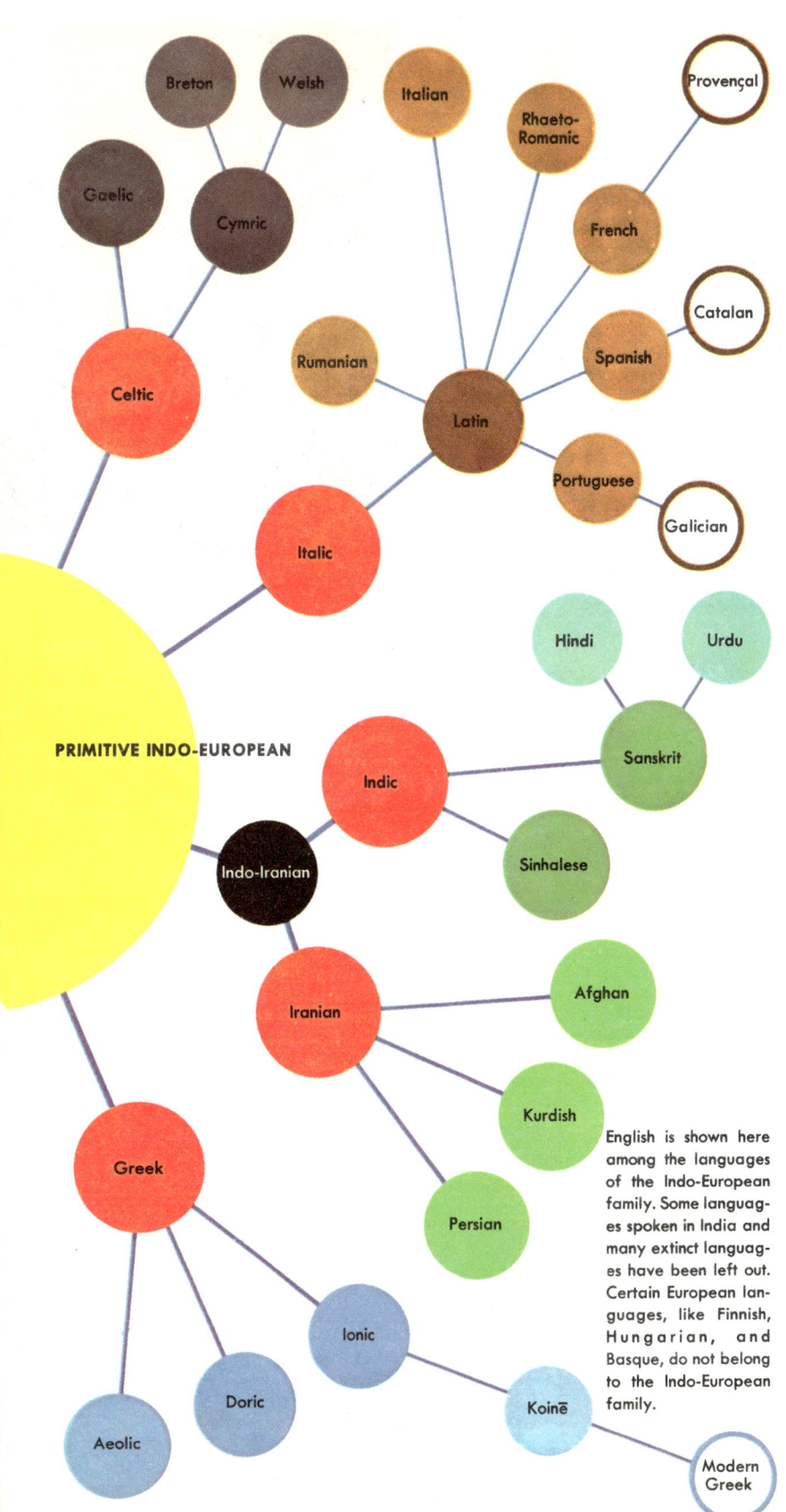

LANIER, SIDNEY (1842-1881), American poet, was born in Macon, Ga. He early showed an interest in a musical career, but his studies were interrupted by the Civil War. He served in the war and suffered a four-month imprisonment at Point Lookout, Maryland.

In 1867 he published his novel *Tiger-Lilies*, and ten years later appeared his *Poems*. Lanier was a flutist with the Peabody Orchestra in Baltimore. At this time he also delivered lectures, which earned him a teaching position at Johns Hopkins. His work as a teacher resulted in two publications, *The Science of English Verse* and *The English Novel*. His complete *Poems* were issued in 1884; and his early lectures, in two volumes, were published in 1902. Lanier's best known poems, "The Symphony" and "The Marshes of Glynn," are notable experiments in the application of musical effects to verse.

LANSING, the capital of Michigan, is located in the south-central part of the state, at the junction of the Red Cedar and Grand rivers. Automobile manufacturing is the principal enterprise, but diversified manufacturing is carried on. Lansing is also the trade center for the rich farming area of southern Michigan. In 1960 the city had a population of 107,807.

Places of interest include the state Capitol, which houses a museum, and the State Office Building, which contains the state library. East Lansing, adjoining the capital, is the seat of Michigan State University. Lansing was settled in 1837, and it was selected as the capital of the state in 1847.

LANSING-ISHII AGREEMENT, an agreement reached through an exchange of notes by Secretary of State Robert Lansing and the Japanese diplomat Viscount Kikujiro Ishii on Nov. 2, 1917. Both governments reaffirmed the Open-Door Policy. (See OPEN-DOOR POLICY.) However, the United States also recognized that Japan had special interests in certain parts of China, an acknowledgment, in effect, that the open door was opened more widely for the Japanese than for others. This interpretation, although denied by Secretary Lansing, was accepted by both the Japanese and the Chinese, and it was used by the Japanese as a justification of their interfering activities in northern China. In 1923 the United States repudiated the agreement.

English is shown here among the languages of the Indo-European family. Some languages spoken in India and many extinct languages have been left out. Certain European languages, like Finnish, Hungarian, and Basque, do not belong to the Indo-European family.

LAOS is a kingdom of southeastern Asia. With Vietnam and Cambodia it formerly made up French Indochina. The area of Laos is about 89,000 square miles. Its population is estimated at about two million.

Laos is a backward country. Practically all its people are farmers who work small plots of land to feed their families. They live in villages composed of houses built on wooden poles, with wooden floors and either bamboo matting or thatch for walls and roof.

The country has much rugged, mountainous terrain, particularly in the forested north. The Mekong River, center of Lao life, flows in a broad valley through northwestern Laos, and in the south it forms several hundred miles of the country's border with Thailand. There are two seasons, wet and dry. In the dry season the river practically dries up, but during the heavy monsoon rains the water level rises greatly. The climate is tropical.

An independent kingdom of united Lao communities existed during the 14th century, but the Lao people for most of their history were dominated by neighboring peoples.

The three-headed elephant on the national flag of Laos is the country's national emblem.

In 1707 they split into two separate kingdoms. One of these was later conquered by Thailand. The French gained control of Laos in 1893. During World War II it was occupied by the Japanese. Afterward Laos gradually achieved complete independence. For detailed map, see THAILAND.

In early 1961 Communist rebels, with Soviet-supplied arms, obtained control of much of Laos. After arrangement of a cease-fire, a conference was held in Geneva in an effort to set up a neutral government.

LA PAZ is a picturesque city in western Bolivia; it is the *de facto* seat of government of the country, although Sucre is the legal capital. La Paz, situated at an altitude of 11,909 feet, is the world's highest big city. It is wedged into the deep La Paz River canyon, with the imposing Mt. Illimani towering over it. The city has a population of about 350,000.

Modern buildings vie with Spanish colonial churches and colorful Indian markets in this hilly metropolis. Among La Paz's outstanding buildings are the dignified Capitol; the cathedral, one of the largest in South America; the Church of Santo Domingo, with its fine altars; and the Diéz de Medina Palace.

La Paz is Bolivia's cultural, industrial, and commercial center. Industries include tanning, brewing, distilling, flour milling, and the manufacture of textiles, shoes, paper, soap, and other items. The city is also a trade center for agricultural products of the region.

Aymara Indians were living in the region when Spaniards from Peru settled in La Paz in 1548. The city was named Nuestra Señora de la Paz until 1827, when it was renamed La Paz de Ayacucho, in honor of the decisive Latin American battle for independence.

LAPLACE, PIERRE, MARQUIS DE (1749-1827), a French mathematician and astronomer. The son of a small farmer, Laplace was born at Beaumont. With the aid of the mathematician Jean d'Alembert, Laplace, when he was 18, was appointed a professor of mathematics at the Ecole Militaire of Paris.

He first applied his analytic powers to the problems of celestial mechanics. Between 1773 and 1787 Laplace vied with the brilliant astronomer Joseph Lagrange in proving the stability of the solar system. Laplace discovered the cause of the inequality in the motions of the planets Jupiter and Saturn and the dependence of the acceleration of the moon on the changes in the earth's orbit. Laplace brought together the results of the mathematical investigation of the solar system into his great *Mécanique céleste*, published in five volumes between 1799 and 1825. The *Mécanique céleste* is contained, without the difficult mathematical portions, in the literary masterpiece *Exposition of the System of the Universe*, which made him world famous. In it Laplace discussed his famous nebular hypothesis. See SOLAR SYSTEM.

Laplace contributed to the field of chemistry during the years 1782 to 1784, when he was associated with Antoine Lavoisier. Laplace's *Analytical Theory of Probabilities* (1812-1820) perfected the science of probability. A more popular version of this intricate work was the *Philosophical Essay on Probability*.

LAPPS, a group of people inhabiting the arctic region called Lapland. Of some 35,000 Lapps, most live in northern Norway and Sweden; the remainder live in Finland and on the Kola Peninsula of the U.S.S.R.

The word *Lapp* is probably of Finnish origin; the Lapps call themselves Samelats. The Lapp language belongs to the Finno-Ugric family, which includes Finnish and Hungarian. The folklore of the Lapps speaks vaguely of lands to the east, and

La Paz, Bolivia, lies nearly 12,000 feet above sea level in a canyon of the Andes.

Ewing Krainin—Alpha

Lapps may have originated in the region around the Ural Mountains. They occupied Lapland about 2,000 years ago. Short and stocky, with broad heads, high cheek bones, flat noses, and swarthy complexions, they are basically Mongoloid.

The Lapps once lived exclusively by hunting and fishing. Later some of them turned to reindeer herding. Reindeer acquired great importance for the Lapps, for these animals supplied them with skins, meat, and horns for personal use as well as for purposes of trade. Ownership of deer was private, but herding was communal. Lapps who tended the forest deer settled in permanent log or turf dwellings and moved with their herds only in the winter. Others who herded the mountain deer, however, had to follow them the year round. Today these nomads are a minority. Only some 20 percent of the modern Lapps herd reindeer. Most of them live by fishing along the Arctic and Atlantic oceans or by raising hay, potatoes, and livestock in small communities on lakes

A few Lapps of northern Norway still follow the nomadic life of reindeer herders.

Rosemary Stopar

and rivers. The Lapps on the Kola Peninsula, for example, are almost all fishermen.

Attempts to Christianize the Lapps began as early as the 11th century. Today, most of them follow the Lutheran and Greek Orthodox religions. Originally, the Lapps held animistic beliefs. They worshiped the spirits of the dead and developed rituals concerning the bear. Sacrifices of animals were made to nature gods such as the sun, the moon, the wind, and the northern lights. The shaman, or priest, mediated between the people and the spirit world. The shaman's soul was supposed to travel at will during a trance, which was induced by the beating of drums. These unique drums, covered with signs and figures describing the Lappic cosmology, were also used in divination. The Lapps became known as magicians, and medieval courts sometimes summoned them to perform.

As nomadic herdsmen the Lapps developed a unique tent (*kata*), a boatlike sledge (*akja*), lassos, and harness for pack deer. The structure of their society was patriarchal. The authority of the father over all family affairs was absolute and passed on his death to the eldest son.

After centuries of cruel exploitation and peaceful assimilation the once-unique culture of the Lapps is gradually merging with the cultures of the nationalities with which they are in contact.

LARK, a small bird famous in literature for its sweet, flutelike song, which it delivers while high in the air as well as on the ground. The lark family consists of 75 species; most are inconspicuous birds in protective brown or gray plumage. Often they have crests or little tufts of feathers on the head. Usually the sexes are colored alike.

Larks are birds of the open areas —deserts, beaches, plowed fields, and prairies. In many regions their numbers have increased because of man's clearance of forested areas. The species are most numerous in Africa, only one being found in the New World and only two in the Australian region. Larks in the northern parts of their range often migrate in winter.

The lark nests on the ground in a little scraped depression, often near the base of a clump of grass. The grass-cup nest may have a hair lining, and it is sometimes partially domed. Three to five spotted eggs are usually laid, and there may be two or more broods annually. Incu-

The brownish bird on the post is the skylark of Europe, a bird with a notable song. With it is shown the horned lark of North America. The horns are small tufts of feathers.

bation requires about 11 or 12 days. The male brings food to the nesting female and later assists in feeding the young. Larks feed largely on insects and their larvae and on small crustaceans, but they also take some plant food and small berries.

The only true lark in North America is the horned lark, a brown bird 7 or 8 inches long, with a definite head pattern, a black collar about the white throat, and two small tufts of head feathers, which look like black horns when they are erected. Viewed while flying overhead, the horned lark looks light with a dark tail. It is often seen walking about on a field or a golf course. It nests as far north as the arctic tundra of Canada and migrates southward in winter.

The meadowlark, a common bird in North America, does not belong to the lark family. It is a member of the blackbird family. See BLACKBIRDS, GRACKLES, COWBIRDS.

The most famous lark in literature, the skylark, is one of the most plentiful birds in Europe. It is noted for its long-sustained song, often delivered as the bird soars upward until it is out of sight. Hence Shakespeare writes: "Hark! hark! the lark at heaven's gate sings."

Other larks not found in North America are the wood larks of Eurasia and Africa, the bush larks of the Old World, and the black larks of northern Europe and Asia. The black lark differs from other species of larks in that the sexes are differently colored—the male all black and the female brownish.

LARKSPUR

Larkspur blooms in tall, clustered spikes.

LARKSPUR, the popular name given to certain plants of the buttercup family. Gardeners usually call the annual forms larkspur and the perennial sorts delphinium. One of the petal-like sepals is elongated to form a distinct, spurlike structure. The flowers are borne in long, showy spikes. Although shades of blue are most frequent, the color range extends from white through yellow, including red. Most larkspurs are tall, upright plants, but the height ranges from 1½ to 8 feet. All larkspurs have more or less poisonous juice, and some western North American species are especially poisonous to cattle. Larkspurs are found in the Northern Hemisphere around the world.

LARVA, an early stage in the development of those animals that undergo a metamorphosis, or series of changes, in their progress from the egg to the mature state. Insects present many familiar and excellent examples of larval forms, and the metamorphic process is typically represented in these forms. Thus, the egg of the butterfly gives origin, not to the perfect winged creature, but to a crawling grub, or caterpillar, which is the larva. Through the subsequent transformations and development of this larva, the adult form, or imago, is produced. The word *larva* is derived from a Latin word meaning a mask. The word thus indicates the semidisguised or temporary nature of the organism when in the larval state. Larvae are rare among vertebrates and appear only in the lower forms, such as lampreys, eels, salamanders, and frogs.

LA SALLE, ROBERT CAVELIER, SIEUR DE (1643-1687), French explorer, was born in Rouen. He was educated by the Jesuits. At the age of 22 he went to Canada and established a trading post on the island of Montreal. In 1669 he was a member of an expedition that explored the Niagara River and Lake Ontario. He became a close associate of Count de Frontenac, governor of Quebec; both of them envisioned North America as a splendid land for French colonization. Returning to France, he obtained Louis XIV's authorization to probe and develop the West. In January, 1680, he established Fort Crevecoeur near what is now Peoria, Ill.; the following year the fort was reestablished near the present city of Ottawa, Ill. Early in 1682 he led an expedition the length of the Mississippi River and reached the Gulf of Mexico on April 9. He claimed the whole region for France and named it Louisiana after the king. He returned to France to report his explorations and was appointed viceroy of North America, with jurisdiction over the territory from the Illinois River to the Spanish territorial borders. In 1684 he set out from France for the mouth of the Mississippi with four ships and 280 men to establish a permanent French settlement on the Gulf and ensure France's claims to the Mississippi Valley. This time La Salle met with no success. He mistook Matagorda Bay on the Texas coast for the mouth of the Mississippi and exhausted his supplies before the mistake could be rectified. Two years were spent in unsuccessful journeys to discover the great river, while his colonists and soldiers gradually dwindled away. By 1687 the number of survivors was reduced to 37. His harshness of manner, more than his want of success, embittered his followers, some of whom killed him.

Lassen Peak, in northern California, is seen from Manzanita Lake. The peak is typical of the other Northwest volcanoes, such as Mt. Rainier and Mt. Hood.

LASSEN VOLCANIC NATIONAL PARK in northern California preserves one of the few active volcanoes in the United States, Lassen Peak, and about 165 square miles of volcanic exhibits. The peak, located at the southern end of the Cascade Range, rises to 10,453 feet. Its latest eruptions occurred in 1914 and 1921. The park contains interesting lava formations and hot sulfur springs. Small lakes are found in the eastern portion of the park. A winter-sports area is in the southwest corner of the park. Lassen Park was established in 1916.

LATHE, a machine tool for turning, shaping, sanding, and polishing articles of metal, wood, ivory, or plastic. Chair rungs, bowls, jewelry, guns, parts of watches, and many machine and automobile parts are made on lathes. Lathes are found in machine shops, woodworking shops, and on jewelers' benches.

The lathe has four principal parts. The first is the bed, the rigid framework on which the other parts are mounted and which determines the overall length of the machine. The

Sieur de La Salle, French explorer

second part is the headstock, which is bolted to the left end of the bed. The headstock totally or partially holds the material to be worked on and spins it toward the operator. The third, the tailstock, slides from the right end of the bed to the left to accommodate the length of the material being shaped. The fourth part is the tool rest, on which or by which the cutting tools are held. The tool rest slides back and forth and across the bed between the headstock and the tailstock. The centers of a lathe are the pins or cuplike holding devices on the inside ends of the headstock and the tailstock. The capacity, or size, of a lathe is determined by the length between the centers and by the working height of the axis of the centers above the bed. Thus a 12-inch lathe is a large machine that will take material 24 inches in diameter. The working length of a lathe is the length of the bed minus the overall length of the headstock and the tailstock.

Bowls, plates, cups, jewelry, and so forth can be turned and shaped on a lathe by attaching a faceplate to the power-driven spindle of the headstock and by swinging the tool rest across the bed and up to within about $\frac{1}{8}$ inch of the surface to be worked on. See ABRASIVE.

The small machine-shop lathe, right, is used by high school students in metalworking courses. The spinning headstock is at the right of the picture. The headstock holds a chuck, in which is clamped the material to be worked. A large industrial lathe is shown below. The headstock is behind the man; the tailstock and bearing supports are at right.

Courtesy of Allis-Chalmers

Washington Park High School, Racine, Wis.

LATIN, one of the ancient languages of the Italic group of the Indo-European family. It developed around the 6th century B.C. as a written language and was based upon the speech in the city of Rome. This speech was a city dialect formed on the basis of the tribal language of the Latins. It was subject to the heavy influence of the neighboring Sabine tribe and the non-Indo-European language of the Etruscans, who ruled the area to the end of the 6th century B.C. After the overthrow of the Etruscans and the establishment of the Roman city government, neighboring tribes that had languages and dialects belonging to the Italic group were swallowed up. Further conquests by Rome absorbed other languages in the Italian peninsula. This process was speeded up during the Samnite Wars in the 4th and 3d centuries B.C. But as late as the 1st century B.C. there existed independent languages on the Italian peninsula, and in southern Italy and Sicily the Greek language, which had been strong from the time of the Greek colonies in the 6th to 4th centuries B.C., persisted.

The conquest by Rome of Gaul, the Iberian Peninsula, northern Africa, Britain, Rhineland Germany, Austria, and large areas of the Balkan Peninsula led to the spread of Latin together with the gradual swallowing up of local languages and dialects. Also, the inclusion within the Roman Empire of areas of Greek culture in Asia Minor, Syria, and Egypt led to the squeezing out of the Greek language.

With the collapse of the Roman Empire in the West in the 5th century A.D. and the weakening of economic and political relations between its parts, Latin broke up into a series of Romance languages, which were based on the vulgar Latin spoken by the Roman troops stationed in the area. These languages include Italian, Sardinian, Provençal, French, Catalan, Spanish, Portuguese, Dalmatian, and lastly, Balkan-Romance (from which developed Rumanian and Moldavian). In Britain and western Germany Latin was dislodged by German dialects and in certain areas of Austria and Yugoslavia, by Slavonian. Romance languages did not develop in these areas. In northern Africa Latin was replaced by Arabic.

Together with the Romance languages, which in the 8th and 9th centuries finally separated out, Latin continued to exist until the 15th and 16th centuries, not only as a written language of the church, science, jurisprudence, and medical practice in all Catholic countries, but as a living, spoken language by the clergy, scientists, jurists, priests, and doctors. It was the most important second language in these countries. It also continued to exist as the international language of literature and poetry in the Byzantine Empire. The literary norms differed sharply from those of Latin in ancient times and gradually became the norms for living languages.

The development of the literary languages of the Romance nationalities in the 15th and 16th centuries and the unsuccessful attempts of the humanists to tear apart the living literary norms of the Latin of the Middle Ages restored the norms of classical Latin prose but killed Latin as a literary language. The use of Latin, however, has continued in Catholic worship services, in medicine, and, in part, in natural sciences and law.

LATIN AMERICAN ART

LATIN AMERICAN ART includes the architecture, sculpture, painting, and popular crafts of Central America and South America. It is an art extremely diversified in character, owing to varying geographical conditions and to the mixtures of native Indian styles with those of Spain and, in Brazil, with those of Portugal. In countries where the native Indian arts were most highly developed, the richest and most productive artistic achievements arose. Toltec, Aztec, and Mayan civilizations underlay the colonial settlements of Spain in Mexico and Guatemala; likewise the Incas were the forerunners of the Spaniards in the mountainous countries of Peru and Bolivia. The three chief centers of colonial culture were Mexico City; Quito, in Ecuador; and Cuzco, in Peru.

Courtesy of City Art Museum of St. Louis
This poncho (a man's cloak and blanket) is decorated with a simple linear pattern.

Courtesy of City Art Museum of St. Louis
Diego Rivera's painting "Yucatan Indian"

From the 16th to the 19th century, while Latin America was colonial, a great many architects and sculptors emigrated from Europe to Spanish America. As a result, structures in the New World were based on late-Gothic, Renaissance, and baroque styles. (See BAROQUE ART.) Although art was fostered by the church and the Spanish aristocracy, most of the craftsmen employed were native Indians; they infused their own styles into the statuary and ornamentation of buildings.

Typical of the 16th-century architecture was the fortress-church, a massive type of stone building with thick walls, a few windows, low towers, and carved doorways. These churches were built in spacious courts surrounded by sturdy stone walls. Chapels stood at the corners and at the entrance of the church. In contrast to the rather bare exteriors of these churches the interiors contained colorful polychrome statues in wood and stone. Choirs and altars, as well as doors, were ornately carved. Ceilings were vaulted in the Gothic manner or were carved in the elaborate designs of the Moorish style. The Indian workmen showed a tendency to flatten figures in their carving and to keep surfaces unbroken. This manner of expression is typical of their indigenous reliefs.

Late-Gothic, plateresque, baroque, and ultrabaroque styles were adapted to Latin American buildings in quick succession. By the 17th century elegant private mansions and magnificent cathedrals abounded in Mexico and in several of the other Latin American colonies. Cathedral domes were tiled in colorful geometric and floral designs. Silver was used in designing church ornaments and tableware. In cathedrals of ultrabaroque style, altarpieces of gold blended with carved ornamentation of vivid colors.

Cathedrals in Bolivia and Peru, set in the Andes with their high valleys, were placed in a rather somber setting. They had the solid walls of Mexican cathedrals but were otherwise more restrained. Paintings and wood carvings again showed the influence of Indian designs, with their flat, unbroken surfaces and their geometrical, animal, and floral motifs.

Brazilian cities, as might be expected, bore the marks of Portuguese styles in architecture, although there was not the burgeoning of architectural forms that existed in Mexico and Peru. A noteworthy example of fine sculpture in wood and stone is the work of Antônio Lisbôa, known as O Aleijadinho, or "The Little Cripple." He is also said to have designed the church of São Francisco in Ouro Prêto, Brazil.

On the whole, painting in the Latin American colonies was less impressive than their architecture and sculpture. Of course, there was not the challenge of a distinctive developing culture to stimulate creativity, nor was there as urgent a need for paintings. Painters were technically proficient, but they contented themselves with imitating styles on the Continent, particularly those of Spanish painters. Ribera, Zurbarán, El Greco, Velázquez, and Murillo all influenced the Hispanic-American painters. Religious murals decorated church walls. The 18th-century painters Miguel Cabrera and José Ibarra, both Mexican, turned to portraiture. Where the

This is a stylized clay figure of an Indian warrior. Latin American flower and animal designs are also highly conventionalized.
Courtesy of City Art Museum of St. Louis

Indian influence was strong, as in Cuzco, a more powerful and original expressiveness in painting arose. And in the cities of Mexico *retablos* were painted in great quantities by the common people. They were votive pictures that narrated a miraculous healing or a rescue from danger.

Courtesy of City Art Museum of St. Louis
Rufino Tamayo's "Girl with Flowers"

During the 19th century the Latin American colonies of Spain and Portugal fought for the status of independent republics. It was only natural that the impact of this fever and unrest would make itself felt in Latin American art. Painting became charged with military and politically conscious subjects. At the same time it was common practice for painters and sculptors to go abroad to study; thus European styles of painting were perpetuated in Latin America. In the 20th century this legacy from Europe has not been abandoned. One by one, the styles of impressionism, cubism, futurism, and now abstract painting have been brought home to Central American and South American countries.

In Mexico the real awakening came after the revolt of the people against the greedy and corrupt Díaz regime in 1911. In the wake of the people's revolt came a revolt of painters against traditional styles of painting. Among those artists who became socially conscious in their work were Alfaro Siqueiros, Diego Rivera, and José Orozco. Rivera's murals and paintings draw upon the wellspring of native traditions. Not only are his subjects urgent ones, but his mode of expression differs sharply from the traditional ones taught. Earth colors are used in his works; the flattened forms show a strongly linear style of painting; the figures are large scale. In the work of Orozco, another revolutionary Mexican painter, all is intense energy, even violence. Scenes of revolutionary soldiers and common laborers are charged with vivid colors; clashing lines of movement animate the figures. The subjects of these paintings—of Rivera's, Orozco's, and others'—bear witness to a deep sympathy for the proletariat. Indeed many of them are designed to teach the peoples they depict so forcefully.

Mexico was not the only country that initiated a revival in the arts. A number of other painters, drawn to new subjects and techniques, appeared on the scene—Carlos Mérida from Guatemala; Emilio Pettoruti of Argentina; Cândido Portinari from Brazil. The indigenist school of Peru likewise presented in painting an interpretation of contemporary life.

Modern architecture took root quite suddenly in Latin America, most noticeably in Brazil. In 1930 a group of young architects trained in France took over a great building enterprise in Rio de Janeiro and later, in 1936, Le Corbusier visited Brazil as a consultant. (See MODERN ARCHITECTURE.) As a result, the

Courtesy of City Art Museum of St. Louis
A ceremonial incense burner

house with patio soon gave way to tall modern apartments with their straight horizontal and vertical planes and series of windows. A great number of public buildings, such as Rio de Janeiro's Ministry of Education and Health and Brazilian Associated Press Building were also built. Windows in these structures were designed so as to admit air while shading the inside

Courtesy of City Art Museum of St. Louis
Ancient Indian relief carving

from the glare of the sun. Concrete was used in the construction; supports were sheathed in granite. The walls were covered with blue and white tiles, and the shutters for the windows were also blue. Great public housing and university-city projects have sprung up all over Central America and South America since World War II. In many such projects the painting and sculpture of famous artists are integrated into one harmonious whole.

Mention should be made of the folk arts in Latin American countries, where Indian traditions still thrive. Woven articles and pottery abound in Mexico, Guatemala, Ecuador, Peru, and Bolivia. Carvings, knitted dolls, silver ornaments, and jewelry are among the articles produced. The making of masks for religious festivals is also an important craft. The votive pictures of Mexico, which date from colonial times, if not earlier, are still a popular art with the inhabitants. They are usually painted on canvas, wood, or tin. There is perhaps no better example of native art, which shows simple but dramatic expression, an expression that springs from the deepest feelings of a people.

Typical Indian ceramic bowl
Courtesy of The City Art Museum, St. Louis

LATIN AMERICAN INDEPENDENCE.

Toward the end of the 18th century Spanish Americans began to complain about Spain's heavy taxation and discrimination against them. They read much about the ideas of Voltaire and Rousseau. These ideas, together with the North American and French revolutions, made them determined to be free.

The first successful call to independence was raised by Toussaint L'Ouverture, a Negro slave who liberated Haiti from France in the 1790's. The first Mexican attempt at liberation from Spain was led by Father Miguel Hidalgo y Costilla. His poor and ragged army stood before the gates of Mexico City but turned back. Hidalgo continued the revolt until his death before a firing squad in 1811. Mexican Independence Day is celebrated on September 16, the day on which Hidalgo raised his cry for independence. But Mexico was successfully freed from the Spanish by Agustín de Iturbide in 1821. Iturbide proclaimed himself Emperor Augustín I, and Mexico was not rid of him until 1823. A second war of independence had to be fought in the 1860's, this time against France. It was led by Benito Juárez, who is regarded as the George Washington of Mexico. See MAXIMILIAN.

The independence of the Central American countries was a quiet result of the Mexican revolution that Iturbide led. Even the Spanish captain general joined in proclaiming Central America's absolute independence from Spain in 1821.

The liberation of South America was the accomplishment of Simón Bolívar and José de San Martín. From 1811 to 1812 Bolívar was the leader, with Francisco Miranda, of a short-lived independence proclaimed in Caracas. Miranda was imprisoned by the Spanish, and Bolívar was exiled. Bolívar, however, returned with a few hundred volunteers from his exile in what is now Colombia. By 1814 he was proclaimed liberator and dictator of Venezuela. However, independence was not to be so easy. Bolívar's armies were defeated by the royalists, and he took refuge on the English island of Jamaica. Bolívar made new plans there. Equipping a small army in friendly Haiti, he returned to Venezuela in 1816, but only long enough to decree freedom for the slaves. Soon Bolívar's strength became irresistible. He was joined by the *llaneros* of José Antonio Páez. These tough, fearless horsemen turned the tide against the Spanish. Englishmen, Scotsmen, Irishmen, and Germans crossed the sea to join Bolívar. From his stronghold at the mouth of the Orinoco River he fought Pablo Morillo, the leader of the Spanish forces. Before the war was over in Venezuela, Bolívar led his forces over jungles and mountains to Bogotá, where he surprised and defeated the Spanish. On his return to Venezuela he took advantage of an armistice to march against the Spanish. His victory at Carabobo assured Venezuelan independence. Next, Bolívar marched to Ecuador, where José Antonio Sucre defeated the Spanish at Quito, in Ecuador, in a "battle above the clouds" in 1822. Bolívar then moved to join San Martín in Peru.

San Martín had been chosen military commander of the United Provinces of La Plata (now Argentina), which had proclaimed independence from Spain in 1816. In 1817 San Martín crossed the Andes to aid the Chilean revolt, which was going badly. The crossing of the Andes may be compared to Hannibal's crossing of the Alps. The hardships were immense: lack of oxygen, no pasture for the horses, and no roads. The howitzers had to be hauled by hand over the higher peaks. San Martín's army was tired but enthusiastic when it descended from the mountains. It crushed the Spanish at Chacabuco in 1817 and at Maipù in 1818. Bernardo O'Higgins, the Chilean patriot, was left as head of his nation; and San Martín turned north into Peru, Spain's last stronghold. With the help of the English naval commander Lord Cochrane, he entered Lima in 1821. But San Martín's force alone could not crush the Spanish. Bolívar and San Martín met in 1822, and San Martín quietly retired from the scene. Sucre and Bolívar were left to defeat the Spanish in 1824 at the battles of Junín and Ayacucho. The last Spanish stronghold was Callao, the port of Lima, which was taken in 1826. South America was free, but Bolívar died discouraged. His dream of a single South American republic was never realized.

Brazil's independence came in 1822. The regent, Pedro, refused to return to Portugal at his father's command. Instead, he drew his sword, announced Brazil's independence, and became Emperor Dom Pedro I. Cuba did not win independence from Spain until the Spanish-American War. See BOLÍVAR, SIMÓN; HIDALGO, MIGUEL; JUÁREZ, BENITO PABLO; SAN MARTÍN, JOSÉ DE; SPANISH-AMERICAN WAR.

LATIN AMERICAN LITERATURE

consists of the literature of Portuguese-speaking Brazil and of the Spanish-speaking countries of Central America and South America. The literature of these countries falls into historical periods that include the colonial period (from 1492 to 1808), the revolutionary period (from 1808 to 1824), the romantic period (from 1824 to 1888), the period of modernism (from 1888 to 1910), and the contemporary period (from 1910 to the present). Since Indian stories, poems, and legends were never set down, the language of Latin American literature is entirely Spanish and Portuguese.

Literary works in the colonial period consisted of chronicles and histories that narrated the high exploits of the conquistadors. In many cases the descriptions of people and places in the New World are extremely detailed. The attention of these writers, many of whom were markedly responsive to nature, was fixed on actual, concrete conditions. Government officials, friars, even soldiers were the literary figures of this period. In the midst of these historical accounts there appeared epic poems of some merit. Alonso de Ercilla y Zúñiga's *La Arauncana* is the most distinguished work of this type. Literary fashions throughout this period continued to be dictated by the canons of Spanish literature. Through the first half of the 17th century the Spanish poet and critic Góngora was extremely influential in the colonies. However, nothing more than imitations of his style were produced, and most of the literature written under his influence was artificial and overblown.

Gabriela Mistral, the Chilean poet, was awarded the 1945 Nobel prize for literature.

Rubén Darío, Nicaraguan lyric poet, is one of Latin America's leading modern writers.

By the second half of the 18th century—the age of enlightenment on the Continent—new ideas from the mother country were circulating among the colonists. Native writers began to question a way of life that had been dominated by centuries of Spanish rule.

In the wars of independence during the 19th century literary preoccupations became intensely political; hence, journalism flourished in this period. Where earlier Latin American writers had concerned themselves with nice matters of taste, the new intellectuals gathered around literary and artistic societies to discuss political and social problems. One of the celebrated political leaders of the day was Simón Bolívar. His *Letter from Jamaica* shows an acute awareness of the problems of newborn republics. The first Hispanic-American novel, which deals with good and bad aspects of Mexican society, was *El Periquillo sarniento*, written by José Fernández de Lizardi. He was also a journalist of some repute and an outspoken defender of the cause of the revolution. With the increase in published periodicals a new reading public arose. Gaucho poetry, an Argentine form that was based on the Spanish popular ballad, was much in demand.

Following the independence of the Latin American colonies came a period of romanticism in literature. The peculiarity of the romanticism in Latin America may be attributed to the welter of European influences that preceded the movement. Thus, the origins of romanticism in Venezuela were Spanish; those in Colombia, English; and those in Chile, Argentinian. In the area of the Río de la Plata the origins of romanticism were French.

Two writers who anticipated the romantic movement were José Olmedo of Ecuador and José de Heredia y Campuzano of Cuba. The former wrote a tribute to Simón Bolívar entitled *La victoria de Junín: Canto a Bolívar*. Heredia was better known for his lyrics; they are charged with feeling for the beauty of nature. Another figure in the early romantic period was Andrés Bello, actually a more classical than romantic type of poet and author. Born in Venezuela, he later lived in Chile. His *Gramática castellana* bespeaks the breadth of his scholarship and erudition. Sarmiento, a rival of Andrés Bello, was a fiery, energetic reformer, whose energies were directed against the Rosas tyranny in Argentina.

Among the romantic novels that appeared in the 19th century was Jorge Isaac's *María*. Like many others of the period it shows a sentimental attachment to the Indian. Its tender and idyllic love story has made it a favorite with young Latin Americans. Among the popular Gaucho writers the most notable is José Hernández, whose poem *Martín Fierro* ranks as an Argentine epic.

The short narratives of the *costumbrista* writers drew upon the customs and habits of the common people; in these works can be found the germ of the realistic novel that came later. Alberto Blest Gana of Chile, Ignacio Altamirano and José López-Portillo y Rojas of Mexico, and the Colombian writers Eugenio Díaz, Lorenzo Marroquín, and Tomás Carrasquilla all wrote in this early realistic strain. The naturalism of the French novelists Zola and Flaubert also left its mark on South American writers. *Juan Criollo*, by Carlos Loveira of Cuba, was the finest novel of this type to appear on the scene. Although not published until 1927, it was a direct historical descendant of late-19th-century naturalism. The latter part of the 19th century found its most satisfying literary expression in essayists who were champions of liberty and social reform. Poetry too, which was based on purely native impulses, came to a sudden flowering at the end of the century.

Varying influences gave rise to modernism in Latin American literature. Social reforms had led to the rise of a middle class. Positivism was the prevailing philosophical viewpoint. Realism and naturalism, already present in the previous literary period, burst forth in vigorous expression. Aesthetic sensibility, purity of language, and beauty of form were the concerns of modern writers. The greatest figure to emerge in this movement was Rubén Darío; his influence was felt throughout the entire Spanish-speaking world. His *Prosas profanas* is regarded as the epitome of modernism. The outstanding essayist of modernism was José Rodó of Uruguay. His essay *Ariel* gave voice to South America's plea for recognition and esteem.

Two women poets who made outstanding contributions to modern Latin American poetry were Juana de Ibarbourou and Gabriela Mistral. Madame Mistral was the first Latin American to receive the Nobel prize for literature. Concern with the plight of the frustrated and downtrodden Indian peon and Negro was a significant new development in narrative fiction. Important short-story writers were Ventura García Calderón, Horacio Quiroga, and Javier de Viana. Ciro Alegraí's *El Mundo es ancho y ajeno* is a noteworthy novel of social consciousness.

The Mexican thinker Alfonso Reyes shared with others his hopes for seeing established in Mexico a solidly rooted national culture, which would combine local and universal elements. A recent Mexican novel, *La region mas transparente* (1958), deals with the discontent and social unrest of life in Mexico today. More and more throughout Central America and South America there is a clamoring for national and individual expression, expression that is independent of North American and European influence.

LATIN LITERATURE. Exclusive of its intrinsic worth, Latin literature, though almost wholly imitative of the Greek, is important for its powerful influence on the culture of Europe over a span of more than 2,000 years. Latin literature is conveniently divided into three broad periods: the anteclassical period (350–80 B.C.), embracing the beginnings and early development of the literature to the time of Marcus Tullius Cicero; the classical period, or Golden Age (80 B.C.–A.D. 14), extending from Cicero through the principate of Augustus; and the Silver Age (A.D. 14–138), lasting through the reign of the emperor Hadrian.

The anteclassical period produced a considerable number of writers. Mention should be made of the father of Roman poetry, Quintus Ennius (2d century B.C.), who is remembered chiefly for his *Annales*, in which he attempted to compose a national epic—like that of Homer —on the rise and glorious progress of Rome. This was the first Latin poetry in hexameter verse. The extant fragments reveal much moral earnestness and a style vigorous and lofty, yet rough and crude. Cato the Elder (2d century B.C.) should also be mentioned. In his *De Re Rustica* he established Latin prose and began the development of Roman oratory, which reached its climax later in Cicero. But it is in drama that the anteclassical period is best represented. The important dramatists were Plautus (3d century B.C.) and Terence (2d century B.C.), both writers of comedy. Of the comedies of Plautus there are 21 extant, the best being perhaps *Captivi*, *Menaechmi*, and *Miles Gloriosus*. Plautus is noted for his broad farce and boisterous fun. The six plays of Terence are more quiet in action and have better developed plots. Terence, who unlike Plautus wrote chiefly for a literary circle, has a style marked for its elegance, grace, and finish. Both drew upon the Greek New Comedy of manners, sometimes combining two Greek plots in one play, but Roman elements often appeared, especially in Plautus. There is no other distinguished name in the history of Latin drama with the exception of Seneca, in the Silver Age, who composed several tragedies, all modeled on the Greek and very influential in subsequent Italian, French, and English tragedy.

The Golden Age was remarkable in both prose and poetry. In prose the outstanding men were Cicero, Julius Caesar, and Sallust (all of the 1st century B.C.), and Livy (1st century B.C. and 1st century A.D.).

This is a bust of the Roman Cicero.

Cicero's writings were many and varied but of four general kinds: orations, letters, rhetorical treatises, and philosophical works. His was the first artistic prose, a blend of the full, rich, sometimes ostentatious Asiatic style of Isocrates, tempered by Attic soberness and chastity. The long, rounded periods of Cicero's orations have been admired and imitated for more than 2,000 years. His letters, which were not intended for publication, reveal the author's character in all its strength and weakness. The *De Oratore*, a dialogue on the various aspects of rhetoric and oratory, is usually considered Cicero's greatest work. His philosophical productions show little originality or profound thought, but in both style and content his influence was felt for centuries.

Caesar's works were memoirs, or *Commentaries:* They included seven volumes—*De Bello Gallico*, an account and justification of his military activities in Gaul, and three volumes, *De Bello Civili*, a history of the civil war. Caesar's Latin is noted for its clearness, simplicity, purity, and vigor. Sallust and Livy were historians. Of Sallust there are extant his monographs on the *Conspiracy of Catiline* and the *History of the Jugurthine War*, in which he adopted Thucydides as his model. His diction was at once archaic and colloquial; his sentences, short and broken. This was a reaction to the exuberance of Cicero, and Sallust's influence in this respect is seen in later writers like Tacitus. However, Sallust's work was marred by historical inaccuracy and an excess of the dramatic. Augustan prose was enriched by the Roman history of Livy. He celebrated the glories of Rome with a moral purpose, but he neglected historical criticism and was extremely partial to his own country. As a rhetorical narrator, however, Livy has few equals, and he was particularly effective in his descriptions. His language was often poetical, foreshadowing the Latin of the Silver Age.

The poets of the Golden Age, all of whom wrote in the 1st century B.C., were more numerous: Lucretius, Catullus, Albius Tibullus, Sextus Propertius, Ovid, Horace, and Virgil. Lucretius exhibited genius in his *De Rerum Natura*, a poem in hexameters expounding the nature of the universe and man. For the physical side of the work Lucretius followed the atomistic theory of Democritus; for the philosophical, his master Epicurus. His object was to free man from his fear of divine punishment on earth or in the hereafter. John Dryden said of him that he was so much an atheist that he sometimes forgot to be a poet. Yet his great work has had a profound influence on many poets from the time of Virgil. Catullus, Tibullus, and Propertius were lyric and elegiac poets. On the familiar themes of love, the simple life, and the swift passing of human existence, they wrote with grace and charm. They addressed their ladyloves, whose names were fictitious and, some believe, their identities also. In Ovid Rome had its most facile and animated poet. His *Amores* and other love poetry, despite immoral frivolity, won him great favor with the social elite of his day but were at least partially the cause of his ultimate banishment by Augustus. In his *Metamorphoses* Ovid narrated tales of legendary adventure and transformation. The most important poets of the Golden Age were Horace and Virgil. Early in his career Horace wrote *Satires*, which for the most part held no personal invective but were discourses denouncing human faults in general terms. His *Ars Poetica* prescribed rules for literary composition. His *Odes* have been famous ever since the day of their appearance, particularly because of the genial spirit of their philosophy, which was mainly Epicurean with some degree of Stoicism. Horace was remarkable for the elegance and urbanity of his carefully polished poetry. A number of his odes were patriotic, recalling to the Roman people the virtues responsible for the uninterrupted growth of their state. This regenerative aim was also voiced by Virgil. Just as Cicero is considered the greatest of the writers of Latin prose, so Virgil is held the greatest Roman poet. His epic, the *Aeneid*, tells of the wanderings of the Trojan Aeneas and of his battles in Italy in his at-

An early book illustration showing Virgil

tempt to establish a new Troy. Modeled on the *Iliad* and the *Odyssey*, it lacks their carefree abandon and love of the active life but is distinguished for its lofty style, its memorable phrasing, its imaginative power, its patriotism, and its deep melancholy. No less mellifluous were Virgil's *Georgics*, which were about farming. The *Eclogues*, ten idylls, are considered inferior to those of Theocritus, which they imitated. No poet has had a more continuous and profound influence on subsequent generations than Virgil.

In the third period of Latin literature, the Silver Age, content was subordinated to form. Language was molded by the schools of rhetoric and took on a spurious glitter. Among the writers in prose the chief were Lucius Annaeus Seneca, Quintilian, Pliny the Elder, Pliny the Younger, Gaius Petronius, and Cornelius Tacitus. The most famous author of the Silver Age was Seneca. He wrote both in poetry, as has been already mentioned, and in prose. His prose illustrates all the faults and the virtues of the style of the period: ornament, conceits, affected simplicity, versatility, novelty of manner, and a tendency toward epigram. His philosophical essays greatly influenced the thought and style of his period. A reintroduction of Ciceronianism as a reaction to Seneca's pointed style is observed in Quintilian's *Institutio Oratoria*, a wholesome treatise on the training of an orator. The indefatigable Pliny the Elder published *Historia Naturalis*, consisting of 37 books and containing a wealth of information. The ten books of *Letters* of his nephew Pliny the Younger reveal the writer as a vain but cultured gentleman, mirroring from its best side the upper society of his generation. Petronius' *Satyricon*, a medley of prose and verse, ridiculed Roman manners and is studied for its colloquial language. Tacitus is usually regarded as Rome's greatest historian. He is most renowned for his *Annals* and his *Histories*, which together narrated the events of the reigns of the emperors from Servius Sulpicius Galba to Domitian. His *Germania* was an account of the life and manners of the ancient Germans; and his *Agricola*, the life of his father-in-law, the conqueror of Britain, was a fine biography. Tacitus was usually sound in facts but partial in interpretation. The brevity, variety, and poetic color of his style are unique and arresting.

The poets of the Silver Age turned to epics, satires, and epigrams. The *Pharsalia* of Lucan, a brilliant epic poem marred by conceits and antitheses, discussed the civil war between Julius Caesar and Pompey the Great. It was followed by a mildly successful epic, the *Thebaid* of Publius Papinius Statius. More representative of the period perhaps are the scathing satires of Juvenal and the biting epigrams of Martial.

With the decline of the Silver Age, postclassical Latin was at hand, to be succeeded by medieval Latin. See ROME AND THE ROMAN EMPIRE.

LATITUDE AND LONGITUDE. Position on the earth is determined in terms of latitude and longitude. Parallels (imaginary lines parallel to the Equator) are used to indicate latitude. Meridians (similar lines through the poles) are used to indicate longitude. Both latitude and longitude are measured in degrees.

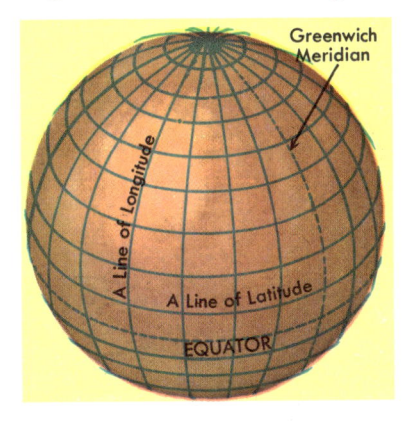

Latitude is measured from the Equator; longitude, from the Greenwich meridian.

Latitude is measured both north and south of the Equator. The Equator is the first parallel and is considered to be 0° latitude. There are, in all, 90 degrees of latitude from the Equator to the North Pole. Likewise, there are 90 degrees of latitude from the Equator to the South Pole. The length in miles of a degree of latitude at the Equator is 68.7; at the poles it is 69.4. The difference is due to the fact that the earth is slightly flattened at the poles.

Longitude is measured both east and west of the prime meridian, which runs through Greenwich, England, the location of the Royal Greenwich Observatory. This site was chosen as the point for projecting the prime meridian in 1884. The prime meridian represents 0° longitude. Westward the degrees are indicated to 180° west longitude; eastward the degrees are indicated to 180° east longitude. The international date line runs through but does not coincide with the 180th meridian. The length of a degree of longitude is 69.17 miles at the Equator. This length gradually reduces to zero as the meridians converge toward the poles.

LATVIA, a northern European country on the shores of the Baltic Sea, since 1940 a part of the Soviet Union. It has an area of about 25,000 square miles and a population of about 2,000,000. The capital is Riga; other chief towns are Liepaja, Daugavpils, and Jelgava. The country is mostly lowland, with hills in the east rising to 1,017 feet. The climate is moderately cool and damp. Dairy farming and livestock-raising are the principal occupations. Rye, barley, oats, potatoes, and flax are the main crops. One-fifth of the land is covered by forests, and lumbering is an important industry. Other industries are flour milling and meatpacking.

The Latvian S.S.R.'s flag shows Soviet ties.

About 60 percent of the people are Letts and belong to the Lutheran Church. About 15 percent are Latgals, speaking a dialect similar to Lettish, and are Roman Catholic. The rest of the people are Russians, Jews, and Lithuanians. There is a university at Riga, and there are six other schools of higher education in the country.

The independent republic of Latvia was founded in 1918 and became a member of the League of Nations in 1921. In 1940 an ultimatum from the Soviet Union led to the formation of a Latvian government friendly to Soviet control. This government asked for the admission of Latvia to the U.S.S.R. The U.S. government does not recognize the Soviet annexation. For detailed map, See UNION OF SOVIET SOCIALIST REPUBLICS.

LAUDER, SIR HARRY (1870-1950), was a Scottish actor, singer, and songwriter. He became one of the most popular entertainers of his day.

Lauder was born in Portobello, Scotland. He first worked as a coal miner, but his talent as a singer and actor soon caused him to choose entertaining as a career. Lauder joined a troupe of traveling players and made his first appearance in London in 1900. His clever songs, sense of humor, and comical appearance in kilts made him a quick success. Lauder specialized in singing Scottish songs. He wrote the words and music of many of them, including "Roamin' in the Gloamin'" and "I Love a Lassie."

Lauder made the first of his many tours of the United States in 1906. Two years later he sang before King Edward VII of Britain. He was knighted in 1919 for his work in entertaining the British armed forces in World War I. He again entertained troops in World War II.

LAUGHTER is a movement of the facial muscles, especially in the vicinity of the mouth, that is accompanied by a series of movements expelling air from the lungs and producing inarticulate sounds. Laughter is usually associated with relaxation of mind and body and a reduction in nervous tension. The psychology of laughter is not yet fully understood. There are many kinds of laughter, and it is difficult to generalize about the reasons for laughter. Only human beings have the nerve and muscle structures for laughter, although other animals may express similar feelings in other ways.

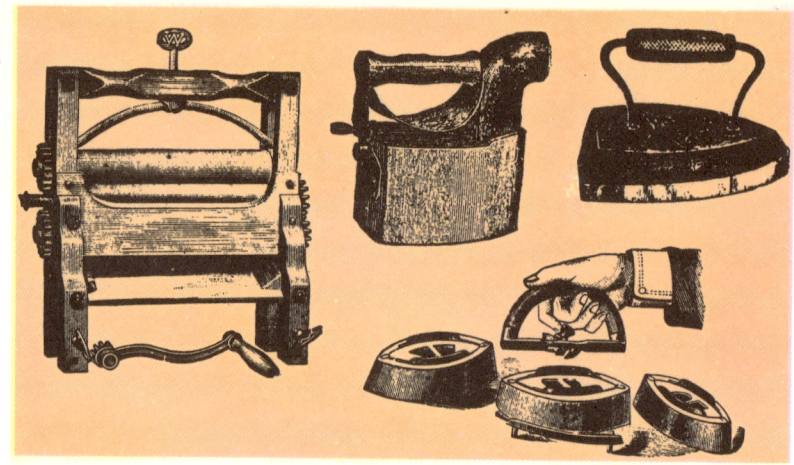

Courtesy of Montgomery Ward & Co.

This wringer and these irons were marketed in 1904. The wringer was turned by a hand crank. The iron with the high base was heated by charcoal that was put inside.

LAUNDRY AND IRONING. Laundry is the washing and drying of wearing apparel, household linens, and furnishings to remove dirt and to restore such items to a clean and usable state. Ironing is the process of pressing the surface of a newly laundered item, by the application of moisture and heat, into a smooth, even finish. Although there are commercial establishments that do this work, we are interested here in these activities as they take place in the home.

Centuries ago women took their soiled clothing and linens to the banks of the nearest stream or river to wash them. Here they knelt and beat the wet fabric against a rock to loosen the dirt. Women of early Gaul and Rome rubbed their laundry with a soap made of goat tallow and wood ash. After a few rinsings in the river, the clean laundry was spread out on the grass to be dried by the sun.

There are many areas of the world today where laundry is still done at the riverbank on a rock and dried in the sun. Ironing, if it is done at all, is with a heavy flatiron heated on a wood stove or in an open fire.

To do the laundry in grandmother's day, you needed wooden

African natives are washing their clothing at a public laundry in Mombasa, Kenya, Africa. Clothes can be washed free in the square tubs and then hung to dry in the ocean breeze.

Hans von Meiss—Photo Researchers

washtubs, a scrubboard, buckets of water boiled on the kitchen stove, lye soap, drying racks or clotheslines strung in the basement or yard, and a strong back. When ironing day came, two or three flatirons were heated on the stove simultaneously to maintain a constant supply of hot irons. Doing the family laundry was a long, hot, tedious job that took several days and left grandmother wilted and tired.

In those countries where the standard of living is high, science and technology have come to the aid of the homemaker, making her tasks easier and less time consuming. This is especially true in the United States, where home appliances designed for laundry and ironing needs are plentiful and may be purchased at relatively low cost.

The major appliance used for home laundry is the washing machine. There are three general types of machines on the market today: the automatic washer, requiring a minimum of attention; the semiautomatic washer, with hand-controlled operations; and the nonautomatic, noncycling (or conventional) type with a wringer. The nonautomatic washer can be used in any household that has electricity. The automatic and semiautomatic types require certain facilities that may not be available in all homes. Selection of a washing machine may depend upon personal preference, finances, and available facilities.

In addition to the washing process a method of drying the laundry is necessary. Here, too, a major home appliance is available. A washer-dryer combination is made in some models of automatic and semiautomatic washing machines. Separate-unit dryers are also popular. For the homemaker without a dryer a sufficiently large area, indoors or outdoors, is needed in order to stretch clotheslines high enough from the ground to allow the larger pieces of the laundry to hang freely. Clothesline poles of wood or metal may be needed to supply additional height. Clothespins of wood or plastic are used to fasten the laundry to the line. Even the user of a dryer may prefer to dry certain pieces on a clothesline, since not all fabrics or items of laundry may dry in the unit to the homemaker's satisfaction.

There are many types of soap and detergents sold. Some are made for specific washing machines, fabrics, or water conditions, while others take care of general laundry. It is up to the individual homemaker to select the product that gives her the cleanest laundry with the least amount of effort on her part.

The general procedure for doing the family laundry should start with the sorting of the clothes and linens. Items that require special washing are put to one side for later hand washing or for delicate-fabric cycling in the automatic washer. The machine-washed pieces are usually separated into loads of white cottons and linens, light-colored garments, dark-colored garments, very dirty pieces, and extremely heavy pieces, such as small rugs or blankets. Manufacturers' tags on new garments should be retained and checked before a first laundering to be sure that the garment can be washed and does not require special care.

After sorting the entire laundry, small tears should be mended. Machine washing may enlarge an unmended rip. Stains should also be removed before washing. Water and detergent may set a stain so it can never be removed. Snaps and zippers should be closed to prevent damage during washing.

Very dirty clothes may need soaking. The soaking method and the length of the soak depend on the condition of the clothes. Soaking for 10 to 15 minutes in soapy lukewarm water may be sufficient for some pieces, while others may need an overnight soak in clear cold water. Heavy stains may also be removed by the application of a paste, made of detergent and water, to the soiled area just prior to laundering.

The machine is filled with water, soap, and detergent after the load of laundry is put in. Manufacturers' instruction booklets have helpful directions as to the amount of soap and water to use and the weight of the load that the machine can efficiently wash. After the machine is started, it is wise to time the length of the washing period. An average of 10 minutes to 20 minutes for each load is usually sufficient.

New automatic washing machines are being tested for performance in an experimental laundry. Fabrics of all kinds and even washable rugs are laundered in the machines to make certain that the washing does not injure any fabric or fade its colors.

Courtesy of The Maytag Company

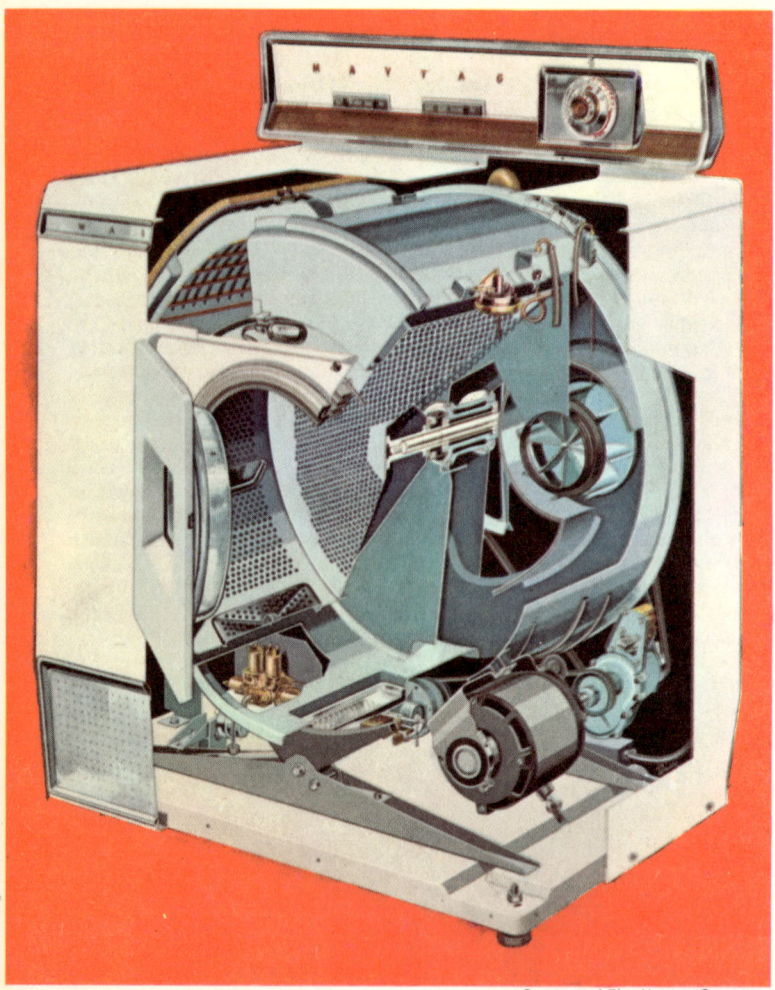

LAUNDRY AND IRONING

Courtesy of The Maytag Company

Clothes can be washed and dried at home in an automatic washer and dryer. The internal mechanism of this machine is shown above.

Courtesy of General Electric

Housewives have been pressing garments with electric hand irons for many years. To press garments properly without wrinkling them is a task that requires skill.

One of the two seemingly identical machines shown below is an automatic washer; the other is an automatic dryer. The chief tasks of the housewife who uses them are to load and unload them and to turn dials.

Courtesy of Westinghouse Electric Corporation

An automatic or semiautomatic washer has at least one deep-rinsing cycle, followed by a removal of excess water. The operator of a nonautomatic washer uses the wringer to remove the soapy water and then may use the washer tub or a laundry tub to rinse the pieces. A second rinse is good practice, especially if clothes are hand rinsed. Laundry should be wrung out after each rinsing.

Any items to be given a special finish are generally removed from the rest of the laundry. The original finish that the textile manufacturer gave to the fabric may be replaced by starching. This treatment is also an aid in ironing. The amount of starch needed depends on the stiffness desired, the kind and construction of fabric, the manner in which garments are to be used, and whether they are to be wrung by machine or by hand. Diluted solutions of gelatins, gum arabic, and gum tragacanth are often used to refinish voiles, organdies, batistes, and silks.

The laundry goes into the dryer for a controlled cycle, which depends upon the weight and texture of the load, or it is hung outside. Some laundry, such as prints, dark colors, and synthetics, should be hung in the shade. After the laundry is dry, it is well to fold the various items neatly, as some things may not require ironing if care is taken with the initial folding from the line or dryer. This is, however, a matter of personal taste.

Hand washing is often required for silks and synthetics, woolens, noncolor-fast prints, laces, combination synthetic and natural-fiber fabrics, and delicate personal apparel. Although each fabric may require special treatment, gentle sudsing with no rubbing or wringing is best for all of them. Garment manufacturers recommend drip drying for some synthetics. Woolens and knits are often dried flat to prevent stretching. Silks and prints may be wrapped in a towel to prevent colors from running.

Like laundry equipment, ironing equipment has found its place in the home-appliance market. The three types of electric hand irons that are now in use are the automatic iron, with a thermostat to control the temperature; the nonautomatic iron, with a simple heat-limiting device; and the steam iron, with a constant stream of steam emitted onto the ironing surface. The automatic steam iron combines the best features of both models into a steam-and-dry iron. While old flatirons depended upon the weight of the iron for efficiency, the modern electric hand iron weighs from 2 to 5 pounds, and it is more efficient.

Another appliance is the electric ironer, or mangle, which is made in a rotary model and a flat-press model. Ideal for flatwork, the ironer can also be used for more complicated pieces.

The user of a hand iron also needs an ironing board. Boards are of wood or metal, with a tapered end, and they usually have a height-adjustment mechanism in the legs. Proper height of the board is important in eliminating the "back-breaking" part of ironing. Sleeve-boards are portable miniatures of the ironing board. Both boards are covered with padding, and a piece of muslin or old sheeting is stretched over the entire board and fastened underneath. Silicone-treated covers, used over the padding, have greater heat reflection, but care must be taken when ironing synthetics that require cool temperatures.

It is well to sort the items to be ironed according to the required heat of the iron. A hotter iron may be used on cottons and linens. Rayons, synthetics, and combination fabrics must have a cooler iron. Some pieces, such as starched items, must be dampened before ironing; some acquire a better finish if dampened a small portion at a time as they are ironed; others are not dampened at all if pressed with a steam iron. Each fabric and garment requires individual attention to iron temperature, dampening, and procedure, and no hard and fast rules may be set for any entire ironing job. Personal preference may dictate more or less care of a particular item.

Proper folding and airing after ironing helps preserve the ironed finish of the laundry. A piece still damp or warm from ironing will not retain its crisp appearance if immediately placed in a closet, nor will improperly folded garments from an airtight drawer be ready to wear.

LAUREL, any tree of the laurel genus, especially the bay tree, or true laurel. The name *laurel* is also applied to some unrelated trees and shrubs similar to the laurels, including the mountain laurel and the great laurel.

The bay tree, which is the laurel of ancient Greek tradition, is an aromatic evergreen tree that grows from 40 to 60 feet high. Native to the Mediterranean region, this laurel has stiff, dull-green, pointed, oblong leaves between 2 and 4 inches long, small greenish-white flowers, and small black berries. In ancient Greece the leaves of this laurel were woven into garlands with which poets and the victors in athletic games were crowned. In later times the recipients of academic honors were crowned with laurel wreaths. Dried bay leaves have long been used to season soups, meats, and vegetables. Oil extracted from bay leaves is used in medicines.

The great laurel, an evergreen tree that may grow 40 feet high, is native to the woods and stream banks of eastern North America. Its flowers, which are 2 inches wide, range in color from rose to white and are spotted inside with yellow or orange. Its leaves, which contain the poison andromedotoxin that is used in medicine, may harm or kill sheep or other animals that eat them. The mountain laurel, an evergreen shrub that may attain a height of 30 feet and form dense thickets, grows in rocky, sandy, barren regions of eastern North America. Wreaths and strands of mountain laurel are used to decorate city streets at Christmas.

LAURIER, SIR WILFRED (1841-1919), Canadian statesman, born in St. Lin, Quebec. He was educated at McGill University and practiced law in Montreal and Arthabaska; he edited a French-language weekly newspaper at the same time. In 1871 he entered the Quebec legislature and in 1874 was elected to the federal Parliament at Ottawa as a Liberal. He soon made a reputation as a speaker and in 1877 was appointed to the Cabinet as minister of inland revenue. A few months later his party was defeated and remained out of office for 18 years. In 1887 Laurier was chosen leader of the Liberal party. In the election of 1896 his party was returned to power, with Laurier as prime minister, the first French-Canadian to serve in that office.

Although loyal to Great Britain, Laurier devoted his political life to guiding Canada toward an independent position in the British Empire. Under his government the last British troops were withdrawn from Canada, a Canadian navy was built, and Canada organized its own defense system and gained the right to negotiate its own treaties. In 1913, although out of office, Laurier helped defeat a bill for the gift of three battleships to the British navy. At the outbreak of World War I, when Canada joined in support of the mother country, Laurier gave the government his full support.

This is a sprig of a California laurel tree.

The photograph shows liquid lava in the crater of Kilauea, a volcano on the island of Hawaii, during the 1952 eruption. Usually the lava breaks through the side of the volcano and flows quietly down slope. Lavas that flow from Kilauea are very hot and fluid.

Above is a map showing exposures of igneous rocks in the United States. Many of the rocks are ancient lavas. On the top, right, is a lava called pahoehoe, which consists of ropelike, twisted masses. The rough, jagged lava in the middle is called aa. It is formed when thin crusts of flowing lava break, turn over, and are stuck together by liquid lava. Aa and pahoehoe are Hawaiian names. On the right, bottom, is a volcanic bomb, formed when a mass of liquid lava was thrown into the air by a volcano.

LAVA is molten rock that flows from a volcano or a fissure onto the earth's surface. Lava is also the solid rock that forms when the molten rock cools. Lava is an extrusive igneous rock.

Lavas of many different compositions, textures, and structures have been found. The names and compositions of the commonest lavas are listed in the entry on igneous rock. See IGNEOUS ROCK.

Lavas are often so fine grained that individual mineral crystals cannot be seen except with a microscope. Such fine-grained rocks have an aphanitic texture. They have a dull, stony appearance. Some lavas, or parts of a lava flow, have a glassy texture. Glassy rocks are smooth and compact. They are not made up of mineral crystals, like most rocks, but of a homogeneous congealed liquid. Many lavas have porphyritic textures. Larger mineral crystals, called phenocrysts, are included in a mass of much smaller mineral crystals, called the groundmass. The groundmass in some lavas is glassy rather than crystalline. Porphyritic lavas look spotted.

Rhyolite is a dense, light-colored lava when it has an aphanitic texture. It is often porphyritic with phenocrysts of quartz, potassium feldspar, and plagioclase feldspar. Rhyolites may be streaked or banded. The streaks or bands are groups of mineral crystals that were segregated from the rest of the rock while the lava was flowing. Obsidian is a glassy rock that has the same composition as rhyolite. A thick piece of obsidian looks black, but a very thin piece is translucent. Pumice is rhyolite glass that has many holes and sealed tubes created by expanding gases in the molten lava. There are so many cavities in pumice that a piece is very light for its size.

Trachyte is similar to rhyolite but never has quartz phenocrysts. Phonolite is lava that contains nepheline or other feldspathoid minerals.

Most andesites are dark gray or greenish gray and porphyritic with an aphanitic groundmass. Some andesites have a glassy groundmass. Andesites may have phenocrysts of plagioclase feldspar, pyroxene, amphibole, and biotite. The last three minerals are dark colored. Andesite lava may have flow banding or streaks.

Basalt is a medium-gray to black lava. Most basalt is aphanitic but not porphyritic. If the basalt is porphyritic, the phenocrysts are plagioclase feldspar, olivine (a greenish, glassy mineral), a pyroxene, and, in a few basalts, brown hornblende. Basalt glass, or tachylyte, is not common. It is black like obsidian. Unlike obsidian, a very thin piece of tachylyte is not translucent.

Rhyolite, trachyte, and phonolite are extruded from some types of volcanoes. Yellowstone National Park, in Wyoming, is on a plateau made up of rhyolitic lavas. Andesite lavas are very abundant in some volcano-capped mountain ranges, such as the Andes, the Cascade Range, and the Carpathian Mountains. Andesite was given its name because so much of it is found in the Andes. Basalts are the commonest lavas, and in many regions tremendous quantities of basalt lava can be found. Nearly all the lavas from Hawaiian volcanoes are basalt. In fact, the Hawaiian Islands are built almost entirely of layers of basalt.

Pahoehoe forms when stiffer surface lava is dragged forward by more liquid flowing lava.

Many great flows of basaltic lava did not come from volcanoes but from fissures not associated with volcanoes. The Columbia Plateau in Oregon, Washington, and Idaho is an area of 250,000 square miles built up by repeated outpourings of basalt from fissures.

Some rock structures are typical of lavas. Most rock with many holes, or vesicles, is lava. In some lavas the holes have been filled with minerals deposited after the lava was solid. Many basaltic lavas have a peculiar pattern of breaking, called columnar jointing. The whole lava flow may have a pattern of cracks that break the rock up into many-sided columns. The columns are upright. Not all rocks that show columnar jointing are lavas. Lava flows have rough, rugged surfaces unless they have been smoothed by erosion and weathering.

LAVOISIER, ANTOINE LAURENT

LAVOISIER, ANTOINE LAURENT (1743-1794), a French scientist and the founder of modern chemistry.

Lavoisier was born in Paris, the only son of well-to-do parents. He was educated in law at the Collège Mazarin. After he was graduated he turned to the study of the physical sciences and became a member of the Royal Academy of Sciences in 1768. He held public offices under both the French monarch and the revolutionists. Lavoisier was appointed director of the state gunpowder works in 1776. He became a farmer-general (a member of a private company that collected taxes for the monarchy) in 1779 and was appointed in 1790 to the commission that established the metric system. He became a commissary of the treasury in 1791. During the Reign of Terror Lavoisier was arrested as a former farmer-general and was guillotined.

Lavoisier is famous for his experiments with combustion. He discovered that combustion is a chemical reaction during which oxygen combines with a combustible substance. He disproved the phlogiston theory that materials burned because phlogiston escaped from them. He determined that water is a compound of oxygen and hydrogen and propounded a theory of the formation of chemical compounds. Lavoisier studied respiration and body heat in animals and correctly concluded that animal heat results from a process of slow combustion in the body. With three other scientists he devised the system of naming chemicals that is the basis of the present system.

Lavoisier investigated the relationship of human oxygen consumption to physical activity.
Courtesy of and © 1959, Parke, Davis & Co.

LAW

LAW is the body of rules for human conduct set up and enforced by the state, or in some cases by a religious organization. The rules may be derived from customs, from legislation, or from decisions of the courts. Contracts, registration and transfer of land ownership, inheritance and wills, marriage and divorce, partnerships and corporations, mortgages, bankruptcy, and trespassing are only some of the items regulated by law. Most of these subjects are classified as private law because they concern relationships between individuals. However, other types of law, such as constitutional law and criminal law, directly concern the state. The state prosecutes a burglar or a murderer because all crime is regarded as injuring the security of the whole society as well as an individual. In contrast to criminal law private law is sometimes called civil law.

Law has existed in every politically organized society. In some primitive societies the infraction of certain rules calls forth a penal sanction by the community. Scholars know of Egyptian and Babylonian law dating from 3000 B.C.; the famous law code of the Babylonian king Hammurabi was written on stone about 2100 B.C. The Greek city-states also had their individual laws, but the best known and most important of all the ancient systems of law was the Roman, for from it developed, directly and indirectly, much of contemporary European law. The latter is also called civil law.

Two great landmarks in the development of Roman law were the Twelve Tables, written about 450 B.C., and the *Corpus Juris Civilis*, codified under Justinian, A.D. 528-534. In the Twelve Tablets the law of Rome was first put into writing. Roman law had grown tremendously by the time of the Emperor Justinian, who ordered it organized and clarified. Thus, one of the books of the *Corpus Juris Civilis*, the *Codex*, contained all enactments (of previous emperors) still valid at Justinian's time; the *Digest* consisted of selections from the writings of legal scholars, writings that began about A.D. 150; the *Institutes* was an introductory legal textbook; and the *Novels*, published in 535 and after, contained new legislation.

After the fall of the Roman Empire some aspect of Roman law continued to hold in parts of Europe. Furthermore, canon law, the law of the Roman Catholic Church, which included much Roman law, governed many matters in medieval Europe that are today regulated by the state. In its turn, canon law contributed new theories and practices to European law, particularly in the spheres of marriage, con-

---

OCCUPATION: Lawyer

NATURE OF WORK: Representing private and business clients and advising them of their legal rights and duties

PERSONAL FACTORS—ABILITIES, SKILLS, APTITUDES: A high degree of intelligence, a genuine interest in law, an understanding of human nature, and the ability to reason and correlate are essential.

EDUCATION AND SPECIAL TRAINING: Two to three years of prelaw training, followed by three years in an approved law school, are required. Specialization in civil law, corporate, or criminal may follow law school. In all states a written examination must be passed before admission to the bar.

WORKING CONDITIONS:
1. **INCOME:**
   COMPARED WITH OTHER CAREERS WITH EQUAL TRAINING: Average
   COMPARED WITH MOST OTHER CAREERS: Average to high
2. **ENVIRONMENT:** Comfortable indoor surroundings; possible travel; various types of clients
3. **OTHER:** Possibly irregular hours

RELATED CAREERS: Insurance adjuster, tax collector, probation officer, credit investigator, claims examiner, land agent

WHERE TO FIND MORE INFORMATION: The American Bar Association, 1155 East 60th Street, Chicago 37, Ill.

tracts, and court procedure. In the 12th century growth of trade required new laws, and scholars turned to the collection of laws later called *Corpus Juris Civilis.* As a result, more Roman law was adopted and adapted throughout Europe. This process culminated in the 19th century with the codification of French law in the Code Napoleon and other codes, and the codification of German law. The French codes were imitated all over Europe and in Latin America, and the German code of 1900 influenced law in Switzerland, Greece, Turkey, and Japan.

In addition to canon law two other religious legal systems have been influential—Jewish law and Islamic law. Both laws contained many subjects other than strictly religious ones. Until the 18th century, Jewish law regulated not only religious and family but commercial life in Jewish communities throughout Europe. At present it operates for the Jewish community in Israel in matters of marriage, divorce, and probate of wills and among Orthodox Jews in religious, matrimonial, and a few other matters. Islamic law governed the world empire of Islam in the early Middle Ages and still governs many Islamic communities throughout the world. In Pakistan a government commission has been established to examine legislation for contradictions with the traditional Islamic law.

The only other legal system as important as the Roman is the English. English law, or law derived from it, prevails in England and the Commonwealth Nations and in all countries, such as the United States, that were English colonies (except such places as Louisiana, Quebec, and South Africa originally settled by the French or the Dutch).

English law has two main divisions, the common law and equity. The common law is so named because, unlike local custom, it was common to the whole country. The development of English common law became possible only in the 12th century when the king's courts, whose decisions formed the common law, became the highest courts of the country. By the 18th century the common law had emerged as a distinctive system, having its own trial procedure, which included trial by jury, and principles of law. This law (which began with local Anglo-Saxon customs, Norman law, and some Roman law) grew mostly through the decisions of the judges. A judge would often base his decision on previous decisions in similar cases. This manner of making law is a distinctive characteristic of the whole English law, whether in England, the United States, Canada or elsewhere. The decisions to which judges refer are called precedents. Frequently no previous ruling fits a new case, and the judge makes an independent decision which may in turn become a precedent.

The other division of English law, equity, grew out of certain lacks in the common law. For example, under common law a person could usually obtain only damages for harm already done; the common-law courts could not prevent someone from doing harm—from breaking a contract, for instance. Therefore people who could not obtain justice in the common-law courts began to appeal to the king, who referred the cases to the chancellor, the king's chief secretary. By the 15th century these cases went directly to the chancellor, who heard them in a special court, the court of chancery. Not only did equity law as developed in the court of chancery provide special remedies, but the entire procedure differed from the common-law courts. The chancellor questioned the parties directly, and there was no jury. By the 17th century it was decided that in case of conflict between rules of equity and the common law, equity was supreme. By the 19th century both equity and common-law systems had become complicated and cumbersome. Laws passed in England in 1873 and 1875 merged the common-law courts with the chancery court, along with the admiralty court and the court handling probate and divorce cases. Now any judge can administer either equity or common-law, whichever suits the case, and courtroom procedure is usually the same. In the United States various state acts, beginning with the New York Code of Procedure of 1848, have joined equity and common law to a large extent. In the federal courts and in many states, however, there are still separate procedures for equity and common-law cases.

There remains one important system of law not yet mentioned, that of the U.S.S.R. It consists of various codes—criminal, civil, family, marriage and divorce, labor, and others —based upon the Marxist analysis of the law as the tool of the state. See INTERNATIONAL LAW; MARITIME LAW.

LAWNMOWER, a machine used to cut the grass of lawns. A lawnmower consists of a framework set on wheels, a series of cutting blades, gears, and a handle for steering or propelling the mower. Power mowers also have a motor or engine.

The simplest lawnmower is the reel-type hand mower. It has two wheels joined by an axle. A long handle is attached to the axle. A number of curved blades, usually five, six, or seven, are attached to the axle and are called the reel. There is also a roller at the back of the reel and a bar at the front. The bar is to protect the reel and to prevent children or pets from being injured by the blades. As the mower is propelled forward by a person pushing on the handle, the wheels turn. The wheels, through gears and bearings, cause the blades to turn and cut grass.

Reel mowers are sometimes powered by internal-combustion engines. The engine is placed on a frame above the reel. Reel power mowers are available in several sizes. The engines are usually about 2 horsepower.

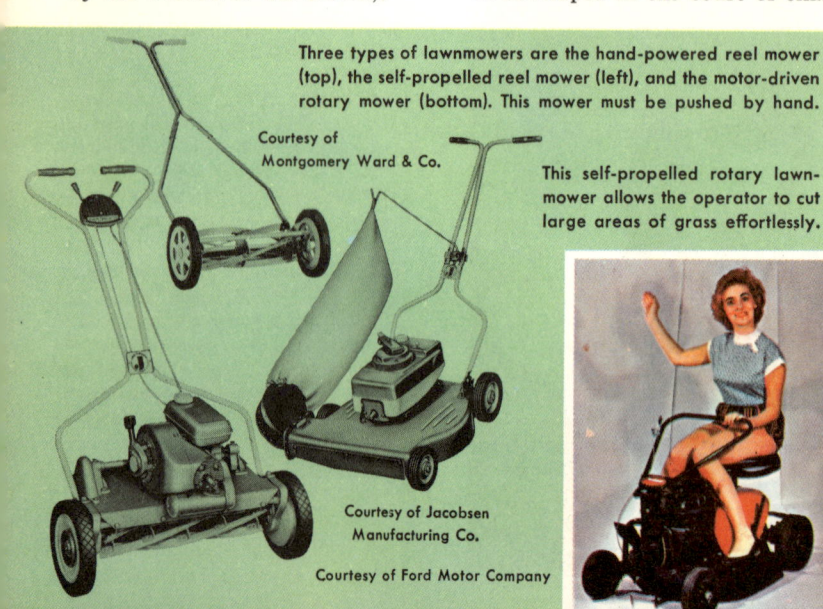

Three types of lawnmowers are the hand-powered reel mower (top), the self-propelled reel mower (left), and the motor-driven rotary mower (bottom). This mower must be pushed by hand.

Courtesy of Montgomery Ward & Co.

This self-propelled rotary lawnmower allows the operator to cut large areas of grass effortlessly.

Courtesy of Jacobsen Manufacturing Co.

Courtesy of Ford Motor Company

Most power lawnmowers are rotary mowers. A rotary mower usually has three flat blades. The blades, which operate something like fan blades, are fastened on the underside of a frame and engine. The blades are rotated parallel to the ground. The blades are designed to create a current of air when they are in motion and cutting grass. The air current picks up cut grass and carries it out one side of the mower.

Rotary power mowers are manufactured in several styles. In some, the engine drives only the cutting blades. The mower must be pushed by handles from place to place. Other rotary power mowers are self-propelled. The engine turns the wheels as well as the blades. Self-propelled mowers have handles for steering. The engines develop about 3 horsepower. Some self-propelled power mowers are built so that the operator rides on the mower. Riding mowers have engines that develop 4 to 7 horsepower. The more expensive riding mowers are capable of cutting several acres of grass an hour and are elaborate machines.

Most power mowers have internal-combustion engines. A few are made with electric motors. Such a mower has a long cord to connect the motor to a source of electricity.

LAWRENCE, D. H. (1885-1930), in full David Herbert Lawrence, a 20th-century English novelist. His novels are an indictment of industrial society and the effect industrialism has on the relationship between men and women. This was apparent in Lawrence's first mature novel, *Sons and Lovers*, published in 1913. It is an autobiographical work of Lawrence's early life in Nottinghamshire, where his father was a coal miner and his mother was a schoolteacher.

Lawrence's almost mystical belief in the communion possible between man and woman appears, perhaps better than anywhere else, in his novel of 1920, *Women in Love*. From that year until the year he died, Lawrence traveled in Europe and America with his wife, Frieda. He was in these ten years enormously prolific. His novels include *The Plumed Serpent* (a haunting novel of Mexico) and *Lady Chatterley's Lover*. Other works include the short stories in *The Woman Who Rode Away;* poems in *Birds, Beasts, and Flowers;* a book of travel, *Sea and Sardinia;* and a reevaluation of American literature, *Studies in Classic American Literature.* Always weak, Lawrence sought the warm climates of Mexico and Arizona in the last years of his life. He died of tuberculosis.

LAWRENCE, ERNEST (1901-1958), American physicist, born in Canton, S.D. He received his doctorate in physics from Yale University in 1925 and joined the University of California faculty in 1928. In 1930, in collaboration with Milton S. Livingston, Lawrence perfected the cyclotron, a device used to bring about transmutations of elements and to produce artificial radioactivity. In 1932 Lawrence founded a radiation laboratory at Berkeley, Calif., in conjunction with the university. He became its director in 1936. During the following years successively larger and more powerful cyclotrons were built. The usefulness of the cyclotron to medicine, particularly in the field of cancer treatment, became apparent largely as the result of research commenced during the late 1930's by Ernest Lawrence's brother John Lawrence.

On the eve of World War II Ernest Lawrence was appointed to the project that developed the uranium-fission bomb. The isolation of the isotope uranium-235, a process crucial to the project, was accomplished by means of several especially adapted cyclotrons.

Postwar advances in nuclear research that occurred at the Berkeley laboratory during Lawrence's directorship include the creation in 1948 of the first artificial (manmade) meson. After 1946 Lawrence served as an adviser to the Atomic Energy Commission and the Knolls Atomic Power Laboratory. He received the Nobel prize for physics in 1939.

LAWRENCE, JAMES (1781-1813), American naval officer, born in Burlington, N.J. Lawrence entered the Navy in 1798 as a midshipman aboard the *Ganges*. His reputation for gallantry, which increased in later years, was established during the Tripolitan War by his participation in several daring naval operations. Promoted steadily following the war, he commanded successively the *Vixen, Wasp, Argus,* and *Hornet.* During the early months of the War of 1812 the *Hornet* captured several British merchant ships and sank the *Peacock*, British brig-of-war. In March, 1813, Lawrence received his final promotion, to the rank of captain, and was later assigned to the *Chesapeake*. Although ordered to intercept British merchant ships en route to Canada, Lawrence decided instead to attack the *Shannon*, a British frigate blockading Boston Harbor. During the ensuing battle, which resulted in the defeat of the *Chesapeake,* Lawrence was mortally wounded. His words, "Don't give up the ship," uttered as he was carried below, became a rallying cry of the Navy of the United States.

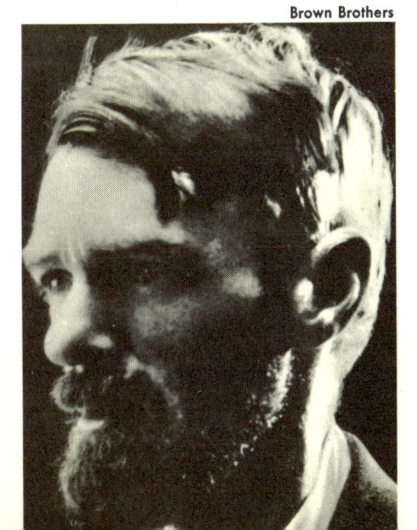

Franklin D. Roosevelt Library, Hyde Park, N. Y.
Hand-to-hand fighting ensued when the British boarded Lawrence's ship, the *Chesapeake.*

D. H. Lawrence
Brown Brothers

LAWRENCE, THOMAS EDWARD

(1888-1935), known as Lawrence of Arabia, British scholar, soldier, and author, born in Wales. He won legendary fame as a leader of the Arabs in their revolt against Turkey during World War I.

As a promising young archaeologist he visited the old castles of the crusaders in Palestine, about which he planned to write a doctoral dissertation. The Near East made a profound impression on him. Lawrence learned Arabic and took a liking to the Arabian people. At the outbreak of World War I he was employed in Egypt as a British intelligence officer. In 1916 he was sent to help the Arab leader Faisal, who later became king of Iraq, in his revolt against the Turks. Lawrence dressed, ate, and spoke as an Arab. He trained an efficient Arabian army that was suited to desert warfare and traveled on camels. This army drove the Turkish garrisons from the Arabian cities and cut their lines of communication by destroying many railroads and bridges. Lawrence's Arabs pushed the Turks far to the north, and in 1918 he was the first to enter the important city of Damascus, now in Syria.

In the peace treaties following World War I the British and their allies refused to grant the Arabs the freedom they had been promised. Lawrence was so angered at what he considered a great injustice to the Arabs that he retired from public life and even changed his name to T. E. Shaw. He came out of retirement to work as a mechanic in the Royal Air Force. He formed friendships with Winston Churchill and Bernard Shaw. Lawrence died in a motorcycle accident. The fascinating account of his adventures, *The Seven Pillars of Wisdom*, was published for the general public only after his death.

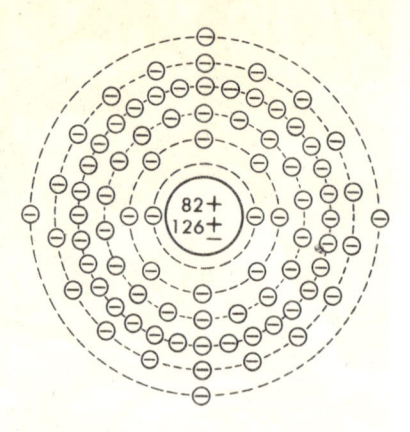

Galena crystals

Anglesite

This diagram of a lead atom shows how the 82 electrons (−) are arranged around a nucleus of 82 protons (+) and 126 neutrons. Lead has atomic number 82; the atomic weight of the most abundant isotope is 208. Lead is in Group IVB, Period VI of the periodic table of the elements.

LEAD, a silvery metallic element, with the symbol Pb (from the Latin *plumbum*, meaning "lead"). The principal ore of lead is galena, lead sulfide, PbS. Lead and zinc are commonly associated in mineral deposits. Major deposits are in the United States, Mexico, Australia, and Canada. There are also deposits in Europe, Asia, and Africa.

Lead is one of the heaviest of metals and also one of the softest. It is easily cut, cast, rolled, and extruded. Small amounts of other elements, such as copper, increase its hardness. The melting point of lead is low, 327° C. Lead oxidizes rapidly, but the oxide coating protects it from corrosion. It also resists attack by many acids. For these reasons lead is useful in building construction and for pipes and cable sheaths and for making lead chambers in chemical plants. Lead is also used in storage batteries, paint, shot, solder, and type metal and other alloys. Because of its high density, lead is used for protection against X-rays.

Lead as a useful metal dates from prehistoric times. The Egyptians used it for glazing pottery as early as 5000 B.C., the Chinese used it before 3000 B.C. An important use of lead by the Romans was for plumbing.

All soluble lead compounds are very poisonous. Lead poisoning, or plumbism, is one of the oldest of all industrial diseases. All persons

Galena, a lead mineral, can be easily recognized by its cubic cleavage, softness, and heaviness. Anglesite, $PbSO_4$, may form concentric earthy layers around galena cubes.

handling products containing lead should take special precautions. However, the mere presence of lead in a product such as paint does not mean that the user will get lead poisoning. Atmospheric contamination is the source of lead poisoning, and when adequate amounts of lead are present in the atmosphere, or when lead accumulates on the hands and is taken into the mouth, lead poisoning will result.

LEAF, a plant organ wherein, by means of photosynthesis, food is manufactured and solar energy is converted into chemical energy. Leaves grow on all angiospermous and gymnospermous trees, bushes, and herbs, on ferns, and on some plants lower in the evolutionary scale.

A typical leaf is composed of a broad, green, paper-thin blade that is mounted on a slender, round stalk called a petiole. Some leaves have no petiole; their blade is attached directly to the stem. Such leaves are termed sessile. A leaf contains a complex network of veins that ramify from the petiole. The petiole connects the veins with the stem. The veins conduct water and dissolved minerals from the petiole to the leaf; they also conduct manufactured food from leaf to petiole.

Leaf blades vary in size. There are the small ones of the violet and the large ones of the catalpa tree. They also vary greatly in shape. Their margins may be without indentation, as are those of the lilac bush. The margin of the elm leaf has many tiny indentations, which resemble the teeth of a saw. The oak leaf has a few broad, deep indentations, which extend almost to its midline. The needles of the pine, spruce, and other evergreens are really their leaves. The leaves of grasses are their tall, slim blades. The iris leaf is tall and sword-shaped. The leaf of the onion is a tall, slender tube.

A simple leaf has a blade that is all in one piece. Elm, maple, and oak leaves are simple. The blade of a compound leaf is composed of three or more distinct leaflets. Walnut, rose, and chestnut leaves are compound. The compound leaves of sumac and ash look like plumes.

A typical leaf consists of four distinct layers of tissue, each of which is composed of many microscopic cells. The top and bottom layers prevent the evaporation of water from the leaf and protect the softer internal layers. One internal layer of tissue is called the palisade layer because its oblong, vertical cells resemble the posts of a palisade. The palisade cells are filled with tiny bodies that are called chloroplasts because they contain the green pigment chlorophyll, which imparts to the leaf its green color. Within the palisade cells occurs photosynthesis, which is the manufacture of sugar from carbon dioxide and water and the conversion of solar energy into the chemical energy of this sugar. Chlorophyll is the essential agent for photosynthesis. The other internal layer of tissue consists of spongy, thin-walled cells that contain chloroplasts. Photosynthesis also occurs within these spongy cells.

A leaf is a vitally important organ because by means of photosynthesis its chlorophyllose cells manufacture the food and obtain the energy that is required for the life and growth of a tree, bush, or herb.

In the Temperate Zones the leaves of deciduous trees change color during autumn from green to yellow, orange, red, or brown. Soon afterward they fall to the earth. Botanists have discovered many of the causes of these phenomena.

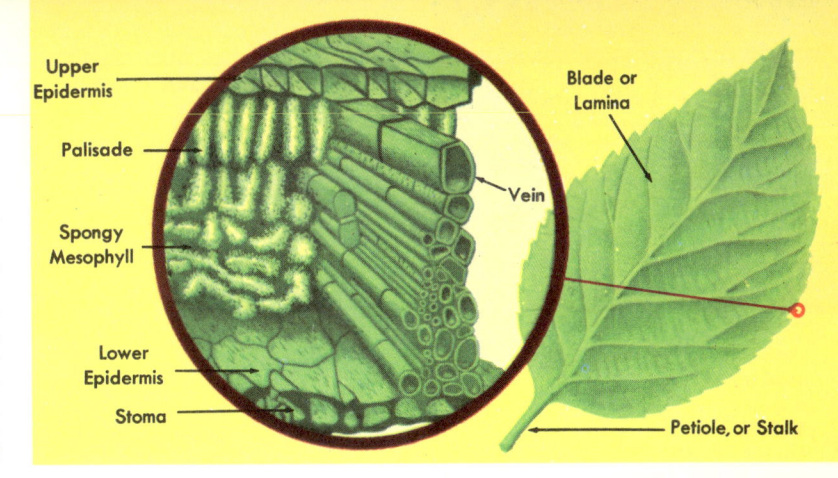

Besides chlorophyll the chloroplasts of the leaf cells also contain yellow and orange pigments. During summer the green chlorophyll obscures these other pigments. However, as autumn approaches and the air becomes colder and the days shorter, the chloroplasts are no longer able to replace chlorophyll that has been destroyed by sunlight, and the yellow and orange pigments finally become visible. Certain leaves turn red because the colder air and the increased atmospheric moisture of autumn cause a red pigment to form for the first time in the vacuoles of their cells. Leaves turn brown when their tissues die and tannic acid forms within them.

Leaves fall during autumn because of the disintegration of a thin layer of cells, called the abscission layer, that is located near the base of their petioles. Cool air and decreasing soil moisture cause gradual disintegration of the abscission layer until it becomes so weak that the wind breaks it and the leaf falls. Frost sometimes hastens the disintegration of the abscission layers and the fall of leaves. See CHLOROPHYLL; PHOTOSYNTHESIS.

Leaves differ greatly in shape and size. The leaf of the primitive ginkgo, or maidenhair, tree is fan shaped and indented. The leaves of the balsam fir and white pine are needle shaped. The leaves of the honey locust and the tree of heaven are compound.

The League of Nations was housed in these buildings in Geneva, Switzerland.

LEAGUE OF NATIONS, an international organization founded as a part of the peace settlement after World War I and formally inaugurated at Paris on Jan. 10, 1920. The formal dissolution of the League was voted by League Assembly on Apr. 18, 1946, at which time its activities were transferred to the United Nations.

According to the League's covenant the signers of the document agreed to refrain from war, to organize the peace, to discharge those special duties imposed upon them by the peace settlement of 1919-1920, and to promote international cooperation. Moreover, permanent machinery was established to implement these pledges. That machinery included the Assembly, which was to meet at Geneva in neutral Switzerland. However, the Assembly, which was supposedly something of a parliament, had little power. Not even its cabinet, the Council, was responsible to it. Within the Council the great powers exercised the controlling influence, for the great powers were designated permanent members. Such members at first included Great Britain, France, Italy, Japan, and the United States, although the last eventually refused to join the League; later the U.S.S.R. and Germany were accorded permanent seats. (The refusal of the United States to participate was based on Senate opposition to Article 10 of the covenant, which the Senate leadership feared would involve the United States in unnecessary and disastrous foreign wars.) The third major arm of the League was the Secretariat, which was the office force of the League. In close association with the League was the Permanent Court of International Justice, which had as its meeting place The Hague. The other important associate of the League was the International Labor Office, which was designed to improve the conditions of labor throughout the world.

While the prevention of war was the primary purpose for which the League was created, war was not altogether forbidden. Even when an armed conflict was obviously an illegal war, the League, which had no armed forces, could act only through moral sanctions and economic boycotts. This limited power, however, enabled the League to mediate with considerable success in disputes between the lesser powers. In 1920, for example, a dispute between Finland and Sweden over the Aland Islands in the Baltic Sea was settled by awarding the islands to Finland. On the other hand, the League was highly unsuccessful in mediating disputes involving great or near-great powers. In 1931 Japan, recognizing the weaknesses of the League, invaded and occupied Manchuria, and in 1935 and 1936 Fascist Italy attacked Ethiopia. In both instances the League was virtually powerless to cope with the situation; France and Britain, the main supporters of the League, could not even agree on the advisability of applying economic sanctions against Benito Mussolini, the Italian dictator. Seeing the impotence of the League, Adolf Hitler and the Nazi party, which had seized control of Germany, embarked upon a program that eventually destroyed the League. In 1940, after the fall of France, Secretary General Joseph Avenol of France and his staff resigned. See INTERNATIONAL LAW; UNITED NATIONS.

LEAR, EDWARD (1812-1888), an English author and artist, born in London. He is best remembered for his limericks, a type of nonsense verse. (See LIMERICK.) He became well known in his day as an illustrator of animals, particularly birds, and as a landscape painter. He also traveled frequently and wrote several books about his tours. His fame, however, rests on his limericks and other verses, which he published in such volumes as *The Book of Nonsense* and *Nonsense Songs, Stories, Botany, and Alphabets*.

The basic types of learning curves represent different patterns of learning: 1, convex curve—rapid, then slower learning; 2, S-curve—rapid learning, almost no learning, then rapid learning again; 3, concave curve—slow, then more rapid learning.

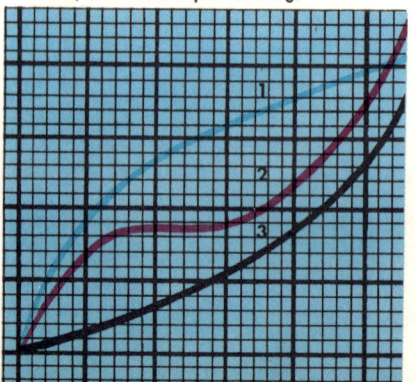

LEAGUE OF NATIONS

LEARNING AND FORGETTING. Learning is the modification of later behavior by earlier behavior. Psychological studies of learning involve attempts to measure learning and to clarify the relationship of learning to motivation, practice, transfer of training, and so forth. Forgetting is the loss of what has been learned.

In the commonest sense learning is improvement through practice in the performance of an act. In a broader sense learning is any change in response to the environment resulting from previous experience. In this sense learning includes both improvement and decline, or the acquiring of bad habits. Psychologists generally distinguish between verbal learning, or memory, and motor learning, or the acquiring of skills. However, this distinction is not clearly defined.

Man's greater capacity and need for learning give him a tremendous advantage over lower animals. Although lower animals may be able to learn, they are almost completely dependent on their instincts for survival. On the other hand, man has few instincts and so must learn almost all his ways of behaving. A change in instinctive behavior may require millions of years in the course of evolution. But through his capacity for learning man is able to adapt readily to new situations and to transmit a culture from generation to generation.

Since about 1920 experimental psychologists have devoted more research to the subject of learning than to any other subject. They measure learning in terms of accomplishment, as expressed by increases in amount, speed, or accuracy. Results of experiments on learning are often shown by learning curves, or graphs on which amount, time, or errors are plotted against the number of trials.

Learning is affected by several factors, including motivation, practice, and transfer of training. Motivation is essential to the learning process because it causes the activity that leads to learning and, accompanied by reward for desired activity and punishment for undesired activity, it gives direction to the learning process. Among human beings the intent to learn and the knowledge of results are important.

Repetition, or practice, is necessary for learning most activities. Distributed practice, or practice occurring at time intervals, is consistently found to be superior to massed practice, or practice occurring all at one time. Transfer of training is the effect of practice in one activity on performance of another. Positive transfer, or facilitation of learning by previous learning, occurs in a variety of learning situations.

Forgetting is measured by decrease in accomplishment. It was once thought that behavior is forgotten only according to the amount of time that has passed since the behavior was learned. The first serious studies of forgetting, by the 19th-century German psychologist Hermann Ebbinghaus, showed that forgetting is very rapid at first and then less and less rapid with the passage of time. Ebbinghaus constructed forgetting curves—graphs showing how material was forgotten with the passage of time—to show his results.

Later research has shown that rates of forgetting depend upon activity after the learning occurs. Thus less is forgotten during sleep than during waking hours. This fact indicates that forgetting is the obliteration of old associations and behavior patterns by new impressions. However, there is evidence that a person never forgets anything completely but retains a trace of everything he has ever learned.

LEATHER, hides and skins of animals prepared for manufacture into useful and artistic objects. *Hides* generally refers to the skins of larger animals, such as horses and cattle; *skins,* to those of goats, sheep, pigs, and calves. Leather is also made from the skins of the seal, ostrich, snake, and shark.

Leathermaking is probably man's oldest manufacturing industry. The Chinese, Egyptians, Greeks, and Romans all made leather. Nowadays newly developed chemicals and dyes are used in the production of leathers that are stronger and more beautiful than any the world has ever known. (See TANNING.) Most often a tannery will produce leather from only one type of hide or skin: cattle hide, calfskin, kidskin, goatskin, horsehide, or even alligator skin. This is so because quite different equipment and chemical processes are required to produce different types of leather. The various leathers are used for different purposes. For example, cattle and calf leathers are produced for shoes, luggage, and upholstery; sheepskins are converted into leather for garments, handbags, slippers, shoe linings, and bookbindings. About 83 percent of the leather made in the United States goes into the tops and soles of shoes.

Courtesy of American Cyanamid Company, Organic Chemical Division

The basic principles of tanning, as shown in this old print, have not changed.

A cross section of calfskin is shown (top) just after the packer removes it from a carcass. The bottom picture shows a cross section of the finished calf leather.
Courtesy of B. D. Eisendrath Tanning Co.

Below is shown one of the last of many operations at the tannery. These workers are polishing the grain surface of the leather. The leather will then be ironed and examined by expert sorters, who will sort it into skins of varying thickness and quality.

The workers above are trimming off those portions of the skins that are not suitable for making good leather and are sorting the skins preparatory to their processing. The skins will next be soaked to remove curing salt. This is the first of many processes.
Courtesy of Leather Industries of America

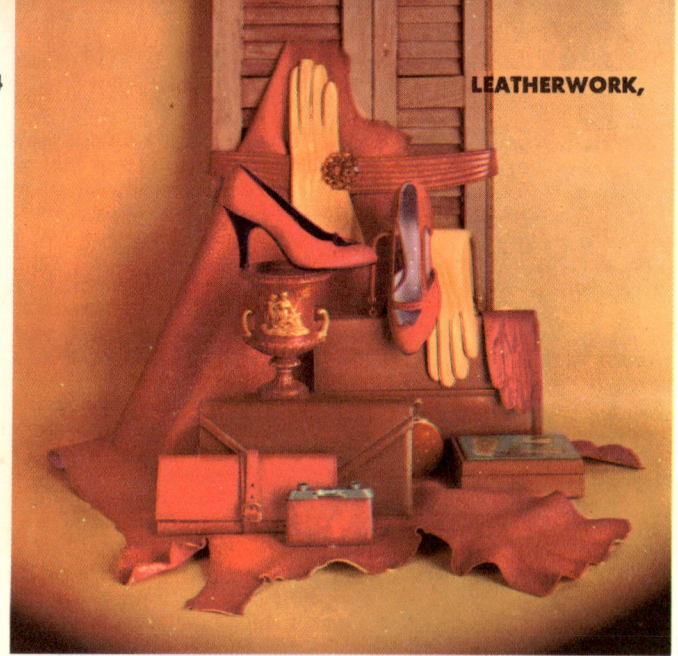

LEATHERWORK,

Courtesy of Leather Industries of America

This collection represents the wide range of quality consumer goods made from leather.

Despite the intense competition that it now faces from rubber and the artificial textiles, leather is still a premium product and in great demand. The United States does not produce enough different types of hides and skins to satisfy its needs. Millions of hides—goat, sheep, kangaroo, and reptile—are imported annually from all parts of the world and tanned in U.S. plants. Leather is popular because it is tough and resists scuffing but is soft, beautiful, and easy to clean. Supple leather is used in shoes, belts, jackets, and coats that must take hard wear but keep their neat appearance. Leather is a comfortable shoe material because it "breathes in" fresh air through millions of tiny pores in the natural skin. Leather's strength and flexibility make it useful for sporting goods such as baseballs, footballs, and bowling shoes, as well as for belts for industrial machinery. Leather goods can be bought in many permanent, washable colors.

LEATHERWORK, the making of articles from vegetable-tanned leathers. Animal skins most commonly used in leather handicraft are from the calf, cow, sheep, morocco goat, steer, and pig. The softer, more pliable of these skins are also useful for linings. The different properties of tanned leathers—their pliability, texture, and strength—should be known before any actual work is begun. Thus, calf is soft and smooth; its surface is lustrous, and it wears well. Cowhide is tougher and heavier; its surface has a dull gloss. Sheepskin is soft and porous; it tools very well but is not suitable for carving. Morocco goatskin is a durable leather used for billfolds, purses, and other small, useful articles. Its hand-grained texture is very pleasing.

Leather skins or hides have two surfaces—the grain side, or outer surface, and the flesh side. The grain side is usually used as the outer surface of a finished article.

The skins of unborn sheep and lambs retain the natural hair of the animal and are therefore excellent materials for linings.

Tooling and carving should be done on leathers tanned by vegetable bark, for these skins absorb moisture and retain imprints after they have dried. Tooling consists in making impressions on moist leather. A design is transferred from paper, or some other medium, to the damp leather by means of a sharp-pointed tool. The background may be depressed or stippled, or the design itself may be embossed for further decorative effects. Designs may also be stamped on leather or carved by hand. In carving, unlike tooling, the surface is cut with a sharp knife, not merely dented. Then the background is stamped flat to make the design stand out. Dyed leather is not appropriate for carving, since the undyed layer shows through when the surface is cut.

Various types of articles may be made by the beginner in leatherwork. Wallets, coin purses, and comb cases are some of the simpler ones. More ambitious projects include making moccasins, suede jackets, and book covers. Patterns for leatherwork may be drawn by hand or copied from another source.

This handsomely finished knife sheath is one of a number of useful articles that can be made by the beginning leatherworker. The diagrams show how you can make your own tools. Interesting designs can be developed by using the two stamps in different combinations.

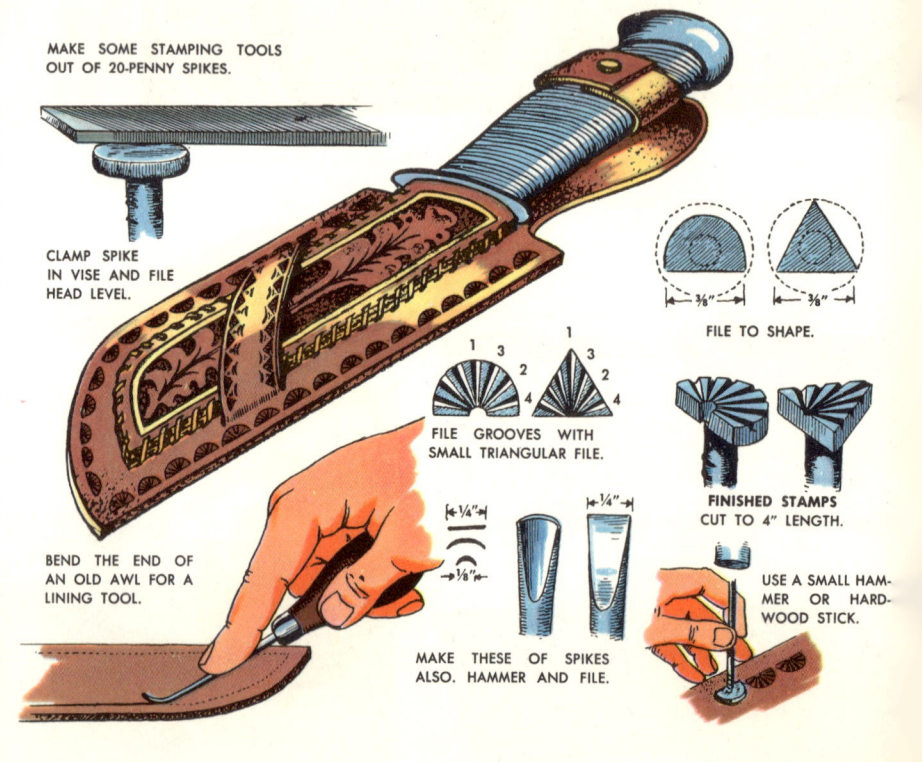

MAKE SOME STAMPING TOOLS OUT OF 20-PENNY SPIKES.

CLAMP SPIKE IN VISE AND FILE HEAD LEVEL.

FILE TO SHAPE.

FILE GROOVES WITH SMALL TRIANGULAR FILE.

FINISHED STAMPS CUT TO 4" LENGTH.

BEND THE END OF AN OLD AWL FOR A LINING TOOL.

MAKE THESE OF SPIKES ALSO. HAMMER AND FILE.

USE A SMALL HAMMER OR HARDWOOD STICK.

LEBANON

LEBANON is a small independent republic of western Asia located on the eastern shore of the Mediterranean Sea. A long and colorful history, a pleasant climate, and magnificent scenery make Lebanon a favorite country for tourists. The republic's area is about 4,000 square miles. Its population numbers about 1,600,000.

About 70 percent of Lebanon is mountainous. Behind the narrow coastal lowland rise the Lebanon Mountains, which reach 10,000 feet and run the entire length of the country. Farther east the Anti-Lebanon chain runs along the boundary with Syria. Between the two mountain ranges lies the fertile Bekaa. This high valley, watered by the Litani River in the south and the Orontes River in the north, is the principal farming area.

Lebanon has mild, wet winters and warm, rainless, but humid summers. The coastal region is semitropical. Since the mountain slopes and interior valleys are cooler, they have many summer resorts. Rainfall is heaviest on the western side of the mountains. During the winter, frosts and snow occur in the high elevations.

Trade and agriculture have always been the basic economic activities in Lebanon. But because the country is so mountainous only a little more than one-fourth of its area is suitable for farming. Olives, grapes, oranges, apples, bananas, and other kinds of fruit are among the chief crops. Wheat, corn, barley, potatoes, and tobacco are also grown. The variations in altitude and climate make it possible to grow crops of both subtropical and temperate climates. Goats are the principal livestock. In general, Lebanon's industries are small and devoted chiefly to producing light consumer goods.

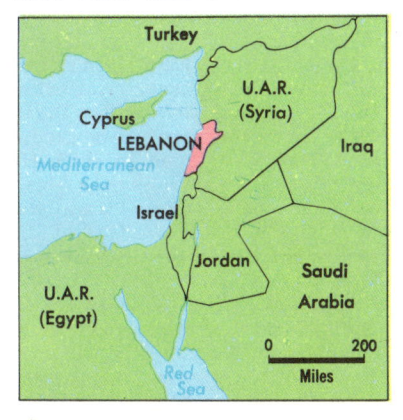

A little more than half the Lebanese people are Christians. Most of the rest are Moslems. Arabic is the official language, but French is also widely spoken. Foreign trade and agriculture provide the largest share of the nation's income. The chief products produced in Lebanon for export are fruits and vegetables, tobacco, wool, hides, and skins. Considerable income is received from petroleum and merchandise shipped through Lebanon.

In ancient times the Lebanese coast was the site of the great cities of Phoenicia, from which Phoenician traders ranged all over the Mediterranean. Having come under Roman control, Syria, of which Lebanon is historically a part, was later included in the Byzantine Empire. By the 7th century Syrian Christians, called Maronites, had established themselves in Lebanon while Islam was taking over Syria. Lebanon was visited by the crusaders.

Later it came under the domination of the Ottoman Empire of the Turks and so remained until World War I. The slaughter in 1841 and 1860 of Maronites by Druses, a sect of Moslems, led France and other European powers to obtain some self-government for Lebanon. After World War I Lebanon and Syria were under French administration. Independence was achieved in 1944. For detailed map, see TURKEY.

LEBANON

Area: 4,000 sq. mi.
Population: 1,600,000
Capital: Beirut
Largest cities: Beirut, Tripoli, Zahle, Saida (Sidon)
Highest mountain peak: Qurnet es Sauda (10,131 feet)
Chief rivers: Litani, Orontes
Climate: Warm, rainless summers and mild, wet winters
National flag: Three horizontal stripes of red, white (wider), red —green cedar in center
National anthem: *Kulla na lil watan lil 'ula lil 'alam*
Form of government: Republic
Unit of currency: Lebanese pound
Languages: Arabic, French
Chief religions: Christian (Maronite), Moslem
Chief economic activities: Agriculture (including livestock raising), international commerce
Chief crops: Fruits (including grapes, apples, oranges, bananas), olives, wheat, other grains, tobacco
Chief exports: Fruits and vegetables, tobacco, wool, hides and skins
Chief imports: Foodstuffs, textiles and clothing, machinery and automobiles, gold

Beirut, the capital of Lebanon, is a port on the Mediterranean Sea.

The cedar of Lebanon tree is used in the center of Lebanon's flag, adopted in 1944.

LECOMPTON CONSTITUTION, a constitution for Kansas that provided for its admission to the Union as a slave state. It was framed between September and November, 1857, by a convention composed of proslavery Kansans. In February, 1858, U.S. President James Buchanan recommended that Kansas be admitted under the Lecompton Constitution, but the proposal was defeated in the House of Representatives. The constitution was then submitted to the voters of Kansas, who on Aug. 2, 1858, rejected it 11,300 to 1,788. See KANSAS-NEBRASKA ACT.

LE CORBUSIER (1887-   ), the pseudonym of Charles Edouard Jaenneret, French architect, artist, and writer. He was born in La Chaux-de-Fonds, Switzerland. He received his training in architecture in the studios of Auguste Perret and Peter Behrens. Le Corbusier and Pierre Jaenneret (his cousin and, after 1921, his business partner) were among the founders of modern functional architecture in Europe. Le Corbusier's best known single project was the design for the Palace of the League of Nations at Geneva. Although it won first prize in the 1927 competition, the design was never executed.

Almost from the beginning of his career he was interested in the sociological aspects of housing. During the period between the two World Wars he attained recognition as an authority on urban planning and renewal and was a consultant during the replanning of cities in Europe, South America, and Asia. In 1945 Le Corbusier was appointed to the French Ministry of Reconstruction. In 1946 he was a delegate to the commission concerned with building the United Nations headquarters in New York.

Although overshadowed by his career in architecture, Le Corbusier's contributions to the fine arts, both as a painter and as a critic, were significant. His writings include *Toward a New Architecture* (1923) and *The City of Tomorrow* (1925).

LEE, RICHARD HENRY (1732-1794), American statesman, was born in Westmoreland Co., Virginia, and was educated there and in England, where he studied law, history, government, and politics. He apparently envisioned a career in public life; and in 1757, when he was 25 years old, he became a justice of the peace in his home county. The following year he was elected to the Virginia House of Burgesses, where he gradually reached a position of considerable influence and prominence. He became noted for his belief in progressive measures and for his firm upholding of colonial rights of self-government. He was one of the principal allies of Patrick Henry in the House of Burgesses.

In 1764 Lee was among the most outspoken opponents of British tax policies, and in his home county he organized a boycott of British goods as a means of forcing repeal of the Stamp Act of 1765. This was the first of many similar boycotts throughout the colonies. (See STAMP ACT.) From 1765 to 1774 Lee, with Henry and Jefferson, was a leader of the Virginia protests against British rule as well as a leader in efforts to promote intercolonial resistance to British policies.

Lee was a member of the Continental Congress, where he served on several important committees and was a leading agitator for independence. On June 7, 1776, he introduced before the Congress the motion for independence that led to the Declaration of Independence the following month. He then went to Virginia to help organize the state government but returned to the Continental Congress, where he devoted his attention principally to foreign affairs. In 1779 he resigned from the Congress and the following year became a member of the Virginia House of Delegates. In 1784 Lee returned to the Congress and served one year as its president. He was a leader in the formation of the Northwest Ordinance, but he declined to participate in the Constitutional Convention. He led the opposition to ratification of the Constitution, maintaining that it had several serious faults that should be changed before, rather than after, ratification. Following its ratification, he was chosen senator from Virginia in the First Congress and devoted his efforts to the adoption of the first ten amendments, the Bill of Rights, which embody many of his ideas. In 1792 he resigned from the Senate because of ill health and retired to his Virginia estate, where he died two years later.

Richard Henry Lee

Newberry Library
Robert E. Lee

LEE, ROBERT EDWARD (1807-1870), American army officer, was born in Westmoreland Co., Virginia. He was a son of Henry ("Light-Horse Harry") Lee, a famous cavalry officer of the Revolutionary War. Lee began his army career after he was graduated from West Point in 1829. He served with distinction in the Mexican War (1846-1848) and from 1852 to 1855 was superintendent of the United States Military Academy at West Point, New York.

When the Civil War began in April, 1861, Lee was a colonel in command of the 1st U.S. Cavalry. He was firmly opposed to both slavery and secession, believing that the Union should be preserved. However, he could not bring himself to fight against his home state. Consequently when President Lincoln offered him the field command of the United States Army he declined and, after having heard of Virginia's decision to secede, resigned from the army (Apr. 20, 1861). Three days later he was appointed major general in command of the Virginia forces. During the summer he was appointed military adviser to Jefferson Davis, president of the Confederacy, and was promoted to general.

On June 1, 1862, he was put in command of the Confederacy's Army of Northern Virginia, which command he held until his surrender to General Grant at Appomattox Court House, Va., on Apr. 9, 1865.

Lee's conduct of his campaigns has won him universal esteem as a great general and probably the greatest American strategist. Although his adversary, the Union's Army of the Potomac, was well commanded and both larger and better supplied than the Army of Northern Virginia, Lee succeeded in defending Richmond, Va., the Confederate capital, for over three years. Among his most famous victories were the battles of Fredericksburg (December, 1862) and Chancellorsville (May, 1863). He twice invaded the North, but both campaigns were checked, the first at the Battle of Antietam in Maryland (September, 1862) and the second at Gettysburg, Pa. (July, 1863), where Lee suffered his greatest defeat.

After the war Lee became president of Washington College (now Washington and Lee University) in Lexington, Va. He accepted the defeat of the South with great nobility and devoted the last years of his life to attempting to make the country once again a union of loyal states.

LEECH is a common name for a class of small, segmented worms, well known for their blood-sucking habits. They differ from other annelid worms in having a short, rather broad body, usually with 32 segments, and two suckers (one around the mouth and the other at the posterior end). The leech hangs on by the posterior sucker but also fastens its anterior sucker to a host to get its blood meal. The alimentary tract is pouched to hold its blood meal.

The common American leech is about 2 inches long and is usually found on stones and other submerged objects. The leech formerly used by physicians to draw blood was a European leech about 8 inches long. This leech may now be found in some streams in the eastern United States.

LEEUWENHOEK, ANTON VAN (1632-1723), a Dutch natural scientist and early experimenter with microscopes, was born in Delft. He made over 247 microscopes, some capable of magnifying subjects 270 times. He was the first man to see bacteria and protozoa and the first to give a complete description of red blood cells.

LEGUME, an angiospermous, or flowering, plant that belongs to the family Leguminosae. This family contains more than 5,000 species, including clover, alfalfa, beans, peas, peanuts, and lespedeza.

Clover, alfalfa, soybeans, lespedeza, and some other legumes are especially important to agriculture because, by means of certain bacteria that become associated with their roots, they effect the conversion of atmospheric nitrogen into solid nitrates, which then are added to the soil and enrich it. These bacteria live in small, round lumps called nodules, which form on the roots of the legumes as a result of the bacterial invasion. The bacteria absorb gaseous nitrogen from the air contained within the soil and combine it chemically with water, oxygen, and carbohydrates to form proteins. The proteins may then be assimilated into the tissues of the legumes. When the legumes die, their tissues decompose, and the nitrogen of their proteins is converted into solid nitrates by a series of chemical changes.

The conversion of atmospheric nitrogen into solid nitrates of the soil by means of leguminous bacteria is nitrogen fixation. Botanists estimate that certain species of nitrogen-fixing bacteria living in the roots of a legume can add between 100 and 200 pounds of nitrogen to an acre of soil in a single season. After the solid nitrates have been added to the soil, they are utilized in subsequent years by corn, wheat, or other crops, which are unable to utilize directly free atmospheric nitrogen. See NITROGEN FIXATION.

LEIBNIZ, GOTTFRIED VON (1646-1716), a German philosopher, scientist, and statesman, who contributed significantly to mathematics, natural science, theology, philosophy, legal history, political science, language, logic, and economics. He was born in Leipzig, where his father taught ethics. As a child he educated himself in history, logic, theology, Latin, and Greek. By the age of 21 he had obtained a law degree and had acquainted himself with the chief modern thinkers. Impressed by Leibniz' legal essays, the elector of Mainz placed him in a political position. In this capacity Leibniz labored to preserve peace in Europe. An official trip to Paris brought him into contact with other thinkers, notably Christian Huygens, who instructed him in mathematics. Leibniz visited London on a diplomatic mission in 1673 and was elected to the Royal Society for his improvements on the calculating machine. In 1676 he transferred to Hanover, stopping in Holland on the way to meet Spinoza. In Hanover Leibniz became official librarian for Duke John Frederick of Brunswick-Lüneburg. He worked on a history of the Brunswick-Lüneburg family, which necessitated research trips into Italy. He also sought to unite the Protestant and Roman Catholic churches, for which purpose he wrote the *Theological System*. In 1700 Leibniz's plan for the Berlin Academy of Science was adopted, and he was made president of the new academy for life. To the end of his life Leibniz energetically contributed to most areas of human knowledge.

Leeuwenhoek, the first man to observe bacteria, is peering through a lens that he ground.
Courtesy of and © 1959, Parke, Davis & Co.

In science Leibniz did basic work in mechanics, suggested the principle of the aneroid barometer, and contributed to optics, hydrostatics, and pneumatics. He also discovered the differential and integral calculus, for which work he shares honors with Isaac Newton.

Leibniz is best known in philosophy for his concept of monadology and preestablished harmony. Leibniz's monads were individual centers of immaterial force, the elements of all things. Each monad acted independently of others, but each monad mirrored the universe and was itself a miniature universe. Monads harmonized with the actions of all other separate monads because as mirrors of the universe they reflected the harmony of the universe preestablished by God. In his work criticizing John Locke's view of the relationship between the body and the soul Leibniz stated that the body and soul harmonize in the same way that two separate clocks may be synchronized. Leibniz's idea of preestablished harmony was optimistic and led him to declare that this was the best of all possible worlds, a view that was mercilessly satirized by Voltaire in *Candide*. Leibniz's philosophy had a profound effect on German thinkers.

LEISURE, time free for voluntary pursuits on the part of the individual. Leisure activities are innumerable and range from the constructive to the destructive. The search for meaningful ways to use leisure is crucial to societies in the age of automation. The requirements of constructive leisure are the absence of coercion and propaganda; the freedom to set goals; the opportunity to join with others in common pursuits; the chance to develop the skills needed to use leisure time wisely; and above all the capacity for enjoyment.

Athens developed a society in which some people lived from the labor of slaves and artisans. These fortunate few sometimes used their leisure for philosophy, art, drama, and politics. They regarded leisure as a time to learn, and the English and Latin words for *school* stem from the Greek word meaning "leisure." During the Renaissance people blessed with leisure often used it creatively: Rabelais, Montaigne, Erasmus, Thomas Hobbes, Francis Bacon, and Spinoza may be regarded as persons who used their leisure to contribute to society. The early Industrial Revolution forced many people to work long hours at unsatisfying tasks. The few who could afford not to work were regarded as fortunate. Thorstein Veblen's *The Theory of the Leisure Class* told how some people spent this leisure uselessly in order to show off the fact that they were wealthy, well bred, and above menial labor.

Industrial automation can allow ample leisure for everyone. In effect, everyone will be in the position of the few in Athens, except that our slaves are machines. Professional recreationists, unions, employers, and agencies like the International Recreation Service or the National

In the future there will be more leisure for everyone. Some leisure may be well spent in just plain relaxation. Group activities such as boating or individual skills such as swimming are other possibilities. Boredom will not afflict the imaginative person.

Courtesy of Johnson Motors

Family life, as this picture indicates, is the source of much leisure-time activity.

Recreation Association are seeking to provide constructive outlets for leisure. Industries may want to revise the traditional working schedules; city planners will want to develop more adequate systems of parks, playgrounds, open areas, museums, and libraries; and individuals must learn to enjoy leisure. One French watch factory, with the collaboration of owner and employees, decided not to reduce the workweek but to devote time to voluntary courses in engineering, physics, religion, languages, or recreation. The company and its workers also bought a farm, on which the workers and their families might spend vacations close to the soil, a condition that this group decided was essential to human fulfillment.

The imaginative person need not fear boredom. For young and old there are innumerable participant sports, such as tennis, cycling, swimming, and fishing. Hobbies can develop into the mastery of whole new fields of knowledge and may include raising and studying plants and animals, collecting, crafts, music, study groups (such as the Great Books groups), photography, weaving, and "ham" radio operation. Some people put on amateur theatrical productions, often of high quality; attend gym classes, an idea originating in Germany and Sweden; or master foreign languages. There is also a wide field for political activity, civic-improvement groups, and the development of leadership and teaching ability through the boy scout and girl scout programs.

LEITZEL, LILLIAN (1891-1931), was a circus performer. She became famous for her daring act, which consisted of swinging and performing acrobatic stunts on flying rings suspended high above the ground.

Miss Leitzel was born in Breslau, Germany. As a child she studied music in Breslau and Berlin, but she soon decided to give up music in favor of the circus. Her mother and two of her aunts performed an aerial ballet act on trapezes, and Lillian joined the act as a young girl. The act was disbanded on a tour in the United States in 1911, and Lillian decided to establish herself as a solo performer.

After playing several years in American vaudeville theaters, Miss Leitzel joined the Ringling Brothers Circus in 1915. She soon became a leading attraction and was a star performer during the 1920's. Besides swinging on flying rings, she developed a specialty of rotating her body many times around a horizontal rope stretched near the top of the circus tent. She held the rope with only one hand.

Miss Leitzel married Alfredo Codona, an outstanding Mexican trapeze aerialist, in 1928. Three years later, while she was performing in Copenhagen, Denmark, a ball-bearing swivel that supported one of her rings broke while she was swinging through her act. She fell to the floor and died two days later.

LEMMING, a small, prolific rodent, distributed in the circumpolar regions. The lemming is 4 to 5 inches long and has furry feet, small ears, and a very short tail. There are several kinds of lemmings. One is tawny yellowish in color, varying to blackish and reddish. Another is similar but turns white in winter; in this species, called the collared lemming, some animals have a light, brown-bordered collar. The best known European species is the Norway lemming, notable for its crop-devastating migrations, which occur at intervals of several years, when the lemming population has grown enormously. The lemmings move in large numbers; they do not stop for cities nor bodies of water but push steadily onward. Naturally, many perish on the way.

LEMON, a citrus fruit that is pale yellow when ripe, has many seeds, and is oval in form. The fragrant oil of lemon, extracted from the rind, is used as a flavoring in candies. The rind is often candied or preserved. Lemon juice is the chief source of citric acid and, being very rich in vitamin C, has long been used in the prevention and cure of scurvy. Lemon juice is used in pies, cakes, cookies, and salad dressing.

The common lemon tree is a stout, thorny shrub, growing 10 to 15 feet high. Unlike the orange, its foliage is sparse, and its shape is irregular. The commercial tree bears fruit prolifically practically the year round. In the United States the fruit is harvested green and is ripened in dark chambers to improve the flavor. Lemons keep well and are easily transported when properly ripened.

The lemon tree is found wild in the mountainous regions of northern India. It was introduced into Europe from India and Iran, probably by the crusaders. Its cultivation spread rapidly in the Mediterranean region, and it is now grown in most tropical and subtropical countries. The United States and Italy are the main producers of lemons and are the major exporters to the rest of the world. California and Arizona grow virtually all of the lemons grown in the United States.

LEND-LEASE, a policy adopted by the United States during World War II for the purpose of supplying aid to nations that were helping to defeat the Axis.

When war broke out in Europe, the United States was bound by the neutrality legislation of the 1930's to supply munitions to other nations only on the basis of immediate cash payment, known as "cash and carry" under the Neutrality Act of 1939. Great Britain and its few surviving allies were unable to continue the staggering cost of buying war materials for the battle against Nazi Germany. To remedy the situation the Lend-Lease Act was passed (not without isolationist opposition) by Congress on Mar. 11, 1941.

Eligibility for lend-lease was not limited to belligerents but was determined by the president in the light of overall strategy. Assistance was granted to 38 countries, including 19 American republics.

Almost 50 billion dollars was spent. (At today's price levels goods and services provided in that program would cost nearly twice as much.) About 65 percent went to Great Britain and the Commonwealth, 25 percent to the Soviet Union, and the rest mainly to France and China. Over one-half of the lend-lease goods were munitions, and the rest were largely petroleum, ships, raw materials, machinery, and foodstuffs. The United States received 8 billion dollars' worth of reverse lend-lease, which was made available to the American Armed Forces by other governments, mostly Great Britain and the British Commonwealth countries. About 4 billion dollars was received in repayments and return of surplus goods. The net cost of lend-lease to the United States was approximately 37 billion dollars. The United States agreed to accept the cost as a contribution to the war effort.

Lemons ripen during all seasons of the year.

LENGTH

FOUR DIGITS ONE PALM

ONE CUBIT SEVEN PALMS

ONE FOOT

Units of length range from those used to measure wavelengths to those used to measure astronomical distances. The angstrom is approximately equal to the diameter of an atom (left). At the other extreme, the parsec is slightly less than the distance from the earth to the nearest star (right).

Length was measured in ancient Egypt by comparison with certain dimensions of the body.

LENGTH is a measure of distance. Of the many units men have selected for measuring distance, some are large enough to span interstellar space, others are of a size convenient to the everyday experiences of men, and some are microscopic.

The largest units are those used by astronomers. For distances within a single or multiple star system the astronomical unit is often used. It equals the earth's mean distance from the sun, or 92,900,000 miles. For distances between star systems the light-year and the parsec are needed. The light-year equals 5,880,000,000,000 miles (nearly six trillion miles), and the parsec about three times that, or 19,200,000,000,000 miles (about 19 trillion miles). *Parsec* is a word taken from the phrase "parallax second." See LIGHT-YEAR.

At the opposite extreme of length are the unimaginably small units used in measuring wavelengths of radiation (other than radio waves) and the distances within atoms. These units are particular fractions of the meter (39.37 inches), which is the base for all units of length in the metric system. (See METRIC SYSTEM.) The micron measures one millionth of a meter (10^{-6} meter), the millimicron one billionth of a meter (10^{-9} meter), the angstrom one ten-billionth of a meter (10^{-10} meter), and the X unit one ten-trillionth of a meter (10^{-13} meter). Very small distances like these are frequently expressed in units of a meter divided by 10 raised to any required power, as shown by 10 with a negative exponent before the word *meter*.

The most commonly used units of length for the English-speaking world are the inch, the foot (12 inches), the yard (3 feet), and the mile (5,280 feet; 1,760 yards). The line ($\frac{1}{12}$ inch) and the league (3 miles) extend the system a step in each direction but are not often used.

In surveying, the link equals 7.92 inches, and 25 links make up a rod ($5\frac{1}{2}$ yards; $16\frac{1}{2}$ feet). Four rods equal a chain (66 feet), 10 chains equal a furlong (660 feet), and 8 furlongs equal a mile. The mile contains 80 chains or 320 rods.

Depths and distances at sea are measured in fathoms (6 feet), cable's lengths, and nautical miles. The cable's length in the U.S. Navy equals 120 fathoms (720 feet); but in the British Navy, 608 feet (about 100 fathoms). The British nautical mile is 6,080 feet, or exactly 10 of its cable's lengths. The U.S. Coast Survey mile is 6,080.20 feet. A proposed international nautical mile of 6,076.097 feet has been adopted by some countries.

Many industries use special units to measure their particular product. For instance, cloth is measured by the 40-yard bolt; wallpaper, by the 16-yard bolt or roll. In printing, the size of type is measured by the point (.0138 inch, or $\frac{1}{72}$ inch), and column width and length, by the pica (12 points, or $\frac{1}{6}$ inch). Wire is measured by the mil (.001 inch), buttons by the line ($\frac{1}{40}$ inch), leather by the iron ($\frac{1}{48}$ inch) and the ounce ($\frac{1}{64}$ inch). Special units for cotton yarn are the thread (1½ yards), the lea (80 threads, or 120 yards), the hank (7 leas, or 840 yards), and the spindle (18 hanks, or 15,120 yards). Linen yarn is measured by the cut (300 yards) and the spindle (48 cuts, or 14,400 yards).

LENIN, NIKOLAI (1870-1924), real name Vladimir Ilich Ulyanov, Bolshevik leader, Marxist theoretician, and founder of the U.S.S.R. He was born in Simbirsk (now Ulyanovsk), the son of an inspector of schools. The execution of his eldest brother in 1887 for his part in an attempted assassination of Czar Alexander III affected Lenin deeply. He studied law at the universities of Kazan and St. Petersburg (1887-1891), but he was expelled from Kazan for revolutionary activities. He went abroad in 1895 and made the acquaintance of prominent Marxist exiles. Returning to Russia, he busied himself with spreading Marxist propaganda and organizing revolutionary societies. He was exiled to Siberia for three years in 1897. While there he married a coworker, Nadezhda Konstantinovna Krupskaya. In 1900 he went to Switzerland, where he published *The Spark*, a revolutionary journal that was smuggled into Russia. In 1902 he wrote *What Is To Be Done?* This laid down a blueprint for party organization and described the procedure for overthrowing the czarist regime. In 1903, at the London meeting of the Russian Social Democratic party, the party split because of differences about revolutionary procedure. Lenin led the majority faction called Bolsheviks (the Russian word meaning "majority") and Georgi Valentinovich Plekhanov led the Mensheviks (Russian word meaning "minority"). Lenin returned to Russia during the 1905 revolution, but, unable to secure his ends, he again went abroad. He worked on various books. *Imperialism: the Highest Stage of Capitalism* (1916) was a significant example. He continued to organ-

UPI
Nikolai Lenin, founder of the U.S.S.R.

ize the Marxist movement. During World War I, at a congress of Socialist parties in Switzerland (1915), he called on the workers of all countries to lay down arms and fight their capitalist enemies at home. In March, 1917, a revolution in Russia deposed the czar and set up a parliamentary government. Lenin went to Russia in April and tried to organize the workers and soldiers councils (soviets) into supporting a Bolshevik revolution. His first effort to overthrow the new government, in July, 1917, failed. He fled to Finland but returned in October after publishing *The State and Revolution*. The Bolshevik Revolution of November, 1917, succeeded. As head of the new government Lenin resolved a civil war and reorganized the national economy. When he was wounded by a would-be assassin, his flagging health gave way, and he died.

LENINGRAD, the capital of Leningrad oblast and the second largest city of the U.S.S.R., was formerly the capital of Russia. The population is over 3,000,000. It was founded in 1703 by Peter the Great and was called St. Petersburg until the start of World War I, when it became Petrograd; it was given its present name in 1924. The city was built on the site of an old Swedish fort on the delta of the Neva River. Many canals and streams run through Leningrad, and the city has hundreds of bridges. The lower portion of the city is sometimes flooded in the fall, and levees of granite have been constructed along the banks of the river. Among its famous buildings and monuments are the Hermitage, containing one of the world's finest collections of painting and sculpture, the fortress of Saints Peter and Paul, the Alexander column, the Kazan Cathedral, the Admiralty building, St. Isaac's Cathedral, and the former Winter Palace. (The last two are now museums.) The city is one of the leading cultural centers of the Soviet Union, having industrial and trade schools, an academy of arts, a university, and a polytechnical college. It is also the Soviet Union's chief manufacturing center for machine and electrical goods. Turbines, generators, diesel engines, cranes, linotype machines, light bulbs, and telephone and radio equipment are some of its products. It excels as a shipbuilding center and also produces rubber goods, chemicals, and textiles. There is an annual international fur auction. It was besieged by the Germans from August, 1941, to January, 1943, during World War II.

Leningrad, a city of many canals and bridges, is a Soviet cultural and historical center.
Mary Jo Read

LENS, a thin, transparent substance, usually glass, generally circular, with one or both of its surfaces rounded. A surface that rounds outward is termed convex; one that rounds inward, concave; one that is flat, plane. The two surfaces of a lens may be combinations of any of these types and are accordingly named double convex, double concave, planoconvex, planoconcave, convexo-concave, and concavo-convex. Lenses are used in microscopes, telescopes, cameras, and other instruments. They are also used to correct defects in the natural crystalline lens of the human eye. They have the property of bending beams of light to produce images of objects from which light emanates or is reflected.

This specific property of lenses depends on refraction, the change in direction of a beam of light when it passes from one medium into another, as from air into glass or from glass into air. The angle at which the beam of light passes through the surface of the glass is called the angle of incidence; the angle at which it travels through the glass is the angle of refraction.

An image is formed by a double-convex lens in this way: Light is radiated from the object in all directions; some of the rays strike the lens. A line from the object through the center of the lens is called the axis; any ray along this line passes through the lens without changing direction. All other rays are bent toward the axis as they enter the lens and again as they leave it; as a result all the light rays coming from a particular point on the object are reunited or focused at a point on the opposite side of the lens, and if a screen is placed at this point, an image of the object will appear on it. This image is inverted compared to the object.

An image that can be cast upon a screen is called a real image. One that cannot is called a virtual image. A typical example of a virtual image is that produced by a concave lens. It spreads the parallel beams of light coming from a distant object in such a way that they appear to the eye to be coming from a small object close to the other side of the lens. Such a lens is therefore sometimes called a reducing glass.

The simple magnifying glass provides another example of a virtual image. When an object is brought within about 8 inches of the eye, the light scatters so widely that the lens of the eye is unable to focus it. If, however, a convex lens is interposed between the object and the eye, the rays will be bent inward; the eye will see, not the object itself, but a large virtual image of the object at a convenient distance.

A compound microscope consists essentially of two lenses. One, called the objective, forms a real image of the object. The other, called the eyepiece, magnifies this real image so that the eye sees a large virtual image of it. The telescope is similar to the microscope. Its object lens focuses the parallel rays of light from a distant object; the real image thus formed is viewed through an eyepiece. See EYEGLASSES.

LENT, in certain Christian churches, the 40-day fast before Easter. Lent is observed in the Roman Catholic Church, the Eastern Orthodox Church, the Church of England, and the Lutheran Church. The fast begins with Ash Wednesday and extends through Holy Week, the week preceding Easter.

The institution of Lent was possibly influenced by the Hebrew Yom Kippur, or the Day of Atonement. Lent is regarded as a time of spiritual purification, of penance, of contemplation of the Passion, and of sorrow in commemoration of Christ's suffering during his last days on earth. It is an imitation of Jesus' retreat in the desert (Matt. 4:2). The word *Lent* is derived from words in Old English, German, and Dutch that meant "spring," for the fast is in the early part of the year.

In early Christianity fasting in preparation for Easter did not last for 40 days. The number might have been suggested by the 40-day fasts of Moses, Elijah, and Jesus, though it is still reckoned differently in different churches. In the Eastern Orthodox churches Lent is observed for 36 days. The Roman Catholic Church has observed a 40-day Lent since the 7th century. During the Middle Ages the observance of Lent was very strict. Only one meal a day was allowed, and flesh, and in some places even fish and milk products, was forbidden. In modern times less stringent rules have been adopted.

In many countries Lent is preceded on Shrove Tuesday by a carnival (the word *carnival* means in Latin "put away meat"). On this day people eat, drink, and dance, for festivities are forbidden during Lent. The carnival, also called Mardi gras (fat Tuesday), has its origin in festivals held in ancient Rome.

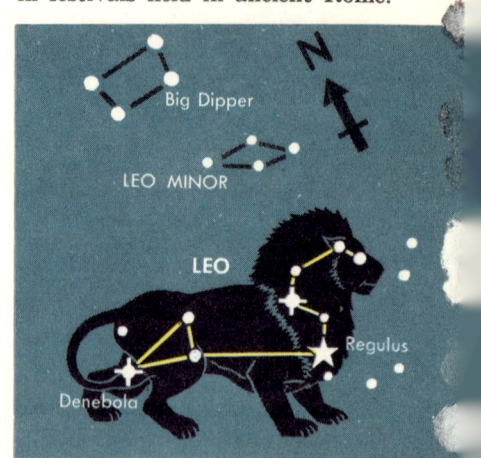

The constellation Leo, or the Lion, is one of the most ancient constellations. Leo was worshiped by the early Egyptians because the sun entered this constellation every year at the time when the Nile waters rose to renew the fertility of the fields.

LEO, or the Lion, is an important constellation of the zodiac between Virgo and Cancer and south of Ursa Major. It includes the first-magnitude star Regulus, which—with the stars of the Lion's head—forms a sickle shape. Leo is visible in the evening sky from midnorthern latitudes between February and July. However, it is still visible during the early morning hours of November 14 or 15, when, each year, the famous meteor shower, the Leonids, takes place. The meteors of this shower seem to radiate from the Lion's head. See REGULUS.

LEONARDO DA VINCI. See VINCI, LEONARDO DA.

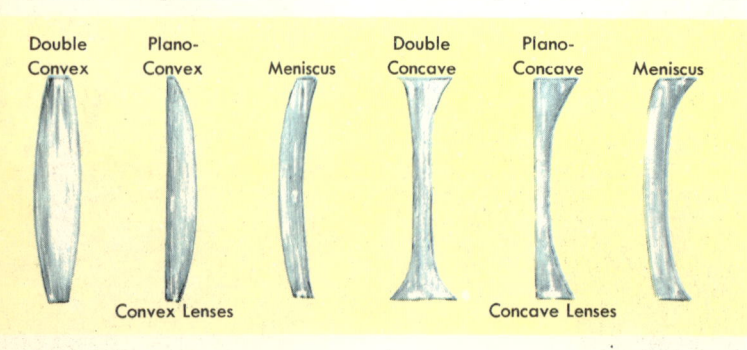

Convex Lenses: Double Convex, Plano-Convex, Meniscus

Concave Lenses: Double Concave, Plano-Concave, Meniscus

Most leopards are spotted; a few are black.

The snow leopard of the Himalayas.

The clouded leopard hunts birds in trees.

LEOPARD, a carnivorous mammal found only in Asia and Africa, though in prehistoric times it ranged as far west as Spain, France, and Great Britain, as is shown by remains. The leopard shares with the lion and the tiger the honor of being one of the three largest cats of the Old World. However, individual leopards differ greatly in size, ranging in total length from 5 to 8 feet. Its tawny yellow fur is speckled with large black rings and spots. Some Asiatic leopards have solid black fur. African leopards have smaller and more solid spots than Asian leopards.

Next to the tiger and the lion the leopard is the most formidable and destructive of the flesh-eating mammals. In some respects it is more dangerous than the tiger, for it is more easily aroused and is more courageous in attacking those who molest it. It inhabits thick forests or wooded, rocky hills, where it lurks in caves or under sheltering ledges, from which it descends toward sunset to pick up straggling animals from herds on their way home. It preys upon antelopes, deer, monkeys, and domestic livestock. It is stealthy and silent and seldom roars except when disturbed or when charging an enemy. Leopards usually go singly or in pairs; but in Africa several full-grown ones, probably members of a family, are sometimes seen together. Cubs are born usually in the spring, a litter being composed of two, three, or four.

LEPROSY, or Hansen's disease, is an infectious disease caused by a specific germ. The disease is believed to be of very ancient origin, and records of its occurrence in Greece date from the 4th century B.C. In Europe the prevalence of the disease began to decline in the 14th century. However, it was spread to the New World by explorers and traders from Europe and from the Orient. Today the highest incidence of the disease is in the western Pacific and in various parts of Africa. The world incidence is estimated at five million cases.

The causative agent in the disease was described by Armauer Gerhard Hansen in 1874, but the organism has resisted all efforts to cultivate it, and experimental attempts to transmit leprosy to animals and men have failed.

The manner in which leprosy is transmitted is also unknown, although the infection is thought to arise from direct contact with infected skin and mucous membranes. Leprosy is not transmitted from parents to children if a child is taken away from the parents at birth. Otherwise the child is likely to manifest the disease early in life.

The initial skin eruptions in leprosy usually appears on the face, extremities, feet, or buttocks. The disease primarily involves the skin and mucous membranes and the peripheral nervous system. The incubation period varies from months to years, the average being three to five years. Nerve involvement leads to numbness, tingling, and pain and in the late stages to destruction of terminal small bones of hands and feet and painless ulcers on the extremities.

Occasionally, leprosy undergoes spontaneous arrest. Temporary remissions can also occur. In the control of the disease early treatment and isolation are essential. In treatment the principal agents are chaulmoogra oil and the sulfones. The former drug has a long history of use in Asia for the treatment of leprosy and began to be used in the Western world during the 19th century. The sulfones are derivatives of sulfonamides.

The United States government maintains hospitals for lepers at Carville, La., and at Kalaupapa, Molokai, Hawaii.

LEPUS, or the Hare, is a small constellation just south of and below Orion. None of its stars is brighter than third magnitude. It is visible in the evening sky from midnorthern latitudes between January and March.

Lepus, the hare, was the animal that Orion most liked to hunt. Accordingly, Lepus appears in the skies beneath the feet of Orion. When Corvus, or the crow, rises, Lepus sets; thus the ancients believed that the hare hates the call of the raven.

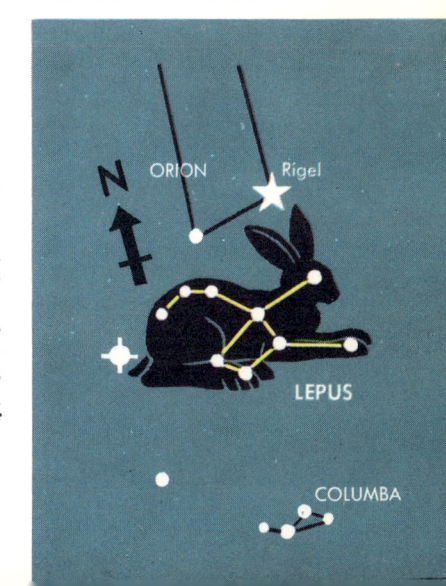

Ferdinand, Viscomte de Lesseps

LESSEPS, FERDINAND, VICOMTE DE (1805-1894), French engineer and diplomat, was born in Versailles. After spending two years in the French army De Lesseps chose a career in the diplomatic service of the French government, a following in which several members of his family, including his father, had achieved distinction. Between 1825 and 1849 De Lesseps represented the French government in several cities in western Europe and northern Africa. In 1848 and 1849 he was French minister to Madrid. In 1849 he went to Rome on a mission that involved negotiation with the Vatican and the government of Rome. A sudden reversal in French policy caused De Lesseps' recall, and he retired from the diplomatic service soon afterward.

In 1854, on the invitation of Said Pasha, the Egyptian viceroy and a longtime friend, De Lesseps traveled to Alexandria, Egypt (then theoretically a part of the Ottoman Empire), and opened negotiations to obtain the concession to build a canal across the Isthmus of Suez. Negotiations were terminated Nov. 30, 1854, and the Suez Canal project was accepted by an international commission of engineers in 1856. De Lesseps disregarded the criticism of Lord Palmerston, the British prime minister, who feared that French control of what would be the shortest route to India would hinder British commercial interests. Other critics held that the geography of the isthmus made construction virtually impossible. Nevertheless, with the backing of the French government a company was organized, and construction was begun. On Nov. 16, 1869, the Suez Canal was opened to traffic between the Red Sea and the Mediterranean.

During the years that followed De Lesseps became involved in several large-scale engineering projects, none of which was successful. One of these was a scheme whereby Europe and Asia would be connected by means of an intercontinental railroad. In 1879 De Lesseps organized, and became president of, the Panama Company, which attempted, unsuccessfully, to carry through the construction of a canal across the Isthmus of Panama. After political and financial difficulties the company failed. De Lesseps and one of his sons, a company director, were sentenced by the French government to be fined and imprisoned for the misappropriation of funds. However, the sentences were never carried out.

LESSER DOG, THE (constellation). See CANIS MINOR.

LETTER, a written communication addressed to a person or to a group of persons. The earliest known letters were inscribed on clay tablets; later, pen and ink and papyrus were used. Most letters are personal and of no interest to others. However, the personal letters of certain important individuals—poets, novelists, philosophers, statesmen, and so forth—often are of interest to the public for their biographical content and their literary and stylistic merits, for their interest as human documents, or as historical records of the social, cultural, and intellectual climate of the particular age in which they were written.

The correspondence of famous men was first collected and published by the Greeks and Romans. Outstanding among the many letters that have come down to us from the Roman period are those of Cicero and Pliny the Younger.

Much early Christian writing was epistolary—for example, in the New Testament, the Epistles of St. Paul and the other apostles. The religious epistles of such early church fathers as St. Augustine and St. Jerome and, during the Middle Ages, those of St. Bernard of Clairvaux and St. Catherine of Siena are also of importance.

The letter reached its highest degree of excellence as a literary form in France during the 17th century, sometimes called the Golden Age of Letterwriting. Outstanding writers of this period included Nicolas Boileau-Despréaux, Pierre Corneille, René Descartes, François de La Rochefoucauld, Blaise Pascal, and Madame de Sévigné. During the 18th century Jean Jacques Rousseau and Voltaire in France and Lady Mary Wortley Montagu in England wrote letters of distinction. The popularity of the letter as a literary form led Samuel Richardson to write the first successful epistolary novel, *Pamela*, in 1740.

The open letter, as distinct from the private, personal letter, has for a long time been an effective medium for publicity and propaganda. The open letter is addressed to a single person or group, but because it concerns some public matter, it is really intended by its author for general publication in a newspaper, magazine, or other periodical. Outstanding examples of the open letter are Pascal's *Les Provinciales* (1656-1657), the letters of Junius (1768-1772), and Emile Zola's "J'accuse" (1898). Many modern newspapers and magazines publish the open letters they receive from their readers under the heading "Letters to the Editor."

HOW TO WRITE A LETTER

All letters, whether they are personal letters to friends, business letters, or letters of thanks, of congratulation, of condolence, of introduction, or of application, have the same general form, or outline. The five parts of this form are (1) the heading, (2) the salutation, (3) the body of the letter, (4) the complimentary close, and (5) the signature. In the business letter only, the firm's name and address precede the salutation and constitute a separate part of this outline.

The heading consists of the writer's address and the date. The date always appears under the address. The heading is placed in the upper-right-hand corner of the page, and the lines may be either even or indented. If the stationery being used already has a printed or engraved address, all that is needed is the date.

The salutation appears about half an inch below the heading at the left-hand margin in a straight line with the body of the letter. The standard form of salutation is the word *Dear* followed by the name of the person to whom the letter is addressed. When writing a formal letter, "My Dear" should be used instead of "Dear."

The body of the letter is the message and is the most important part of the letter. The reason for writing the letter should be kept in mind, and the writer should express himself as clearly and simply as possible and always keep to the point.

The complimentary close is written two or three spaces below the last line of the message, beginning at the middle of the page. Only the first word is capitalized, and the phrase is finished with a comma. The wording varies according to the type of letter and the degree of friendship and intimacy with the person addressed. The forms most generally used for informal letters are "Sincerely yours," "Yours very sincerely," "Yours cordially," "Most cordially yours," and "Faithfully yours." "Yours truly" or "Very truly yours" are used for business letters and very formal letters.

The signature is handwritten in ink below the complimentary close.

LETTERING, ways of writing various types of alphabetical letters so as to form a clear, legible, and attractive design. Most styles of handwriting and printing used in Europe and America today developed from Latin writing. Inscriptions in stone and other hard materials were skillfully drawn and carved on lasting monuments. For writing documents and manuscripts, however, a more convenient manner of lettering was necessary. Brushes or reeds were dipped in ink and applied to papyrus. Later, quills and pens were found to be more suitable, since they made letters bolder and more rounded. The handwriting of professional scribes was of course clearer and more regular than that of other educated citizens in Rome and was more resistant to change. Indeed, their manuscript styles are the ancestors of our roman lettering, the most widespread type of lettering in use on the Continent and in America today.

Modern printers and letterers recognize four basic letter forms, although an infinite variety of shapes and sizes are actually in use. They are called text, roman, italic, and script. Further variations within each of these forms result from differences in sizes, spacing, and weight of letters, weight being lightness or darkness of color.

Text letters are black letters, or Old English letters. Roman letter forms are familiar to everyone. Newspapers, books, magazines, official notices and documents, posters, and display heads all use this style of lettering. Gothic letters, although easy to draw, are less legible than other forms and therefore are not widely used. Their decorative flourishes make them appropriate for Christmas cards, religious texts, and formal invitations. Italic letters are most commonly used with roman letters for emphasizing particular letters or words and for marking subheadings. Script is a variation of the italic form based on handwriting styles. It is the most difficult letter form to draw well. As in handwriting, all the lowercase letters are connected. Since script is less legible than the roman and italic forms, it is used for short pieces, such as invitations and formal announcements.

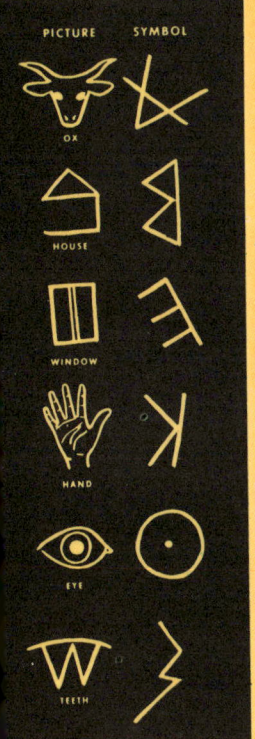

Lettering has become increasingly refined as it has developed. Phoenician letters were pictorial, abstracted from pictures of objects (above, left). Innovation through refinement is seen in the evolution of lowercase letters until A.D. 900 (above, middle). Present-day lettering is based on the classical Roman alphabet (with J, U, and W added) and the lowercase alphabet in classical spirit (above, right). The advertisement and illuminated page at right show a contrast in uses of lettering.

A head of lettuce consists of many large leaves folded together to form a ball.

LETTUCE, a widely cultivated salad plant. A native of Europe and Asia, it has been under cultivation for 2,500 years. The three common classes of lettuce are crisp-head, or iceberg, lettuce; leaf lettuce; and loose-head lettuce, including Cos, limestone, and butterhead lettuce.

Head lettuce has a cabbage-like head, a few outside green leaves, and a solid head of crisp, white leaves. Leaf lettuce, or garden lettuce, has a less compact head than head lettuce and many more outer green leaves. Cos lettuce, often called romaine lettuce, has a long head with rather loose leaves. Limestone, or bibb, lettuce has a small head with a dark-green rounded leaf. Butterhead, or Boston, lettuce has a rounded loose head with creamy yellow leaves.

Lettuce favors a cool growing season and plenty of moisture. Accordingly, it is grown in the early spring and late summer unless the entire growing season is cool. Lettuce has become an important commercial crop since refrigerated railroad cars made long-distance marketing possible.

LEUCITE is a white or gray, translucent mineral found in distinct crystals in some light-colored igneous rocks. Leucite is a potassium aluminum silicate. It is about as hard as a steel knife and is quite light for its size. Leucite crystals are roundish.

Leucite is a rather rare mineral. It is chiefly found in recent lavas. It occurs only in rocks that have no free quartz. Leucite occurs as phenocrysts (large crystals embedded in a mass of much smaller crystals) in the lavas on Mt. Vesuvius. It is also found in rocks of the Leucite Hills, in Wyoming, and in the Bear Paw Mountains, in Montana.

LEUKEMIA, a disease of the organs that form the blood. It is so named because one of its symptoms is an excess of leucocytes, or white blood cells. Leukemia may be regarded as a cancer of the blood-forming organs —the bone marrow, the lymph glands, and the spleen and liver. Tumorous cells crowd out the normal blood-producing cells of these organs. Anemia, lowering of immunity to infections, and numerous complications result. The cause of leukemia is unknown, and it is considered incurable, although treatment with X-rays and chemotherapy helps to prolong life.

LEVEE. See Dike and Levee.

LEVEL. When the surface of anything is parallel to the surface of still water or is perpendicular to the direction of the plumbline, it is said to be level, and an instrument for finding out when a thing is level is called a level. A plumbline is a line or cord to one end of which is fastened a metal weight, usually of lead. When the string is held by the other end, the weight, or plummet, will point to the center of the earth, the same direction in which bodies fall when attracted by gravitation. The simplest instrument for finding a level is the plummet level or plumbline level, a wooden frame shaped somewhat like an inverted T with a plumbline attached to the upright. When the line shows that the upright is exactly perpendicular, the lower or horizontal limb, which is at right angles to it, will be level.

The spirit level is a frame with a glass tube that is closed at the ends and is filled with alcohol or a mixture of ether and alcohol, with a small bubble of air inside, which naturally tries to get to the highest possible point. When the instrument is level, the bubble of air will be exactly in the middle of the tube, which is marked by a line on the glass. In using the level it is proper to take two observations, reversing the level for the second, so that if there is any inaccuracy in the level itself, it can be discovered. This kind of level has now largely taken the place of the plumbline level, which is used only for coarse work.

The spirit level is a part of all surveying instruments, as it is necessary that the bases of the instruments be horizontal when observations are taken. The surveyor's level is a telescope with a spirit level attached and is mounted upon a tripod. It is used for measuring differences in heights.

LEVER, one of the fundamental machines. It is a bar of wood, metal, or other rigid substance, having a fixed point (or fulcrum) and used to overcome a certain resistance (or weight) at some part of the bar by means of a force (or power) applied at another part. Common examples of a lever are the clawhammer and the can opener.

The parts of the lever divided by the fulcrum are called the arms of the lever. When the arms are in the same straight line, the lever is called a straight lever; in other types it is called a bent lever. The plane in which the lever can move is called the plane of the lever. For a force to be effective in overcoming the resistance, it must be applied within this plane. Levers are divided into three classes according to the positions of the points of application of the power and the weight of the fulcrum. In the first class the power and the weight act on opposite sides of the fulcrum. In the second class the power and the weight act on the same side of the fulcrum with the weight nearer the fulcrum. In the third class the power and the weight also act on the same side of the fulcrum, but the power is nearer to the fulcrum.

The advantage of using a lever is that it enables a person to lift a heavy load with a rather small effort. Thus, with a particular lever, one may be able to lift a load of 300 pounds by applying a force of only 30 pounds. With a lever, as with any other machine, the ratio of the resistance overcome to the force applied is called the actual mechanical advantage. In the example the actual mechanical advantage is equal to $\frac{300}{30}$ or 10. Because of friction the actual mechanical advantage of a machine is always less than the ideal mechanical advantage, found from the dimensions of the machine. The ideal mechanical advantage of a lever is equal to the ratio of two distances—the distance from the fulcrum to the point where the force is applied and the distance from the fulcrum to the point where the resistance is applied.

The lever increased man's natural strength.

LEWIS, JOHN L. (1880-   ), American labor leader, born in a mining community near Lucas, Iowa. His parents came from mining communities in Wales, and his father had been active in the Knights of Labor. Lewis left school after the seventh grade to work in the mines. After work he managed a baseball team and a debating society. He eventually developed into a powerful orator. Myrta E. Bell, his future wife, helped Lewis in his program of reading; and a trip throughout the nation begun in 1901 acquainted him with labor conditions elsewhere.

He was a delegate from an Iowa mine to the national convention of the United Mine Workers' Union (UMW) in 1906. In 1917 he became a vice-president for the UMW, and in 1920 he became the union's president. He was offered the job of secretary of labor in the cabinet of President Calvin Coolidge for his plan of reducing the number of uneconomic mines, but he refused the appointment. Lewis had long been in favor of the industrial pattern of organization, and in 1935 he organized the Committee for Industrial Organization (later the Congress of Industrial Organizations). Lewis guided this organization into militant membership drives. His opponents within the union were displaced or ignored, although Lewis allowed subordinates a wide latitude in administration.

Angered at President Franklin D. Roosevelt's stand regarding the violence on both sides in the drive to unionize the little steel companies, Lewis refused to support Roosevelt in his third bid for the presidency. Lewis resigned his presidency of the CIO after the election.

In 1943 Lewis threatened a strike of the UMW, and the government seized the mines. In 1946 Lewis ignored an injunction forbidding a strike, and he and his union were fined for contempt of court. However, Lewis' daring policy won unparalleled concessions for his miners. Outraged at the Taft-Hartley Act, he withdrew the UMW from the American Federation of Labor, as he had earlier withdrawn from the CIO. Lewis resigned the presidency of the UMW in 1960 but retained the chairmanship of its welfare fund. See LABOR MOVEMENT; LABOR UNION.

William Clark (right) and Meriwether Lewis (far right) led an expedition through the new territory purchased from France by President Thomas Jefferson in 1803.

LEWIS, MERIWETHER, (1774-1809), American explorer was born in Albemarle Co., Virginia, and grew up there and in Georgia, where he spent a great deal of time outdoors and became an expert hunter. He returned to Virginia for his education. When he was 20 years old, Lewis joined the local militia and liked military life so much that in May, 1795, he enlisted in the regular army. By 1800 he had attained the rank of captain and had served in several army frontier posts.

In 1801 Thomas Jefferson, about to be inaugurated third president of the United States, chose Lewis to be his private secretary. While serving in this position, Lewis lived in the White House and took part in many official functions. In 1803 he was selected by Jefferson to lead an expedition to discover an overland route to the Pacific Ocean; Lewis chose William Clark, a fellow army officer, as his companion on the expedition. Lewis and Clark left St. Louis in the spring of 1804 and eventually reached the Pacific by way of the Missouri and Columbia rivers. Returning by a similar route, they arrived at St. Louis in September, 1806. See CLARK, WILLIAM; LEWIS AND CLARK EXPEDITION; LOUISIANA PURCHASE.

After the successful completion of the journey Lewis traveled to Washington to report to President Jefferson. At that time Lewis resigned from the Army, and Jefferson appointed him governor of the Louisiana Territory, which included all of the Louisiana Purchase except what is now the state of Louisiana. In 1809 he found it necessary to go to Washington to resolve a financial problem; on the trip he was murdered, presumably by robbers, at an inn in central Tennessee.

Charles Willson Peale, Independence National Historical Park Collection

Brown Brothers

LEWIS, SINCLAIR (1885-1951), American novelist, was born at Sauk Center, Minn. He was graduated from Yale in 1907 and then worked as an editor and writer in New York. His first novels, *Our Mr. Wrenn* and *The Trail of the Hawk*, were little noticed, but he gained wide recognition with his 1920 publication, *Main Street*. In 1922 he added a new word to dictionaries with his novel *Babbitt*, and in 1925 he published *Arrowsmith*. For *Arrowsmith* Lewis was awarded a Pulitzer prize, which he declined.

In 1927 Lewis published *Elmer Gantry* and in the following year *The Man Who Knew Coolidge*. *Dodsworth* appeared in 1929. In 1930 Lewis became the first American to be awarded the Nobel prize in literature.

Later works of Lewis' include *Ann Vickers*, *It Can't Happen Here*, and *Kingsblood Royal*. His letters were published in *From Main Street to Stockholm* and his essays in *The Man from Main Street*.

LEWIS AND CLARK EXPEDITION, an expedition sent out by President Thomas Jefferson in 1803 to find a route across the continent and to cultivate the trade and friendship of western Indians. Some of the territory explored was part of the Louisiana Purchase, which had been made after the expedition was planned.

Meriwether Lewis was in charge of the trip, with William Clark as coleader. The company gathered near the mouth of the Missouri River, where they wintered. The expedition left St. Louis on May 14, 1804, and proceeded up the Missouri River to the lands of the Mandan Indians near what is now Bismarck, N.D. Here they spent the winter

Above is the route taken through the wilderness by Lewis and Clark.

and picked up a French-Canadian interpreter and his Shoshoni Indian wife, Sacagawea, who was to be a great help to them. On Apr. 7, 1805, the expedition continued up the river to what is now Great Falls, Mont. They disembarked, carried their supplies around the falls, and built canoes in which they traveled on to what is now Three Forks, Mont. Here the Jefferson, the Madison, and the Gallatin rivers, named by Lewis and Clark, join to form the Missouri. The expedition then followed the Jefferson River and met the Shoshoni Indian tribe. The Shoshonis were overjoyed to see Sacagawea and provided the expedition with horses and guides. Alternating travel by land and by water, the expedition reached the mouth of the Columbia River at the Pacific Ocean in November and remained for the winter. Beginning the return trip in March, 1806, they followed the route by which they had come until they traversed Lolo Pass near what is now Missoula, Mont. The expedition then split. One group, led by Lewis, took a shortcut to Great Falls, explored the valley of the Marias River until attacked by Gros Ventre Indians, and then hastened back to the Missouri. The other group, led by Clark, continued along the old route to Three Forks, where Sacagawea guided them across Bozeman Pass to the Yellowstone River. They then traveled along that river until it joined the Missouri River, where they met the Lewis group, The expedition returned to St. Louis on Sept. 23, 1806.

LEXINGTON AND CONCORD, BATTLES OF, the first armed conflicts of the Revolutionary War.

Upon the secret orders of Thomas Gage, the military governor of Massachusetts, about 800 British troops under Lieutenant Colonel Francis Smith set out from Boston on the evening of Apr. 18, 1775, to confiscate the colonists' military stores at Concord, 17 miles away. However, Whigs detected the British movement and sent Paul Revere and William Dawes as couriers to arouse the countryside. Revere arrived in Lexington, 5 miles from Concord, about midnight and warned John Hancock and Samuel Adams, patriot leaders sought by the British. While in Lexington the two riders were joined by a third, Samuel Prescott, who alone managed to elude the British and carry the message through to Concord.

When the advance British troops, under Major John Pitcairn, arrived in Lexington at dawn on April 19, they were confronted by about 70 minutemen mobilized on the common. Pitcairn's demand that the Americans disperse was followed by a brief skirmish, during which eight Americans were killed and ten were wounded. One British soldier was wounded. The British then marched on to Concord, where they destroyed the few remaining military stores that had not already been either hidden or removed by the colonists. Later in the morning between 300 and 400 minutemen attacked and repulsed a British platoon at the bridge spanning the Concord River. About noon the British withdrew from Concord and began the march back to Boston by Lexington, where they were reinforced by between 900 and 1,000 troops under Lord Percy. The rapidly growing band of minutemen, firing from the shelter of trees, stone walls, and fences, kept up a running battle along the route until the British reached Charlestown that evening.

British casualties numbered 73 killed, 174 wounded, and 26 missing. Of the approximately 4,000 Americans who participated, 49 were killed, 39 were wounded, and 5 were reported missing. Shortly after the battles of Lexington and Concord the British commenced the siege of Boston, which was continued until March, 1776.

The map at left shows the location of Lexington and Concord, the two Massachusetts towns where the first shots were fired in the warfare for American independence.

LEYDEN JAR, a glass jar lined on the inside and covered on the outside with tinfoil to form a condenser in which an electrical charge can be held. It was invented at the University of Leiden in 1745 and was one of the principal tools of the early pioneers in electricity. An electrostatic machine was used to charge it. Today its use is confined largely to the school laboratory, where it is used to demonstrate a simple form of electrical condenser.

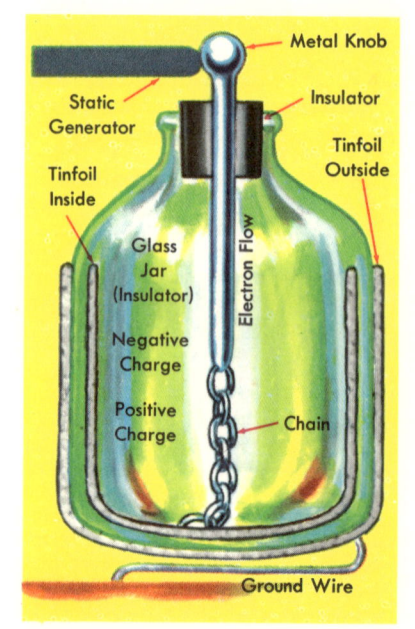

LIBERAL PARTY, CANADIAN, one of the two major political parties of Canada. It was formed by George Brown, editor of the Toronto *Globe*, and first formed a government in 1874 under the leadership of Alexander Mackenzie. In its first term of office the Northwest Mounted Police (now known as the Royal Canadian Mounted Police) was organized, the Supreme Court of Canada was set up, and voting by secret ballot was substituted for the previous open voting system. The party was defeated in the elections of 1878 and remained out of power until 1896. The Liberal party won the election of 1896 and returned to office under Sir Wilfrid Laurier. It lost to the Conservatives in 1911 and returned to power in 1921 with William Lyon Mackenzie King as prime minister. The Liberals maintained their control of the government from then until 1957 except for a few months in 1926 and the period from 1930 to 1935. After King's retirement in 1948 Louis St. Laurent was leader of the party and prime minister from 1948 to 1957.

LIBERIA is a republic at the southwestern edge of the great bulge in western Africa. It was founded in 1847 as a home for freed Negro slaves from the United States. Liberia is still underdeveloped, and health conditions are poor. The republic's area is about 43,000 square miles. Its population is estimated to be about 2,500,000, but estimates vary widely.

Above are the national flag and the seal of Liberia. The 11 stripes on the flag represent the 11 signers of Liberia's declaration of independence. The flag was raised in 1847 when the country became independent. For over a century it was the only independent Negro republic in Africa.

From a narrow strip of level coastal land, cut by lagoons, creeks, and marshes, the rolling country rises toward the interior in a series of plateaus. Low mountains, rarely more than 3,000 or 4,000 feet high, occur here and there. Liberia's rivers are navigable for only short distances because of steep falls and many rapids. The country lies in the tropical-rain-forest belt of Africa's west coast. More than a third of its area is forested, but lumber production is limited.

The climate is hot and humid, with distinct wet and dry seasons. Rainfall is heavy, and nearly all of it occurs between April and November. It is heaviest near the coast. During the dry season the dry, dust-carrying winds, called harmattans, blow in from the Sahara.

Liberia's economy is based on agriculture, but farming methods are generally primitive. Machetes, and often hoes and axes, are the chief farming tools. No work animals are used. Rice and manioc (cassava) are the two main food crops. Rubber is Liberia's principal export. Iron ore is the leading mineral export, but gold and diamonds are also mined. In addition to rubber and iron ore, Liberia also exports such agricultural products as palm kernels and oil, piassava fiber, cacao, and coffee. The United States is its leading trading partner.

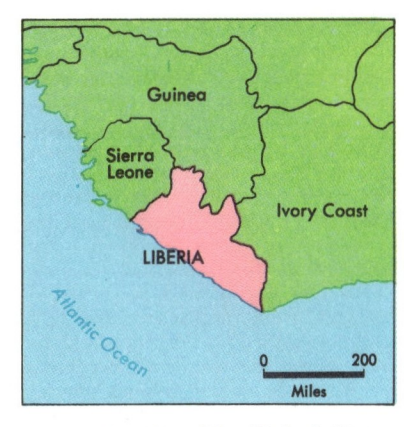

In 1822 a colony of freed American Negro slaves was established near the present location of Monrovia. The republic of Liberia was set up in 1847. In the early 1900's the government went bankrupt and required support from the United States. Economic development began in 1926, with the rubber-plantation concession to the Firestone Tire and Rubber Company. For detailed map, see ALGERIA.

LIBERIA

Area: 43,000 sq. mi.
Population: 2,500,000
Capital: Monrovia
Largest city: Monrovia
Chief rivers: Cavally, Cess, St. Paul
Climate: Hot and humid with wet and dry seasons—heavy rainfall during wet season
National flag: Six red stripes alternating with five white—blue square containing white star in upper left
National anthem: All Hail, Liberia, Hail!
Form of government: Republic
Unit of currency: U.S. dollar
Languages: English, tribal languages
Chief religion: Pagan
Chief economic activity: Agriculture
Chief crops: Rice, manioc, rubber
Chief minerals: Iron ore, gold, diamonds
Chief exports: Rubber, iron ore, palm kernels, diamonds
Chief imports: Manufactured goods, machinery, automobiles, foodstuffs

LIBERTY BELL, the bell used to proclaim United States independence. It rang from the State House in Philadelphia after the Declaration of Independence was read there on July 8, 1776. The bell was originally ordered by the Provincial Council in 1751 to celebrate the Golden Jubilee of William Penn's 1701 Charter of Privileges. Cast in London by Thomas Lister, the bell was cracked during its testing in Philadelphia in 1752 and was recast there by Pass and Stow. From 1777 to 1778, while the British were in possession of Philadelphia, the bell was hidden at Allentown, Pa. During subsequent years it was rung frequently for celebrations; but in 1835, while tolling for the funeral of John Marshall, the bell was greatly strained. Eleven years later it cracked while being rung for the birthday of George Washington.

The Liberty Bell is now in Independence Hall in Philadelphia. It weighs over 2,080 pounds and cost £60. The bell was given its name in 1839 by members of the antislavery movement, who derived the name from the bell's inscription. That inscription, which was taken from Lev. 25:10, reads, "Proclaim Liberty Throughout All the Land unto All the Inhabitants Thereof."

LIBRA, or the Scales, is a constellation of the zodiac south of the celestial equator and between Scorpio and Virgo. It is visible in the evening sky from midnorthern latitudes between May and August. Its two brightest stars are of third magnitude.

The ancient Hebrews and Indians regarded this constellation as a celestial balance scale, possibly because when the sun enters Libra in the fall, the days and nights are of the same length. The Greeks later combined Libra with the constellation Scorpio. The Latin name Libra refers to the balance of Astraea, Roman goddess of justice.

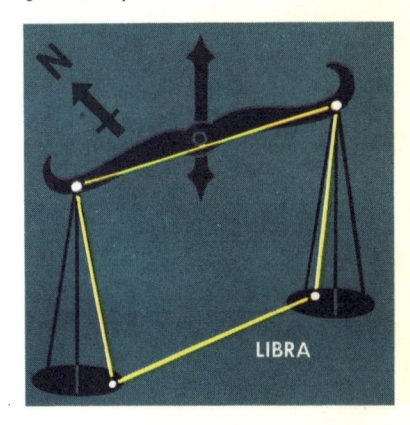

LIBRARY, a collection of books and other reading materials intended for use instead of for sale; also, the building in which such a collection is housed.

The earliest books, documents, and records (which in Babylonia and Assyria were clay tablets; in China, wooden tablets; and in Egypt, rolls of papyrus) were usually stored in palaces and temples.

The first systematic collector of books was the Greek philosopher Aristotle. The greatest library of the Hellenistic world was founded at Alexandria, Egypt, by Ptolemy I. It contained several hundred thousand papyrus and vellum rolls, and it is supposed to have been modeled on Aristotle's library. Another great library of the time was located in Asia Minor in the city of Pergamum.

Cicero and many other Romans had large private libraries. Gaius Asinius Pollio established the first public library in Rome in 39 B.C. Many of the Roman emperors, including Augustus, Tiberius, Vespasian, and Trajan, set up libraries. Attached to such public buildings as temples and baths, they served as meeting places for scholars.

Constantine I set up the imperial library in his new capital of Constantinople (formerly Byzantium) during the 4th century. Much Greek and Latin literature was preserved in it; it also contained important early Christian texts.

When the Western Roman Empire collapsed, many of its libraries were destroyed. Fragments of Greek and Roman books were preserved by the Christian church. For a time, monasteries served as libraries and monks as librarians. In the 13th and 14th centuries the great universities established their own libraries. Because books were very expensive and relatively few in number, the monastic and university libraries remained the chief collectors of books until the late Middle Ages. With the invention of printing and the growth of commerce more books were available, and more people could afford them.

The 17th and 18th centuries were marked by the establishment of several important libraries, including the Bibliothèque Mazarine and the Bibliothèque du Roi in France and the British Museum (1753) in England. Circulating and subscription libraries were founded in the 18th century; they were developed chiefly in England and America. Benjamin Franklin started a famous one in Philadelphia in 1731. The free public library began during the 19th century and developed in Great Britain and the United States.

The national library of England is the British Museum in London; there are also excellent libraries at Oxford and Cambridge. In France the Bibliothèque Nationale and the Bibliothèque de l'Arsenal, both located in Paris, are the two most important libraries. The Bibliothèque de l'Université de Paris, which includes the Bibliothèque de la Sorbonne, is also noteworthy. The Library of Congress is the national library of the United States. (See LIBRARY OF CONGRESS.) Other outstanding American libraries are the Army Medical Library (the largest of its kind in the world), the New York Public Library, the Harvard University Library (the oldest in North America), and the Yale University Library.

HOW TO USE A PUBLIC LIBRARY

Most public libraries issue a card to those who wish to withdraw books and can meet certain basic requirements, such as residence within the city or the county. This card is obtained by applying to the librarian.

The reference section of the library is an information center where one can find all kinds of facts about people, places, and things. It contains such books as dictionaries, encyclopedias, atlases, and directories. These reference books cannot be removed from the library.

One of the most important parts of a library is the card-catalog index. In this file there exists a card for every book in the library. These cards are filed in alphabetical order according to author, title, and subject matter.

The number that appears on each card helps to locate the book quickly. In small libraries it is often possible to go directly to the shelves and find the desired book. In most larger libraries you write the number, title, and author on a slip of paper and give it to a library helper, who then gets the book for you.

There are a number of systems in use for the classification and arranging of books. These include the system of the Library of Congress, the Universal Decimal Classification (established by the Institut International de Bibliographie), and the Dewey Decimal System. The last system, which was devised by Melvil Dewey, is the commonest.

There are ten numbered subject classes in the Dewey Decimal System. They are as follows: 000-099, general and reference; 100-199, philosophy; 200-299, religion; 300-399, social sciences; 400-499, language and linguistics; 500-599, science; 600-699, practical arts; 700-799, fine arts; 800-899, literature; 900-999, history and biography. Fiction is usually arranged alphabetically by authors. The basic plan of this system is a division by subject and an orderly progression from the general to the specific. The above-mentioned main classes are each divided into ten subgroups. Thus, 720 is the number of architecture, one of the divisions of the fine arts, the number of which is 700.

A library card serves as a pass to the many services a public library offers. The library patron should know how to use the card catalog files, 1. Here, a card, 2—either title, 2A, author, 2B, or subject card, 2C—gives him the call number of the book he wants, 3.

Wilson & MacPherson Hole

The Library of Congress in Washington, D.C.

LIBRARY OF CONGRESS, the national library of the United States, founded on Apr. 24, 1800, by and for the Congress. Its services have since been extended to other government agencies, other libraries, scholars, and the general public. The library is housed in two buildings on Capitol Hill, Washington, D.C. Together the buildings contain 270 miles of bookshelves. It has six main departments: the Legislative Reference Service (Congress' main information and research center), the Processing Department, the Reference Department, the Administrative Department, the Copyright Office, and the Law Library (probably the most comprehensive in the world). The librarian of Congress is appointed by the president.

Each year, library experts answer thousands of questions and prepare numerous studies on foreign and domestic matters for congressmen and congressional committees. The library also provides books and reference services to hundreds of thousands of individuals and libraries.

Materials in the library were acquired by purchase, gift, exchange, official transfer, and the operation of the copyright law, which requires that two copies of most types of copyrighted materials be filed with the library.

In 1960 there were over 38 million items in the collections of the Library of Congress. These items included many rare books; historical manuscripts; original musical compositions; maps; phonograph recordings of music, speeches, and poetry readings; bound newspaper volumes; photographic items, including motion pictures, kinescopes, and microfilms; "talking books" and books in braille and Moon type for the blind; fine prints and reproductions of paintings; rich collections of Japanese, Chinese, and Russian books; and scientific materials obtained from sources all over the world.

LIBYA is an independent kingdom of North Africa. It consists of three historic provinces: Tripolitania in the northwest, Cyrenaica in the northeast and east, and Fezzan in the southwest. Libya achieved independence, by resolution of the United Nations, on Dec. 24, 1951, for the first time in its long history.

Libya has an area of about 680,000 square miles, or about one-fifth the size of the United States. It is bounded by the Mediterranean Sea on the north, Tunisia on the northwest, Algeria on the west, Niger on the southwest, Chad on the south, the Sudan on the southwest, and Egypt on the east. The two capitals are Tripoli and Benghazi. A third capital is being built at Beida. The country has a population of about 1,250,000, of which about 95 percent are Moslem Arabs.

The greater part of the country is unproductive, arid land, most of which is part of the Sahara. Only the immediate coastal areas at the western and eastern ends of the 1,000-mile coastline contain useful land, and it is here that the bulk of the population is concentrated. Yearly rainfall reaches 15 inches in these areas. Summer temperatures go up to 115° F. even in these more favored regions.

Natural resources, other than possibly oil, are scarce, and there is very little industry except for agriculture. Esparto grass (for papermaking), barley, olives, citrus fruits, dates, and wheat are the chief crops.

The colors represent Libya's three provinces.

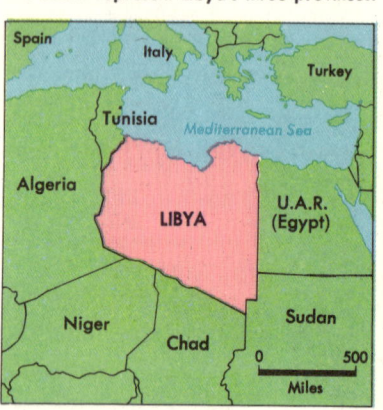

Because most of Libya lies in the Sahara, camels are very important to the country. They are used not only for transportation but also for pulling old-fashioned plows.
Tom Hollyman—Photo Researchers

These large, brightly colored lichens grew naturally on some arctic island. Lichens flourish in the arctic zone during its short but warm summers.

Stockraising is common among the many nomadic Berbers and Arabs. Foreign companies have concessions to develop Libya's oil reserves. United States and British military bases are of major importance to the country's economy.

Libya was the Greek name for northern Africa in olden times. The country's history dates from 1100 B.C., when the Phoenicians assumed control. Before the Italian occupation in 1911 the Ottoman Empire was in command of Libya's strategic position. The country was a major battlefield in World War II; after the Allied victory it was placed under British and French administration. Libya joined the Arab League in 1953 and the UN in 1955. For detailed map, see UNITED ARAB REPUBLIC.

LIBYA

Area: 679,358 sq. mi.
Population: 1,250,000
Capitals: Tripoli, Benghazi
Largest cities: Tripoli, Benghazi, Misurata
Climate: Hot and dry—desert conditions in most of the country
National flag: Three horizontal stripes of red, black (wider), green—white crescent and white star in center
Form of government: Constitutional monarchy
Unit of currency: Libyan pound
Language: Arabic
Chief religion: Moslem
Chief economic activity: Agriculture, including livestock raising
Chief crops: Barley, wheat, olives, dates, oranges
Chief exports: Esparto grass, peanuts, sheep, wool, hides and skins, sponges
Chief imports: Foodstuffs (mainly wheat flour, tea, sugar), machinery, automobiles, electrical equipment, cotton textiles

LICHEN, a natural plant structure and association that consists of certain types of algae growing within a mass of filaments of fungus. The association between the algae and the fungus is symbiotic. This means that the green algae, which contain chlorophyll and manufacture food by photosynthesis, provide food for the fungus. The fungus is incapable of manufacturing its own food. The fungus reciprocates by sheltering the tender algae from direct sunlight and by keeping them moist so they can grow on the dry, sunny, exposed surfaces of rocks and tree trunks. The symbiotic association between the algae and the fungus developed naturally, and individual lichens will form naturally wherever the proper conditions for their formation exist.

Lichens often form on rocks and dead tree trunks in meadows and woods and on rocks along the seacoast. They grow abundantly on rocky mountain summits, where it is too high and too cold for trees and shrubs to grow. They grow abundantly in arctic areas, where also it is too cold for most other kinds of vegetation. A certain arctic lichen is called reindeer moss because it serves as an important food for reindeer.

LIEBIG, JUSTUS VON (1803-1873), German chemist, born in Darmstadt. In 1824 Liebig was appointed professor of chemistry at the university at Giessen (now the Justus Liebig Institute for Agriculture and Veterinary Medicine). From 1852 until his death he held the position of professor of chemistry at Ludwig Maximilian University at Munich. While teaching at Giessen Liebig established the first laboratory to be used in conjunction with the classroom teaching of chemistry.

In the field of organic chemistry Liebig introduced several methods of analysis that are now considered fundamental. He discovered several chemical substances, including chloroform and aldehyde, and conducted research into the construction of fluids of the human body. Primary among his contributions, however, was his work in developing methods of artificial fertilization to revitalize depleted soil. He is considered the founder of agricultural chemistry.

Green lichens often grow on boulders lying in the woods. A microscopic examination of a piece of green lichen would reveal many tiny green dots, which are the algae, surrounded by a tangled mass of white threads, which are the filaments of the fungus. Some green lichens resemble moss.

LIECHTENSTEIN, a principality located between Austria and Switzerland, has an area of 62 square miles. Its population is about 14,000. The capital and largest town is Vaduz.

The valley of the Rhine River is diked, irrigated, and planted in corn and potatoes. Three-fourths of the land is steep mountains. The slopes are planted with orchards and vineyards. Cattle are raised. Small factories make precision tools, lenses, and pottery. One-third of the national income comes from the issuance of postage stamps. Over 1,000 international companies and trusts have their official headquarters in Liechtenstein to take advantage of the low tax rate and to maintain secrecy of identity. The people speak German and are largely of the Roman Catholic faith. The House of Liechtenstein has ruled since 1719. The principality became independent in 1866. It had a customs union with Austria until 1919 and formed a similar union with Switzerland in 1924. It has been a constitutional monarchy since 1921.

Vaduz, the capital of Liechtenstein, is a charming little town near the Rhine River. The picturesque old white castle that towers above it has been the home of Liechtenstein's royal family for many centuries.
Swiss Natl. Trav. Off.

Above are the national flag and the coat of arms of Liechtenstein. Designs on the coat of arms represent historic regions.

LIFE. Any abstract definition of life must be somewhat arbitrary; however, scientists have found that practically all known life is associated with certain specific substances and activities. The basic living substance, called protoplasm, is organized into small units called cells. Through these units living organisms carry on certain vital processes and other processes that serve to characterize living substance.

The difficulty of defining life is demonstrated in the case of the viruses; scientists are not presently agreed on whether viruses are living organisms. However, with the possible exception of viruses, all known life is associated with protoplasm. In fact, life has been defined as "the activities of protoplasm." (See PROTOPLASM.) Protoplasm is chemically complex and highly organized within the cells. See CELL.

Vital processes are those processes without which life cannot continue to exist. These processes all originate in the protoplasm of the cell, and unless the protoplasm is able to carry out these processes, it is no longer alive.

Probably the processes most essential to life are metabolism and reproduction. Metabolism, or the breakdown of energy-bearing molecules, is in turn dependent on nutrition, or taking in food and breaking it down into molecules that can be used in metabolism. (See METABOLISM.) Similarly, reproduction is dependent on the process of growth. Reproduction may occur simply by a division of the protoplasm when it grows to a certain size or, as in most multicellular organisms, by a sexual process. See REPRODUCTION.

Other processes characteristic of living organisms include autonomous movement, irritability, and continuity, or heredity. Movement includes not only the visible actions of animals but also the movements of plants—such as raising leaves to sunlight—and even the microscopic streaming of protoplasm within cells. The reaction of plants to sunlight also illustrates irritability, or responsiveness to changes in the environment. The ability of roots to respond to light, gravity, moisture, and chemical changes; the ability of the retina of an eye to respond to light; and the ability of muscle cells to respond to nerve stimuli—these are also examples of irritability. Heredity, a special aspect of reproduction, insures that the form and activity of an organism will follow the same pattern from one generation to the next. See HEREDITY.

LIFE BEYOND THE EARTH. No form of life has yet been identified beyond the earth. Observations within our solar system suggest that life may perhaps exist on Mars, probably not on Venus, and almost certainly not on any of the other planets. So far it has not been possible to observe planetary objects outside our solar system. However, present theory of how stars and planets are formed suggests that millions of other stars may possess planets with conditions similar to those on earth. If so, life may well exist on such planets. Radio telescopes may eventually receive signals that would confirm the presence of intelligent life on such planets.

Instruments for obtaining from points on the earth information about other space objects are severely limited, not only by the enormous distances between earth

LIFE BEYOND THE EARTH

Seasonal changes on the face of Mars are considered strong evidence that some forms of life exist there. Mars's year, almost twice as long as the earth's, is divided into seasons. During the Martian winter (left) the planet's icecap becomes 3,000 miles wide; the green areas over the rest of the planet shrink. Each summer (right) the ice cap shrinks to 150 miles wide, and the green areas spread.

E. C. Slipher, Lowell Observatory

and other space objects but by the drastic screening effect of the earth's atmosphere. Those observations that have been possible indicate that very few other bodies in our solar system combine the necessary conditions of temperature and material that would support life as it is known on earth. Temperature extremes alone rule out most of the planets and other bodies.

Mercury and Venus lie closer to the sun than does the earth. Mercury has no atmosphere, and because it holds the same face always toward the sun, it has one enormously hot hemisphere and one enormously cold one in permanent shadow. Venus has a dense atmosphere, part of which may be water vapor. However, Venus' surface temperature has been estimated at nearly 600° F. Jupiter, Saturn, Uranus, Neptune, and Pluto are all extremely cold planets.

Mars is the only other planet of our solar system that shows signs of possible life. Mars's surface color changes with the Martian seasons from green or bluish in the spring to brown or reddish in autumn. Certain areas of its surface absorb infrared radiation in the same wavelength as some earth vegetation. Both of these observations could mean that some form of plantlike life exists on Mars, but the same observed conditions could be caused by nonliving processes. Mars is also the only planet whose surface temperature at all approaches the earth's. In the Martian summer in the tropics the temperature rises to about 60° F. by noon. However, the nightly plunge of temperature far below zero makes the climate still far from moderate. Mars has water in small quantities in clouds and in polar icecaps.

Observations within our solar system will greatly improve with advancing space technology. Placing telescopes in orbit around the earth will overcome the screening effect of the earth's atmosphere. Unmanned rocket probes will send back information across the enormous distances. Eventually space probes may take human observers along. If such probes are to observe the natural conditions on other planets, great care must be taken not to introduce earth organisms accidentally. The same care will be needed to prevent accidental contamination of the earth by possibly harmful organisms from those planets.

Beyond our solar system the distances to even the nearest stars are so great that the most powerful optical telescopes cannot resolve the reflected light of possible planets from the glare of the stars themselves. However, present ideas of how stars are formed suggest that planetary systems like that of our sun may be a common product of star formation. If this is true, then—despite the apparent rarity of life on the planets of our sun—there may be millions of other solar systems, each of which contains one planet—similar to the earth—that could support life.

If intelligent life exists on planets in other solar systems, it may have developed a technology capable of sending radio signals in an attempt to contact life elsewhere in space. With the help of computers, our present radio telescopes are capable of separating such radio signals from the general radio noise of a planet's local star. The chance of actually discovering such signals is considered good enough so that one radio telescope is already being used for this purpose. In 1960 it began scanning those stars in the sun's vicinity that are most like the sun.

Like a giant ear turned toward the universe, a radio telescope listens for possible signals from intelligent life beyond the earth. The first attempts to detect such signals were directed toward promising stars within 12 light-years of the earth.

LIFE EXPECTANCY, the average number of years people in any given age group will live, computed on the basis of mortality tables recording past experience. Life expectancy varies in accordance with such factors as race, sex, and age. It is the death rates in the mortality tables rather than the life expectancy derived from them that are used in life insurance underwriting.

At the time of the Roman Empire the average person lived about 22 years. Life expectancy in medieval cities in Europe had risen to about 35 years, but overall the lifespan remained what it had been in the ancient world. Estimates for France in 1795 indicated a life expectancy for males of about 23.4 years, and conditions were less favorable elsewhere. Toward the middle of the 19th century new medical and surgical techniques, better public health services, and new drugs began to increase the average lifespan. For example, in the United States life expectancy for white males rose from 48.0 years in 1901 to 59.9 years in 1930 and to 66.5 years in 1950. The life expectancy of women is generally several years more than a man's at all ages. The following figures from the 1950's (except where otherwise indicated) show the life expectancy at birth for males in several nations:

The Netherlands	71.0
Sweden	70.5
England and Wales	67.5
United States (white)	67.3
United States (non-white)	61.2
Australia	67.1
France	65.0
Japan	63.9
Congo Republic	37.6
Egypt (1936-1938)	35.7
India (1941-1950)	32.4

LIFE ON EARTH lies in a shallow layer of earth, water, and gases scarcely 10 miles thick that stretches around the surface of our planet. This zone is called the biosphere, the sphere of life. Compared with the nearly 8,000-mile diameter of the earth, the biosphere is hardly more than a film on its surface. Beneath the film is the great mass of the earth, impenetrable to life. Above it—a surprisingly short distance away—lies the dark severity of space itself. There, emptiness opposes life. No elements are clustered to participate in the changing processes of life. Impossible cold would bring any life process to a stop. Intense solar radiation would destroy life processes. Even though the earth's atmosphere extends several hundred miles above the surface of the earth, the protected conditions of the biosphere fail against the severe aspects of space within but a few miles of the surface. If a person could walk straight upwards, he could walk out of the biosphere in little more than one hour.

Within the cocoon of the biosphere the innumerable forms of life have penetrated relatively extreme environments. Fish live in the deepest ocean trenches, while birds wing high in the atmosphere. Penguins nest on the ice shelves of Antarctica, while the kangaroo rat survives in the desert even without drinking water. Yet even in these extreme environments life is utterly dependent on the fundamental protections that the biosphere possesses against the extremes of space. Such protections include the stability of gravitation at a constant strength, a plentiful supply of the elements used in life processes, atmospheric protection from the lethal rain of radiation and meteors, and regulated temperatures. All of these conditions are made possible by highly particular features of our planet that are primarily astronomical in character, such as the particular mass of the earth, the earth's rotation, its location near a star such as the sun, its particular distance from the sun, and so forth.

All life is, of course, ultimately dependent on the energy received in the sun's radiation. It also depends on the relative constancy of the sun's radiation. Any considerable variation in the amount of the sun's radiation would radically change the earth's temperature ranges.

The particular mass of the earth is critically important to life. Had the earth's mass been considerably less, its gravitation would have been too weak to retain an atmosphere. Aside from the dependence of plants and animals on the air, the earth without atmosphere would be exposed to all the wavelengths of radiation from the sun, some of which are deadly to life. The millions of meteors that daily burn up in our atmosphere would instead fall destructively against the earth's surface. And temperatures on an airless earth would range so widely as to make life impossible. Our moon stands as an example of what the earth might have been like had it been smaller.

Outside the earth, temperatures range from hundreds of degrees below zero in space to thousands of degrees above zero at the surface of stars and millions of degrees in stellar interiors. Yet life on earth can exist only within a narrow temperature span. Above a mere 150° F. most compounds involved in living processes break up. At low temperatures most life processes are destroyed or become dormant. Some life forms survive even at extremely low temperatures, but these forms depend ultimately for food on other forms of life from the warmer temperature range. Life also depends upon the availability of liquid water, yet water exists in this form only within a similarly narrow range of temperature.

The earth's narrow temperature range is regulated in several ways. Part of the energy received from the sun's radiation is retained by the atmosphere in the form of heat instead of being radiated back into space. Circulation of the atmosphere helps equalize extremes of temperature at different parts of the earth's surface. The rotation of the earth is equally important in producing regular temperatures. If the earth were not rotating, one side would be continuously exposed to the sun's radiation, while the other side would lie in permanent cold. Temperatures on either side of the planet would then almost certainly be impossibly extreme for life.

Although the earth's atmosphere and the effect of the earth's rotation together produce a relatively even temperature, they do not necessarily bring about temperatures within the specific range required for life. The specific range is the result of the earth's particular distance from the sun. From observations of the two planets nearest the earth scientists can conclude that the earth would be too hot for life processes at Venus' distance from the sun and very cold at Mars's distance. The nearly circular shape of the earth's orbit also contributes to the evenness of earth temperatures. If the orbit were more elliptical, the earth would experience sharp extremes of temperature as its distance from the sun changed.

Just why the earth possesses not only its particular mass, rotation, and distance from the sun but its proportions and kinds of elements is a question that cannot yet be answered. This complex coincidence of physical conditions is apparently unique in our sun's planetary system. Whether there are parallel conditions in possible planetary systems of other stars is an open question. See LIFE BEYOND THE EARTH.

LIGHT

SAVING FROM DROWNING

Using underwater approach, lifeguard turns victim around and grasps by chin. The sidestroke is then used with the lifeguard stroking with his free arm.

SAVING FROM ELECTRIC SHOCK

The wire is removed with a dry pole or rope before touching victim. This is for protection against shock. Symptoms are like those of burns. Victim is often rigid.

SAVING FROM BREAKING ICE

A ladder, or long pole, tied to a rope may be used to rescue a skater. The skater can help himself by heaving and extending body forward to avoid breaking ice at edge. A human chain may also be used by pushing prone men forward behind each other to edge.

Lyle R. Salvo

Above are lifesaving methods used in firefighting, in saving the drowning, in rescue from breaking ice, and in electric-shock cases.

LIFESAVING. The rescue of persons in danger from shipwreck, fire, and other disasters has been greatly increased in efficiency in recent years through the development of new techniques and equipment. In addition, old types of lifesaving equipment with modern improvements continue to play a large role.

In nearly all maritime countries there are some organized means for saving shipwreck victims. In the United States this work is done by the Coast Guard, the largest lifesaving service in the world and one of only three supported wholly by governments. The other two government rescue services are those of Belgium and Denmark. In all other countries the service is maintained by private organizations, which are assisted and controlled by public authorities.

The most important pieces of equipment of the Coast Guard are surfboats, powerboats, lifeboats, rafts, and breeches buoys. A breeches buoy is of invaluable aid in getting people off a sinking ship when the seas are too rough for a lifeboat to be sent out. It consists of a life preserver with canvas breeches attached, and it runs on a trolley arrangement rigged between ship and shore or between ships. The latest addition to rescue equipment is the helicopter, which can pluck people off a ship or out of the ocean. The speed with which the helicopter can rush an injured person to the shore has saved many lives. Life preservers and lifejackets, carried aboard all seagoing ships, often have lights attached.

The latest development in firefighting and rescue equipment is the so-called snorkel, a tall ladder attached to a firetruck. It can be raised and lowered mechanically and turned in any direction.

Modern rescue organizations, aided by modern lifesaving techniques and rapid communication and transportation facilities, save many lives each year. Yet even with all these aids the rescuers risk their lives constantly that others may live.

LIFT PUMP. See PUMP.

LIGHT. The nature of light has been explained in different ways by scientists of different times. Until the middle of the 17th century light was considered to be streams of corpuscles emitted by light sources, such as the sun or a candle. In 1678 Christian Huygens, a Dutch physicist, showed that the reflection and refraction of light could be simply explained if light were thought of as a wave motion. Huygens' theory was not readily accepted. Later, Thomas Young and Augustin Fresnel found behavior in light (interference and diffraction) that could not be explained by the corpuscular theory. Interference and diffraction can be easily explained by a wave theory. In 1873 James Clerk Maxwell proposed that light was an electromagnetic radiation of very short wavelength. Heinrich Hertz later proved Maxwell's theory. In 1905 Albert Einstein, using an idea of Max Planck's, proposed that the energy in a beam of light is concentrated in small packets, called photons. This idea is almost a return to the corpuscular theory, except that photons have some properties of waves, such as frequency. The photon theory was devised because the electromagnetic-wave theory was not able to explain photoelectric emission. (Photoelectric emission is the emission of electrons from an electrical conductor when light falls on the conductor.) It is thought that when a photon hits the conductor, the photon's energy is transferred to an electron. The electron acquires so much energy that it escapes from the conductor.

Scientists today accept both the electromagnetic-wave and the photon theories. The commoner phenomena of light can be explained by the electromagnetic-wave theory.

Light has definite properties. It travels through empty space with a velocity of about 186,000 miles per second. It travels through air at about the same velocity. In other substances it travels at different velocities. Under ordinary circumstances light travels in straight lines and does not bend around objects. Ordinary white light can be divided into the colors of the rainbow, or the visible spectrum, by passing it through a suitable substance—a phenomenon known as dispersion. Light can be reflected; it changes its direction of travel when it strikes a reflecting surface. Light can be refracted; when light passes from one substance to another substance with a change of velocity, the direction of travel of light is changed. Light also has more complicated properties.

Light occupies a definite place in the electromagnetic spectrum. (See ELECTROMAGNETIC SPECTRUM.) All electromagnetic waves, including light, have certain characteristics. Light waves are transverse waves—the electric and magnetic field intensities vibrate at right angles to the wave's direction of travel. When a light wave spreads out from a small source in a uniform material, it travels in all directions at once with the same velocity. At any one instant, the wave has reached the same distance from the source in all directions. This distance can be represented by a sphere. The sphere is called the wave front. Any straight line drawn from the wave source to the wave front is perpendicular to the wave front, represents a direction in which the wave is traveling, and is perpendicular to the directions of vibration of the magnetic and electric-field intensities. Such an imaginary line is called a ray and is used in diagrams to represent a direction of travel of light waves.

The directions of the vibrating electric, **E**, and magnetic, **H**, fields along three rays of a light wave from a point source are shown.

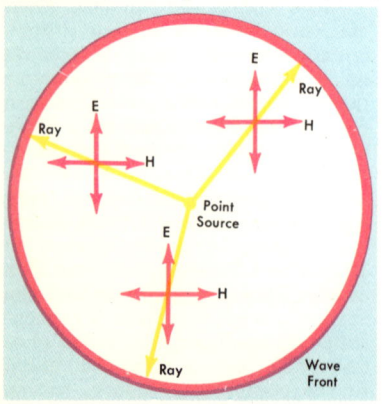

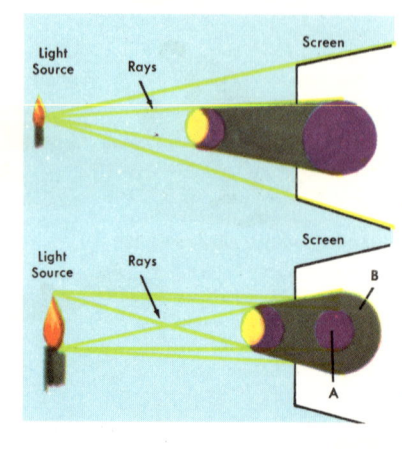

An object in the path of light from a point source casts an even shadow—an area that no light hits. The same object in the path of light from a large source casts a shadow with an umbra (an area that no light hits) and a penumbra (an area that a little light hits).

The relation between wavelength, velocity, and frequency is the same for all waves. If v is the velocity, n the frequency, and λ the wavelength, the relation is $v = n\lambda$. Light wavelengths range from 0.00004 to 0.00007 centimeter. Because the wavelengths are so short, it is convenient to put them in smaller units. Light wavelengths are usually expressed in microns, μ; millimicrons, mμ; or angstroms, A. The wavelengths of light range from 400 to 700 millimicrons and from 4,000 to 7,000 angstroms.

Probably one of the first-noticed properties of light was that light travels in straight lines. This can be easily demonstrated if an object is placed between a point source of light and a white screen. A black enlarged shadow of the object appears on the screen. A straight line can be traced between any edge of the shadow and the point source. Such a straight line is tangent to the object. If the light source is too large to be a point source, a more complicated type of shadow is cast. Such a shadow has two regions. In the darker region no light rays reach the screen. In the lighter region some rays from the source reach the screen. The region of total shadow is called the umbra. The region of partial shadow is the penumbra.

REFLECTION

Every particle or object visible is either a light source or a light reflector. We can see a candle flame or the sun because they are light sources. The light they give off comes directly to our eyes. We can see people, rocks, and trees because they reflect light to our eyes. All reflecting objects absorb some part of the light that strikes them. Glass mirrors and highly polished metals absorb little light. White objects are good reflectors. Black objects absorb most of the light that falls on them.

When a ray of light strikes a reflecting surface at an oblique angle, the light is reflected at an equal angle. The angle between a line perpendicular to the reflecting surface (the normal to the surface) and the incident ray is the angle of incidence. The angle between the normal and the reflected ray is the angle of reflection. One of the most important laws of optics is that the angle of reflection is always equal to the angle of incidence. (Optics is the study of light.) This law is true for light rays striking any reflecting surface at any angle.

Surfaces that reflect light to form images are called mirrors. The commonest mirrors are plane mirrors, convex spherical mirrors, and concave spherical mirrors. (A spherical mirror is shaped like a part of a sphere.) Plane mirrors and convex mirrors always form virtual images. Light rays only seem to come from a point to form virtual images. Depending on how far the object is held from a concave mirror, the mirror may form either a virtual or a real image. Reflected light rays actually pass through a point to form a real image.

All spherical mirrors have a principal focus and a principal axis. The line through the center of curvature and the middle point of the mirror is the principal axis. When all the incident light rays are parallel to the principal axis, the reflected light rays meet, or appear to meet, at the principal focus. The focal length of

LIGHT

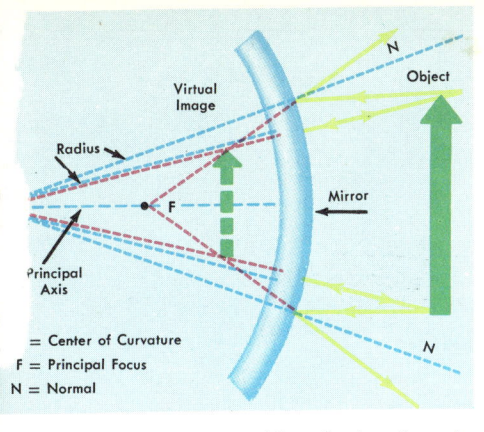

An image is formed by reflection of an object in a convex spherical mirror. C is the center of curvature. F is the principal focus.

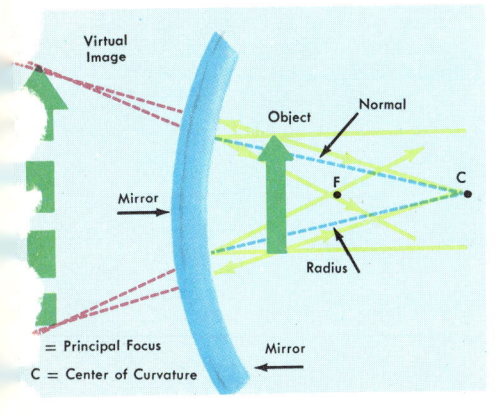

A virtual image is formed by the reflection in a concave mirror of an object between the mirror surface and the principal focus, F.

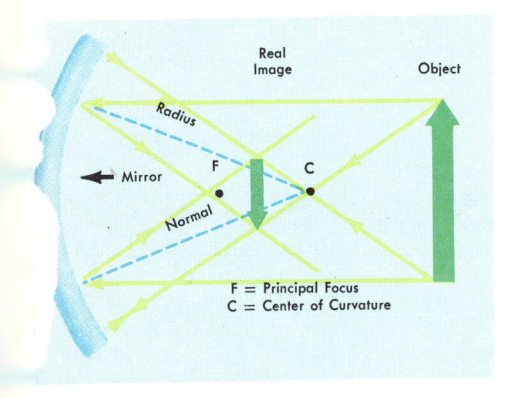

A concave mirror reflects an inverted, real image of an object more distant than the mirror's center of curvature, C.

a spherical mirror is the distance along the principal axis between the principal focus and the mirror. The focal length of a spherical mirror is one half the radius of curvature of the mirror. If the incident rays are parallel to the principal axis, a concave mirror forms a real image at the principal focus. A convex mirror forms a virtual image at the focus, which is behind the mirror.

A plane mirror always forms a virtual image the same size as the object. The image appears to be as far behind the mirror as the real object is distant from the mirror. If the object before the mirror is upright, the image is upright.

A convex mirror forms diminished, upright, virtual images of objects at any distance. An image appears to be between the principal focus and the surface of the mirror. The image is behind the mirror.

If an object is placed between the principal focus and the surface of a concave mirror, an enlarged, upright, virtual image appears. If an object is placed between the principal focus and the center of curvature of a concave mirror, an enlarged, real, inverted image is formed. If an object is placed farther away from a concave mirror than the center of curvature, an inverted, real, diminished image is formed.

To find the distance of an image from a convex or concave mirror, the distance of the object from the mirror and the focal length of the mirror must be known. The formula

$$\frac{1}{D} + \frac{1}{d} = \frac{1}{f}$$

expresses the relation between object distance, D, image distance, d, and the focal length of the mirror, f. The object distance, D, is always positive. The image distance, d, is positive for real images and negative for virtual images. The focal length, f, is negative for convex mirrors and positive for concave mirrors. Suppose an object is placed 12 inches from a concave mirror that has a focal length of 3 inches. The object is farther away than the center of curvature, twice 3 inches. What distance is the image from the mirror? Substituting into the formula, one arrives at

$$\frac{1}{12}\text{ in.} + \frac{1}{d} = \frac{1}{3}\text{ in.}$$

$$\frac{1}{12}\text{ in.} - \frac{4}{12}\text{ in.} = -\frac{1}{d}$$

$$-\frac{1}{4}\text{ in.} = -\frac{1}{d}$$

$$d = 4 \text{ inches}.$$

The image is 4 inches in front of the mirror.

If the relation between object and image distance is known, it is possible to determine the image size from the object size.

$$\frac{\text{Image size}}{\text{Object size}} = \frac{\text{Image distance}}{\text{Object distance}}$$

If, in the example above, the object is 6 inches high, the image height can be found as follows:

$$\frac{S}{6 \text{ inches}} = \frac{4 \text{ inches}}{12 \text{ inches}}$$

$$\frac{S}{6 \text{ inches}} = \frac{1}{3}$$

$$3S = 6 \text{ inches}$$

$$S = 2 \text{ inches} = \text{image size}.$$

REFRACTION

Refraction is the change of direction of light rays that happens whenever light rays pass obliquely from one medium into another in which the velocity of light is different. When a light ray enters a medium perpendicularly to the medium's surface, the light ray may change its velocity but its direction remains the same.

Refraction can be explained by the wave theory. Suppose a plane wave front of light traveling through air is approaching a piece of glass. (If the light source is not close, the curvature of the wave front is so small that the front can be considered a plane.) Suppose the glass has two plane surfaces. If the wave front approaches the glass at an oblique angle, part of the wave front enters the glass before the rest of the wave front. Imagine that one can stop the light wave front and examine it just after it has entered the glass. Because the velocity of light is less in glass than in air, the parts of the wave front longest in the glass have fallen behind their original positions with the rest of the wave front. The parts of the wave front that have been in the glass the least time are close to their original relative positions. In other words, the plane wave front has pivoted and changed direction. The light ray, or direction of travel, is always perpendicular to the wave front, so it has changed direction with the wave front. The same process happens in reverse when the wave front leaves the glass at the other plane surface.

When the wave front pivots in traveling from air into glass, its direction becomes more nearly parallel to the plane surface of the glass. The light ray becomes more nearly perpendicular to the surface. The opposite change takes place when light travels from glass into air. This predictable change is one of the most important rules to remember in the study of refraction. It can be simply stated: A light ray entering a medium in which its velocity is less is bent toward the perpendicular to the surface. A light ray entering a medium in which its velocity is greater is bent away from the perpendicular to the surface. The imaginary line perpendicular to the surface is called the normal.

The angle between a ray striking a plane surface and the normal to the surface is the angle of incidence. The angle between the normal and the ray in the refracting medium is the angle of refraction.

The index of refraction of a medium is the ratio of light in air to the velocity of light in the medium.

$$\frac{\text{velocity of light in air}}{\text{velocity of light in glass}}$$

= index of refraction of glass

The index of refraction can also be stated in a second ratio.

$$\frac{\text{sine of angle of incidence in air}}{\text{sine of angle of refraction in glass}}$$

= index of refraction of glass

Because it is easier to measure the angles of incidence and refraction than the velocity of light in substances, the second ratio is more commonly used. The fact that the two ratios are equal for the same two mediums and are constant for all angles of incidence is known as Snell's law.

A light ray traveling through a triangular prism is refracted twice—once when it enters the prism and once when it leaves the prism. After the light ray leaves the prism, it travels in a different direction than before it entered the prism. The angle by which the direction of the ray has been changed is called the angle of deviation.

When light rays traveling from a medium of lesser velocity to a medium of greater velocity strike the surface separating the two media at a certain angle, the rays have an angle of refraction of 90 degrees. The refracted rays travel along the surface between the two media. The angle of incidence for which the angle of refraction is 90 degrees is called the critical angle. The critical angle is different for different media. If light rays traveling in the medium of lesser velocity strike the surface at an angle slightly less than the critical angle, the rays are refracted into the medium of greater velocity in the usual way. If rays strike the surface between the two media at an angle greater than the critical angle, the rays are not refracted but are reflected back into the medium of lesser velocity. This reflection of light at the surface of a medium of lesser velocity is called total internal reflection. The critical angle and total internal reflection can be present only when light travels from a medium of lesser to a medium of greater velocity.

A lens is a transparent object that alters the path of, or refracts, light rays in a predictable manner. Two common types of lenses have spherical surfaces (surfaces shaped like

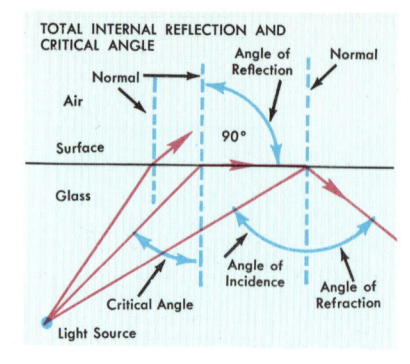

This diagram shows the relation of the critical angle to total internal reflection.

parts of a sphere). These lenses are convex or concave. A convex lens has a thicker center than edges; a concave lens has a thinner center than edges. A convex lens is a converging lens—it refracts light rays so that they meet. A concave lens refracts light rays so that they spread out; it is a diverging lens.

A double-convex or double-concave lens has two centers of curvature—one for each surface. Symmetrical lenses have surfaces of equal curvature. Each lens has a principal axis—an imaginary line that includes the two centers of curvature. Most rays that pass through a lens have their directions changed. However, rays that follow the principal axis and rays that cross the principal axis at a certain point do not have their directions of travel changed. The point on the principal axis through which all rays of unchanged direction pass is called the optical center of the lens.

Light rays entering a convex lens parallel to the principal axis are refracted to meet at a point after leaving the lens. This point is the principal focus. Light rays entering a concave lens parallel to the principal axis are refracted so that the rays appear to come from a point (the principal focus) in front of the lens. The focal length of a lens is the distance from the optical center to the principal focus along the principal axis. The focal length of a lens depends upon the size, curvature, and index of refraction of the lens.

Simple concave lenses form only one type of image of objects—virtual, upright, diminished images. Simple convex lenses form virtual, enlarged, upright images of objects closer than their principal focus. Convex lenses form real, inverted images of different sizes of objects farther away than their principal focus.

The same formula,

$$\frac{1}{D}+\frac{1}{d}=\frac{1}{f}$$

can be used to find image distances from both mirrors and lenses. When using the formula on lens problems, the object distance, D, is always positive. A concave lens has a negative focal length, f. The focal length of all convex lenses is positive. Real images have a positive image dis-

C and **C'** are centers of curvature; **F** is the principal focus; **P** is the optical center.

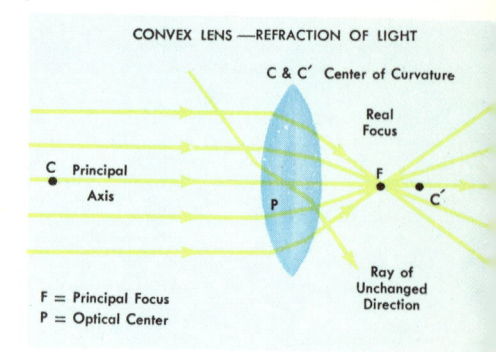

Parallel rays are brought to a virtual focus by concave lens; real focus, by convex lens.

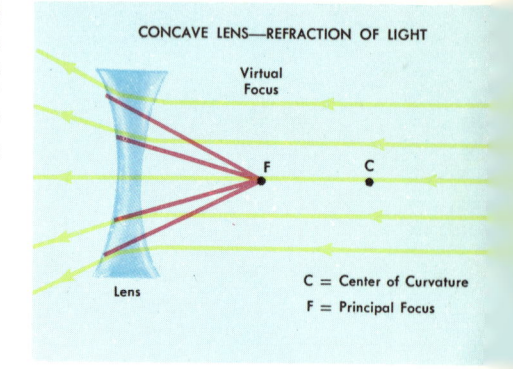

Concave lenses form only one type of image —virtual, upright, and reduced in size.

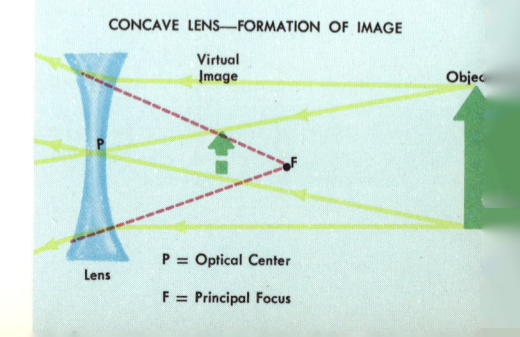

tance, *d*. Virtual images have negative image distances. Lens image sizes are found by the same method as mirror image sizes.

Light of all wavelengths travels at the same velocity in space; but in substances some wavelengths of light have a greater velocity than others. When a beam of white light, a mixture of all wavelengths, enters a substance, the wavelengths that have the greatest velocity in the substance are the least bent. The wavelengths that have the least velocity are refracted the most. Each wavelength has its own angle of refraction in a substance. Each different wavelength acquires a separate direction of travel because of its separate angle of refraction. The separation of wavelengths of light by refraction is called dispersion.

Different wavelengths of light affect the human eye as different colors, so we can see dispersion. When a beam of white light enters a prism, the prism bends the violet light the most and the red light the least. Violet light has the shortest wavelengths and the highest frequencies. Red light has the longest wavelengths and the lowest frequencies. We see the separated wavelengths of light as the colors of the rainbow, or a spectrum. The colors are arranged in the order of their wavelengths. See COLOR.

Polarized light has electric and magnetic field intensities that vibrate only in one direction perpendicular to its direction of travel. In ordinary light the field intensities vibrate in all directions perpendicular to the path of travel. A polarizing substance, such as Polaroid, stops all light trying to pass except light vibrating in one special direction. The light that gets through is polarized. Many crystals have the property of polarizing light.

LIGHT FILTER, a substance or combination of substances that absorbs some colors, or wavelengths of light, or that absorbs light waves vibrating in certain directions. (See COLOR; LIGHT.) Color filters absorb certain wavelengths of light and allow others to pass unchanged. A red filter, for example, transmits red light but absorbs blue and green light. Polarizing filters allow only light waves vibrating in one plane to pass. Light that has passed through a polarizing filter is called plane-polarized light.

Color filters can be used to produce special lighting effects. Both color and polarizing filters are much used in photography. See PHOTOGRAPHY.

The yellow filter shown below transmits red and green light. It absorbs blue light.

LIGHTHOUSE, a structure built on or near the coast of navigable waters to serve as a landmark by day and a warning light by night to guide shipping. Lighthouses are usually placed at salient points on the coast, on coastal islands, shoals, reefs, and sandbanks. A stone and reinforced concrete tower, circular in section, is the general form; but open structural-steel framework is used to advantage in some cases, as in the American Shoal Lighthouse off the Florida coast at Saddlebunch Key. This light is 109 feet above the water and is visible on a clear night for 16 miles. The brightest U.S. lighthouse, at Oak Island, North Carolina, has a candlepower of 14,000,000. There are many with more than a million candlepower.

The earliest recorded lighthouse was maintained in Asia Minor before 660 B.C. The Pharos, a lighthouse reported to be 100 feet square, was built at Alexandria, Egypt, about 280 B.C. It was one of the Seven Wonders of the World, and from its name was derived the word *pharology*, meaning "science of lighthouse construction."

The three types of apparatus used are: the catoptric, in which metal is used to reflect the light; the dioptric, in which glass is used and the light rays are refracted; and the catadioptric, in which both glass and metal are used.

To identify the light for the mariner there are nine different types of signaling: the fixed light; the slowly revolving light that flashes as it passes; the timed flashing light; the red or green light; the intermittent timed light; the intermittent light of unequal periods; the group flashing light, two or more in succession with an interval; fixed lights covering the whole horizon but with intermittent characteristics over certain areas; and the intermittent flashing light with a darkened period.

Lighthouses are now equipped with fog signals, radio, and radio beacons that enable the ships' officers to get their bearings through rotating antenna. The control and supervision of lighthouses is part of the service of the U.S. Coast Guard.

Lightships are stationed where it would be impractical or impossible to erect a lighthouse. All U.S. lightships are provided with radio telephone or telegraph. Lightships are self-propelled and carry electrical powerplants for the lights. These lightships are also under the control of the U.S. Coast Guard.

Warning lights of lighthouses guide ships.

Sketch shows image formed by convex lens of object farther away than principal focus.

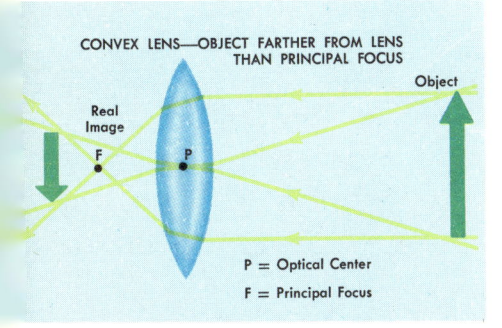

If object is closer to lens than principal focus, an enlarged, virtual image is formed.

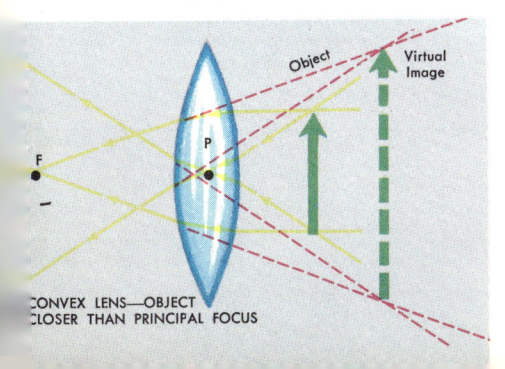

LIGHTING, or illumination, is the process of supplying light. Artifical lighting generally supplements or replaces natural daylight.

A foot-candle, the most commonly used measure of lighting, is the amount of light received from a source of 1 candle at a distance of 1 foot. (Originally, the standard of 1 candle was an ordinary candle of specified composition, wick structure, and rate of burning. The present candle, adopted by the International Committee of Weights and Measures, is the luminous intensity of 1/60 square centimeter of a black body radiator—one that absorbs all radiation falling upon it—operating at the temperature of solidification of platinum.) Sunlight on a clear day provides illumination ranging from 5,000 to 10,000 foot-candles.

The laws of illumination must be considered in designing the lighting to be used for a particular area. These laws state that the illumination for a given area increases with the intensity of the light source, and that the intensity of illumination decreases as the square of the increasing distance from the light source. This can be expressed in terms of foot-candles:

$$\text{number of foot-candles} = \frac{\text{candlepower of source}}{(\text{distance in feet})^2}$$

These laws and the equation that expresses them are used in designing lighting for the home or office and are also used by astronomers to calculate the distance of a star once the absolute brightness is calculated from the star's spectrum.

Desirable levels of lighting vary with use. A hotel lobby might have about 5 foot-candles; a library reading room, 30 foot-candles; an industrial drafting room, 50 foot-candles; and a hospital operating room, as high as 1,000 foot-candles. Light sources also vary. A 60-watt incandescent light produces 835 lumens; a 100-watt, 1,630 lumens; a 40-watt fluorescent tube, depending on its shade of white, 1,840 to 2,600 lumens. The fluorescent light has largely replaced the incandescent light in commercial, industrial, and some home lighting because of the more even lighting at lower cost that it provides. A newer type of lighting, called panel lighting or panelescent lighting, produces a gentle, even glow from large panels and promises to be even more efficient than fluorescent lighting. It is particularly adapted for use in decorative lighting.

Incandescent lights are operated by passing electric current through thin wire filament to make the wire white hot. The wire then emits visible light. Oxygen is sealed out by the glass bulb, and the wire in the bulb is thus prevented from burning up.

Fluorescent lights have a thin coating of a fluorescent phosphor on the inside of the tube. The tube contains mercury vapor from a drop of liquid mercury. This vapor conducts electricity through the tube; in so doing, it becomes heated, and the mercury atoms are excited and emit radiation, which is primarily ultraviolet. The ultraviolet radiation causes the phosphors to fluoresce and give off visible light.

Panel lighting, or panelescent lighting, employs a fixture that consists of a sheet of metal coated with three layers. It operates like a large condenser. The layer next to the steel contains phosphors that fluoresce in the electric field set up by current traveling in the steel and in the transparent conducting layer just above the phosphor. The third layer is electrical insulation. See LAMP.

LIGHT METER, an instrument that converts light energy into electrical energy and then indicates the strength of that current on a graduated scale. The light meter that photographers use is often called an exposure meter. Though several types of light meters have been designed, the only type commonly used today is the light meter that employs a photoelectric cell to convert the light energy into electrical energy. When light strikes the photoelectric cell, it generates a tiny electric current. This current, in turn, moves the needle of a sensitive microammeter across a graduated scale. The movement of the needle is proportional to the amount of light striking the photoelectric cell. This cell, by the way, does not run down, as a dry cell or other type of battery does. The reason is that the electrical energy it gives out is entirely derived from the light energy that falls upon it.

In photography a light meter is not generally needed for taking black-and-white snapshots. Black-and-white film allows for a wide margin of error in exposure time. Color film, however, demands more care. Really good color pictures can be taken only if the lens of the camera is correctly accommodated to the amount of light showing on the subject. The light meter is, therefore, a necessity for anyone regularly using color film. This meter may be built into the camera, or it may be a separate piece of equipment.

LIGHTNING is the flash of light caused by a discharge of atmospheric electricity between two clouds, between parts of clouds, or between a cloud and the earth. Lightning is a direct discharge lasting 0.00002 to 1 second or more. The current may be as much as 100,000 amperes, and the potential difference is about 100,000,000 volts. Lightning is a natural phenomenon associated with thunderstorms.

When a thundercloud forms, strong currents of air circulate within the cloud. Some air currents move upward. The rising air carries minute water particles that gradually grow as moisture collects on them. When the water has collected into large raindrops, it begins to fall. If the raindrops are very large, however, they fall so fast that they split into several smaller drops.

A photographer's light meter indicates light intensity on a graduated scale. Proper camera adjustments are read from a round dial.

Courtesy of Weston Instruments, Division of Daystrom, Inc.

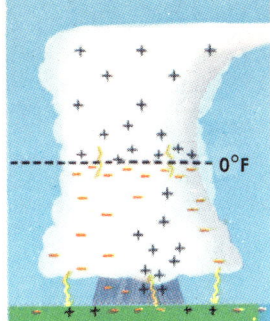

The cause of lightning (above) is the attraction of unlike electrical charges. Airplane and car passengers and people in houses fixed with lightning rods are relatively safe from lightning.

When a raindrop splits, its balanced charges of electricity get separated. The smaller particles of the split raindrop have one kind of charge; the larger, an opposite charge. The smaller particles are carried upward by the rising currents of air; the larger particles fall to the ground or collect near the bottom of the thundercloud. Soon tremendous charges of static electricity are built up in different parts of the cloud.

Opposite charges are always attracted to each other. When a large enough number of opposite charges are accumulated to overcome the insulating effect of the air, an electric discharge takes place. This discharge is lightning. Most lightning takes place between two parts of a cloud where opposite charges have accumulated. Discharges, or lightning strokes, also take place between two different clouds. Sometimes, about once out of every hundred discharges, a bolt of lightning travels between a cloud and the ground.

When a thundercloud passes over the earth, the ground beneath the cloud becomes highly charged. The charge of the ground is the opposite of that in the lower part of the cloud. The ground has the opposite charge because of electrostatic induction. If the lower part of the cloud is negatively charged, the negative component of the earth's balanced charges is repelled from the area under the cloud, and the earth is left with a positive charge. This condition makes possible a stroke of lightning.

Each year some people are killed by lightning. People can protect themselves from lightning by taking a few simple precautions during thunderstorms. Go inside a steel-framed building or a building protected by lightning rods. Even if lightning strikes the building, it will pass harmlessly to the ground and not hurt a person inside. A closed car also provides very good protection from lightning. Do not take shelter under an isolated tree during a storm—lone trees are just the sort of object lightning is apt to hit. Do not walk about open country, such as golf courses and beaches, and do not go swimming. If you are caught in open country during a thunderstorm, stay away from small hilltops, wire fences, and isolated shacks. The best thing to do is to find a hollow and sit or lie down in it.

Buildings are protected from lightning by lightning rods. Lightning rods are metallic conductors. The part of the conductor on the roof of a building has a sharp point. The rest of the conductor extends from the top of the building down into moist earth, which is also a conductor. The function of a lightning rod is to prevent a buildup of electrical charge on a building. Remember that charges are induced in the ground and on buildings by a passing thundercloud. The charges on a building are attracted to the opposite charges in the cloud, but the charges on the building cannot escape from the flat building surfaces unless there is a sudden electrical discharge, a stroke of lightning, between the building and the cloud. However, it is easy for such charges to escape from the tip of a pointed conductor like a lightning rod. The gradual escape of charges produces a gradual electrical discharge and prevents a sudden discharge.

LIGHTNING BUG. See FIREFLY.

LIGHT-YEAR, an astronomical unit of measurement equal to nearly 6,000,000,000,000 miles. It is defined as the distance traveled by light through a vacuum during one year. The speed of light—approximately 186,300 miles, or 299,800 kilometers, per second—times the number of seconds in a year—31,558,150 (365 days, 6 hours, 9 minutes, 10 seconds) —gives the value of the light-year as approximately 5,879,000,000,000 miles, or 9,461,000,000,000 kilometers. (See YEAR.) Some idea of this distance may be obtained from the fact that light leaving the sun reaches the earth in only eight minutes, passes our outermost planet, Pluto, in about five hours, and is 1,600 times farther than Pluto after a year. Yet light takes over four years to reach even the closest star. It is this enormous distance between stars that requires such a large unit of measurement. Astronomers also use a still larger unit, the parsec.

LILAC, shrubs and small trees of the olive family. They are widely planted for their colorful, fragrant flowers and attractive foliage. The small, single flowers are tubular with four lobes, but double forms are also grown. The flowers are borne in large, dense clusters in April, May, or June, according to variety. Colors are white, pink, lavender, and purple. Lilacs should be planted in sunny locations. The flowers are forced into bloom during the winter and early spring in greenhouses in The Netherlands and are shipped by airplane all over the Western world. They are also important in the perfume industry. Most lilacs are native to southeastern Europe, but some are found in Asia Minor and northern Asia.

Blooming lilac bushes have become a traditional poetic symbol of spring.

White flowers of the regal lily are tinged with pink. The orange and yellow flowers of the tiger lily are speckled with black.

LILY, one of the most important garden-plant families. Included in this family, in addition to the true lilies, are these valuable flowers: day lily, hyacinth, narcissus, and tulip. Vegetables in the lily family are asparagus and onion. The true lilies include over 100 species native to many parts of the world. True lilies grow from scaly bulbs and have upright stems with slender leaves. The flowers have six equal parts, which are often united to form funnel shapes. The showy flowers vary in color from white to yellow, pink, red, or orange and are often spotted or banded on their inner surfaces. They are usually borne in clusters at the top of the stem.

The tiger lily, a native of China and Japan, has 5-inch-wide, black-spotted orange flowers. The Easter lily has white, fragrant, trumpet-shaped flowers. Although originally native to Asia present-day Easter lilies are the result of hybridization. The Madonna lily, which has white, waxy flowers and is native to Greece and Asia Minor, was depicted in Renaissance paintings to symbolize the Annunciation to the Virgin Mary. Other popular garden lilies are the regal lily, the Japanese lily, the gold-banded lily, and the candlestick lily. Among many nonlily plants are the water lily and the calla lily.

LILY OF THE VALLEY, a dwarf perennial herb of the lily family, is native to northern Europe and Asia. The tiny, white, fragrant, bell-shaped flowers appear in May on slender spikes about 5 to 8 inches long. The attractive oval leaves arise directly from underground rootstalks. The lily of the valley grows best in shady or partly shady places. It is a favorite for bridal bouquets. To supply this continuous demand florists use greenhouses to force the budded rootstalks, called pips, into flower throughout the year. The pips are kept in cold storage until needed. The flowers are much used in France in making perfume and toilet water.

LIMA is the capital and by far the largest city of Peru. It is the leading city of the country; the administrative, cultural, financial, and commercial center. Lima is situated on the Rímac River in west-central Peru, 7 miles east of Callao, its Pacific port. It has a population of about 1,200,000.

Lima is a modern city with a rich historic background. Among the noteworthy public buildings and institutions are the cathedral (on the site of the cathedral for which Francisco Pizarro laid the cornerstone in 1535), the lavish monastery of San Francisco, San Marcos University (founded in 1551, and one of the oldest in the Americas), and more than 60 churches. Elaborate colonial palaces and mansions, striking government buildings, and many beautiful parks and monuments are outstanding attractions. Lima has a pleasant, dry, semitropical climate with little rain and an average temperature of 66° F. Fogs are prevalent in the winter.

The city is an industrial center with foundries, oil refineries, textile mills, food-processing plants, and tanneries among its important manufacturing establishments.

Founded in 1535 by Francisco Pizarro, Lima was for nearly three centuries the seat of Spanish culture and authority in South America. It was a stronghold for Spanish resistance until 1821, when San Martín entered the city and proclaimed Peru's independence.

Key limes are yellow and round. Persian limes are green and oval shaped.

LIME, a citrus fruit that is closely related to the lemon and is used similarly. The lime tree is native to southeastern India but is now extensively grown in southern Europe, Florida, the West Indies, and Mexico. It rarely reaches a height of over 10 feet. Its cultivation is similar to that of the orange and lemon.

Limes are used to flavor candies and beverages and are a source of

The Cathedral (right) and the President's Palace can be seen on Lima's Plaza de Armas.
Courtesy of PANAGRA

The white cliffs in Wind Canyon, South Dakota, are chalk, a type of limestone. Chalk consists of minute calcareous remains of animals and plants that lived in shallow seas.

citric acid. They are rich in vitamin C. In the days of sailing vessels sailors on long voyages ate limes in order to prevent scurvy. British sailors were dubbed "limeys" because of their practice of eating limes when at sea.

There are two distinct groups of limes, acid and sweet. Only acid limes are grown commercially in the United States. The sweet limes, however, are much prized by the peoples of Egypt, South America, Central America, and Mexico.

LIMERICK, a comic-verse form consisting of five lines in anapest rhythm with the rhyme scheme *a a b b a*. The third and fourth lines have two feet; the others, three. The name for this type of verse is probably derived from the town of Limerick in southwestern Ireland, although the reason for the association is not known. The limerick became popular in the 19th century, especially as a parlor game. Sometimes the group of persons present would compose one of these humorous stanzas. Sometimes one person would recite a nearly completed limerick to the others and ask them to think of a good last line. Limericks cover a wide variety of subjects. Two of the best known writers of limericks are Ogden Nash and Edward Lear, many of whose limericks contain references to ridiculous or eccentric behavior. See LEAR, EDWARD.

LIMESTONE is a sedimentary rock composed chiefly of calcium carbonate, $CaCO_3$. Some limestones also contain calcium magnesium carbonate, $CaMg(CO_3)_2$, or dolomite. (See DOLOMITE.) Limestone is a common rock; extensive deposits are found in many parts of the world.

Limestone is usually white, light gray, dark gray, tan, or bluish gray. Limestones are soft. They can easily be scratched with a knife. They all react vigorously with hydrochloric acid. The texture depends on the variety of limestone. Exposed surfaces of limestone have rounded corners, and the joints and cracks of the rock have been widened by solution. Limestones occur in layers, called beds, which may be less than 1 inch or more than 100 feet thick. Some limestones are interbedded with shale or sandstone. Some limestones contain nodules or layers of flint. Fossils are abundant in most limestones.

Some limestones are composed chiefly of the fossil shells and hard parts of organisms, such as corals, mollusks, crinoids, brachiopods, bryozoans, and foraminifers. Fine-grained calcite cements the shells and hard parts together. Other limestones are composed of dense, fine-grained calcite chemically precipitated from sea water.

Most limestones contain some impurities. The commonest impurities are quartz sand and clay minerals. If a limestone contains large amounts of clay minerals, it is called an argillaceous limestone. If it contains much quartz sand, it is called arenaceous limestone. Some limestones contain considerable amounts of organic matter. These limestones are dark colored and give off a disagreeable odor when they are broken. They are called bituminous limestones.

Coquina is a limestone made of loosely packed and cemented shells and fragments of shells. It is a porous and fragile rock.

Oolitic limestone consists of small spheres, called oolites, of calcium carbonate. Each sphere is made up of concentric shells of calcium carbonate. The spheres are cemented together by fine-grained calcite.

Travertine is calcium carbonate precipitated at spring mouths, especially at the mouths of warm springs. Travertine is porous, loose, and crumbly. It is often stained red or yellow by iron oxides. Calcium carbonate is deposited from spring water because some of the water evaporates or because the water loses most of its carbon dioxide content. Carbon dioxide in the spring water originally converted nearly insoluble calcium carbonate into soluble calcium bicarbonate. When the carbon dioxide is lost, calcium carbonate is precipitated. Algae that secrete calcium carbonate help deposit calcium carbonate from warm spring waters.

For a discussion of other varieties of limestone, see CHALK; STALACTITE AND STALAGMITE.

Limestone is used for many purposes. It is used as a building stone and as road metal. Limestone is quarried for use as a flux in making iron and steel. Large quantities of limestone are used in the manufacture of portland cement, lime for plaster, and fertilizers.

LINCOLN, ABRAHAM (1809-1865), 16th president of the United States, was born in Hardin Co. (now Larue Co.), Kentucky, Feb. 12, 1809. Most of his boyhood was spent in Spencer Co., Indiana, where his mother, Nancy Hanks Lincoln, died in 1818. In 1831 Abraham settled at New Salem, Ill., where he remained for the next six years. During that time he clerked in a store, managed a mill, split rails, served as village postmaster, and worked at a number of odd jobs. At the same time he studied law. During the Black Hawk War he served as a volunteer captain, and from 1834 to 1841 he sat in the state legislature, where he was floor leader of the Whig party.

In 1842 he married Mary Todd. His political interests continued, and he was elected to Congress, serving the term 1847-1849. At this time he became known for his opposition to

Abraham Lincoln

Abraham Lincoln was born in this log cabin in Hardin (now Larue) Co., Kentucky.

the Mexican War. His constituents disapproved of his stand, and he did not seek reelection. He seemed to have retired from politics until the Kansas-Nebraska Bill brought the extension-of-slavery issue to a head in 1854. Lincoln attacked the bill and in 1856 joined the new Republican party. In 1858 he became his party's candidate for the U.S. Senate against the country's leading Democratic contender for the 1860 presidential nomination, Stephen A. Douglas, who was senator from Illinois.

In a series of debates with Douglas, Lincoln argued against the extension of slavery into the territories. He opposed any interference with slavery in the South but thought that if the extension of slavery were prohibited, the institution would eventually die out. Though Lincoln lost the election, he was now a national figure. He gained popularity as a possible nominee for the presidency with his Cooper Institute speech in New York in February, 1860, in which he called for reconciliation and the preservation of the Union. Nominated by the Republican party convention that year, he was elected president.

The South regarded Lincoln's election as a deadly threat to slavery, and the secession movement was well under way before his inauguration. Thus, when he assumed office, the Confederacy had already been organized. Lincoln was determined to preserve the Union. The fall of Fort Sumter in April, 1861, led to a call for troops. Although hampered by the activities of a hard core of demagogues in Congress (the Radical Republicans), who sought to undermine his conduct of the war, and harassed by the zealous abolitionists, whose cause was being subordinated to the war effort, Lincoln steered a steady course. Preservation of the Union was his sole aim. The emancipation of the slaves in 1863 was primarily a war measure. Difficult generals, bumptious and ambitious politicians, disloyalty behind Union lines, possible war with England and France, violation of the Monroe Doctrine in Mexico, and several years of defeat for the Union forces constituted his chief difficulties. He prevailed in the face of all obstacles. The hard core of radicals within the party sought to prevent his renomination in 1864. But a burst of military victories and a consequent surge of Lincoln popularity forced them to drop their opposition. Since the Southern states did not vote in the election of 1864, Lincoln had both popular and electoral majorities. The war seemed to be nearly over. The Hampton Roads Conference (February, 1865) failed to produce peace, but Robert E. Lee surrendered to Ulysses S. Grant at Appomattox on Apr. 9, 1865. Lincoln was planning statesman-like reconstruction policies based on moderation and reconciliation, when, on the evening of Apr. 14, 1865, he was assassinated at Ford's Theater by John Wilkes Booth. He died the following morning.

At Lincoln's second inauguration, shown below, the President counseled Americans ". . . to do all which may achieve and cherish a just and lasting peace . . . ."

Library of Congress

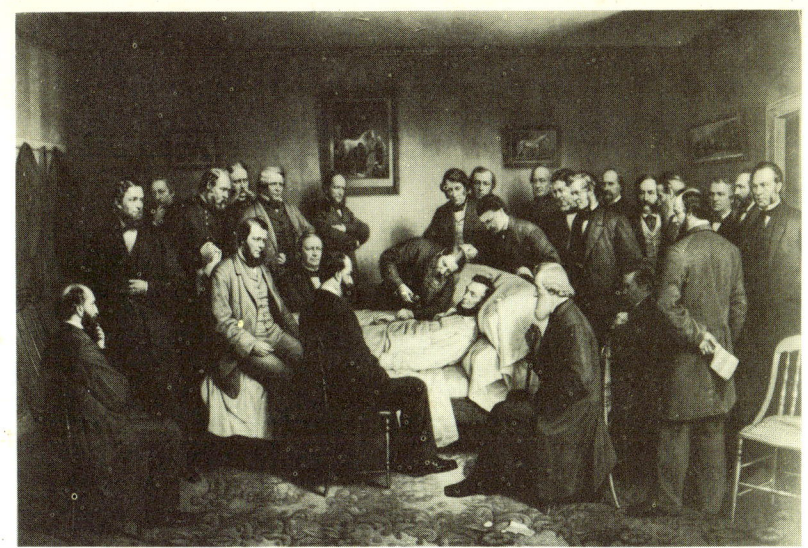

Lincoln was shot by John Wilkes Booth. Above is an artist's conception of Lincoln's death.
Library of Congress

LINCOLN, the capital of Nebraska, in the southeastern part of the state, 50 miles southwest of Omaha. It is the shipping center for a large farming district, and its chief industries are meatpacking, canning, and the manufacture of bricks and tiles. As a railroad center it also has large

Lincoln, the capital of Nebraska

railroad-repair shops. Lincoln is an important insurance center and is the leading educational center of the state. It is the seat of the University of Nebraska, Nebraska Wesleyan University, and Union College. The city is noted for its skyscraper Capitol, completed in 1932. Lincoln is the site of various state institutions, including a penitentiary, an orphans home, and an orthopedic hospital. The city began as the village of Lancaster, which was chosen as the state capital in 1867. The name was changed in the same year to Lincoln. In 1960 the population was 128,521.

LINCOLN-DOUGLAS DEBATES, a series of debates that took place between Abraham Lincoln and Stephen A. Douglas in 1858, when both were candidates for U.S. senator from Illinois. Lincoln and Douglas conducted their debates amid growing tension over the slavery issue. The most recent event to rouse public excitement had been the Dred Scott case. It implied that slavery could be carried even into free states.

Lincoln had opened his campaign with a speech containing the famous words, " 'A house divided against itself cannot stand.' I believe that this nation cannot endure half slave and half free. I do not expect the Union to be dissolved . . . but I do expect that it will cease to be divided. It will become all one thing or all the other." In the first of the debates Douglas attacked this speech as a threat to the unity of the nation.

Lincoln counterattacked at the next debate, which occurred at Freeport, Ill., by asking Douglas whether a state could exclude slavery. If Douglas, in order to support his doctrine of popular—or squatter—sovereignty, had answered yes, he would have opposed the Dred Scott decision and thereby infuriated Southern Democrats. If Douglas had answered no, he would have denied his own doctrine. Douglas avoided the dilemma by giving a practical answer that became famous as the so-called Freeport Doctrine. He said that slavery could not exist in a state unless it had special laws protecting the property rights of slave-owners. This answer won the election for Douglas but lost him Southern support in the presidential election two years later.

Lincoln went on to claim at the debate in Quincy, Ill., that the question of slavery was a moral one and that slavery was wrong. Douglas replied that slavery was not a moral issue but simply a political matter for each of the various states to settle in its own way.

Lincoln, in calling slavery a wrong, did not mean that the federal government should take action against slavery in the states where it was already established. He did not oppose a fugitive-slave law so long as it would not extend slavery to free states or territories. He favored legislation that would prevent the spread of slavery and hoped that slavery would eventually die out in the slave states.

The Lincoln-Douglas debates of 1858 gave Lincoln a national reputation.

LINCOLN MEMORIAL, a monument, generally considered the finest piece of memorial architecture in the United States. It stands in Potomac Park, Washington, D.C., at one end of the long grassy strip called the Mall. It was designed by Henry Bacon and contains a statue of Abraham Lincoln by Daniel Chester French. Built mostly of white marble, it was dedicated in 1922. The 36 columns in the colonnade surrounding the building stand for the 36 states in existence at the time of Lincoln's death. The names of these states appear in the first row of decoration above the columns.

The Lincoln Memorial, in Washington, D.C.
L. B. Prince

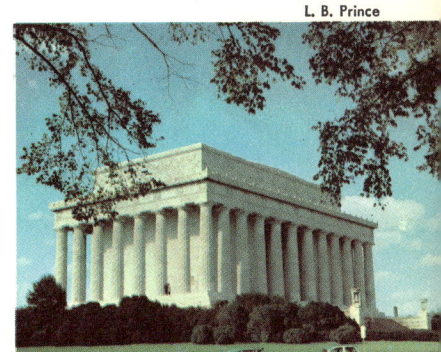

LINCOLN'S BIRTHDAY is a holiday in many parts of the United States. It is celebrated each year on February 12, the birth date of Abraham Lincoln, who was born in 1809. The first celebration of the day occurred in Washington, D.C., in 1866, the year after Lincoln's death. Officials in Washington honored Lincoln with a memorial service and speeches. In 1892 Illinois declared Lincoln's birthday a legal holiday and was the first of 30 states to do so.

LIND, JENNY (1820-1887), a Swedish soprano, was born in Stockholm. She studied singing in the Stockholm Conservatory and then in Paris and in the German city of Dresden. In 1838 she made her debut in the role of Agathe in the opera *Der Freischütz* at the Court Theater in Stockholm. She sang in operas throughout Europe until 1849 and then devoted all her time to concert work. From 1850 to 1852 she toured the United States, an event sponsored and managed by P.T. Barnum. She gained success and renown throughout the world and became popularly known as the Swedish Nightingale. She made her last public appearance in 1883.

LINDBERGH, CHARLES (1902-   ), American aviator, was born at Detroit and grew up in Little Falls, Minn., and in Washington, D.C., where his father was a member of Congress for ten years. He enrolled in a flying school at Lincoln, Neb., in 1922; two years later he entered the Army Air Service as a cadet at Kelly Field, Texas. After securing his commission as a second lieutenant in 1925 he became an airmail pilot and was engaged on the night service between St. Louis and Chicago.

Attracted by the offer of $25,000 for a flight across the Atlantic nonstop from New York to Paris, he set out from Roosevelt Field, Long Island, on May 20, 1927. He successfully accomplished the journey of 3,600 miles of Le Bourget airfield at Paris in 33½ hours in a single-motored plane, the *Spirit of St. Louis* (which is now in the Smithsonian Institution in Washington, D.C.). This exploit won him immediate fame; he became a popular hero and received honors from the French, Belgian, British, and United States governments. He made a good-will air tour of Latin America in 1928. With his wife, Anne Morrow Lindbergh, he flew to Japan by way of the Arctic Circle in 1931, and in 1933 he visited 21 countries on four continents. In 1932 the nation was grieved by the kidnaping and death of the Lindberghs' first-born son. The publicity that followed the kidnaping and the trial and conviction of Bruno Hauptmann resulted in the passage of new kidnaping laws with more severe penalties than had previously been in effect. Lindbergh lost much of his popularity in 1941 by joining the isolationist America First group, but he partly recovered it during World War II by his services as a civilian flyer and technician. In 1954 Lindbergh was appointed brigadier general in the reserve. He is the author of *We*, *Of Flight and Life*, and *The Spirit of St. Louis*, for which he won a Pulitzer prize. His wife has published several books of prose and verse.

Brown Brothers

The various species of linden trees range in height from 50 to 120 feet.

LINDEN, the popular name of a genus of deciduous trees that includes about 30 species native to the North Temperate Zone. The three species of linden most widely cultivated in Europe are not the same as the one that is most widely cultivated in North America. However, all of these species are somewhat similar.

Most species of linden are tall trees with a broad, symmetrical crown of heart-shaped leaves. They have small, fragrant, yellowish-white flowers that grow in drooping clusters and attract many bees. The flower stalk is joined to a strap-shaped bract, which helps disperse the mature fruits. Honey made from linden flowers has a distinctive flavor.

Because of their stateliness, graceful form, and abundant shade, lindens are often planted in public parks and in rows along boulevards throughout Europe and North America. The famous Unter den Linden of Berlin is a wide avenue bordered on each side by linden trees. The name of this avenue comes from German words meaning "under the lindens." Some lindens are also known as lime trees or basswoods.

LINDSAY, VACHEL (1879-1931), American poet, was born in Springfield, Ill. He went to Hiram College and was an art student in Chicago

American aviator Charles A. Lindbergh stands beside the *Spirit of St. Louis*. This photograph was taken at the time of his record-making transatlantic solo flight.

and New York. Lindsay took tramp tours through the United States and spent part of his winters lecturing on temperance and art.

Lindsay's first book, *General William Booth Enters into Heaven and Other Poems*, was published in 1913. Besides the title poem it contains "The Eagle That Is Forgotten." The following year he published *The Congo and Other Poems*, which included his noted poem "Abraham Lincoln Walks at Midnight." *The Chinese Nightingale and Other Poems* appeared in 1917. It contained the poem "The Ghost of the Buffaloes." Two editions of Lindsay's *Collected Poems* appeared, one in 1923 and a revised edition in 1925. His prose works include *A Handy Guide for Beggars* and *The Litany of Washington Street*.

LINEAR ACCELERATOR. See Particle Accelerator.

LINEN includes all the yarns spun, and the fabrics woven, from the fibers of the flax plant. The term *linen* is also used to refer collectively to such household items as sheets, towels, and tablecloths.

The history of linen is long. Before 4000 B.C. the Egyptians were wrapping their dead Pharaohs in linen, and the Bible records the weaving of linen for fine garments and for religious ceremonies. The Romans brought flax to Gaul and Britain and thus laid the cornerstone for a world-renowned industry. By the 11th century Flanders was noted for the manufacture of fine table linens. The real beginning of the Irish linen industry can be traced to the exiled French Huguenots who settled near Belfast in 1694 and who brought with them the knowledge of how to make fine linen. The Pilgrims carried flaxseed to the New World, and every early American family spun and wove its own linen for household use.

During the Industrial Revolution cotton began to be produced rapidly and cheaply. Because of this it largely displaced linen, with its high costs of cultivation and labor. The first successful factory for weaving linen by power was established in London in 1812. Yet, the whole process of producing linen remained slow, painstaking, and costly.

Today machines have been developed for cultivating flax, but much work is still done by hand. Only once in five years may a field be planted with flax. When the flax is ripe, it is pulled, never cut, to keep the entire plant, top to roots, intact. Separating the flax fibers from the core and covering, a process called retting, takes at least seven days, during which the fibers are soaked in water to loosen them from the rotted core. Rollers at the mill break and discard the useless woody portions of the stalk. Hackling, or cleaning and straightening, the flax is done by a series of combs. This combing separates the flax fibers into two types: line, which are long, smooth, top-quality fibers; and tow, which are shorter, fuzzy fibers, used in lower priced goods frequently known as crash. In roving, the fibers are loosely twisted to hold them together. The fibers are then spun into yarn, which is woven into linen fabrics. Hundreds of weaving variations produce different textures and patterns. Bleaching, once done by spreading the cloth outdoors on the grass, is now often accomplished by modern chemical methods. After bleaching, linens are vat dyed to produce a color that is fade resistant in wear and washing. The fabric may be printed by roller, screen, or hand-block processes.

Linen has many characteristics that are well liked. It has a smooth and lustrous finish; it does not soil easily and is a cool fabric; it launders and wears evenly and well; and it has double the strength of any other natural fiber.

The leading world producers of linen are Ireland and Belgium, which are noted for the artistry of their designs as well as the quality of their textiles. England, Scotland, and the U.S.S.R. also produce large quantities of linen. The United States manufactures linen thread in the Pacific Northwest, but it uses imported yarn for textile weaving.

LINE OF DEMARCATION, a geographical line drawn May 4, 1493, by Pope Alexander VI. It divided the world not ruled by other Christian kings between the kings of Spain and Portugal. Such a division was a consequence of Christopher Columbus' discovery of the New World. The pope set the line at 100 leagues west of the Azores and the Cape Verde Islands. All land west not held by a Christian prince on Dec. 25, 1492, was to belong to Spain. By the Treaty of Tordesillas on June 7, 1494, between Spain and Portugal, the Line of Demarcation was moved 270 leagues westward; Portugal was to have all lands east of it and Spain all west of it. Thus Portugal acquired Brazil.

LINNAEUS, CAROLUS (1707-1778), the Latinized name of Swedish naturalist Carl von Linné. The son of a Lutheran pastor, Linnaeus was born in Smaland province and received his early education in the grammar school and gymnasium at Vaxjo. He continued his studies at the universities of Lund and Uppsala. At the latter place his interest in the natural sciences, botany in particular, was encouraged. He was appointed an assistant lecturer on botany at Uppsala in 1730. Two years later Linnaeus made a botanical expedition to Lapland under the sponsorship of the university. Soon afterward he traveled to The Netherlands for further study. While there he took a degree in medicine from the University of Harderwijk. After journeying through England and France he returned to Sweden in 1738 and established a medical practice in Stockholm. In 1741 he was appointed professor of medicine at Uppsala and, later, professor of botany, a position that he held for the remainder of his active life. The immense popularity of Linnaeus' botany lectures caused a marked increase in the university's enrollment. In 1761 Linnaeus was raised to the Swedish nobility.

The founder of systematic botany, Linnaeus is remembered for introducing the system of binomial nomenclature, which, in principle, is in use today. First applied to the vegetable kingdom, the system was was later extended to the animal kingdom as well. Today every plant and animal is identified by a name consisting of two Latin words. The first is the name of a genus; the second, of a species. Although subsequent study modified certain aspects of the system, its fundamental principles survive.

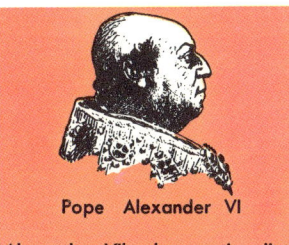

Pope Alexander VI

Alexander VI's demarcation line (broken line at right) was moved west to the solid line. Spain then had the zone west of the solid line.

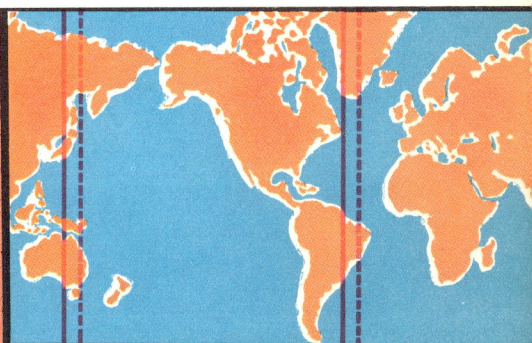

1480

LINOLEUM, a waterproof floor covering made from an oxidized vegetable oil, powdered cork or wood flour, and a backing of asphalt-impregnated cloth or felt. Linoleum manufacturing began in 1860, when Frederick Walton, of England, observed that a useful paste could be made from the surface scum of dried linseed oil. He mixed ground cork and colors into the linseed paste and applied the mixture to a cloth backing placed between heavy rollers. Thirty years later the same inventor developed the rotary laying machine, which made possible the great inlaid-linoleum industry. The pattern in inlaid linoleum goes through to the backing.

Inlaid linoleum is sold in two forms: tiles 9 by 9 inches and strips 6 feet wide. Linoleum should be laid over a felt base and laid down with a special linoleum paste. Before it is laid, the roll of linoleum should stand in a warm room overnight because cold linoleum cracks easily. The felt base should first be fitted to corners and around obstructions. Then, using the trimmed felt base as a pattern, the linoleum may be cut with a curved linoleum knife to exact shape.

In cleaning or waxing linoleum it

Long-wearing, easy-to-clean, brightly patterned linoleum is ideal for kitchen floors.
Photograph Courtesy Armstrong Resilient Floors

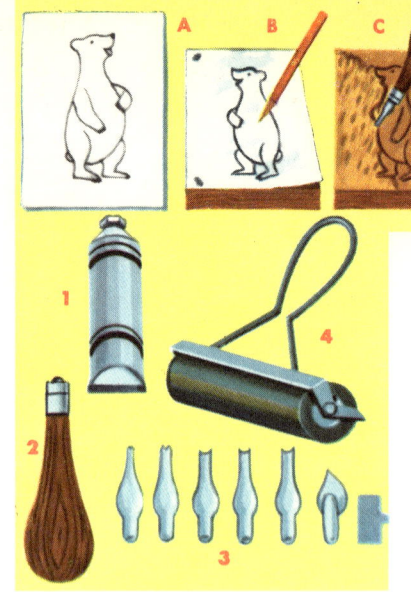

At left are shown materials needed for making linoleum block prints: **1**, ink; **2**, gouger handle; **3**, gouging blades of various shapes; **4**, a brayer to ink the design for printing. The drawings above show the stages in making the print. The original drawing, **A**, is copied on a piece of tissue, which is reversed, **B**, and placed on the block, and the design is transferred by tracing over a carbon. The design, **C**, is cut into the surface of the linoleum. All the surface outside the design is also trimmed away to a depth of about 1/8 inch. The design is inked, **D**, and a sheet of thick white paper is pressed on it. Last, **E**, is the finished print.

is necessary to avoid the use of any product that will dissolve the bonding materials in the linoleum.

The linoleum industry is absorbing many of the latest developments in foam rubber, the new adhesives, and the vinyl compounds. Rolls and tiles of asphalt, cork, and rubber laid over foam rubber and asbestos underlayments may provide greater foot comfort and total quietness in a building than is possible with plain wood or cement floors. In one of the new tiles colored vinyl chips embedded in translucent vinyl appear to be floating, but the surface is smooth, tough, and resilient. Another type has multicolored and translucent vinyl chips fused to give a soft jewel tone suggestive of fine china.

LINOLEUM BLOCK, a square or rectangular piece of linoleum with a design cut into the surface. The design is gouged out of the linoleum with a sharp tool in much the same way that a wood block is engraved. Linoleum itself is a hard and fairly durable material, made of powdered cork or wood flour and whiting, color pigments, and linseed-oil paste, which holds the various particles of the mixture together. More recently soybean oil has come to be used in place of linseed oil. Strips of felt, burlap, canvas, or similar fabrics serve as backing for the linoleum mixture.

Block printing on linoleum is a way of making prints from the design engraved on the block. The block can be inked in any color and pressed down firmly on a piece of paper or cloth, or it may be left face up as the paper is rubbed evenly with a spoon to receive the impression of the original design.

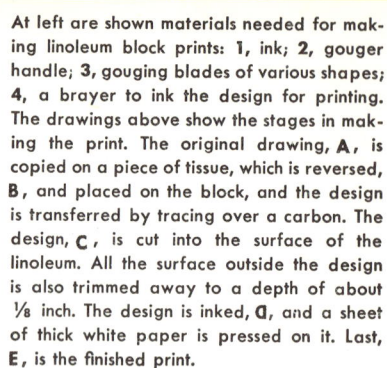

Until the hand becomes skilled in cutting, designs cut into the block should be fairly simple. Even so, linoleum is not the best medium for doing intricate work. Details may be painted in after the print has been made from the block and is thoroughly dry. This engraving technique is a popular one nowadays, especially for use in the home. Many people like to make their own Christmas cards and to monogram their stationery with linoleum blocks. Posters and bookplates can also be printed this way.

LINOTYPE, a trade name for a typesetting machine, on which an entire line of type is composed and cast at one time. The individual letters and symbols, called matrices, are small brass molds with depressed characters. They are stored in containers, called magazines, above a power-driven keyboard of 90 keys. As the operator touches the keys, the desired matrices are released from the magazines and automatically assembled in a line, along with extensible steel spacing devices (called spacebands) between words or other groups of characters. When the line of matrices and spacebands has been completely assembled, the operator presses a lever, and all subsequent actions pertaining to that line are carried on automatically.

The line of matrices and spacebands is carried before an adjustable steel mold and a metal pot. The spacebands between the character groups are driven upward, which extends the line to the exact width desired and evenly spaces the words.

Molten metal is forced from the metal pot into the mold and against the casting edge of the matrices and spacebands, thus forming a bar of type, or Linotype slug. The slug, which quickly cools, is trimmed and delivered onto a container, called a galley, and is ready for printing. In the meantime the matrices and spacebands have been returned to their containers for use over and over again. When a Linotype slug has served its purpose, it may be melted; and the metal is used indefinitely for new and made-to-order lines of type.

Linotypes are used in all parts of the world—in fine book-publishing houses, in high-class commercial printing plants, on oceangoing vessels, and by nearly all newspapers—and are producing composition in more than 70 languages.

Although the Linotype bears the name of Ottmar Mergenthaler, its inventor, it is a product of many minds. After nearly ten years of trial and error Mergenthaler completed the first commercially successful Linotype machine. This machine began producing type in the plant of the New York *Tribune* on July 3, 1886. Whitelaw Reid, at the time the leading spirit of the *Tribune*, gave the machine its name—Linotype. The coming of the Linotype was hailed the world over as the greatest event in the history of printing since the invention of movable type.

A mated lion and lioness and their cubs often live together and cooperate in hunting prey.

LION, most celebrated representative of the carnivorous mammals and chief member of the cat family. The lion is distinguished by the great mane that covers the head, neck, and shoulders of the male; the uniform, unmarked, tawny skin (without the stripes common in cats); the long tuft of hair at the end of the smooth tail; and the loud and characteristic roar. The African lion is up to 8 feet in length, including a 3-foot tail, and stands 4 feet high. The female is smaller and lacks the characteristic mane of the male. Though some authorities believe the lion not so strong and fierce as the tiger, he is certainly the most imposing of the cats. In prehistoric times lions ranged much more widely than now, over almost all of Europe. Even in historical times they were perhaps still in Greece. Now the African continent is their chief habitat, although some are found in India, Iran, and Iraq.

Lions are generally nocturnal, sleeping during the day and at night stalking their prey through the brush or lurking in the brushwood near a waterhole to spring upon animals coming to drink. Lions will at times attack man, but man-eaters are less common than among tigers. Sometimes found solitary, lions often go in pairs or small troops. They apparently mate for life, two to four cubs being born at a birth once each year. In captivity lions are less fierce than tigers and breed more readily. Exhibitions of lions and combats between gladiators and lions were outstanding features in the ancient Roman arenas. Lucius Cornelius Sulla and Hadrian were said to have each exhibited 100 at one time, and Pompey the Great as many as 600. In the persecutions the Christians were frequently condemned to be cast to the lions in the arena.

LION, THE (constellation). See LEO.

LIQUID describes the physical state of any material that is characterized by an ability to conform to the shape of the containing vessel (unlike a solid) and by having a definite volume and surface (unlike a gas). Water is the commonest liquid.

A liquid is made up of many small particles, called molecules, which move about in a random fashion, frequently bumping into each other.

A liquid flows when an outside force causes an appreciable portion of the liquid to move in a particular direction. Some liquids, like water, flow easily, while other liquids, such as glycerol and molasses, offer considerable resistance to flow. The extent of this resistance to flow is indicated by the viscosity of the liquid.

Freezing usually takes place when a liquid, through cooling, is changed to the solid state. When a liquid is heated, it eventually changes to a vapor or gas. The temperature at which this conversion primarily takes place is the boiling point of the specific liquid.

An operator sits at the keyboard of a Linotype, striking a key for each character to be printed. Matrices are released from the magazine (seen above and to the right of the operator's head) and sent, one line at a time, to the casting mechanism (to the operator's left).

Lisbon, the capital of Portugal, is an ancient city. With one of the best harbors in Europe, it has been a seaport since early times.

LISBON, seaport, capital of Portugal, of the province of Estremadura, and of the district of Lisboa, on the Tagus estuary, 10 miles from the river entrance into the Atlantic Ocean. It has a population of just under 1,000,000.

The city lies in a valley surrounded by hills and is built on a series of terraces. A few of the ancient or important buildings are the castle of St. George, the cathedral of St. Vincent, the palace of the Necessidades, the tower of Belém, and the church of São Roque. An aqueduct built in the 18th century and still in use lies outside the city. Lisbon's harbor, almost a landlocked bay, is one of the world's finest. From it Lisbon exports chiefly wine and cork. Imports are grain, sugar, cotton, coal, petroleum, iron, and steel. The city has sugar refineries, ironworks, and textile and chemical factories. It has a vital airport on the route from London to the Azores, Bermuda, and New York.

Lisbon has been under the rule of the Romans, Visigoths, Moors, and Spanish. In 1755 an earthquake and tidal wave took the lives of from 30,000 to 40,000 persons and damaged vast sections of the city. Before and during World War II the city was one of the last contact points in western Europe, and many refugees from the Axis escaped through the port.

LISTER, JOSEPH (1827-1912), the founder of antiseptic surgery, was born in Essex, England. After receiving his medical degree from the University of London in 1852, Lister served at the Royal Infirmary, Edinburgh. In 1860 he became professor of surgery at the University of Glasgow; in 1867, professor of clinical surgery at the University of Edinburgh; and in 1877, professor of surgery at King's College, London. He was a fellow of the Royal College of Surgeons and a president of the Royal Society. Lister was created a baronet in 1883 and raised to the peerage in 1897.

Although his observations on the coagulation of blood and on the early stages of inflammation were significant, Lister's major contribution was the introduction of antiseptic surgery. Lister followed the lead of Pasteur in assuming that germs cause infection. While at the University of Glasgow Lister devised a technique employing a mist of carbolic acid as a local germicide during the course of a surgical operation. Although remarkably effective this original technique was soon improved by Lister himself. Lister devoted much of his later career to the perfection of antiseptic surgery.

Joseph Lister performs a surgical operation (below); an assistant sprays the incision with antiseptic mist. Two other assistants are administering anesthetic to the patient.

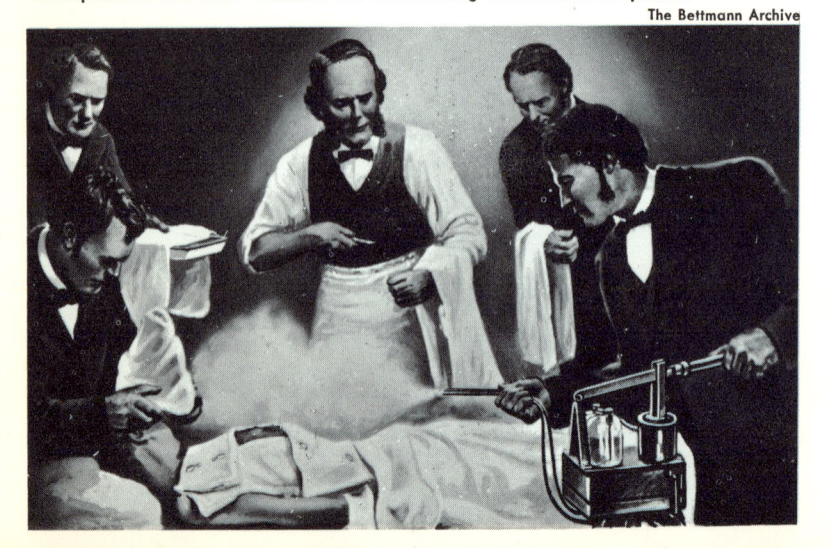

The Bettmann Archive

Library of Congress
Franz Liszt

LISZT, FRANZ (1811-1886), a famous Hungarian pianist and composer, born in Raiding. The strange rhythms and weird, sweet melodies of wandering gypsy bands of his childhood home in western Hungary no doubt influenced much of Liszt's music. As a child he studied piano in Vienna under Czerny and began to play in concerts when he was nine years old. At the age of 12 he performed so brilliantly in Vienna that Beethoven congratulated him with a kiss.

Liszt spent years in traveling on the Continent and in giving concerts in the capitals of Europe. His friendships with such French writers as Victor Hugo, Lamartine, George Sand, and Sainte-Beuve bore fruit in his work. Many of his musical compositions were inspired by their verse. The paintings of Delacroix, too, appealed to Liszt's romantic imagination. He was also on intimate terms with Chopin and Wagner; indeed Liszt is largely responsible for the reputation Wagner gained in music during the 19th century. The friendship of these two composers was further cemented by the marriage of Liszt's daughter Cosima to Wagner.

From 1849 to 1859 Liszt acted as musical director in the little German town of Weimar. In 1865 he entered the Roman Catholic Church and became known as Abbé Liszt, although only minor orders were conferred on him. He died at Bayreuth, Germany, on July 31, 1886.

Liszt was one of the greatest pianists and teachers of the pianoforte ever known. The catalogue of Liszt's compositions includes a variety of works, but he stands out as the originator of the symphonic poem and as the composer of hauntingly beautiful pieces for the piano. *Les Préludes*, several Hungarian rhapsodies, *Liebesträume*, *Todtentanz*, and *Mephisto-Waltz* are some of his works that are most popular with modern audiences.

LITERACY RATE, in statistics, the percentage of people in a given group able both to read and to write a language. When considering the percentage of people unable to read and write, statisticians speak of the illiteracy rate. The groups of people studied are selected on the basis of any one, or a combination, of the following criteria: age, sex, race, nativity, nationality, and geographic area or region of habitation.

The most comprehensive study of illiteracy, *World Illiteracy at Mid-Century* (1957), was made by the United Nations Educational, Scientific and Cultural Organization (UNESCO). Based primarily on population censuses, this report revealed that 44 percent of the world's adult (15 years old and over) population in 1950 was illiterate. In terms of worldwide distribution 75 percent were in Asia, 14 or 15 percent were in Africa, about 6.5 percent were in the Americas, and 4 to 5 percent were in the U.S.S.R., Oceania, and Europe. Illiteracy rates are lowest in northern, western, and central Europe and northern America.

A high level of literacy is a consequence of, and a requirement for, educational and industrial development, as is evidenced by such countries as Great Britain, Germany, France, and the United States, whose urban-industrial development began with the Industrial Revolution. Their respective illiteracy rates in 1950 were 1 to 2 percent, 1 to 2 percent, 3 to 4 percent, and 3 to 4 percent. Japan and the U.S.S.R., two countries that have relatively recently become major industrial powers, have shown a marked improvement in mass literacy since the beginning of the 20th century; their respective illiteracy rates for 1950 are estimated at 2 to 3 percent and 5 to 10 percent.

Countries less advanced in education and industry tend to have high adult illiteracy rates; for example, Afghanistan (95-99 percent), Ethiopia (95-99 percent), India (80-85 percent), China (50-55 percent), Pakistan (80-85 percent), and Brazil (50-55 percent).

The best means of increasing the literacy of a people is to improve educational facilities for children. The report prepared by UNESCO states that "If all children of school age in any country attended school for a sufficient length of time, there would eventually be no adult illiterates except those mentally deficient and incapable of learning to read and write."

LITERARY FORMS. Many terms are used conventionally to describe literary works. Because these terms make it possible to talk about literature on a very general level, they are useful. But one must not think that they divide the realm of literary works among them, that they are precise definitions, or that they name watertight compartments. It is often the case that one descriptive term applies correctly to several very different works, while a number of names can be applied to one work. A literary work is not understood simply by applying a few qualifying labels to fit it. Each novel, play, short story, and poem must be investigated as an individually created thing, in all its complexity and uniqueness. The kind of literary criticism that conceives as an end in itself the lumping together of literary works into convenient categories is inadequate.

This entry is concerned with the criteria and terminology pertinent to the classification of fictional writings, that is, of works of the imagination in which characters, emotions, states of mind, and events professing to represent those of real life are portrayed. See FICTION.

The most general distinction made for the purpose of classifying fictional works is between those written in prose and those written in verse. Simply stated, the difference between verse and prose is that words are arranged to form regular and recurrent sound patterns in the former, and in the latter they are not. It should be noted, however, that although the terms verse and poetry are often interchangeable, measured language alone does not qualify literary works as poems. Conversely, some poems, notably those in free verse, do not employ regular rhythms or meters. The language of such poets as Walt Whitman, Ezra Pound, and William Carlos Williams, is as close to prose as to verse, and yet their works are called poems. See POEM.

The two broad categories of prose and poetry (or verse), which were established on the basis of a difference in the choice and arrangement of words, are subdivided through the application of another criterion —the compositional forms appropriate to each. In prose some of these forms are the essay, novel, letter, short story, play, and oration; in poetry, the poem, epic, metrical romance, ballad, play, lyric, sonnet, ode, epigram, and limerick. See ESSAY; LETTER; RHETORIC.

CLASSIFICATION IN FICTION

While *fiction* includes all imaginative writing, the word is used in a specific sense to refer to novels and short stories as distinct from plays and poems. The novel is a most important form of prose fiction. A bewildering multiplicity of descriptive terms is applied to novels, and no one of them adequately characterizes any given novel. Care must be exercised in their application because they can be misleading. The student must become familiar with them because they appear repeatedly in conversation, book reviews, and literary histories.

Attempts to distinguish the subject matter of novels have given rise to the following classifications: The picaresque novel tells the story of a clever and romantic picaro, or rogue, who wanders aimlessly from adventure to adventure. Regional novels depict the lives of people in particular locales, or regions, of the country. The historical novel represents real or fictitious characters participating in verifiable historical events. The novel of manners portrays the behavior and customs of a specific social class at a certain time in history. Westerns, science-fiction stories, mysteries, and supernatural tales all have their respective kinds of subject matter; also, certain conventions of form and certain plot devices characterize these works.

Consideration of the kinds of narrative and stylistic devices authors utilize to tell their stories also leads to classification. The unfolding of a plot through the letters written by characters is characteristic of the epistolary novel. The dominant technique in the stream-of-consciousness novel for revealing character and action is to record the unordered stream of the characters' thoughts.

Novels can be further described in terms of the period of literary history in which they were written. The sentimental novel and the Gothic novel are preromantic types. The romantic novel was a popular form of the 19th century. The realistic novel, which came into existence at the end of the 19th century, purported to picture life as it really was; it rejected high-sounding diction and the sentimental and melodramatic and emphasized the more disagreeable aspects of life. The naturalistic novel developed from the realistic and is often indistinguishable from it. The modern novel is an all inclusive name designating certain new trends in prose narration of the 19th and 20th centuries.

Most of the classifications of the novel apply as well to the short story. It is, however, an entirely different form. The chief difference between the two is the compression of the short story, which does not make use of the elaborate plot structure that characterizes the novel. The short story can simply be a character sketch or a slice of life. See NOVEL; SHORT STORY.

CLASSIFICATION IN DRAMA

Any kind of writing that tells a story is called narrative. A play is narrative in the sense that it relates a sequence of events; but because it has a special manner of doing this, it is a very different form from the novel or the short story. In a play characters and actions are presented physically on a stage by actors moving about and speaking dialogue—an audience sees and hears the story taking place before it. This is not the case with a novel, where the actions are presented as if they had already taken place. These two types of story presentation are known as the narrative and the dramatic forms.

It should be noted that the two ways of telling a story can be combined in any given literary work. Elements of the narrative form appear in plays, and elements of the dramatic form appear in both novels and short stories. Narration in a play is technically known as exposition; an example of this is found in Shakespeare's *Hamlet*, when Ophelia's drowning is not shown (dramatized) but is told about (narrated) by Hamlet's mother, Gertrude. In novels a sense of the immediacy that is so characteristic of drama is achieved through the use of dialogue: The characters "speak" to one another.

The terms *romantic, sentimental, realistic, naturalistic,* and *symbolic* (which describe the literary period, treatment, and selection of subject matter of novels) have the same meanings, for the most part, when applied to plays. *Tragedy, comedy, melodrama, farce,* and *tragicomedy* are all words that designate specific types of plays, but they are also used in connection with novels. The drama developed historically before the novel, so that originally when one spoke of a tragedy, he was referring to a play with a specific compositional form that presented serious subject matter in a serious manner. Gradually it became common to use the term *tragedy* for any literary work in which subject matter was treated seriously. The terms *comedy, melodrama, farce,* and *tragicomedy* were also subjected to this type of extension of meaning and application. See COMEDY; DRAMA; FARCE; MELODRAMA; PLAY; TRAGEDY.

CLASSIFICATION IN POETRY

Poetry has been traditionally classified as narrative, dramatic, and lyric.

Narrative forms like the ballad, epic, metrical romance, lay, and tale tell stories. The ballad is generally short and has a precise stanzaic form. The epic, which relates heroic deeds and events, is one of the oldest and longest forms of the verse narrative. The medieval metrical romance was shorter and dealt with adventure, chivalric love, and war; the heroes of the three great cycles of metrical romances are King Arthur, Alexander the Great, and Charlemagne. The lay and tale had a wider range of subject matter and were more compact in form. Because of their complexity, scope, subject matter, and length, many great narrative poems by such poets as Edmund Spenser, Robert Browning, and Robert Frost do not fit into any of the types just named. See BALLAD; EPIC.

Dramatic poems present actions directly in monologue or conversation. The dramatic monologue was a form used often by Robert Browning and later by Robert Frost. Dramatic poems intended for reading rather than for acting are called closet dramas. Shelly's *Prometheus Bound* and Milton's *Samson Agonistes* are examples of this type.

Lyric, like most of the other terms under discussion, has both a general and a specific meaning. On the one hand *lyric* denotes an emotional, musical quality; on the other, it is a specific name for poems composed in stanzas, expressive of the poet's feelings, and not distinctly narrative or dramatic. But lyrics, again like all other types, are seldom pure; many of them have a narrative framework and use action and incident. Classification of a poem depends finally upon a determination, or judgment, as to what the dominant characteristic is.

Lyrics usually have fixed stanzaic forms: precise line rhythms and lengths, definite rhyme schemes, and predetermined repetitions of lines. Some important French forms, which have to some extent been imitated in English, are the triolet, rondeau, ballade, rondel, and villanelle. The Limerick is a light nonsense poem with an ingenious play on words in its rhyme scheme. A short verse form expressing tersely and wittily a single thought is the epigram. See LIMERICK; VERSE FORMS.

The subject-matter criterion is used in the classification of lyrical forms. Almost any poem about death is an elegy. Lyrics about rural country life filled with talk of shepherds and maidens are called pastorals (also *bucoliques*, eclogues, or idyls). See ELEGY.

Other types of lyrics include the ode (a thoughtful, formal, and dignified poem), the song (poem simple in diction and suitable for singing), and the sonnet (a fixed verse form of either the Italian or the English type). Each of these labels needs extension of definition when applied to particular poems. See ODE; SONNET.

OTHER CRITERIA OF CLASSIFICATION

Length is often a consideration in classification of literary forms. Plays, for instance, are divided into full-length and one-act plays, a distinction similar to that made between the novel, or long story, and the short story. The word *novelette* is sometimes used to denote a short novel; it is supposed to lie in length somewhere between the short story and the full-length novel and to have the construction of a novel.

Literary works intended by their authors to teach the reader some lesson are called didactic. Compositional forms employed for the metaphorical presentation of single ideas or morals are the allegory and the fable. When certain problems of human society are singled out for exposé by novelists and playwrights, the result is either a propaganda novel or a problem play. Satire is a device authors use to hold something up to contempt, scorn, or ridicule; the mock epic is a poem in which trivial subject matter is treated satirically or comically in a pompous and grandiose epic style. See ALLEGORY; FABLE; SATIRE.

LITHOGRAPHY. The inventor of lithography, or printing from stone, was Aloys Senefelder (1771-1834). In his attempts to produce music sheets cheaply he came upon the idea of writing the notes on stone and making the impression from it. In 1818 he published his handbook on lithography, covering all processes of stone lithography. The entire process of lithography rests on the way in which grease and water are repelled by each other and the way in which greasy substances

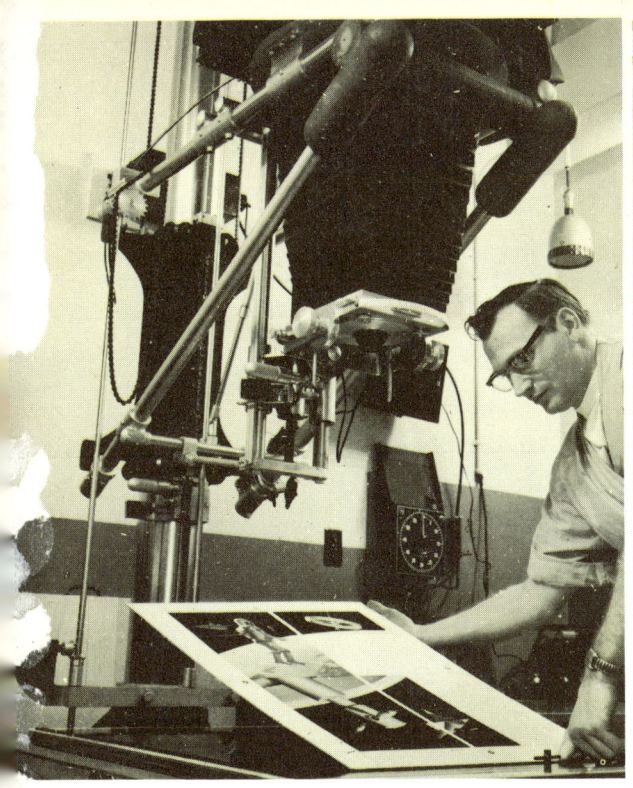

The first full-color pictures were printed by the lithographic process, above. Negatives of pictures and type are stripped into place, below, as they will appear in the printed product.

Modern lithography employs a camera to photograph original artwork, eliminating much handwork.

The thin press plate is clamped to the lithograph plate cylinder.

Proofing plates are made from the stripped up flats in a lithograph proofing press, above. After all corrections have been made, the final press plates are made in a composing machine, below.

This is a large, five-color, sheet-feed, offset lithographic press. It can print five or six thousand full-color sheets in an hour.

tend to adhere to each other. In illustration, a drawing is made on a smooth stone with lithographic ink, which is a greasy substance. The drawing is first treated with weak solutions of acid and gum; then it is subjected to a process of charging, in which gummed water is freely used. After this the stone is again wet, and an inking roller is passed repeatedly over it. The parts of the stone not occupied by the drawing are protected by the water and gum, repelling the printing ink and remaining clean. But the greasy lines, or marks forming the drawings, reject the water and receive the greasy ink, which adheres to their surfaces in sufficient quantity to give off an impression upon paper when subjected to the action of the printing press.

Instead of stone, zinc and aluminum plates are now extensively used for lithographic printing. Modern lithography also employs photographic techniques. The desired material, instead of being manually drawn on a plate, is photographed, and a negative is made that is then exposed to the metal plate, specially coated with a light-sensitive emulsion. To develop this plate a greasy developer is used that leaves a black impression on the surface of the plate. The ink adheres to this black impression, just as it does when the design is made with a lithographic crayon, and is repelled by water where the developer leaves no black impression.

When only a small number of copies are desired, lithography is less expensive than other forms of printing. Lithography is also desirable when many illustrations must be reproduced. Lithography may be used for any number of desired colors.

LITHUANIA, a small country of northern Europe, on the Baltic Sea, since 1940 a part of the Soviet Union. It is bordered by Latvia on the north, Belorussia on the east, and the Kaliningrad oblast of Russian S.F.S.R. on the south. The area is 25,200 square miles, and the population is about 3,000,000. Lithuania's capital is the old city of Vilna, in the southeastern part of the country.

The land is generally flat and is dotted with many lakes. Most of the people are farmers and stock raisers.

The Lithuanian S.S.R.'s flag and coat of arms are similar to those of the other constituent republics of the U.S.S.R. The United States does not recognize Lithuania's annexation.

The principal crops are rye, oats, potatoes, and flax. Hogs, dairy cattle, and poultry are raised in large numbers. Dairy farming and meat-packing are important industries, and their products form the main items of the export trade.

Four-fifths of the people are Lithuanians; the remainder are Russians, Jews, and Poles. Most of the Lithuanians are Roman Catholics.

In the late Middle Ages Lithuania was a part of Poland; it was occupied by the Russians in the 18th century, when Poland was divided between Russia, Austria, and Prussia. The country gained its independence following World War I and remained independent until World War II. In 1940 a pro-Soviet government applied for admission to the Soviet Union. The United States did not recognize the Soviet annexation of Lithuania. For detailed map, see UNION OF SOVIET SOCIALIST REPUBLICS.

LITTLE BEAR, THE (constellation). See URSA MINOR.

LITTLE HORSE, THE (constellation). See EQUULEUS.

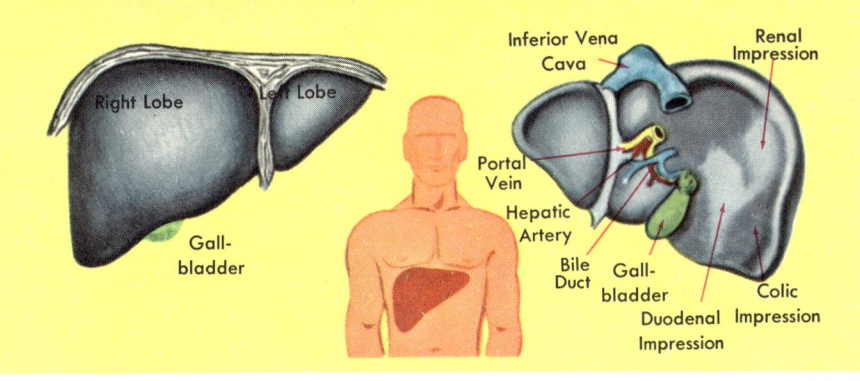

The liver is shown in posterior view at the left, and its position in the human body is indicated by the red area on the human figure at center. The view at right, from underneath the liver, locates the gallbladder, major blood vessels, and the impressions made by the duodenum, the kidneys (renal impression), and the large intestine (colic impression).

LITTLE ROCK, the capital of Arkansas, in the central part of the state, on the Arkansas River, 130 miles west of Memphis, Tenn. It is the commercial center of the state. It manufactures cottonseed oil and lumber products and is near the largest bauxite mines in the United States. It is the seat of the school of medicine of the University of Arkansas, Philander Smith and Arkansas Baptist colleges for Negroes, schools for the deaf and blind, and a U.S. veterans hospital. Among its important buildings are the state Capitol and two cathedrals. Albert Pike House here dates from 1840. Little Rock was laid out in 1820 and became the territorial capital in 1821. In 1960 the population was 107,813.

LIVER, the largest organ in the body and one that performs more essential functions than any other organ. It is located in the upper right part of the abdomen, just under the diaphragm. It is composed of four lobes. The gallbladder, a pear-shaped sac 3 to 4 inches long, is located on the undersurface of the right lobe. The liver changes simple sugars, after absorption from the digestive tract, to a more complex form known as glycogen, which is stored in the liver until it is needed. The liver maintains a constant level of blood sugar by breaking down this glycogen store as required and changing it back to a simple sugar (glucose). The liver also has the following functions: the excretion of bile; the manufacture of fibrinogen and antithrombin (heparin), which are vitally necessary in the coagulation of blood; the formation of antibodies; the production of heat for body warmth as a result of the numerous chemical reactions occurring in the liver; the formation of vitamin A from carotene; the storage of vitamin B; and the production of substances necessary for the maturation of red blood cells and for the prevention of pernicious anemia.

The liver is composed of many small units, called lobules, each of which has blood vessels in close connection with secretory cells and ducts, through which the secretion is carried away. In most animals and in man bile is secreted constantly by the liver cells and passes from the hepatic duct to the cystic duct and to the gallbladder for temporary storage.

Fresh mammalian liver or its extracts are used to treat pernicious anemia, certain obscure anemias, and sprue. Since liver has a high protein, vitamin, and iron contect, it should be a frequent dietary component. Injury to the liver and a resulting decrease in its secretions may be caused by various poisons, acute and chronic liver diseases (such as acute yellow atrophy, cirrhosis, and inflammation of the bile passages), bacterial toxins, and cardiac failure. Jaundice is a common result of damage to the liver.

This is the waterfront of the great English port of Liverpool. The ocean liner at the left is tied at the floating landing stage.

LIVERPOOL, a large seaport city in northwestern England, near the mouth of the Mersey River, 180 miles northwest of London. With more than 750,000 inhabitants, it is the third largest city in England and the second greatest port in the British Commonwealth. Its docks, which extend for 6 miles along the river, are among the largest and most modern in the world. In the center of the dock area is a floating landing stage 2,534 feet long and 80 feet wide. The stage is supported by 200 iron pontoons and is connected with the river wall by ten hinged bridges and a slanting roadway 550 feet long. A tunnel under the Mersey connects Liverpool with the city of Birkenhead on the opposite bank.

Among the chief imports of Liverpool are cotton, wheat, flour, fresh meat, sugar, fruits, palm oil, olive oil, wine, tobacco, and wool. The products of its own factories and the factories of nearby industrial towns are shipped from the port. Among the most important of these are machinery, cotton and woolen goods, ironware, clothing, and chemicals.

Liverpool has a university, a fine art gallery, a large public library, and other notable public buildings.

Liverpool was founded by King John early in the 13th century but remained only a small hamlet until the 17th century. After that time it began to share in the West Indian trade, and its prosperity and growth began. Liverpool developed rapidly in the 18th and 19th centuries and took the place of Bristol as the leading port on the west coast. The city was made a bishopric in 1880 and in the same year received its city charter. During World War II the city suffered great damage from German air raids.

B.I.S.

LIVERWORT, a member of the class Hepaticae of the bryophytes, the most primitive of land plants. The liverworts resemble and perhaps are related to the mosses. Their plant body is forked, or lobed, in a manner suggestive of liver lobes, hence their name. The plants are green and can manufacture their own food, but they cannot live far from water and are found only in wet places. The production of many-celled sex organs, which produce the reproductive cells, is an adaptation to their land environment and represents an advance in the method of reproduction over that of the thallophytes. The union of the sex cells, or gametes, is called fertilization and gives rise to a spore-producing structure called a sporophyte. These spores from the sporophyte then grow into the original type of green liverwort plant. This represents alternation of generations, a characteristic feature of all higher plants. Liverworts, in general, are of no direct importance to man.

LIVINGSTONE, DAVID (1813-1873), a Scottish medical missionary, born in Lanarkshire. He devoted his life to exploring the uncharted regions of central Africa. When he was only ten years old, David Livingstone worked in a local factory 14 hours a day, six days a week. For 13 years he spent his days surrounded by the crash of machinery and his nights attending school or studying on his own. Finally, in 1840 Livingstone qualified as a medical missionary and went with his wife to Bechuanaland, where he worked for about ten years.

For their own health and safety, Livingstone's wife and children then returned to England. Livingstone, a man devoted to his work, remained in Africa. In 1851 he undertook the first of his three major expeditions: the search for a practical trade route to the coast. On another expedition in 1855 he discovered and named Victoria Falls.

In 1858 Livingstone was commissioned by the British government to explore eastern and central Africa. By this time Livingstone's outstanding work had brought him international fame, and his book *Missionary Travels and Researches in South Africa* was widely read. On this second trip he discovered Lake Nyasa. He also realized the necessity of abolishing the Arab slave trade, widely practiced in the region of Zanzibar.

Despite endless personal hardships and bitter disappointments Livingstone undertook his third major expedition in 1866. He traveled great distances into the African interior. The theft of his medicines left him no means of controlling a fever that wracked his body. He and his party were in constant danger from their enemies, the Arab slave traders. Cut off from the world, Livingstone carried on his work in isolation. Finally, in November, 1871, Henry Morton Stanley, an American newspaperman, found the explorer and uttered the now famous words, "Dr. Livingstone, I presume?"

The world's joy at rediscovering the famous man was short lived. On Apr. 30, 1873, his devoted natives found him dead kneeling beside his bed. These loyal followers preserved Livingstone's body and carried it, along with his precious papers and journals, 1,000 miles to Zanzibar. From there it was transported to England and to Westminster Abbey, Livingstone's final resting place.

Fed. Inf. Dept., So. Rhodesia
David Livingstone

LIZARD, a scaly, usually limbed reptile that somewhat resembles a miniature crocodile. Ranging in length from a few inches to 10 feet, lizards usually have long, slender bodies with long, slender tails. The bodies of most terrestrial species are flattened vertically, whereas those of most aquatic ones are compressed laterally. Although most species have four short, widespread legs that terminate in claws, some species have only two legs, and a few that resemble snakes have none. Many lizards are brightly and variously colored, and a few species can change their colors. Most species inhabit tropical and subtropical regions, including both jungles and deserts.

The iguana, a lizard that reaches a length of 6 feet, looks like a living relic of the remote geologic past. Native to the American tropics, the iguana climbs trees, rests on their branches, and plunges into the water when danger threatens. Its white flesh is relished by some Indian tribes and is said to taste like chicken.

The gila monster of Arizona and neighboring desert regions is a fat, vertically flattened, clumsy lizard whose body is covered with small orange, pink, black, or brown lumps, which resemble Indian beadwork. The gila monster can live for months without food while subsisting upon fat stored in its thick tail. It has a venomous bite and can strike quickly at small animals, gripping them like a bulldog.

The chameleon, a small tree-dwelling lizard of North Africa and Asia Minor, is famous for its changes of color, which are caused by changes in temperature and light and by emotions. A decrease in temperature causes the chameleon's color to change from grayish green to dull gray, whereas an increase in temperature causes a change to green. Sunlight induces a dull-black hue; darkness induces a creamy hue. Anger causes the lighter areas to darken, whereas fright causes them to lighten again.

Lizards manifest many diverse anatomical adaptations that facilitate their locomotion in particular environments. Tree-climbing lizards have elongated toes with broad adhesive scales that enable them to cling to smooth bark. Certain lizards that burrow in sand have no limbs whatsoever and resemble snakes. So-called flying lizards can glide through the air by means of thin flaps of skin that are extended laterally from the sides. Each of these adaptations has evolved gradually over a long period of time.

LIZARD

1489

Monitor

True Chameleon

Tuatara

Iguana

Flying Dragon

Komodo

Sonoran Skink

Gila Monster

The wool of the llama makes vicuña cloth. — Natl. Zool. Park, Smithsonian Inst.

LLAMA, a South American cloven-footed mammal, member of the camel family, native to Peru, Bolivia, and the western coast of South America. Mature animals reach a height of 3 feet at the shoulder and are able to carry average loads of about 100 pounds at a speed of 12 miles an hour. Herds of llamas are raised for milk and wool. In color, llamas may vary from black to white. The alpaca is another wool-bearing species of llama also common in South America. Both the llama and the alpaca are descended from the wild guanaco.

The male llama was domesticated by the ancient Incas and was used as a beast of burden, but it was valued chiefly for its flesh and wool. Immense herds of llamas were held by the Incan government and entrusted to shepherds, who conducted them from one part of the country to another, wherever there was green pasture. The animals were sheared at regular intervals, and the wool was dealt out to the people to be made into clothing. After the Spanish conquest the use of the llama as a beast of burden increased greatly, and many thousands of these animals were employed in transporting silver from the mines. Droves of 500 or 1,000 were often seen descending the mountain paths in a single file, each drove in charge of a single native. The Spaniards used these animals so wastefully that in a few years the great flocks of the Incas had disappeared. However, the llama is still used as a carrier by the Indians of Peru and Chile.

LLOYD GEORGE, DAVID (1863–1945), English Liberal leader, was born at Manchester. He entered Parliament in 1890, opposed the Boer War, strongly supported the Welsh Disestablishment Bill, and took an active interest in the Education Bill of 1902. Appointed chancellor of the exchequer in 1908, he reorganized the financial system and placed the burden of taxation on property producing excessive profits, on inheritances, and on nonreproductive property. For merchants, industrialists, and employees he established national insurance and old age pensions. During World War I he was made minister of munitions in 1915, and he became prime minister in 1916. After active participation in the Versailles peace-treaty negotiations in 1919, he aided in establishing the Irish Free State in 1920. He was removed from the office of prime minister in the elections of 1923, the first victory in 17 years for the Conservative party. After his retirement from Parliament late in 1944, with an unbroken record of 54 years of service, an earldom was conferred upon him.

LOAN AND INTEREST. A loan is the transfer of a property right (usually a right to use money) for a length of time, after which the property must be returned to the lender. The borrower is generally charged interest, a sum of money that compensates the lender for the period during which he forwent the use of his property. Loans were common among primitive men, but interest probably did not exist. The idea of interest caught on rather early; by the time of Hammurabi, Babylonian farmers were heavily in debt to the great landowners because of the high rate of interest. This was also the case in ancient Athens in the time of Solon. Solon, however, passed laws to relieve debtors of unjust interest rates. He canceled debts and prohibited creditors from taking debtors into slavery if they could not pay their debts. Solon left the rate of interest up to free contract between debtor and creditor but allowed the creditor only a portion of the debtor's property as security. Julius Caesar established for Rome the same laws governing loans and interest.

The medieval church regarded moneylending for interest as immoral. Christians were prohibited from lending money at interest during the early Middle Ages. One reason was the knowledge that in the ancient world persons sought loans only when they were in desperate straits, a situation that was often exploited. Loans were not a common fact of the economic system. Consequently, the early church frowned on loans with interest. Nevertheless, loans were still sought. After the crusades knights attempted to imitate the luxurious living they had seen in the East, and they borrowed money to do so. Kings were always in need of money to carry on foreign wars. The kings of England frequently pawned the royal crown with Italian and German bankers. Kings were sometimes bad risks—the Bardi, bankers in Italy, were ruined by the bankruptcy of King Edward III of England.

The medieval word for *interest* was *usury*, a word that now means "an exorbitant rate of interest." In the modern world lending money at interest has become a normal and necessary procedure. People borrow money today in order to invest in business enterprises and buy luxury goods. Borrowing for necessities and out of desperation is still sometimes done. The practice of borrowing, however, is socially acceptable and even encouraged by banks and lending institutions. Banks are the common source of loans for businessmen. Individuals can obtain small personal loans at banks, loan companies, or pawnshops, depending upon their character, capacity, and capital. A man must be a better credit risk to borrow at a bank than to pawn some of his property at a pawnshop. The use of the loan, the position of the borrower, and his collateral will determine the amount of interest. Rates vary from 5 percent to 36 percent per year. Personal loans usually cost more than business loans because the risk is greater and the amount borrowed is smaller.

Borrowers should be cautious in seeking loans and should figure out how much interest they will have to pay on a loan. Prior to the passage of small-loan laws in many (but not all) of the states in the United States, loan sharks might charge an interest rate as high as 1,000 percent each year. There are several things to investigate before borrowing money. Is the interest rate quoted on a monthly or an annual basis? A rate of 1 percent a month is 12 percent a year. Does the borrower receive the entire amount of his loan, or is the interest taken out in advance? If the interest is taken out in advance on a $100 loan and the borrower receives only $90, 10 percent interest would cause the effective rate of interest to be higher than 10 percent. Can the borrower repay the loan before the end of the installment period without having to pay the full interest charges? Will the borrower have to continue to pay interest on the portion of the loan that he has already paid in past principal installments? See BANK AND BANKING; CREDIT; DEBT; MORTGAGE.

LOBBY, in American politics, a pressure group that maintains a representative in Washington, D.C., or in a state capital, to obtain legislation favorable to its interests. Lobbying is not new, but it has grown steadily in extent and power since the Civil War period. So important is lobbying in the process of federal legislation that lobbyists are sometimes said to comprise a "third house" within Congress.

Lobbies are maintained by almost every social or economic group in the United States. Veterans, farmers, manufacturers, workers, doctors, bankers, prohibitionists, and real estate boards are but a few of the many interests represented by lobbies. Among the more powerful lobbies are the National Association of Manufacturers, the American Medical Association, the Farm Bureau Federation, the U.S. Chamber of Commerce, the AF of L-CIO, the political action arm of the AF of L-CIO, the National Education Association, and the American Legion. There are about 3,000 organizations or persons registered as lobbyists under the Federal Regulation of Lobbying Act.

The lobbyist is in a position of strength when he presents an argument to a congressman, for he generally knows more about his particular interest than does the legislator. The lobbyist usually knows many people in Washington, and strikes up friendships with congressmen whenever possible. Bribery is seldom resorted to, but lobbyists representing wealthy and well-organized interests can often offer large contributions to the campaign funds of the congressman's party. If a congressman ignores a lobbyist, he may be deluged with letters and calls from his constituents who have heard a particular lobby present its case on television or seen propaganda in newspapers and periodicals.

The main criticism of lobbies in a democratic society is that they may represent a very small interest, but an interest able to make its voice heard above that of the unorganized general public. To deal with lobbies it has been necessary to regulate them. The Federal Regulation of Lobbying Act, passed in 1946, requires all lobbyists to register with the secretary of the Senate and with the clerk of the House of Representatives. A lobbyist must also reveal his salary, his expenses, his employer, and his activities. However, court decisions have made the act ineffectual and the problem of controlling lobbies still exists.

LOBSTER, a salt-water crustacean that is related to the shrimp and crayfish. The common lobster of the Atlantic coast from Labrador to North Carolina may attain a length of more than 2 feet and a weight of 30 pounds. Its color is dark green with irregular red and blue patches. Its large, powerful front claws, or pincers, are used for catching prey and for fighting enemies. Its four pairs of hindlegs are used for swimming and for crawling along the bottom. The body and claws of the American lobster (and of other species) are enclosed in a hard, rigid external skeleton, which consists of a substance called chitin. The skeleton of a young lobster is molted many times to permit growth. Lobsters mate and reproduce in May, and the female lays her eggs in June. She may carry tens of thousands of them under her abdomen for 10 or 11 months before they hatch.

During summer the American lobster inhabits the rocky or sandy bottoms of shallow water near the shore. During winter it inhabits deeper waters. This lobster is the principal edible species of lobster of the Atlantic coast; more than 100 million are captured each year.

Other edible lobsters are the spiny ones of California, western Mexico, Florida, and the West Indies. The spiny lobster is so named because of the sharp spines on top of the thorax and along the sides of the abdomen. These spines are this lobster's only weapon of defense, since it lacks pincers. The spiny lobster also has a pair of unusually long tactile antennae, which enable it to explore the water before it as it moves along. If the antennae touch another animal in the water ahead, the lobster immediately retreats to safety.

The American lobster, whose natural colors are green and yellow, turns red when boiled.

LOCATION means identified position in space. Fundamentally, a position can be identified only by stating its direction and distance from a known physical object. Positions cannot be stated in reference to empty space itself. Even where physical objects are present, no absolutely fixed location can be identified because every object is moving relative to some other object. The position of a mountain peak or of one's home address may be identified relative to the surface of the earth, but these same locations are constantly changing relative to the sun and all other objects in space.

Direction and distance from a physical object can be stated either directly or else indirectly by means of a system of predetermined locations. Animals, as well as human beings, use both the direct and the indirect methods.

The direct method defines direction and distance between two objects without referring to any predetermined system of locations. Animal senses of sight, hearing, and smell are, of course, examples of this method. Human inventions such as sonar and radar are in effect extensions of ears and eyes. They send out sound and radio waves, interpret reflections of these waves from objects within range, and give a continuous report of the position of these objects.

Indirect methods give direction and distance relative to a predetermined system of locations instead of to an object directly. Bees perform symbolic body movements inside their hive in order to communicate to other bees the direction and distance of a newly found flower patch. The human invention of latitude and longitude is perhaps the best known example of an indirect system of location. This system establishes the position of every point on the surface of the earth relative to two artificial lines—the Equator and the zero meridian passing through Greenwich, England. These artificial lines are in turn defined relative to physical objects. (See LATITUDE AND LONGITUDE.) Similar systems have been established for locating objects in space.

Some indirect systems do not give both distance and direction. An altimeter, which measures air pressure, gives the distance above sea level but not the direction of sea level. On the other hand, the location of a star is normally given in right ascension and declination, which determines the direction of the star but not its distance.

LOCKE, JOHN (1632-1704), English philosopher. Locke is noted as a defender of civil and religious liberty. He helped spread the spirit of free inquiry. His political ideas had their greatest influence in the political thought that preceded the revolutions in France and America in the 18th century.

John Locke was born in the village of Wrington. His father, a strict but pleasant Puritan, carefully educated his son at their farm home. Locke entered Christ Church College, Oxford, in 1652. According to his own account he was not overly studious and devoted much time to conversation with urbane companions. He obtained his master's degree in 1658 and became a tutor at Christ Church College. He lectured on philosophy, rhetoric, and Greek. Locke was attracted by Descartes' philosophy. The experimental method was coming into vogue, and Locke himself conducted experiments in meteorology and chemistry. Following a political mission to the elector of Brandenburg, Locke had the good fortune in 1667 to become a personal secretary to Lord Ashley, the first earl of Shaftesbury, a man very active in English political affairs. Locke took up residence in London, where he engaged in numerous informal debates on questions of the day. He was stimulated to begin work on *An Essay Concerning Human Understanding*, which was finally published in 1690.

Locke lived several years in France, and in 1683 he left a politically turbulent England for Holland, where he published several articles in a scholarly journal. The year following the Glorious Revolution of 1688 Locke returned to England. There he published his *Two Treatises on Government* and the *Essay Concerning Human Understanding*. Later, from the country residence of Francis Masham in Essex, Locke published the *Letter on Toleration*, *Thoughts on Education*, *The Reasonableness of Christianity as Delivered in the Scriptures*, works on economics, and letters defending his views.

Locke's rule in all his writing was to seek out the truth only in the light of reasonable evidence. He was a calm thinker with a great respect for facts. In his theory of understanding, Locke was an empiricist, holding that all ideas entered the mind through the senses. However, he founded his politics, which were a defense of the Glorious Revolution, on ideas of natural rights. Society, he believed, was founded to protect one's natural right to life, liberty, and property.

LOCKJAW, or tetanus, a severe infectious disease characterized by spasm of muscles. It is caused by the introduction of spores of the tetanus bacillus into a wound. The disease occurs in all parts of the world where the soil is infected by human or animal excreta. Since the organisms are transmitted by this medium, the disease has commonly occurred during warfare when soldiers' wounds come in contact with infected soil.

Usually it is the dirty, ragged type of wound, such as that made by a rusty nail, that becomes infected. Wounds from blank cartridges and firecrackers seem particularly prone to cause lockjaw. Any type of wound, no matter how small and unimportant it may seem, may be the focus of lockjaw if the spores of the germ get into the wound.

It is not the organism itself but the toxin produced by it that makes the disease such a serious one. This toxin is one of the most powerful poisons known. The incubation period, that is, the time from the introduction of the organisms into the wound until the symptoms of the disease appear, varies from about four days to four weeks.

The first symptoms are slight stiffness of the jaws and neck, restlessness, and irritability. Other parts of the body may seem a little stiff, and the patient may complain of feeling chilly. These symptoms are important because successful treatment of the disease depends on beginning early. The later symptoms, which soon develop if treatment is not begun, are those of severe muscle spasm. The jaws become tightly locked so that the patient cannot open them. If treatment is not given or has no effect, the disease is likely to be fatal within a week after symptoms develop.

The outlook is good, however, if tetanus antitoxin, obtained from immunized horses, is administered soon after a wound is received. This affords temporary passive immunity to the disease. The wound itself should be thoroughly cleansed.

An attack of lockjaw, if survived, does not confer immunity. Lockjaw, however, is a preventable disease. Permanent active immunity to lockjaw can be attained by the injection of a toxoid.

LOCOMOTIVE, a self-propelled railroad engine. A steam locomotive is a steam-operated, self-contained power unit designed to run on rails; it consists of an engine and a boiler powered by water and fuel. By means of a throttle, steam is admitted into the cylinders (through a system of valves), where it acts against the pistons. The pistons move back and forth, transmitting power to the driving wheels through the main rod.

Although a steam-operated carriage was built about 1770 by Nicolas Cugnot, a French engineer, it was not until 1804 that the first successful steam engine running on rails was demonstrated by Richard Trevithick, an English engineer. Trevithick discovered that smooth wheels would provide sufficient trac-

The contrast between the old and the new in railroading is embodied in the contrast between steam (left) and diesel (right) locomotive cabs.

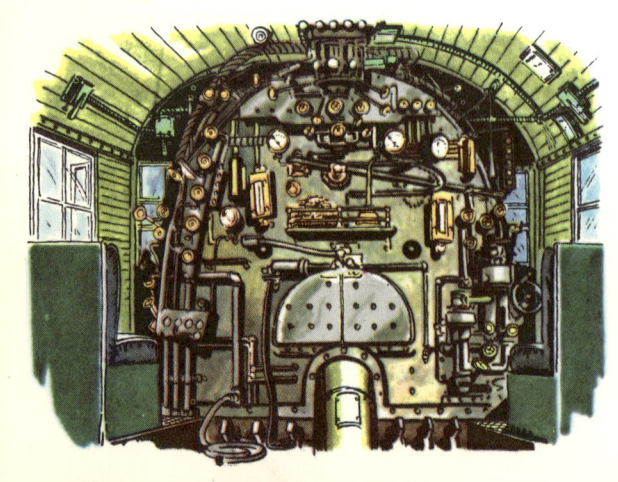

tion and that exhaust steam conducted into the stack would increase firebox combustion. William Hedley's *Puffing Billy* appeared in 1813, followed by George Stephenson's *Blucher* (1814) and prize-winning *Rocket* (1829). The Rocket weighed about 4½ tons, had a boiler pressure of 50 pounds, and achieved an average speed of 15 miles an hour when pulling a load of 13 tons and a top speed of 30 miles an hour when running light. The *Stourbridge Lion* was imported from England by the Delaware and Hudson Canal Company and was the first locomotive to be put into service in the Western Hemisphere (Aug. 8, 1829). In August, 1830, the *Tom Thumb*, a small experimental engine built by Peter Cooper, of New York, was given a trial run on the Baltimore and Ohio Railroad. The American-built *Best Friend* was the first locomotive to pull a train of cars in regular service in the United States (Dec. 25, 1830). It originally ran over 6 miles of track on the South Carolina Railroad, now the Southern Railway. In 1832 Matthias Baldwin's first locomotive, *Old Ironsides*, appeared; it was kept in continuous service for ten years. Other important early contributions to locomotive development included the *De Witt Clinton* (1831) and the *John Bull* (1831).

As the locomotive developed, its construction began to vary according to its intended use. The American locomotive, designed for long trips over irregular terrain, was enlarged and constructed with swiveled trucks. Differentiation between the passenger and the freight engine became noticeable. The former, requiring less tractive force, was built with fewer but larger driving wheels, and its large boiler, necessary for speed, was supported by leading and trailing truck wheels. The position and number of wheels led to a classification of locomotives, and any type can be distinguished by the numerical arrangement of its leading, driving, and trailing wheels. The Mogul type, having two leading truck wheels, six driving wheels, and no trailing truck wheels, was represented by the figures 2-6-0. The ten-wheeled, consolidation type was represented by the figures 2-8-0. Large Mallet (articulated) locomotives included the 2-8-8-2 type and the 2-8-8-4 type. The triple articulated type was classified as a 2-8-8-8-2. The size of the tender or the amount of fuel carried depended upon the distance to be traveled and the kind of fuel used. The loco-

Science Museum, London
William Hedley's *Puffing Billy*, built in 1813, is the oldest locomotive in existence today.

motive designed to travel great distances had to have a correspondingly large tender. A yard, or switch, engine had a small tender. Wood, which was the ordinary fuel for the early American locomotive, was later replaced by coal and oil.

The general trend in locomotive design since 1930 has been away from steam and electric locomotives and toward the compact and versatile diesel electric. With their easy starting, rapid warmup, reduced maintenance requirements, and high efficiency, diesel-electric locomotives have largely replaced all other types in railroad service in the United States. By combining a suitable number of standard power units, a diesel-electric locomotive combination may be given power for switching or commuter service or may be powered to haul a long passenger or freight train of any desired length at any practical speed.

In diesel-electric locomotives powerful diesel internal-combustion engines, running on fuel oil, generate electric power in direct-current transformers. The electricity, applied through electric motors connected to the wheels of the locomotives, produces maximum horsepower at all locomotive speeds. Therefore, a locomotive of this type, pulling a fast freight train up a steep grade, will be slowed but will seldom require an additional standby engine to get up the grade.

Other types of locomotives have arisen to challenge the diesel electric. Steam-turbine locomotives have been tested but are not in regular service at present. However, the gas-turbine locomotive, developing 8,500 horsepower, has proved very efficient in road freight service, especially at high altitudes. An increasing number of gas-turbine locomotives are being put into service. The ignitron rectifier type of electric locomotive, operating where electric power is plentiful, changes easily transmitted alternating line current to more useful direct current in the locomotive. Locomotives using atomic power face the problems of great weight (from the need for radiation shielding) and the high cost of the installation.

Tom Hollyman—Photo Researchers

For over 100 years the steam locomotive provided the power to move passengers and freight in all the world's industrial nations.

The *Catch Me Who Can*, a later model of the first successful locomotive, is seen (right) on an 1808 souvenir card. At left is the *Tom Thumb* (1830), an early American locomotive. Below it is one of the powerful Great Mogul locomotives (1865). At bottom left is the speedy *Locomotive 999* (1893); at bottom right is the locomotive of the *Pennsylvania Limited* (1905), whose speed record for steam locomotives still stands.

TREVITHICKS, PORTABLE STEAM ENGINE.

Catch me who can.

Mechanical Power Subduing Animal Speed

Science Museum, London

Santa Fe Railway Photo

Gas-turbine locomotives, such as the one seen at right being serviced and repaired, show great promise for the future. But over 90 percent of all locomotives in service in the United States in 1960 were diesel electrics (below).

Chicago & North Western Railway Co.

Union Pacific Railroad Photo

The advent of diesel-electric locomotives has dramatically changed the railroading scene. The railroad ahead as it looks to the engineer in a diesel-electric cab is seen above. At left a present-day locomotive and passenger train stand beside a platform in Chicago, the world's greatest railroad center.

Union Pacific Railroad Photo

The leaves, thorny twigs, blossoms, and seed pods of the black locust are shown above.

LOCUST, a genus of deciduous trees and shrubs native to Europe and North America. The compound leaves of locusts consist of many small leaflets and in some species are feather-like. The white or pink blossoms are borne in clusters. The fruit is a pod like that of peas and contains pealike seeds.

The black locust is a large tree cultivated for ornament in yards and parks throughout Europe and North America. The honey locust is so named because of the fragrance of its blossoms and the sweet flavor of its pods and leaves. The carob tree, an evergreen locust native to the eastern-Mediterranean region, bears the sweet-tasting pods allegedly eaten by John the Baptist while he dwelt in the wilderness.

LODESTONE. See MAGNETITE.

LODGE, HENRY CABOT (1902-), U.S. political leader, was born in Beverly, Mass., the grandson of Senator Henry Cabot Lodge. He was educated at Harvard University. As a staff member of the New York *Herald Tribune* (1924-1932) he served in the Washington Bureau and on special foreign assignments. His political career began in the Massachusetts General Court (1933-1936). In 1936 he became the seventh and youngest member of his family to win a seat in the U.S. Senate. The first senator since the Civil War to see military action, he served briefly as major with the British Eighth Army in Libya in 1942. He resigned from the Senate in 1944 and served with the U.S. Army in Italy, southern France, and Germany. He was reelected to the Senate in 1946 and in 1948 served as chairman of the platform committee at the Republican National Convention. He was defeated for reelection to the Senate in the election of 1952 and the following year was appointed head of the United States delegation to the United Nations. He resigned in 1960 after receiving the Republican nomination for vice president.

LOGARITHM. In mathematics it is sometimes useful to express one number in terms of another number raised to a power. For example, 100 can be expressed as 10 raised to the second power, or $100 = 10^2$; and 1,000 can be expressed as 10 raised to the third power, or $1,000 = 10^3$. The idea of logarithms lies in the question, "Are there powers of 10 lying between the second and third power that correspond with numbers between 100 and 1,000?"

The answer to this question is "Yes." In fact, it has been found that all numbers can be expressed as graduated powers of a single number such as 10 or of any other number greater than one. These powers are called logarithms of the numbers. The fixed number that is raised to different powers is called the base of the logarithms. For example, if a base of 10 is chosen, the logarithm of 100 is 2, since 10 must be raised to the second power to equal 100. In mathematical symbols this statement would be written as $\log_{10} 100 = 2$. Notice that the number used as the base is indicated as a subscript after *log*. If no subscript is shown, the base is understood to be 10.

John Napier, of Scotland, discovered logarithms about 1590. He quickly recognized their usefulness and gave much of his time to constructing tables of logarithms. Such tables made possible a much simpler process for solving long problems of multiplication, division, raising to a power, and extracting a root.

In any logarithmic table all the logarithms are exponents of one base. This base is 10 for tables that are to be used for arithmetic computation, although tables with other bases have been constructed for other purposes. Because the logarithms are exponents of the same base, they can be used in computation according to simple arithmetic rules. For example, if two long numbers are to be multiplied, one need only find their logarithms, add the two logarithms, then use the table again to find what number has this sum as its logarithm. Thus, a multiplication problem is converted into an addition problem by using logarithms. By a similar process subtracting logarithms replaces long division, multiplying a logarithm replaces raising to a power, and dividing a logarithm replaces the process of extracting a root.

LOGROLLING is a sport that requires balance and strength. It is popular in heavily forested areas in the United States and Canada. Another name for the sport is birling.

The commonest type of logrolling begins with two men standing on a log that is floating in a body of water. The log is usually about 2 feet in diameter and from 12 to 15 feet long. The men stand at opposite ends of the log. They spin the log under their feet so that it rotates under them at a very fast rate of speed. Each man must be strong and have a well-developed sense of balance to keep from falling off the spinning log and into the water. The contest ends when one of the men falls off the log.

A second form of logrolling is called log poling. Each contestant stands on a floating log and holds a long pole. He then moves the log forward by pushing the pole against the bottom of the stream or lake and races his opponents to the finish line in this manner.

Henry Cabot Lodge
Wide World Photos